Three Modern Italian Poets

SABA · UNGARETTI · MONTALE

JOSEPH CARY

Second Edition

three modern italian poets

three
SABA
modern
UNGARETTI
italian
MONTALE
poets

SECOND EDITION

Joseph Cary

THE UNIVERSITY OF CHICAGO PRESS
Chicago and London

Joseph Cary is professor emeritus of English and comparative
literature at the University of Connecticut, Storrs. He is the author of
A Ghost in Trieste, published by the University of Chicago Press.

The University of Chicago Press, Chicago, 60637
The University of Chicago Press, Ltd., London
Copyright © 1969, 1993 by Joseph Cary
First edition published 1969 by New York University Press.
Second edition published 1993 by University of Chicago Press.
Printed in the United States of America

99 98 97 96 95 94 93   6 5 4 3 2 1

ISBN 0–226–09527–4 (paper)

Library of Congress Cataloging-in-Publication Data

Cary, Joseph
    Three modern Italian poets: Saba, Ungaretti, Montale / Joseph
Cary.—2d ed.
        p.   cm.
    Includes bibliographical references and index.
    1. Italian poetry—20th century—History and criticism.   2. Saba,
Umberto, 1883–1957—Criticism and interpretation.   3. Ungaretti,
Giuseppe, 1888–1970—Criticism and interpretation.   4. Montale,
Eugenio, 1896–   —Criticism and interpretation.   I.   Title.
II. Title: Three Modern Italian poets.
PQ4113.C37   1993
851'.91209—dc20   93–12940
                                                              CIP

⊗ The paper used in this publication meets the minimum
requirements of the American National Standard for Information
Sciences—Permanence of Paper for Printed Library Materials, ANSI
Z39.48–1984.

This "book about books"
is for three who stood and waited
Alicé, Nat and—most of all—Edie

contents

preface to the first
edition (1969)

These pages have been written out of strong feelings of affection and admiration for the three men who are my subject. They have been generous masters, from whom I have learned according to my abilities; they have stirred me and given me enormous pleasure; they have lived—each one so different from the others!—courageous and honorable lives. I hope these feelings are legible throughout what follows. I would like them to be contagious.

I suppose strictly I ought to speak of "works" rather than "men" for I have met none of them personally and never shall. But the distinction is academic; the life that counts for a poet will have to be in his poems. Giuseppe Ungaretti in his fifties contemplated his work and chose to call it—all of it, what was to come as well as what was done—*Vita d'un uomo*: *A Man's Life;* under that legend each single volume of verse or prose could be understood as an installment of biography, the work-in-progress of a lifetime. But his choice simply made explicit what is virtually true in any case. A poet's poems are or ought to be his truest confessions, his peculiar "way," forthright or oblique, confused or acute, at once his astral body and body odor.

I declare my not very remarkable prejudices. I like poetry that, audibly or not, involves a *voice*, a created tone or timbre that seems the authentic expression of a particular consciousness. *What* is expressed—that is, those ideas, attitudes or sentiments with which I personally may quarrel or sympathize—is surely not irrelevant; neither are the various aptitudes, obsessions, accuracies, and graces that amount to a style. But I respond most fully when I am in what I take to be the presence of an "I," the revealed or intimated livingness that "has" ideas, attitudes, and sentiments, and whose utterance of them, said or sung, I am made to feel is genuine, true, and thereby beautiful. Without this nuclear presence, shifting and unstable though it must be, I am left mainly aware of the game of words as a skill or finish, the play of verbal surfaces that implicate a hollow: the subject, routine or pastime of "mere literature."

So I "demand," I suppose, an effect or myth of depth, since strictly speaking words are nothing but surface, conventional signs and sounds on the page and tongue (though "surface" itself, implying something beneath, is part of the myth). At any rate it is a beneficent, life-enhancing myth and a natural one, and it seems to me to be categorically imperative for the lyric experience. Its powers are by no means inevitable; most poets possess (or are possessed by) their voices only intermittently, the rest of their work being derivative, a kind of self-declension in the manner of *ego scriptor*. I think that for the most part each of the poets considered here has mastered his voice and speaks, as a man, from the printed page. Part of my study is to ascertain how this is so. For the rest I try to define each voice by pertinent example and comment, to note developments in range and tone; to provide, in effect, a useful introduction.

In this century there have been two spectacular bursts of national poetic renaissance, one originating in the United States, the other (*pace* Ireland) in Italy. Both begin about the same time, the century's second decade. Both involve broadly contemporaneous generations; Saba and W. C. Williams were born in 1883, Ungaretti and Eliot in 1888, and so on. The first, cosmopolitan and traveled possibly to a fault, is famous and influential. The second has had comparatively little recognition beyond Italian frontiers.

There are several obvious reasons for this, and one of them involves politics. The main stretch of time during which these poets wrote and published their work coincides with what in postwar Italy has been called *il ventennio nero*, the twenty "black" years of Fascist dictatorship (extending from Mussolini's rise to power after World War I to his fall in 1943) when free cultural relations with other countries were minimal, being officially discouraged as unpatriotic. After 1945 this isolation began to be dispersed. The comparable features of both Italian films and novels written after the war involved a sober, pared, quasi-documentary approach to the problems of everyday life. The results were catholic, honest, and immensely moving, easily assimilable by an international audience.

The situation has proven otherwise for poetry. Of the poets discussed in these pages only one, Umberto Saba, could be even remotely characterized as "neorealist"; this would mean merely that his poems deal largely with familiar, everyday life in a relatively open and "democratic" fashion. But Saba's transparencies are deceptive, and the claims made by his peculiar voice are not likely to survive translation; he reads in English like a sub-Wordsworthian.

Through combinations of temperament and outside pressure to be examined further on, the other main poets of the *ventennio*, Ungaretti and Montale, developed distinctly difficult, high, aristocratic styles.*
In the textbooks this tendency is called *ermetismo*, the hermetic movement, but the companionship that a movement implies did not exist for these two poets. Unearthed by certain critics as a pejorative for labeling the cause of their bewilderment or disapproval, the term survives (like *symboliste* or *décadent* in France a half century earlier) as an ironic banner for admirers, a catch-all for literary historians. In any case, the work of Ungaretti and Montale, intricate and at first glance forbidding, and the work of Saba, "easier" perhaps but vast and uneven and peculiarly local, have negotiated the frontiers with indifferent success. Though of course poetry is scarcely a popular commodity, even in the original.

This brings us to the second condition contributing to their relative isolation: Who, after all, reads Italian? When I taught it, my classes were generally composed of two types: Italo-Americans conscientiously boning up in honor or memory of their parents, and music majors with special ambitions in opera. Add the occasional fan of Ezra Pound or an eccentric who wants to read Dante in the original and you have a thoroughgoing fringe.

Italian, pragmatically considered as a useful commercial weapon, is a dead language—English or French will suffice in most countries, Italy included. The unjaundiced literature major will normally gravitate toward French, the language of Villon, Baudelaire and Proust. The truth of the matter is reflected in the paucity and unevenness of Italian instruction in most American and English classrooms. The supply is geared to the demand, and there are few incentives.

I would like this book to be a further one. Especially since the late 1950's (a convenient rough date would be 1959, the year a good but lesser poet, Salvatore Quasimodo, won the Nobel prize for literature) the veil has been slightly rent by a number of translations, of varying scope and worth, of modern Italian poets. It is now possible for a curious reader with little or no understanding of Italian to get his hands on English-language versions of selected lyrics with the originals *en face*, enough to support and guide his

---

* Surely Dante would have called them "illustrious, cardinal, courtly, and curial." The *really* popular style, hortatory, purple, scrumptiously sonorous—d'Annunzio traduced by Marinetti-Mussolini and Co.—was safely in the hands of the regime.

intuitions.* It is the right time for an extended critical study in English.

I hope I have taken nothing and no one for granted. The first chapter is meant to provide summary background materials: the literary-cultural situation at the turn of the century, which these men inherited and had to cope with, the names of relevant poets, periodicals and programs, some prevailing winds and tendencies, some elementary history. (The appendix gives chronological tables of important literary and political events from 1880 to the present.) The body of the book consists of three essays, one for each poet. In these I have felt free to digress or fill in certain gaps when it has seemed pertinent; thus, my main effort to "define" *ermetismo* will be found in the middle of the Ungaretti chapter, apropos of his readings in Leopardi, which is where I am sure it belongs.

So that my remarks may be as serviceable as possible both to the reader and to the poetry, I have quoted from the originals as much as I could. All passages cited in Italian have been translated and all translations are my own. As for the prose, my conscience is relatively easy; it has been the poems that troubled. I finally chose as my model George Kay's fine versions in prose for his *Penguin Book of Italian Verse;* that is, I settled for trying to be as faithful as possible to the literal senses of the poem, leaving all indications of rhythms and "music" for my commentaries. Even this compromise has had its own complexities, as the bracketed materials cluttering my cribs will show. I hereby declare my generic indebtedness to every one of my predecessors (see bibliography) in this tricky area.

The bibliography in fact not only gives something of my reading background but ought to stand as a listing of the sources I am in all conscience able to recall. I particularly value and recommend Giacomo Debenedetti's various essays on Saba, Luciano Rebay's richly documented survey of the formative influences on Ungaretti, and Sergio Solmi's poet's insights into the complex and reticent humanism of Eugenio Montale. Specific bibliographical acknowledgments are numbered in the text and refer to footnotes placed at the end of each chapter; side issues and annexes of more immediate interest are asterisked and dispatched at the base of the page on which they occur.

---

*These are listed in the bibliography. If the reader knows French, he is luckier. Jean Lescure's Ungarettis of 1953 and Patrice Angelini's Montales of 1966, both bilingual and both offering the *complete* poems as of dates of publication, are accurate, usefully annotated, and introduced magnificently by the poets themselves. They do these things better in France.

A grant generously supplied by the Research Foundation of the University of Connecticut enabled me to purchase the proper primary texts needed to begin this study.

To my teacher and friend Robert J. Clements of New York University go my special thanks for a faith and patience I hope not too incompatible with my just deserts. May he and others who read this book find it a constructive guide to what I know to be a remarkable poetic experience.

Joseph Cary

Mansfield Center, Connecticut
London, England
1963–1968

preface to the second edition (1993)

I am pleased and honored that the University of Chicago Press is reissuing *Three Modern Italian Poets* in a revised and slightly enlarged edition. Whatever the merit of the original, an *aggiornamento* can only better it. Errata and simple mistakes can finally be corrected; after a quarter of a century there is a bibliography to be brought up to date and made useful again. But most of all, a new edition offers the opportunity for a final say—three Afterwords—on the trio involved.

It now seems obvious that Umberto Saba was a more complex—even wilier—character than I once believed, . . . taken in, perhaps, by his famous "transparency" as by the cloth-capped *popolano* persona of his latter days. That *Il canzoniere* is a fabrication and work of art rather than a documentary or historical record should not be taken for granted, as I think I did in the 1960s.

I have added two variations on the theme of "Egyptian nominalism" in Giuseppe Ungaretti, exploring aspects of his haunted religiosity and perpetual struggle, as a poet, with the demon of solipsism. This book is not the place to investigate the contrast between his life as a man, with its very human appetite for national and international recognition and honors, and the unworldliness of his poems, the remarkable *Vita d'un uomo*.

As for Eugenio Montale, *poète malgré lui* and doubtful from almost the start as to whether there were any poetry left in him, who could have dreamt that this Nobel laureate would go on to write four more books of verse before his death in 1981? The work of his *senilità*, and its relation to the three great books of his prime, needs to be examined. I have also reflected on what he has called "il *tu*" in his poetry, the second-person intimate who is always a *donna*.

The leopard, even if it would, cannot change its spots. In spite of the critical developments of the past twenty-five years, the author of *Three Modern Italian Poets* persists in believing in voices that can summon up a living "I," in words as real instruments capable of indicating realities. The reader who is uncomfortable with this should proceed no further.

J.C.

Mansfield Center, Connecticut
1993

I TWILIGHT, AND THE CONDITIONS OF NEW DAY

I would shake off the lethargy of this
   our time, and give
For shadows—shapes of power,
For dreams—men. . . .
   —Ezra Pound, "Revolt: Against the
   Crepuscular Spirit in Modern
   Poetry," *Personae* (1909)

The twilight metaphor that begins this chapter holds little novelty in any language, but it has its peculiar utility when applied to the literary scene in Italy for the first decade or so of this century. "Italian poetry grows dim . . . but in a mild and attenuated twilight that perhaps will not be followed by the night." So wrote the young protégé of Croce, Giuseppe Antonio Borgese,[1] in 1911, with a muted pessimism which is itself eminently crepuscular. The title of his article was "Poesia crepuscolare," and it gave the factitious integrity of a name to an assortment of literary symptoms then prevailing. It was in fact an intelligent provisional generalization which, because it was convenient and quotable, begat a nonexistent "school," *i crepuscolari*, though most of the poets involved died too soon to dispute it.

Borgese's antique image was not merely descriptive of a set of common characteristics in the poetry under review. It also implied a certain idea of Italian literary history, and it is this idea that we ought to examine first. Although there is undoubtedly a way of regarding twilight that might be called, in analogy with Shelley's spring-heralding winter, dawn-oriented and "bright," the usual emotions associated with this time of day are dim, melancholy, obsessed with terminals and dust. Highest value is ascribed to *the day that is done*.

Such is the assumption (there is no argument since the author is never in doubt) underlying Borgese's imagery and article. It is very Italian of him. In Italy, Metternich's "mere geographical expression" declined from Roman grandeur, the past has always cast a special spell, sometimes as nourishment and stimulus, sometimes as an opiate or crippling mortgage. Vergil himself worked in Homer's shadow, and

1

it is not surprising that Aeneas' major feature is his piety, his fidelity to the past and the ways of the fathers. Dante, Petrarch, and Boccaccio, bearers of the first tripartite "day" to Italian literature, gazed back to an idealized Latinity for sustenance and guidance, and, as a "third classicism," were in their turn emulated by later waves of writers. The Italian for words denoting renaissance or resurrection (*rinascimento, risorgimento*) requires that particular attention be given to the prefix, for it implies no break or novelty but a metahistorical repeat, the ideal reflux of exemplary old times.

By the same token, nothing is more conservative than literary Italian, effectively "fixed" by the splendor of its *Trecento* beginnings. Renaissance men of letters like Bembo, Speroni, Varchi, or bodies such as the powerful Accademia della Crusca, whose emblem was the sieve, for use in separating out the pure *toscano* from the chaff of lesser dialects, gave good or bad marks for writers' linguistic conformacy to models innocently set by Florentines two centuries earlier. What is usually called in Italy the *questione della lingua* has never been a "question." Leopardi's notebooks are crammed with lists of "un-Italian" words (recent coinages, barbarous compounds, gallicisms, words unsanctified by use in the superb past); Manzoni had to move from Milan to Florence in order to "purify" his tongue of Lombardisms so that he could recast the *Promessi sposi* in the language of the fathers. And as in letters, so in politics; Dante could envisage nothing better for his broken land than a new Augustus; Machiavelli wrote commentaries on Livy for the political enlightenment of his contemporaries; even sad Mussolini cribbed his fasces and salutes from Roman legionaries, wore eagles, and built a shabby "forum."

One has to be strong-nerved and self-possessed to survive and thrive in such a wealth of ruins, and the great Italian poets, from Dante to the present, have been so. Others, Petrarch and Tasso in their epic urges, Chiabrera, Monti, the "serious" Belli, Carducci, caught cold and turned into something as chilly as Carraran marble. The fate of Lot's retrospective and nostalgic wife is exemplary here: the landscapes of Italian literary history are studded with pillars of salt. Reviewing it, Giuseppe Borgese felt that Italian poetry had had its second marvelous day in the period beginning with Parini in the late eighteenth century and compassing the triads at either end of the nineteenth: Foscolo-Leopardi-Manzoni at one end, Carducci-Pascoli-d'Annunzio at the other. After such as these, the dusk.

Within the limits of gross metaphor he was, of course, right; it had been, in his words, a "miraculous flourishing." And the metaphor is not so indiscriminate as it seems at first glance. The image of day invites some attention to the particular hour of day. If meridian is meant to be, as it surely is, the era of Foscolo, Leopardi, and Manzoni extending over the first half of the last century, then the ante- and postmeridians might imply a promise (Parini, Alfieri) and some sort of decline (the most recent triad, still very influential in Borgese's Italy). Thus, the metaphor incorporates a simple grading system.

Still, it mourns the departed day and disconsolately proclaims the end of an age of genius. If d'Annunzio is inferior to Manzoni, d'Annunzio was nevertheless something extraordinary, "an artist to his fingertips," a scintillating, opulent, and formidable energy *hélas*. Carducci died in 1907, Pascoli in 1912; d'Annunzio, though he survived to 1938, had completed his best work by the end of the first decade and was about to become a national monument. What remained were young apprentice poets born in the 1880's; they included Martini, Corazzini, Gozzano, Moretti, and Chiaves, and these, for Borgese, were poets of the dusk, *a lume spento*, the inheritors of aftermath.

❖   ❖   ❖

"Crepuscular" also was intended to describe something of their subject matter and modes of expressing it. Two of their immediate predecessors had been fatally fond of large ideas and sumptuous, sometimes grandiose, effects. Carducci's strenuous classical republican idealism and d'Annunzio's complacent titanism were both skillfully served up in exuberant rhetorics designed for an audience whose tastes ran to the outsized and the sonorous earful. From reaction as well as exhaustion, then, the newest generation tended to take the option exemplified by Pascoli: to write of *piccole cose* (the little things), in a comparatively restrained and low-keyed manner.

Unhappy Giovanni Pascoli had evolved a mystique of Nature and what he felt to be especially natural creatures (swallows, rabbits, children, etc.) as a refuge from what he legitimately conceived to be the inevitable misery of human existence. He celebrated the rural landscape and his own memories of childhood with the eye and ear of an acute naturalist congenitally prone to sentimentality the instant he crossed from the specific to the general. On the one hand he advocated and illustrated a poetics of veristic local color; hence his campaign for a *svecchimento del lessico* (an updating of the poetic lexicon) and his suggestions to contemporaries on how to revive the traditionally Arcadianized landscape of Italian poetry: "a bit of botany and zoology would help." In 1896 he had criticized what he felt to be the vague generality of Leopardi's vocabulary, opposing that poet's famous "canto degli uccelli" (song of the species "bird") with a pluralist serenade by "robins, chickadees, cardinals, larks, nightingales, cuckoos, horned owls, finches, sparrows, wrens, doves, tits, shrikes, chats, swallows and swallows and swallows that come and go and stay. . . ." From there it was but a short step to his famous and faintly comic experiments in onomatopoeic naturalism: *tac tac* (chickadees), *tin tin* (robins), *zisteretetet* (tits), *tellterellltellteretellltell* (sparrows), and so on.

On the other hand his symbolic application of this observed data was frequently teary and self-indulgent. The peroration to the preface of his *Primi poemetti* (*First Little Poems,* or *Poemlets;* the suffix is significant) accurately catches the style of his humanitarian designs upon his readers:

> Oh, no! honest souls! I do not want to *honor myself;* I want—that is I would like—to infuse within you, in the rapid mode that befits poetry, a few sentiments and thoughts of mine that are not wicked. . . .
>
> I would like you to think with me that the mystery in life is great, and that the best we can do is to cling as close as we can to the others, whom the same mystery makes anxious and frightened.
>
> Men, I shall speak as in a fable for children: men, imitate the swallow. Men, above all content yourselves with little . . . and love one another within the limits of the family, the nation, and humanity.

Such is the poetics; it works little better in the poetic instance. But somewhere between the various layers of keen-eyed birdwatcher and avuncular sentimentalist, the slender best of Pascoli can be found in a grey and modest sort of naturalistic mood poem, observant of the country life it deals with and fairly reticent as to the motivations that have brought it there. As its maker advised, it contents itself "with little." At its best its effect is honest and quietly moving.

I suggest that "good" Pascoli, despite the liability to mawkishness, should be considered a rough antithesis or even antidote to the declamatory modes of Carducci or, more sensationally, of d'Annunzio.

> One of the ways by which contemporary verse has tried to escape the rhetorical, the abstract, the moralizing, to recover (for that is its purpose) the accents of direct speech, is to concentrate its attention on trivial or accidental or commonplace objects. . . . [Also] it is not unworthy to notice how often the word "little" occurs; and how this word is used, not merely as a piece of information, but with a caress, a conscious delight.

This is not (as might be supposed) a translation of critical remarks on Pascoli's poetry of *piccole cose* but the young T. S. Eliot writing on Georgian poets in *The Egoist* for September 1917. Between the

Georgians and the youthful "Pascolian" poets described by Borgese as *crepuscolari* there are indeed certain broad resemblances. Neither grouping is programatically revolutionary (and thus quite unlike the Italian Futurists and their cousins the London Vorticists), but both in their quiet way react against the pomp and high circumstance of much of the poetry written in the reigns of Queen Victoria and King Umberto during the closing years of the nineteenth century. Both are suspicious of political or ethical editorializing in verse; both try to steer clear of the big issues or the old sublimities; both value accurate firsthand observation and plain speaking, reservedly rhythmed; both gladly relinquish any claim to being bards or prophets; even the title "poet" smacks of artiness and pretention. Far more preferable are "amateur," "plain man," *poète malgré lui.*

As far as Italians are concerned, standard procedure at this point is to adduce a few well-known lines from a lachrymose anthology piece by Sergio Corazzini, lines forgiven him only because he died of tuberculosis in 1907 at the age of twenty:

> Perchè tu mi dici: poeta?
> Io non sono un poeta.
> Io non sono che un piccolo fanciullo che piange.

Why do you call me "poet"?/I am no poet./I am just a little child who is crying.

I personally prefer the more genial disclaimer of the "nonsense" canzonetta by a contemporary, Aldo Palazzeschi, who when asked for his credentials by an earnest patron of the arts, responds

> Tri tri tri,
> fru fru fru,
> ihu ihu ihu,
> uhi uhi uhi!

closing with a last "Ahahahahahahah" and the reflection that

> . . . i tempi sono molto cambiati,
> gli uomini non dimandano
> più nulla dai poeti,
> e lasciatemi divertire!

. . . times have changed a lot,/People don't ask/Anything from poets anymore,/So let me have my fun!

But whether his public face is unhappy child or everyman, clown or warbler, the poet of this dispensation tries for a direct and seemingly artless verse that can express his modest emotional responses to the minutia of daily life in a quiet conversational style. His virtues and vices are more or less an extension of Pascoli's—on the one hand speech that feels unpretentious and sincere, with a widening of subject and diction to include material traditionally felt to be anti-poetic; on the other, a disingenuousness that can drift dreamily into straight self-pity, a fairly uniform disposition to passive suffering (cloudy skies/easy sighs), a certain dimness.

Often, their "things" are "little" *faute de mieux.* Quite unlike Umberto Saba (who once was written off in Italy as merely a longer-lived *crepuscolare*) or, say, William Carlos Williams, both of whom begin the world again whenever genuinely brushed by the Muse, these poets are frequently world-weary, quite capable of making the normal worldly distinctions between big and little things, disappointed men for whom the commonplace is commonplace. In effect they are *resigned* to little things, and condescend or sentimentalize over them. The grain of sand or wildflower they might contemplate has nothing to do with "big" things like Blake's immanent world or heaven, or only insofar as such objects hint of some blurred loss. More often than not, even this poignance is derivative; not only Pascoli but the lesser fry of late French *symbolistes* (Jammes, Vielé-Griffin, Samain, Paul Fort) float in the middle distance.

All of the so-called *crepuscolari* were born between 1883 and 1887; that is, they were contemporaries rather than predecessors of poets like Saba and Ungaretti. And none of them ever developed. They either dried up, or died young, or (like Palazzeschi) ended as novelists. All this is worth keeping in mind when thinking of the sort of lyricism demarcated by Borgese's epithet, for without exception, all of it is by young men in their early or mid-twenties. I mean that to some extent the phenomenon of *crepuscolarismo* is related to a certain callowness, to rushing into print at an age notorious for its exacerbated sense of isolation and impotence, precipitating a precocious valitudinarianism or premature "acceptance."

At any rate, with the main exception of Guido Gozzano (who like Eliot went to Laforgue for a carapace of saving irony), they are largely remembered in Italy for their negative virtues; that is to say, less for what they did do than for what they did not. The phrasing of Umberto Saba's tribute to Corazzini is a case in point, the more so because Saba himself was extremely sensitive about being called crepuscular.

> His [Corazzini's] poetry is not, nor could it be, given the age of the man who composed it, "great." But it is a precedent and a beginning.

Above all it is poetry, noble poetry. In him, for the first time in more than half a century, a poet spoke Italian verses without amplifications, without soapbox oratory, above all without considering the public too much.[2]

We can add, more positively, that the value of the work of Corazzini and others was to help create a sort of atmospheric hush in which the literary values of clarity, directness, and simplicity could be quietly reproposed—through a modest practice rather than a program.

❀   ❀   ❀

If one of the senses of *crepuscolarismo* implicitly exalted the Italian past, it was the main though concealed seriousness of a more or less concurrent phenomenon, *futurismo,* that condemned it. "Museums: graveyards!" fulminated Marinetti in the famous manifesto published in *Le Figaro* in 1909. And despite the jumping internationalism of the movement—with cells from London to St. Petersburg—it is clear that the stress on things to come and frantic contempt for *passatismo* and *passatisti* are very much Italian matters.

> It's from Italy [Marinetti wrote in French] that we fling into the world this manifesto of impetuous and incendiary violence . . . because we want to liberate that country from its stinking chancre of professors, archeologists tour-guides and antiquarians.
>
> For too long a time already Italy has been a market for second-hand dealers. We want to free it from the innumerable museums that cover it beneath innumerable graveyards. . . .
>
> I declare unto you in all truth that the daily frequentation of museums, libraries and academies . . . is as dangerous for artists as the prolonged supervision by parents would be for certain youths. . . . For the dying, for the sick or for prisoners, it's another thing: the admirable past is perhaps a balm for their ills. . . . But we, we young and strong Futurists, we want to know nothing more of the past!
>
> And therefore let them come, these gay incendiaries with their flaming fingers! Here they are! . . . Up now! set fire to the library shelves! . . . Alter the canals' course so that they may flood the museums! . . . Grab those picks, mauls and sledges and smash, smash without pity those venerated towns!

It would take a tone-deaf reader indeed to bother arguing here that both present and future are seeded in the past, that the leaf cannot "really" abolish its branch, and so on. Marinetti was not a particularly intelligent man, but he knew that much. His manifesto was not offered as a refutation of Bergson but as the first barrage of a propaganda campaign against an attitude that he and his associates felt held Italy in thrall: namely *passatismo,* "pastism," the burden of a great but succubist past that inhibits or drastically qualifies vigorous living in the present. The Futurists' genial polemics in this area (Down with the Uffizi! Down with the Pope! Down with the hendeca-syllable!) were inevitably empty gesturings, but they had a certain local symbolic point as a dramatic focus for the normal patricidal impulses of a younger generation and as an infectious assault upon an important national psychosis. As it tragically turned out, this emetic function of Futurism was quickly absorbed by the advent of genuine, nonsymbolic war.

Filippo Tommaso Marinetti was born and raised in Alexandria, Egypt. So was Ungaretti, but what each of them made of it could not have been more antithetical. If Marinetti liked to talk of the "sainted black teat" of the Sudanese nurse who suckled him it was not out of any particular piety toward his past but in order to make his credentials as a hot-blooded, action-loving sensual African as graphic as possible. He was Italian in nationality, he meant, but exempted by birth from its passéistic virus. He was rich, energetic, extroverted, totally humorless, and supremely self-confident. Like his master d'Annunzio he had an ad-man's flair for publicity and how to attract it. He also had literary ambitions and had read enough recent French literature to have grasped and mastered the external mani-festations of the *vie de bohème:* the mucker poses, the scandal-mongering and bourgeois-baiting *trucs,* the "irreverent" experimenting with traditional grammar and metric, the fire-breathing manifesto.

Marinetti's real genre was the manifesto, for which his congenital exhibitionism, floridity, and knack for sustained vituperation specially suited him. Although his own art was worthless (Cocteau once wrote that Marinetti "spoke of dreadnoughts in the style of Byron"[*]) he

---

[*] He should have said "d'Annunzio." Marinetti was not above publically addressing his roadster as his "Pegasus," his "smithy-eyed formidable Japanese monster nourished by flames and mineral oil," "drunk on space," all of which recalls the plummiest prose-poems of Paolo Tarsis, super-hero of d'Annunzio's Nietzsche-novel *Forse che sì forse che no.* D'Annunzio used to pride himself on his ability to mimic the murmuring of trees and waters in the sound-systems of pastoral poems like those of *Alcione.* So too a great deal of Marinetti's ex-perimentalism boils down to a crude application of the principle of mimicry to more mundane and mechanistic matters. Hence this passage from a description of the Italian bombardment of Adrianopolis during the Libyan campaign of 1911: ". . . Sciumi Maritza o Karvavena ta ta ta ta giii-tumb giii-tumb ZZZANG-TUMB-TUMB (280 colpo di partenza) srrrrrrr GRANG-GRANG (colpo in arrivo) croooc-craaac . . ." etc. And Marinetti's cult of speed, violence and war ("sole hygiene of the world") is a clear derivative of what d'Annunzio called "my anxiety to live, as man and artist, at the utmost limits of what can be ex-pressed by the word and at the threshold of what must be completed by action." Truly, Marinetti reads like a crude parody of d'Annunzio (and often so does Mussolini).

attracted artists, chiefly painters and sculptors already converted by cubist example, to join with him at least until it became clear that *futurismo* was really *marinettismo*.

In the field of poetry the movement's main innovations were the dragooning of so-called "free verse" as a counterblow to the traditional hendecasyllable, eccentric suspensions of normal syntax and punctuation, a plethora of short-lived onomatopoeic coinages, the cultivation (as ejaculation out of "real life") of the fragment, a fondness for addressing racing cars, smokestacks, and locomotives, and an impudent, jazzy, informal "oral" style best illustrated in the early work of Palazzeschi, Cendrars, and Apollinaire. But Futurism's main contribution was an *ambience*, a five- or six-year period of exhilarated and semiserious experimentalism in the name of Novelty that had repercussions throughout the whole of Europe. At home its militancy quickly brought it into the political sphere, an influence from which it never recovered. By 1915 it had become a noisy organ for Intervention; by 1919 Marinetti and his remaining followers were publicity agents for Fascism. But for a while, at least until new labels could be invented, all literary novelties in Italy were regarded as "futuristic"; not only the tiny wartime "fragments" written by the young Ungaretti, but (at least according to the poet's memory of a remark made to him by Borgese) "A mia moglie," Saba's great and sweet pastoral celebration of his wife in terms of barnyard creatures!

❖   ❖   ❖

Much later, in the 1950's, Ungaretti wrote of those years preceding the First World War as a normal and fundamentally constructive "period of bewilderment and confusion":

> The youth of those days felt that after Foscolo, Leopardi and Manzoni, there were no more poets in Italy; that a tradition had been broken and that those poets following them had had nothing to do, aside from the mere use of the language, with our culture. This was exaggerated and unjust but it is in the natural order of things that sons affirm themselves through rebellion against the fathers. . . . Do us the justice of recognizing that it was right that the youth of those days felt the whole debate had to be taken up again from the very beginnings, that everything needed to be renewed.[3]

In their very different ways Futurism and symptomatic "crepuscularism" were important manifestations of that research and ferment, the first a bona fide movement, the second not.

There were of course other groupings, associated for the most part with reviews issuing from Florence. Giovanni Papini's *Leonardo* (1903–1907) was one such, operated with the editorial aid of bright young writer-critics like Giuseppe Prezzolini, Emilio Cecchi, and

Borgese. *Leonardo's* slant was broadly cultural and philosophical; indeed it could have been Papini's attack on positivism, *Il crepuscolo dei filosofi*, which suggested that image to Borgese for use in literary matters. In 1908 Prezzolini founded the very influential *La Voce*, a weekly "cultural review" which drew regular contributors like Papini, Renato Serra, Gaetano Salvemini, and Giuseppe De Robertis. Beside its active concern with contemporary ethical, political, and philosophical affairs, *La Voce* also printed the work of some of the young Italian poets. Saba's second book of poems, for example, was published in 1912 under *Voce* auspices.

Both Prezzolini and Papini were vigorous and self-assertive types, ill-suited both temperamentally and intellectually for work together. By 1913, Papini had broken with *La Voce* entirely, had written a grandiloquent autobiography craftily titled *Un uomo finito* (*A Finished Man*) in which his various quarrels with the world were presented as proof of his genius, had converted to Futurism, and was beginning (with Ardengo Soffici and Palazzeschi) a lively futuristic literary magazine called *Lacerba* which lasted for two years (1914–1915) and was the first to publish the poetry of Giuseppe Ungaretti.

With the coming of war, *La Voce* itself entered a short but important second phase under the editorship of Giuseppe De Robertis. From December 1914 to its demise in December 1916, it operated as a purely literary review, inculcating the "method" of discriminating and knowledgeable reading of texts (*saper leggere*: know how to read, was the famous motto) by precept and magisterial example. The second *Voce* was hospitable to unaligned younger poets of all persuasions: Jahier, Cardarelli, Onofri, Ungaretti, Sbarbaro and Apollinaire published in its pages. It is remembered today as a sensitive and constructive agent for renewal in Italian letters in a very fluid and difficult (wartime) period.

Not the least of De Robertis' contributions to modern Italian poetry was his interest in the work of Giacomo Leopardi, which not only helped desentimentalize and revitalize study of the *Canti* but also had some influence on Ungaretti's reading of that great poet. This, in my opinion, is a capital event in the history of what the critic Francesco Flora later captiously called "hermeticism." In a broad sense Flora was right when, in his big history of Italian literature, he called the second *Voce* an accomplice in the formation of hermeticism, *not* because it pushed a francophile sub-symbolist poetry (Flora's point) but because it encouraged a scrupulous rereading of Leopardi's *opera omnia*.

❖   ❖   ❖

The three years of war from 1915 to 1918, punctuated by the Caporetto disaster of October 1917, effectively silenced the little disputes between literary movements and reviews. That it did not silence individual poets is most movingly demonstrated by Ungaretti's comments on the genesis of his first book, *Il porto sepolto* (*The Buried Harbor*), published in an edition of eighty copies in Udine at the end of 1916. "What is amusing is knowing how this book was made. Written in the trenches, in the mud, written in the midst of the grief of war; gathering water drop by drop from the tentflaps, rusty, turbid, in empty meat cans. . . ."[4] But this historical note on the book's genesis, supplemented as it is by the place names and dates appended to every one of its poems, is misleading. In his *Note on War Poetry* T. S. Eliot questions the expressive potential of the "mere" individual in relation to such an experience:

> Where is the point at which the merely individual
> Explosion breaks
> In the path of an action merely typical
> To create the universal, originate a symbol
> Out of the impact?[5]

For Ungaretti, the details of place and date, the phenomenon of a life lived under combat conditions, were contingencies, external accessories to a crucial inward experience which really deserves to be called "religious"; "One felt oneself a man," he writes, "religiously a man." It is worth reading a later account of it, composed in the coiled baroque periods of his late prose style, for its general relevance to the question of what that war meant to many Italians, some of them poets, of Ungaretti's generation.

> But it was during the war, it was my life mixed with the enormous suffering of the war, it was the primitiveness of those conditions— immediate and unveiled feeling; fear of nature and an open-heartedness (*cordialità*) now made instinctive by nature; a spontaneous and dis- quieting immediatization with the cosmic essence of things—it was the degree to which, of every soldier at grips with the blindness of things, with chaos and with death, there was formed a being who in a flash recapitulated himself from his origins, urgently resurrecting himself in his solitude and in the fragility of the human condition—it was the de- gree to which there was formed a being torn by feeling for his fellows an immeasurable terror and yearning and a paternal solidarity—it was that state, then, of extreme lucidity and extreme passion which made articulate within my soul the goodness of that mission I had already half-glimpsed. . . .[6]

The mission he mentions here is a fundamental poetic reform strictly in line with the experience vouchafed him by life in the Carso trenches.

Before the war, in the *Lacerba* days, Ungaretti had briefly been a Futurist of the blithe Palazzeschian variety. His later retrospective assessment of that movement is conceived entirely on grounds of a subsequent moral awakening:

> In a certain sense the Futurists would have been able to avoid deceiving themselves if they had paid attention—not to the new means given to man by scientific progress—but to the human *coscienza* [consciousness and conscience] which had to dominate these means. They deceived themselves above all by making their own the most absurd illusions promulgated by the decadence, imagining some energy or dignity would be released by war and destruction. So too they fancied that by destroying the language some force or glory would be restored to it.[7]

Montale has written of how Ungaretti was the sole Italian poet able to "profit by the freedom in the air" in those days of this century's second decade.[8] But for Ungaretti, any genuine renewal for Italian poetry would have to begin with a man and his inwardness, his objective consciousness of himself, and his condition as an infinitesimal part of something larger. The *expression* of this consciousness (or, because it involves a moral dimension as well, this *coscienza*) might make of him a poet, and to be a poet would mean, as we shall see, a scrupulous meditation on verbal resources in order that expression translate *coscienza* as precisely as possible.*

Futurism too had contended erratically for a sort of renewed consciousness. A central factor in its polemic against the past had been its view of traditional letters as a reliquary or historical crystallization wholly unrelated to the dynamics of living in the present. The all but suppressed seriousness of the movement lay in its aim of freeing consciousness from the various psychic automatisms or habits relating to the glorious past to which it was felt Italians were especially prey. But, as Ungaretti quickly saw, if Futurism fought against one cult, it fell into another: the cult of action as an end in itself, with all its attendant obsessions with nerve and muscle, speed and violence, the sensual and the instinctive. The liberation proposed by Futurism was ultimately reductive, easily shunted into mindless conformacy with the Fascist rule: "No discussion, obedience only."

* *Coscienza*: the identity of "consciousness" and "conscience," the organic integrity of being and moral awakeness. There is no word like it in English. As a *mot juste* it recurs frequently in these pages.

Following the war there had been other negative responses to Futurism and experimentalism in general. The most important of these was grouped about the literary periodical *La Ronda* (1919–1922), founded by the poet Vincenzo Cardarelli. *La Ronda* was set up as a classicist call-to-order of a much more dogmatic variety than Eliot's *Criterion*. Reacting against what it felt to be the characteristic romantic anarchism of the previous decade, it proposed an end to the "barbaric" worship of immediacy and spontaneity and a return to a purely Italian literary tradition. It declared a moratorium on cross-cultural influences and borrowings and "romantic" egoism with its lexicographic and prosodic infractions of classical rules. Of course it also had certain urgent recommendations of its own: a diligent rereading of Italian classics, *italianità*, and a view of style as the product of study and application, as a *craft* in which the qualities of elegance, formal sophistication, and cultural resonance were stressed at the expense of "content" and personal expressiveness. *La Ronda's* adulation of what it called *lo bello scrivere* can be seen in retrospect to mask, beneath its fervent affirmations of literary patriotism, a certain moral crisis, a despair in the efficacy of the individual thought, act, or expression which finds its refuge in the cult of a "pure" and suprapersonal Italian style. Hence, for example, Cardarelli's sickly definition of style as "total delight, an almost delirious musical *divertimento* for a soul wearied and nauseated by its own thoughts."[9] The *rondisti* also felt that verse was a dead-letter and favored *prosa d'arte*, *prosa numerosa* in Ungaretti's phrase, a highly wrought "prose-poetry" as the appropriately dense medium for the projected new classicism.*

* * *

Though *La Ronda* preached a disciplined *passatismo* that was, in precept and practice, the almost exact antithesis of Futurism, both movements were identical in one thing: they were convinced that health lay in the assimilation of something "outside," in conforming to a declared procedure, attitude, doctrine, or style. In this of course they were in line with most of the literary-artistic *isms* of the first quarter of this century, all of which could be called extroverted in the sense that they advocated *doing certain things*: reading certain

---

* Hence their advocacy and attempted adoption of the prose manners of Manzoni and, above all, Leopardi, whose marmoreal prose dialogues, the *Operette morali*, were their chief admiration. *La Ronda* published a *Testamento letterario di Giacomo Leopardi*, a contentious selection from his notebooks, the *Zibaldone*, which stressed his classicism and formal purity as both theoretician and practitioner of *lo bello scrivere*. The Leopardis of De Robertis and Cardarelli are of course quite different; both of them were of use to Ungaretti.

books or authors, coveting a certain past or future, exploring and exploiting certain ways of seeing—images, cubes, vortices—cultivating a certain energy. To the contrary, Ungaretti could be said to have subordinated *doing* to *being*, according to what had been revealed to him during the war. This was not, obviously, to make a prerequisite of war, which was simply the "occasion" for his personal discovery.

It is not my intention to draw up some *gradus ad Parnassum* with a psycho-spiritual axis for rating poets. But in this century's famous reaction to "romantic" personalism and expressionism (as in Yeats' "all that is personal soon rots; it must be packed in ice or salt"[10]), we tend to cling to the supposedly objective verities of technique and craftsmanship and are absurdly shy of mentioning the qualities of being they are meant to serve. We can say at least that the real "reforms" and novelties in Italian poetry of this century began with the need felt by certain individuals, Ungaretti for one, for an expressive means as adherent and "true" as possible to their sense of their objective being; and that words like "authenticity," "honesty," or "*coscienza*," while wretchedly generic, are more useful terms for indicating vital tendencies than any of more literary origin.

Of the Voceans Borgese had written: "They are more moralists than *letterati*,"[11] and so in a sense they were, at least when compared to the *Ronda* group. The Vocean Renato Serra, a confederate of De Robertis killed early in the war, wrote movingly of his intimations of a new lyricism characterized not by any novelty of form or content but by an enveloping truth-to-oneself purged of all posture and conventional etiquette. "We know that *coscienza* is what counts."[12] But in my opinion, the most eloquent manifesto for the moral renewal sketched here was composed in 1911 for publication in *La Voce* by an all but unknown poet, Umberto Saba, who clearly meant it to be the *ars poetica* for the forthcoming book of his verse put out in 1912 under the *Voce* imprint. The article was rejected and returned to the poet, where it remained among his papers until after his death in 1957.[13]

The title of Saba's article was "Quello che resta da fare ai poeti" ("What Remains for Poets to Do"), and its subject was announced by the abrupt single sentence which constitutes its first paragraph: "It remains for poets to make poetry honest." Theoretically at least the point was very simple:

> Whoever does not write verse out of a sincere need to support the expression of his passion with rhythm, whoever has commercial or otherwise ambitious intentions—he for whom the publication of a book is like winning a medal or opening a shop—such a one cannot

begin to imagine what stubborn force of intellect, what disinterested grandeur of soul, is needed to resist all seduction and to keep oneself pure and honest in front of oneself—this is even when the dishonest line of verse, taken by itself alone, may seem best.

For Saba, the sole criterion for good poetry is its truthful correspondence to its poet's experience. He assumes that the habitual reader of poetry ("he who is able to go ever so slightly below the surface") will instinctively recognize transgressions of this moral imperative, but whether or not the delinquent poet is publicly caught out is really irrelevant—"Quello che resta . . ." was written as a declaration of faith by a poet for poets. And it says that the poet's crucial responsibility lies in the sphere of moral awakeness, *coscienza*, in order that expression may be as faithful as possible to the engendering perception or passion.

At first glance this seems an unremarkable restatement of the traditional view of poetry as a sort of rhythmic truthfulness. In a way it is; Saba was always fond of calling attention to what he called his classical temperament, insisting his classicism was "a profound, prenatal vocation." The important point is that in 1911, the view needed restatement; the major temptation toward literary "dishonesty" in those experimentalist days was the obligation to be new, to be at all costs original. The contemporary villain of the piece for twenty-eight-year-old Saba in 1911 was neither Papini nor Marinetti, though he speaks contemptuously of Futurism's "billboard manifestos," but their common *maestro*, Gabriele d'Annunzio.

"Quello che resta . . ." begins with an invidious distinction contentiously drawn between Manzoni and d'Annunzio, "between two Italians so famous that they lend themselves perfectly as examples of what I mean by literary honesty and dishonesty."

> For whoever can go ever so slightly below the surface, there is apparent in the verses of Manzoni a constant and uncommon scruple never to say a word that does not correspond perfectly to his vision. The same reader will see that the artifice of d'Annunzio is not only verbal but substantial as well; that he exaggerates or entirely fakes passions and admirations alien to his temperament; that he commits this unpardonable sin against the spirit for the sole, wretched end of gaining a more striking stanza or a more resonant line.

It is worth noting here the Saba's attitude toward d'Annunzio was always more complex or "ambivalent" (to use an adjective he favored) than it would seem from this passage. In his study of his own poetry, Saba wrote much later that in his days of apprenticeship he had found that of the famous triad [Carducci-Pascoli-d'Annunzio] he [d'Annunzio] was most poet, but that the touch of falseness, of excessiveness, which could be detected in the center of even his best compositions, kept them [d'Annunzio and Saba] apart as natural opposites. Even so, something of the d'Annunzian hendecasyllable entered, fused with other elements, into Saba's own. Nor did Saba ever join his contemporaries in their total and unjust negation of d'Annunzian value.[14]

In his younger days Saba had adapted a patently d'Annunzian sobriquet ("Umberto da Montereale"), was precociously bald like the *maestro*, sported a d'Annunzian goatee, had even paid an homage-giving visit to his home in Versilia.[15] Thus the rejection of d'Annunzio in "Quello che resta . . ." is in part a fair instance of what Ungaretti called the natural self-affirmation of the sons through rebellion against the fathers.

But d'Annunzio constituted a peculiar problem for poets of Saba's generation. If his moral program, the quadrivial cult of "will, *volupté*, pride, instinct," and his massive egotism were repellent (and they were to some), and if much of his product proved to be a quick-dating brand of *fin de siècle* aestheticism out of Huysmans by way of Nietzsche, he was nevertheless an extraordinarily talented and dynamic artificer, whose verbal sleights still compel a certain admiration. "My language," he once wrote, "my language belongs to me as the most powerful of all my instincts. It is a carnal instinct purified and exalted by the white fire of my intelligence. . . ."[16] In a way this boast is accurate. If "instinct" is primarily a mechanism intimately involved with reactions to sensorial experience, d'Annunzio's peculiar power resides in his ability to mimic this experience through the manipulation of words employed chiefly for their auditory and sonorous suggestiveness. He is manifestly a poet of the "ear," kin in this respect to English-language poets like Poe, Tennyson, Swinburne or Hopkins to whose gifts we frequently (and I think too exclusively) apply the word "musical."

In Italian there are several adjectives derived from the word for ear (*orecchio*). *Orecchiabile* generally refers to a melodic pattern which is "tuneful" and compellingly hummable. *Orecchiante* refers to the ability to play or sing "by ear" without knowing the music, and, figuratively, to repeat with facility what has been heard without much understanding it. D'Annunzio's verse, then, is always richly *orecchiabile* and frequently *orecchiante*, and this is, I think, the real core of Saba's moral objection to it. The *orecchiante* (the "sounding," the sonorous) is perhaps a special danger for a liquid and feminine tongue like Italian, and this can be compounded by what seems to be an almost national predilection for the theatrical gesture. Certainly d'Annunzio's verse is an extremely sophisticated instance of it, for when it is not directly onomatopoeic and thereby controlled by the requirements of auditory naturalism, it tends towards the condition of a "pure" music, a sumptuous and hypnotic mellifluence of sounds almost entirely abstracted from their dramatic occasion or "meaning." Hence Saba's accusation of a "sin against the spirit" in what he feels is d'Annunzio's habit of sacrificing truthfulness to gain "un verso più clamoroso," a more high-sounding line.

So Saba calls for a return to the austerities of Manzoni, not of course meaning a direct imitation of the *Inni sacri* or "Cinque maggio" (for truths differ according to time, place and personality) but a resumption of the moral seriousness he senses in all that master's work, the *coscienza* informing it. Then he develops his idea of what literary honesty would signify:

> . . . first of all, a refusal to force one's inspiration, and secondly not to try to make it seem, for miserable motives of ambition or success, more vast or transcendent than perchance it is. Such an honesty then is a reaction, under work conditions, to that mental sloth that keeps the plumb from touching bottom, or to that sweetness of allowing the rhythm or rhyme or what is popularly called "the vein" to take over. Although *to be original* and *to find oneself* are used synonymously, whoever does not know in practice that the first is the effect and the second the cause, whoever begins not from the need to discover oneself but from an uncontrollable desire to be original, whoever cannot resign himself when necessary to say what others have said . . . such a one will never find his true nature and will never say anything unexpected. It is necessary (kindly understand the spirit of my words) to be original in spite of ourselves. . . .
>
> [So] a long discipline is needed in order to prepare oneself for receiving a moment's grace with one's authentic being; making a daily examination of one's conscience, rereading what one has written in those periods of quiet when analysis is possible, seeking always to recall the state of mind that first generated those lines, noting with heroic meticulousness the discrepancies between what was thought and what was written.

At this point Saba gives an autobiographical instance of such a revision in the interests of honesty; we discuss this passage in the next chapter. After a brief allusion to the political prostitution of some contemporary poetry (he must have had in mind the militarist odes by d'Annunzio and certain Futurists written at the time of the Tripolitan War) he ends with an eloquent exhortation directed towards his fellows:

> For poets of the present generation there remains to be done what ought to be done by sons whose fathers have been sadly prodigal of property and health—that is, to live a life of reparation and penitence without any thought of being the eventual harvesters of the fruits of such activity. . . . It remains for them, through living useful lives and begetting healthy sons, to return to the roots of things, with a life's work characterized more by discrimination and reconstruction than by any radically new sort of creativity. It remains for them to accomplish what up to now has been only rarely and partially achieved: an honest poetry.

*   *   *

I have given considerable space to quoting and paraphrasing a rejected article that influenced nobody because of what strikes me as the importance of its orientation. Its moral idealism, its exclusive concern with qualities of being (*coscienza*, the obligation to be "honest in front of oneself"), its very lack of literary professionalism, these things are exemplary not because they are right-minded but because they make up the approach that will prove of most value to Italian poetry in the decades to come.

Obviously honesty does not in itself make a poet. It is not mere cleverness that gives rise to talk of the artist as fabulist, forger, or white-liar. And in chapters to follow there will be much to observe about matters of "mere" technique. How *sincere*, after all, is a carefully dislocated hendecasyllable, an assonance, the curial citation of a medieval emblem? Questions like these, dealing fundamentally with the moral relation of form to content, will have to be answered as they arise. The point to be made here is that the aspiration towards an expressive mode that would correspond as fully as possible to a particular inwardness, to a man's sense of himself as alive in a world, seems to provide the creative tension that resulted in the major poetry to be discussed in these pages. I gladly grant that this may go without saying for *all* major poetry. But it is the fate of truisms to be repeated.

The end of World War I found Italy in a state of economic and political turmoil. Nominal victory had been won at a great price in men and morale; the consolations of territorial acquisition, the old anti-Austrian dream of *irredentismo*, were quickly frustrated at the conference table. (D'Annunzio's Fiume adventure was an authentic symptom of that frustration.) If poverty and social unrest were widespread and the Giolitti government too rattled to know what to do about it, the possible solution by revolution along recent Bolshevik lines was a frightening prospect to many. It was time for a leader, some *dux* or *duce* of the old Caesarian persuasion with the following prerequisites: a war-wound and a veteran's grievances, vitality, infectious self-confidence, showmanship, the ability to command and get obedience, a superpatriotism which, if anti-Communist, otherwise "rose above party," and whatever the magnetism is we call charisma. The man who plausibly rose to the occasion was Benito Mussolini.*

This is not the place to rehearse the history of the *ventennio*. The chronological tables at the back of this book give a few of its major dates, from the so-called "march on Rome" to the *duce's* death at the hands of a partisan firing squad in 1945. But above all else, Italian Fascism was a totalitarianism that sought adherents by strenuous appeals to brotherhood and fatherland, by instant folklore and singing "Giovanezza," by varieties of imperial bread and circuses, and forced what it could not win—by black-shirted hoodlumism, by dosages of castor oil and *manganelli* (retributive shillelaghs), by severe curtailment of individual liberties through police surveillance and censorship, by imprisonment (for example the Marxist Gramsci) and by murder (for example the socialist Matteotti).

In the early and middle 1920's it was still possible to oppose the regime publicly. The year of the scandal surrounding the death of Matteotti, 1925, was in fact a difficult one for Mussolini and his followers. It was the year of Giovanni Gentile's proclamation of writers' and intellectuals' support of the government, and the strategic need for such a proclamation is itself significant. Even more so were the responses it evoked: Croce's counter-proclamation of non-support drew a far more distinguished list of signatures. Croce, a venerable and international figure, obviously could not be touched. Younger and less-renowned writers and thinkers, like the Turinese socialist Piero Gobetti or the various *letterati* associated with the Florentine journal *Solaria*, were able for a while to voice their disillusionment and opposition without subterfuge.

Eugenio Montale's first book of poems, *Ossi di seppia* (*Cuttlefish Bones*), was published by Gobetti in 1925 and it was for Gobetti's magazine *Baretti* that Montale in the same year wrote his first important essay, "Stile e tradizione" ("Style and Tradition"). Indeed, this piece, with its stress on the moral responsibilities of the Italian

---

* Of whom Saba, who suffered greatly under Fascism, was to write: "Mussolini was not a mysterious man. Take three Italians, remove their many good qualities, multiply their bad ones, and you have Mussolini."[17]

writer, can be seen as the unwitting heir to the position taken in the Saba essay composed and shelved fourteen years before.[18] "Stile e tradizione" is basically a reasoned declaration of values inspired by Benedetto Croce whom Montale regards as *"maestro di chiarezza"* ("master of clarity") and leader in the struggle for honesty and lucidity in the written word, whether employed in politics or literature. Like Eliot, but well before he was acquainted with his work, Montale views tradition here as something living and continuous, an "intimate spirit" rather than *fait accompli* or dead weight of precedent. He understands the specifically *Italian* tradition as that expounded by Croce, "propositions of clarity and concreteness," and sees the writer's present task as allied to Croce's efforts to establish "a language of mutual comprehension" between writer and public, "the creation of a center of resonance that would permit poetry to regain its position as the ornament and pride of our country, no longer a solitary and private shame." Referring directly to Fascism and its pretentions to historic empire and manifest destiny, he writes: "We do not wish to accept *any* mythology; but to the new ones that some wish to impose upon us we decisively prefer those of our past which have a justification and a history."

It is in this context, as a cry for freedom from propaganda and for the full play and expression of intelligence, that Montale presents the famous ideal of "superior dilettantism" with which his essay closes.

> Far more than those who preserve only the appearances of our traditional style . . . they seem to us to be directly in the tradition who, reflecting in their own work the characteristics of our complex and difficult time, tend toward a superior dilettantism, saturated with human and artistic experience. . . . The style, the famous total style that our last illustrious triad of poets [that is, Carducci, Pascoli, d'Annunzio] have *not* given us (sick as they were with revolutionary frenzies, supermanism, messianism and other worminesses) will perhaps come to us from disenchanted savants and informed men, aware of their limits and humble lovers of their art more than of remaking the people. In times that seem stamped with the need for immediate utilization of culture, with polemicism and diatribe, health perhaps lies in useless and unobserved work—style will come to us from good habits. If it once was said that genius is a long patience, we would like to add that it is also *coscienza* and honesty.

Montale's Croceanism is typically independent and nonclerical, a commitment not to any specific aesthetic, ideology or philosophy, but to a style of living out a life with maximum awareness and truthfulness. The fact that phrases like "superior dilettantism" and "useless work" have in them the wry flavor of self-mockery (and we shall see that these are manners belonging to the radically skeptical "Arsenio" side of this poet), should not obscure their fundamental seriousness. Like "Quello che resta da fare ai poeti," "Stile e tradizione" asserts the value of *coscienza* as a ruthless discipline directed towards objective self-knowledge and accurate expression which, if important during the carnival days of Futurism, became all the more so, and perhaps more unusual as well, during the dangerous period of the Fascist *ventennio*.

*   *   *

Among others Cesare Pavese has written vividly of the panicked sense of crisis with which the Italian intelligensia had to live as the 1920's gave way to the 1930's, the "continual awareness of there being no way out" that endowed so much of the art of that era with what he calls its "shadowed, futile or desperate character."[19] In the decade of the 1930's, Europe was reeling into World War II, a dénouement clocked by the rise of Hitler, the successive Soviet purges, the Spanish Civil War. For Italy there was the sordid adventure in Ethiopia, the Rome-Berlin axis, a growing Nazi domination leading to such discoveries as that "real" Italians were genuine Nordic Aryans, that Jews were a peril to the *patria*. Fascist collectivization grew more stringent, individual liberties and freedom of expression were more drastically curtailed. Some succumbed to the *duce's* spell; others had to act as if they had. A few escaped; hence, as I understand it, the tormented Ungaretti's professorship in São Paulo, Brazil, from 1936 to 1942.

For those who stayed and opposed there could be no *direct* resistance to the regime, or only at the price of immediate arrest and imprisonment. For writers so equipped there was the act of translation, which could be, as was so famously the case with Vittorini and Pavese and their "discovery of America,"* a moral gesture in behalf of what seemed to be, in the pages of writers like Melville or Whitman or Twain, an authentic passion for freedom and self-renewal. Montale's introduction to his translation of *Billy Budd*, written in the dark days of the early 1940's, treats it expressly as a "mystery play" with revolutionary implications very relevant to the dilemma faced by Italians at that hour.[20] There was also the technique of the imaginary interview whereby meetings with foreign writers could be invented; Vittorini did one with "Erskine Caldwell,"[21] and the

---

* Pavese's phrase for the inspirational-ideological phase of American studies for young anti-Fascist Italians in the 1930's. See his essay on Richard Wright and above all "Ieri e oggi" in his *Letteratura americana e altri saggi*.

stranger was made to say things not strictly in line with official ideology. The offender, of course, would be the "foreigner."

And there was the act of literary criticism itself. The Florentine review *Solaria*, published between 1926 and 1936, paid homage not only to "non-Aryan" Italians like Svevo and Saba but also to the work of young writers unsympathetic to the regime: Moravia, Pavese, Vittorini, Montale, and Quasimodo among others. Furthermore, it presented sympathetic critical notes on literary developments outside of Italy: the work of Proust, Kafka, Faulkner, Joyce and so on. *Solaria* and its successor *Letteratura* were constrained to remain "cultural" and literary in content. Still, through their hospitality to innovations in other lands and the belief in freedom and individual diversity which their literary choices evidenced, they were able to register a criticism of the absurd and mechanical *italianità* urged from the seats of power which was clear enough to those who wished to understand. " '*Solarian,*' " reminisces Vittorini, "was a word that in the literary circles of those days signified anti-Fascist, European, universalist, anti-traditionalist. . . ."[22]

❖   ❖   ❖

In 1945, at the end of the *ventennio*, Montale described the situation of the disaffected writer under Fascism in this way:

> Basically one could put into prose or verse one's nostalgia for adolescence or for grandfather's carpet slippers, or could reel off a tale in a nineteenth century style. One could converse with one's own transcendent "I" with methods developed by the new *trobar clus*. By no means was it licit to respond directly to one's own time, to be critical of it, to denounce its customs or deride its vices. . . . This was, therefore, a time for writers of "intimate" prose, for exquisite essayists, for ascetic and fakiresque poets—sometimes sincere, more often echoing the experiences of others.[23]

What the regime wanted of writers was what it felt to be a healthy constructivity, happy hortatory songs about fecund mothers, beaming babies, teeming fields; positive thinking, in other words, about the *patria* and its dedicated leadership, neo-Pindaric odes celebrating heroism and sacrifice.

Strictly speaking there was no such thing as a *Fascist* literature. What one often got was what Quasimodo was later to call a literature of evasion, dense and formally elaborate lyrics in which memories of childhood, travelogue, or occult Catholicism provided the exotic occasion. Pier Paolo Pasolini has characterized the so-called "hermetic phenomenon" of poetry of the 1930's as a kind of passive resistance to the regime, and indeed the comparatively difficult and "closed" poetry that is typical of that decade could be seen as a deliberate rejection of the hearty chorales urged by the party. But while charitable, this is doubtful. In the case of the poets who mainly concern us here, Ungaretti and Montale (Saba, a Jew, did not publish in Italy from 1934 to 1945), an increasingly unaccommodating lyric is really a testament to the passionately absorbed confrontation of two markedly diverse beings with themselves and the world they had in common. The sarcasm of Montale's remarks made in 1945 about "the new *trobar clus*" and the bitterness informing Salvatore Quasimodo's concurrent "conversion" to *littérature engagée* both suggest that a good proportion of verse of the 1930's was either *à la mode* or morally inscrutable, if not opportunistic.

Still, a large percentage of what might seem *clus* to a postwar and non-Italian reader was clear enough to an intelligent home public at the time of original publication. For English-speaking readers, perhaps the most famous example of this would be Elio Vittorini's *Conversazione in Sicilia* (written between 1937 and 1939) with its "abstract furies," prevailing stenches, chorus of drunkards, nostalgia for a risorgimental "great Lombard," and so on. Here the author, inspired by lyric opera, devised a simple imagistic prose characterized by a rhythmic repetition of certain key motifs that build into a "Sicily" closer to an expressive allegory of current Italian *coscienza* than to the large southern island where Vittorini grew up.[24] In the same way the storm (*la bufera*) that looms and breaks in Montale's poetry of the decade between 1935 and 1945, the blind times (*ciechi tempi*) or ferocious faith (*fede feroce*) that drives his Jewesses, Liuba and Dora Markus, into exile, are not very oblique references to the regime and its workings.* Specific knowledge of their historical and political dimension is not required to make either the *Conversazione* or *Occasioni* comprehensible and interesting today, though there is no doubt that it augments the human drama of those pages. Good writing is not bound by its occasion. It is the lesser stuff that can be adequately explained by historical or biographical footnoting. As for the censors of those days, they were plainly either overworked or distracted. Witness most of all what was permitted, culminating in the sad farce of Pound's broadcasts to America.

The large tendencies of Italian letters during the *ventennio* were either an archeological formalism on the *Ronda* model of the early 1920's or an esoteric neo-symbolism that mixed gnostic images with

---

* See "*A Liuba che parte*" and "*Dora Markus II*" in *Le occasioni*. Montale's postwar notes now make explicit what his ladies' broadly "middle-European" names could only imply—that both are Jewish.

personal reminiscences. The result of both was to suppress any contact with external conditions in the literature characteristic of the period. Saba, neither exquisite nor exclusive, writes of the effect of those conditions on his own work of the late 1920's: "Not able by any means to react against that which he felt was a baleful error, and suffering greatly both from the error itself and his own impotence, he took refuge in himself more than ever, literally stopping up his ears in order not to hear the voices of the loudspeakers, and hearing instead, with more concentrated attention, other 'voices' that quarreled in his own heart. . . ."[25] In lesser hands a similar retreat gave rise to a merely private poetry, derived on the one hand from Ungaretti's seminal *Sentimento del tempo,* on the other from the abbé Henri Bremond's Valéryan poetics of a *poésie pure.* This fashionable school verse was what Montale had in mind with his sardonic allusion to "the new *trobar clus.*"

*   *   *

If the true Italian tradition lay in "propositions of clarity and concreteness" as expounded by Croce, then it is appropriate that the first major criticism of the new esotericism should come from a disciple. For it was the Crocean literary historian Francesco Flora who in his *La poesia ermetica* (1936) first labelled the trend "hermetic" and pinned the blame for it on Ungaretti's francophilia. "There is not a line of verse in all the Italian tradition from Petrarch to Carducci that can be viewed as the historical premise for Ungaretti's use of analogy [*analogismo*]. The real basis for his tendencies and their development is French, and nineteenth century French at that . . . the poetics of French symbolism."[26]

This assertion is highly questionable. Like *crepuscolare, ermetico* is a critic's pejorative now made commonplace and all but neutralized through heavy use. Ungaretti, Flora's influential demon whose poetry must occupy a central position in any discussion of the term, has evolved his own complex and exclusive understanding of what it signifies—we consider this at some length in the third chapter. Saba, an admirer of both Ungaretti and Montale (as well as one who profited in his later poetry by Ungaretti's early formal experiments), consistently thought of hermeticism as the modern manufacture of French crossword puzzles; also as "impotence in the presence of the Muse. . . . When one cannot move in deep, one fakes and complicates. This is human. But children don't get born this way."[27] As for Montale, often crudely lumped with Ungaretti as cofounder of this "movement": "I have never deliberately sought to be obscure. Therefore I do not feel myself qualified to speak of a supposed Italian hermeticism, even granting (which I do not) that there exists among us a group of writers who have as their objective a systematic non-communication."[28]

For Eugenio Montale most of the difficulties in his own poetry result not from any program but are "born of an extreme concentration or from a perhaps excessive confidence in the material dealt with"—that is, from the poet's erroneous assumption that certain of his allusions will be viable for readers of good will. In such cases it has been Montale's own practice to supply notes. But surely he has critics like Flora in mind when he countercharges that much of the difficulty is of the reader's own making, the result of asking irrelevant questions:

> Confronted with this [so-called obscurity born of extreme concen-
> tration], criticism behaves itself like that visitor to an exhibition who,
> looking at several pictures—for example a still-life with mushrooms
> or a landscape with a man holding an open umbrella—asks himself:
> How much do those mushrooms cost per litre? Were they gathered
> by the painter or bought at market? Where is that man going? What's
> his name? Is the umbrella of real silk or is it synthetic?[29]

We might observe here that all poetry exacts a rare sort of attention, a way of reading that combines care with relaxation, an intelligent responsiveness purged as far as is possible of preconception and the *a priori*. Critics by definition have to carry out their reading in public, and it is the fate of some of them, like Flora in the case of *Poesia ermetica* or indeed like his master Croce in so many of his reactions to modern literature, to stick in the mind as brothers to those who insisted the earth had an edge or who assailed suffragettes with umbrellas: that is, as proverbial instances of dogmatic *passatismo*. Flora in any case has a voluminous and important critical achievement to his credit and has no need of our condescension. His polemic was honestly waged under the banner of clarity (rather than, say, reactionary *italianità*) and is thereby to my mind a misguided but sympathetic one.

We might put aside the whole hermetic controversy as a critical phenomenon having little to do with poetry itself if it were not for the contentious and well-publicized position of an important poet whose conversion from a confessed hermeticism to a postwar "neo-humanist" verse constitutes strong adverse criticism of what he calls "the poets between wars" who occupy us here. For Salvatore Quasimodo as for others, "war changes the moral life of a people, and on his return from it a man no longer finds a measure of security in an internalized way of life, a *modus* either forgotten or made ironic during his struggles with death."[30] With World War II, or in Italy

with that terrible and heroic climax to it called *la Resistenza*, the
key question changes from the metaphysical to the physical scale—
in Quasimodo's phrase, "the problem of *why* one lives was altered
to *how* one lives."[31] And in *Resistenza*, as in war hot or cold,

> the position of the poet cannot be socially passive: he "modifies"
> the world. . . . His strong created images beat upon the heart of
> man more than philosophy or history. Poetry is transformed into
> ethics. . . . A poet is really a poet when he does not renounce his
> presence in a given land, at an exact moment that can be defined
> politically. And poetry is the liberty and truth of that moment—not
> abstract modulations of feeling. . . . After 1945 Italian poetry is
> of a choral nature . . . it flows with spacious rhythms, it speaks of
> the real world with common words. . . .[32]

Questions arise confronting such a position. Is it always possible
for an ethical or social position to find adequate "definition" in terms
of political party? Is a so-called "metaphysical direction" or a concern
with *whys* rather than *hows* inevitably antisocial and inhumane? Is
the individual's *sentimento* or feeling necessarily self-centered, irrele-
vant to broad human concerns?

Clearly the answer to all of these questions is a corporate "Yes"
for Quasimodo, who sees his own development in terms of Dante's
shift from the "exquisite hermetic poems of the *dolce stil nuovo*"
to the larger human, ethical and political concerns voiced in the
Monarchia and *Commedia*. Curiously jealous of Ungaretti's reputation
as hermetic *capo di scuola*, Quasimodo has concurred with Flora in
seeing the older poet's work as basically French in inspiration, at the
same time insisting (quite unlike Flora) that there was an authentic
Italian hermeticism flourishing in the 1930's. "Ungaretti's hermeticism,"
he has said recently, ". . . is of Mallarméan derivation; it is thus not
Italian hermeticism as it took shape in those days, according to which
poetry became a lexically- and stylistically-oriented *datum*."[33]

Of course poems *are* inevitably verbal, as Mallarmé explained to
the poetaster Degas, and everything, rhythms, feelings, ideas, some-
how must pass through the "lexical" filter. However, Quasimodo is
making two related points: that there was an Italian hermetic move-
ment, which he himself began, and that this hermeticism, of which his
Acque e terre (published by *Solaria* in 1930), *Oboe sommerso* (1932),
and *Odore di eucalyptus* (1933) are main examples, was primarily
what he elsewhere calls a *poetica della parola*,[34] a poetics wherein
the suave, moody, musical word took precedence over what he would
later think of as a defined and humane content. The expressive burden
of this phase was characteristically porous: vague dreams, evanescent

moods, nostalgic melancholia, all evoked with a skill that reminds us that Quasimodo was a pupil of d'Annunzio as well as Tasso. Hence his strange, resonant Sicily, his remembered *paese* exfoliating the idyllic landscapes of childhood, the wind at Tindari, the Anapo, papyri, and eucalyptus, his *isola matutina* (dawning isle), components of a love "unable to bid memory to flee those places forever."[35]

His *poetica della parola* thus coalesced almost inevitably with a *poetica della memoria,* "a poetics activated to see the world once again through memory's gentle rhythms and moods."[36] The result is what he came to reject vehemently as part of his cultural as well as political *resistenza.* "Dim landscapes cede to dialogue. . . . The most vital poetics is that which has moved away from purely formal values to search out, through man, the interpretation of the world. Man's feelings, his thirst for liberty and wish to leave his solitude—such are the new contents."[37]

It is not my purpose to adjudicate these contentions and charges in a chapter designed as a broad historical introduction. I have a high opinion of Quasimodo's talents as poet and translator; but it should be clear if only from this book's title that I do not consider him to be the equal, as a poet, of either Saba, Ungaretti, or Montale. He belongs, I think, in the distinguished company of artists like Cardarelli, Solmi, Alfonso Gatto, Leonardo Sinisgalli, and Mario Luzi, some of the men who have made this century's Italian poetic *risorgimento* substantial. I believe that the 1959 Nobel prize for literature was awarded to him largely to make up a symmetrical political package with Boris Pasternak, the previous recipient: a Russian looking westward and a westerner looking towards the U.S.S.R. But seedings and prizes have no intrinsic relation to poetry.

Yet Quasimodo's criticisms of "the poets between wars," himself included, hermetics or not, will have to be answered. As concerns the oddly assorted trio discussed in these pages, I am sure he is wrong; it is up to me to prove it. But certainly there are many ways in which a literature can be *engagée,* and it strikes me that Quasimodo's interpretation of that adjective is excessively doctrinaire and egocentric. Feeling (*sentimento*), a personal aspiration towards some sort of harmony and integrity, the troubled awareness of limit, instants of ecstasy and despair, such elements are all "engaged" in the realm of objective human values, involved in what it is to be a man at any time.

Saba and Montale suffered in their lives for their frank antipathy to the regime. In itself this is not a sufficient answer to Quasimodo, but surely Saba's *Preludio e fughe* (1928–1929) or Montale's work of the 1930's gathered in *Le occasioni* speak for basic human values, "man's feelings, his desire for liberty and wish to quit his solitude," at least as clearly and passionately as Quasimodo's postwar and committed *Giorno dopo giorno.**

Ungaretti, in contrast, formally adhered to, even signed, Gentile's proclamation, dedicated his *Allegria* of 1931 to *"l'Uomo"* ("the Man": Mussolini), and in 1942 was awarded by the government a chair at the University of Rome and membership in the Academy of Italy.** Yet at the same time as he was writing letters to the *NRF* subscribing himself "Ungaretti *poeta fascista*" he was also composing and publishing the great *Inni* (*Hymns*) of the late 1920's, in which a tortured *coscienza* expresses the anguish of those dark days. Again, in 1942, the year of his return from Brazil to an exhausted Italy to accept official honors, he was at work on the lacerated second half of *Il dolore,* his *grido* or cry of remorse, bereavement and stammered love of his fellow men, very far from either party-line or "purely formal values."

Their poems tell the truth about these lives. For the work of all three I have suggested two related perspectives: first, the sense of a human voice warming each distinctive poetics into life; second, a stubborn, sometimes heroic conception of poetry as a discipline drawing on and devoted to *coscienza*, true witness to man's life. What follows is meant to be of use in the reading of their poems, as well as proof of such large claims.

* Thus in a published review of *Le occasioni* in 1939 Vittorini wrote that the book "counts more than so many of the facts told us by the papers for the past year, two years, many years. . . ."[38]

** "Founded by Fascism," wrote Montale, "to keep the poor Italian *letterati* dangling on the hook."[39]

Notes

1. Giuseppe Antonio Borgese, "Poesia crepuscolare: Moretti, Martini, Chiaves," in *La vita e il libro,* second series (Turin, 1911).

2. Umberto Saba, *Prose,* ed. Linuccia Saba (Milan, 1964), p. 781. This sketch was apparently written around 1930 for a projected anthology of modern verse which never was completed.

3. Ungaretti, *Vita d'un uomo: Saggi e interventi* [*SI*], (Milan, 1974), p. 742.

4. From an interview in the Roman paper *Il Tevere,* July 18, 1932, cited in Luciano Rebay, *Le origini della poesia di Giuseppe Ungaretti* (Rome, 1962), p. 14.

5. *Collected Poems* 1909–1962 (New York, 1963).

6. Ungaretti, *SI,* p. 743.

7. Ungaretti, *SI,* p. 742.

8. *Letteratura* #35–36, September–December 1958 (Ungaretti issue), p. 325

9. Cardarelli, *Viaggi nel tempo,* cited by Gigi Cavalli, *Ungaretti* (Milan, 1958), p. 55.

10. "General Introduction to My Poetry," *Essays and Introductions* (New York, 1961), p. 522.

11. Cavalli, *Ungaretti,* p. 54.

12. Cited from Serra's *Epistolario* by Gianni Pozzi, *La poesia italiana del Novecento da Gozzano agli ermetici* (Turin, 1965), p. 17.

13. Now available in Saba, *Prose,* pp. 751–59.

14. Chapter on "Formazione e origini di Saba," *Storia e cronistoria del Canzoniere (Prose,* p. 421).

15. For Saba's humorous personal recollections of d'Annunzio see "Il bianco immaculato signore" and "Versilia," *Prose,* pp. 139–45, 208–11.

16. "Encomio della mia arte," cited in Giorgio Pullini, *Le poetiche dell' Ottocento* (Padua, 1909), p. 343.

17. Saba, "Scorsiatoie disperse 1945–1948," *Prose,* p. 395.

18. Available in Montale's collection of essays on art and literature, *Auto da fé* (Milan, 1966), pp. 15–19.

19. Pavese, "Il fascismo e la cultura," *La letteratura americana e altri saggi* (Turin, 1962).

20. See Eugenio Montale, "An Introduction to *Billy Budd* (1942)," tr. Mrs. Barbara Melchiori Arnett, *Sewanee Review,* LXVIII, 3 (Summer, 1960).

21. Elio Vittorini, *Diario in pubblica* (Florence, 1957), p. 94.

22. Vittorini, *Diario in pubblico,* p. 174.

23. "Il fascismo e la letteratura," *Auto da fé,* pp. 23–24.

24. See Vittorini's 1948 preface to his first novel, *Il garofano rosso,* excerpted in *Diario in pubblico,* pp. 293–301.

25. Saba, chapter on *Preludio e fughe* in *Storia e cronistoria del Canzoniere (Prose,* p. 558).

26. *La poesia ermetica* (Bari, 1947), p. 72.

27. Saba, chapter on *Autobiografia, Storia e cronistoria del Canzoniere (Prose,* p. 504).

28. Montale, *Sulla poesia [SP],* (Milan, 1976), pp. 558–59.

29. Montale, *SP,* p. 87.

30. "Discorso sulla poesia," in Salvatore Quasimodo, *Il poeta e il politico e altri saggi* (Milan, 1960), p. 27.

31. "Poesia del dopoguerra," ibid., p. 39.

32. "Discorso sulla poesia," ibid., p. 36.

33. Quasimodo interview in Ferdinando Camon, *Il mestiere di poeta* (Milan, 1965); see also the title essay in *Il poeta e il politico,* p. 48.

34. "Una poetica," ibid., p. 24.

35. Ibid.

36. "Discorso sulla poesia," ibid., p. 35.

37. "Il poeta e il politico," ibid., p. 49; "Una poetica," ibid., p. 24.

38. *Diario in pubblico,* p. 100.

39. "Il fascismo e la letteratura, *Auto de fé,* p. 21.

II UMBERTO SABA

Nulla riposa della vita come
la vita.

"My dear Linuccia, once upon a time there was an all but fabulous city, under Austrian domination, called Trieste," where "once there lived a young man (by no means fabulous—only a little restless, a little neurotic) called Umberto. . . ." So Saba begins a memoir[1] addressed to his daughter in the very last years of his life, and for the non-Triestine reader whose knowledge of the area is based on recollections of irredentist politics, commercial slogans ("Gateway to the East"), and the novels of Italo Svevo, the ascription of fable, even modified by *quasi*, could seem excessive. "One day is sufficient to visit the town," the Touring Club Italiano advises in its guide. "A crucible of heterogeneous elements attracted by commerce," writes Svevo,[2] executive by day of a marine paint factory, whose *nom de plume* ("Italus the Swabian") testifies to the heterogeneity of both his ancestry and city. But for Umberto Saba at seventy, Trieste was "fabulous" because he had been young there, and for "an old man dreaming" (the title of the memoir), it is perhaps fable enough to have been young at all. For the readers of his poetry, however, it is not where or when he lived but what he made of it that must count, and what Saba made of it can be found in the big, uneven, often fabulous lyric diary of over six hundred pages, kept and published at intervals between 1900 and 1954, which he called, with a bow to Petrarch and an assertion of continuity, his *Canzoniere*.

In his remarkable book-length act of autocriticism, the *Storia e cronistoria del Canzoniere* (History and Chronicle of the Canzoniere), Saba writes: "The *Canzoniere* is the history (we would have nothing against calling it a 'novel,' even, if one wished, a 'psychological novel') of a life relatively poor in external events but rich, at times excruciatingly so, in emotions and inner resonances, in the people whom the poet loved in the course of his long life and out of whom he created his 'characters' [*figure*]."[3] Along with what he liked to call his innately classical formal conservatism, it is the frankly autobiographical, occasional and, at times, documentary nature of Saba's

31

content that most sharply divides it from the work of his contemporaries, both in Italy and abroad.

Certainly any textbook definition of international literary "modernism" for the first forty years of this century would have to include the potent Parnassian ideal of impersonality, wherein the author, cool as the god of Voltaire, strives to transcend his merely "contingent" historical identity through manipulation of mask, myth, or irony. For the English-speaking reader, the *locus classicus* for impersonalism is to be found in Eliot's "Tradition and the Individual Talent," where the requisite process of depersonalizing is icily or "metaphysically" likened to a chemical experiment, and the poem itself is seen as "not the expression of personality, but an escape from personality." Likewise, the ineffable purity sought under the heading of *poésie pure* (out of Mallarmé by Valéry and the *abbé* Henri Bremond) refers in part to the abolition of personal-historical dross by the poet-priest in the course of his "alchemy" of creation.

By such standards, the poetry of Saba is indubitably *periferico e arretrato*, peripheral and backward; the sardonic adjectives are his own. Saba is a personal artist if ever there were one, whose poetry, in the phrase of Giuseppe Ravegnani, "follows his biography like a shadow."[4] Even the table of contents of the *Canzoniere* reads like an autobiographical outline. His "matter" is almost aggressively his life: a childhood and adolescence at once tormented and beatific, military service, courtship and marriage, servitude and grandeur of wedded life and fatherhood, real and imagined erotic adventures with concomitant *tristesse* and pangs of guilt, the bookshop, the experience of psychoanalysis, an old age embittered by Fascist persecution and what he felt to be critical neglect. It is a lifetime lived almost entirely in Trieste. Above all there is Trieste itself: streets, shops, houses, encircling hills and harbor, its men, women and children, citizens and strangers, and all this mass of local detail unified in the strange sensibility and limpid language of one man, the Triestine Saba. As he rightly boasts in 1944, in a period of exile and great personal danger,

> Avevo una città bella tra i monti
> rocciosi e il mare luminoso. Mia
> perché vi nacqui, piú che d'altri mia
> che la scoprivo fanciullo, ed adulto
> per sempre a Italia la sposai col canto.

I had a lovely city between the rocky / mountains and the shining sea. Mine / because I was born there, more than others' mine / who as

a boy discovered it and as an adult / forever to Italy wedded it
with song.

*   *   *

The most beautiful autobiographies no doubt require a certain
egoism or some such sense of special calling. A central problem
for any critical assessment of Saba's work is to weigh to what extent
and by what means he has been able to validate his obsession with
self *as poetry*, so that we read him not as historical symptom or case
history but as he would wish, as our brother, man among other men,
uomo fra gli uomini. He himself had called attention to the liabilities
of self-concern at several points in the course of the *Storia*. Com-
menting on *Il piccolo Berto* (Little Berto), a childhood-fixated
sequence written while he was undergoing psychoanalysis, he remarks
that "here truly . . . the reader didn't exist for Saba. . . . The names
of Aunt Stellina, Elvira and Peppa had an evocative value for him
that clearly they could not have for the reader, to whom they remain
'dead letters.' . . . [Poetic] inspiration there was in some sense, but
born in solitude, destined therefore never to become poetry, or to
become so for the author alone."[5] Giacomo Debenedetti, one of the
earliest admirers and best critics of Saba's work, has written per-
ceptively about this problem.

> There exists in his poetry a kind of egoistic intransigence (if you
> wish one might call it a kind of affectionate claim) in which our
> participation in certain of his ways of feeling is taken for granted.
> Saba believes that his recollection of certain objects is sufficient to
> transmit to the reader the whole gamut of sensations felt by him at
> the sight of them. We are not dealing here with magical resonances
> [the reference is to Ungaretti], but with authentic touches of realism
> which function as complex evocation. I would say that, at certain
> moments, it is enough for Saba to name Trieste for a crowd of
> vibrant and yearning memories to possess him; one notes this wholly
> through the passionate affection with which he pronounces the
> name of Trieste—the rest one has to guess or deduce from his biog-
> raphy. Elsewhere . . . certain figures are merely indicated without
> comment; one must intuit for oneself the thoughts that gravitate about
> them. It is as though his interpretation of the world were univocal,
> completely evident in the simple appearance of things. . . .[6]

If the "affectionate claim" was palpable to Debenedetti, it has not
always been so for others; the formidable Alfredo Gargiulo, for
instance, an important critic and sensitive interpreter of Ungaretti
and Montale, found Saba's *autobiografismo* "persistently prosaic,"
tracing this to the poet's lack of distance—that is, lack of objective

judgment—regarding his materials. It would be ridiculous to assert that there were no dead letters in the *Canzoniere*. There assuredly are, but the miracle is that in this enormous book of a lifetime there are, relatively, so few.

In my opinion one of the fundamental plotlines of the *Canzoniere* as a whole is the poet's largely successful struggle to achieve objective distancing about his life through experimentation with "given" traditional prosodic and stanzaic forms; if ever technique were discovery, it is in the technically ultra-conservative pages of the *Canzoniere*. And the very abundance of his Muse, the considerable volume of poetry that he wrote, builds into a sense of homely continuity or process in which the single "stunning" poem (and there are many) often counts for less than the more massive resonances of its ambiance or autobiographical "stage." Certainly Saba's own description of his book as a novel suggests a different, perhaps less intense, mode of reading it than is usually advised for poetry of the modern variety. However, any conclusions on his poetry in general, or on how best to read the *Canzoniere,* should wait until the end of this chapter, when we shall have examined some of the poems as well as Saba's aims and development in some detail.

*   *   *

Elsewhere Debenedetti writes: "Homage to Saba ought to begin with his biography. He is a man worthy of biography; his life has unforgettable accents and is certainly the most authentic preface to his verses."[7] This seems a curious remark to make about this most autobiographical of poets (for whom "the work of art is always a confession"[8]) whose poems articulate those unforgettable accents in a way no authorized biography ever could. Yet Saba himself clearly agreed with Debenedetti; the *Storia e cronistoria* (written in the difficult years between 1944 and 1947), which he genially called his doctoral dissertation, is not only a nearly poem-by-poem assessment of the *Canzoniere* composed to remedy critical neglect, but also an attempt at a fairly circumstantial biography providing background for the poems. Written in the third person* by a pseudonymous Giuseppe Carimandrei (the real identity of the author was an open secret), the *Storia* provides a fund of concrete information on the circumstances of Saba's life, the conditions under which specific poems were written, his intentions, and his estimates

---

* Anita Pittoni, editor of Signora Livia Svevo's memoir of her husband (*Vita di mio marito*), surmises that Saba's procedure here might have been suggested to him by his friend Svevo's use of the same distancing device in his "Autobiographical Profile" of 1928.

of success and failure. As an informal life history the book is invaluable; as criticism, it is the best thing written on the *Canzoniere* so far. The author's intimate involvement with his work occasionally results in a protective tenderness for certain of the weaker poems. Nevertheless, Saba is not so paranoid as to neglect the sometimes negative judgments of professional critics, so that the *Storia's* claims to a certain objectivity are not as spurious as one might think. Insofar as the basic story line about which his poems accrue is the poet's life, we should follow his example by prefacing an examination of them with a summary account of his biography, that soil to which the gross harvest of the *Canzoniere* is so generous a witness.

Umberto Poli, who later chose to be called Umberto Saba, was born in Trieste on March 9, 1883. This was the same year in which were born the ironic *crepuscolare* Guido Gozzano, and Collodi's *Pinocchio*. Saba, who always resented any attempt on the part of critics to diagnose his poems for symptoms of twilight, felt especially fraternal towards the aimiable Geppetto's masterpiece, who was, like himself, an abnormal outsider. While he was still an infant, his Jewish mother had been deserted by his irresponsible and gentile vagabond of a father. As a consequence his earliest years and childhood were spent in an atmosphere of great poverty and bitterness.* In the 1924 sonnet sequence entitled *Autobiografia* he attempts an analysis of his own ambivalent or split nature in terms of his broken family:

> Mio padre è stato per me «l'assassino»,
> fino ai vent'anni che l'ho conosciuto.
> Allora ho visto ch'egli era un bambino,
> e che il dono ch'io ho da lui l'ho avuto.
>
> Aveva in volto il mio sguardo azzurrino,
> un sorriso, in miseria, dolce e astuto.
> Andò sempre pel mondo pellegrino;
> più d'una donna l'ha amato e pasciuto.
>
> Egli era gaio e leggero; mia madre
> tutti sentiva della vita i pesi.
> Di mano ei gli sfuggí come un pallone.

---

* "Saba" in fact means "bread" in Hebrew; the poet's adoption of this pseudonym in his twenties manifests symbolically his fealty to the lonely woman who raised him and rejection of the patronymic "Poli." Actually "Saba" is the second and the only permanent one of his three pseudonyms: he published his first poems in 1911 under the dandy's name of "Umberto da Montereale" and signed "Giuseppe Carimandrei" to the *Storia*.

We shall query "why *bread*" further on. It is interesting to note that Saba's daughter Linuccia employs "Annetta Pane" as a pseudonym—*pane* being the Italian for "bread."

No. see 345

«Non somigliare—ammoniva—a tuo padre».
Ed io piú tardi in me stesso lo intesi:
Eran due razze in antica tenzone.

My father was for me "the killer" / until, twenty years old, I met him. / Then I saw that he was a child, / and that the gift I have I had from him. /
He had in his face my own blue eyes, / a smile, in his wretchedness, both sweet and sly. / He roved the earth, always the vagabond; / more than one woman loved and nourished him. /
He was gay and blithe; my mother / felt all the burdens of life. / From her hand he spurted like a ball. / "Don't," she warned me, "don't be like your father." / And later within myself I found the answer: / they were two races in an ancient quarrel.

Saba, homerically self-styled *esperto di molti beni e molti mali* (expert in many goods and many evils), locates in the antagonistic figures of his parents the primitive schism out of which his own torn character was fashioned. From his father "vagabondaggio, evasione, poesia" (these astounding synonyms are from a late poem), his so-called "Franciscan" love of things, his sensuality, his infantile egotism, his restlessness; from his mother his sense of the weight of existence, his frequent bitterness and intimations of persecution, his self-pity and "Jewish" cultivation of suffering. Such was the inheritance Saba was aware of, and whether or not it is valid is of no importance compared to the fact that he believed in and accepted it.

In contrast to the misery of the dark home in the Trieste ghetto, "little Berto" found what seemed forever after like paradise in the person of his nurse, the butcher's wife Peppa, with whom he spent most of the first four years of his life while his mother worked at menial jobs in the city. Peppa had lost her own son and found a glad surrogate in deprived Berto. Her house, facing an abandoned Jewish cemetery on a hill overlooking Trieste and its harbor, with its rural peacefulness and domestic sounds and odors, was to become the very first of the recurrent icons of love and community to which the poet returns again and again in the long course of the *Canzoniere*. Yet this precarious idyll was also an early source of guilt. His harassed mother grew jealous and more embittered by her son's clear preference for Peppa; harsh arguments took place between mother and nurse, the son was brought back to the city and his visits to his nurse thereafter had to be furtive "betrayals" of the mother by a son who seemed already, so precociously, to take after his *assassino* of a father. In the period of his psychoanalysis Saba was to feel that another source of his torments came from having been fought over by two mothers without the stabilization or counterbalance that a father might have provided. One also notes that the coupling of love and guilt, his continuing sense of betraying her who loves and needs him most, is repeated in his marriage, where after the newness wears off his wife Lina seems more and more to take on the lineaments of some mourning Rachel, the victimized mother.

In such circumstances, Saba's formal education was minimal and erratic. Largely self-taught, intensely interested in reading poetry from an early age, he experienced the frustration of "living in an ambience where no one spoke to him of good or bad authors," and, at one point, he bitterly "burned in a bonfire of joy the classical texts which had become, through lack of love, too difficult—indeed impossible."[9] Following this he attended vocational school, determined, he says, to become a "good, honest, reputable businessman" (eventually he did) and took a job as clerk, meanwhile continuing to read voraciously.

He began to write poetry in his mid-teens, from "the need to find," as he writes in the *Storia*, "some relief from his troubles." What he has preserved of it in the *Canzoniere* is chiefly of interest in revealing his precocious passion for the Italian classics, Petrarch, Parini, and above all, the Leopardi of the idylls, and his sensitive "ear" for reproducing their modulations in his own work. Very little trace of the latest triad is evident in it. Saba explains this youthful preference for an earlier tradition with an assortment of genetic and cultural possibilities: his classicism, he says, was a "profound and prenatal vocation," the product of a "temperamental" classicist "who came of age in a romantic environment."[10] It also served as a compensation for his own shattered family background: "There was in his deepest nature something requiring support in the most stable, certain and tested past, as ground for the conquest of self." In other pages of the *Storia*, however, it is the cultural peculiarity of his city which is cited as the dominant influence on his conservative tastes, partially through a sort of emotional irredentism ("for the Triestine, the verses of the great Italian poets— that is, of the tradition—had a greater emotional value than for other Italians"), partially through its cultural retardation: ". . . to be born in Trieste in 1883 was like being born elsewhere in 1850. . . . [It was] behind the times, barbaric, primitive."* Hence of course his

---

* But compare Svevo's picture of Trieste in roughly the same period (from his autobiographical "profile"): ". . . a terrain particularly receptive to all intellectual currents. Set at the crossroads of many peoples, the Triestine literary ambiance was permeated by the most diverse cultural influences."

sardonic epithets for his own verses, *periferico* and *arretrato*. The general title of *Canzoniere*, of course, asserts his traditionalism with pride.

In 1902, at the age of nineteen, Saba quit his clerkship in order to devote himself to poetry. For the next six years he tried (as Umberto da Montereale) his absentee father's life of *vagabondaggio*, traveling through northern Italy living from hand to mouth, publishing a book of his poems in 1911. In Florence he came into contact with the *Voce* circle, and *La Voce* published his second book of poems in 1912. One of the sonnets of *Autobiografia* deals with his literary memories of this decade. The resentment of the last tercet derives from Saba's feeling that his book had been "sabotaged" by the Voceans' basic lack of sympathy for his work (despite their publishing it!), their failure to send out review copies, absence of advertising, and so on.

> Vivevo allora a Firenze, e una volta
> venivo ogni anno alla città natale.
> Piú d'uno in suoi ricordi ancor m'ascolta
> dire, col nome di Montereale,
>
> i miei versi agli amici, o ad un'accolta
> d'ignari dentro assai nobili sale.
> Plausi n'avevo, or n'ho vergogna molta;
> celarlo altrui, quand'io lo so, non vale.
>
> Gabriele d'Annunzio alla Versiglia
> vidi e conobbi; all'ospite fu assai
> egli cortese, altro per me non fece.
>
> A Giovanni Papini, alla famiglia
> che fu poi della «Voce», io   appena o mai
> non piacqui. Ero fra lor di un'altra spece.

I was living then in Florence, and once / a year returned to my native city. In his memories more than one can still hear me, / under the name Montereale, speak / my lines to friends, or to a gathering / of the ignorant in rather venerable salons. / From this I gathered praises that now I am most ashamed of; / to hide this from others, when I feel it, would be pointless.

Gabriele d'Annunzio at Versiglia / I saw and knew; to his guest he was / courteous enough; more for me he did not do. / With Giovanni Papini and the *Voce* family / of those days I found scant / favor, or none at all. Among them I was of another species.

In Trieste, in 1907, he met the seamstress Lina, "Lina of the red shawl," one of the central presences of the *Canzoniere* to come. He corresponded with her during his year's military service with the twelfth infantry regiment in Salerno and married her in Trieste a year later. The great sequence gathered under the title of *Casa e campagna* [*House and Countryside*] is Saba's celebration of his marriage and first years with Lina, and it constitutes one of the high points of the *Canzoniere* as well as perhaps the one untrammeled moment of idyll in the poet's long life.

Thereafter, with the brief exception of his army service during the First World War (he worked as an inspector of parts at an airfield) and his underground existence as a refugee from Fascism during the Second, Saba's outwardly uneventful life is tied to Trieste, the world of the *Canzoniere*. In 1919 he bought an antiquarian bookshop, the Libreria Antica e Moderna, with which, lover of books and "good, honest, reputable businessman" that he truly was, he was able to support his little family until the end of his life.

By the later 1920's the emotional crisis that can be seen gathering a long way before came to a head, complicated by the poet's bitter resentment at the comparative neglect of his work by Italian critics. Due to its proximity to Vienna and its largely Austrian political and cultural background, Trieste was one of the first outposts of Freudianism in Europe. In 1929 Saba underwent psychoanalytical treatment and became a doctrinaire Freudian. We shall note the effect of this experience on his poetry later on. Fortunately his genial propagandizing for Freud was confined to conversation and prose.* Saba's "conversion" to Freud no doubt gave him the sort of covering myth or system he required in order to map and bear the conflicts within him. It also furnished him with a tradition for what he liked to call his "affective ambivalence" and excruciated sense of inner flux and dissonance. Perhaps above all his experience of the confessional procedure of psychoanalysis set a scientific seal of approval on his compulsive *autobiografismo*, finding in his obsession with his past the way to reconciliation with his ghosts as well as a possible alliance with the phantoms of health and transfiguring wisdom. "See my childhood?" wryly asks another great Triestine, Svevo's Zeno Cosini, as he sits himself down to comply with his analyst's prescription—and promptly falls asleep. Unlike Zeno, Saba, a true believer, was able to come up with the poems of *Piccolo Berto,* and in the process a more serene acceptance of, or resignation to, his own *dolore.*

For Saba the 1930's were a time of not only psychic but poetic

---

* Once in the days of political tension he was asked to what political party he belonged. Only partially ironic, he answered "To the psychoanalyst party."

renewal. "If" he writes in the *Storia*, "in order to escape from hell, Saba had not experimented on his own skin with the truths of psychoanalysis, we would not have today the limpidity of his last poems. . . ."[11] Saba sees Sigmund Freud as the chief genius presiding over this transformation, but the poems of this decade show also the effect of Saba's study of Ungaretti's early war poems, as, indeed, Saba himself points out.

But this period was also a time of steadily mounting anxiety. Saba's Jewish "blood" and contempt for Mussolini's imperialism made him increasingly *persona non grata* to the authorities. In the years of the war the Libreria was forced to close, and Saba, in his sixties, was driven into three years' wandering exile: first, abortively, in France, then in Milan, Rome and Florence (where he was concealed and aided by Montale among others). The bitter refrain in "Avevo" (I Had) is his cry out of that Diaspora, the single direct reference to politics in all the *Canzoniere:*

> Tutto mi portò via il fascista abbietto
> ed il tedesco lurc. . . .

> . . . The vile Fascist and the swilling German [the adjective is Dante's: see *Inf*. XVII, 21] took all I had. . . .

Now and in the unsettled conditions of the period immediately following the war he turned increasingly to prose; memoirs, the *Storia* and a collection of epigrammatic *pensées* he called "shortcuts" or *scorciatoie* were mainly composed in these years.*

The final decade of his life (1947–1957), though it at last brought him the large public recognition and affection that had seemed to elude him in the course of his long career, was marred by illness and continued poverty. The death of his Lina in 1956 was a blow he survived by only nine months, dying on August 25th, 1957. Saba was never really "cured"; he alternated in moods between a querulous despondency over his life and times, and that wry sympathy for

---

* Saba's prose is conveniently available in the single volume *Prose* edited by his daughter Linuccia. Apart from various prefaces, speeches and occasional articles, this work divides into three sections: 1) memoirs of Trieste in the old days, of acquaintances and friends, of his youth and young manhood, etc., collected as *Ricordi-Racconti* (Memories-Tales); 2) the *pensées*, written between 1934 and 1948, whose "genealogy" he schematically indicates as "Nietzsche-Freud," collected as *Scorciatoie e raccontini* (Shortcuts and Little Tales); 3) the autocriticism, *Storia e cronistoria del Canzoniere*, written between 1944 and 1947. In 1953 Saba wrote some chapters of a novel he called *Ernesto*, the story of a youth of 16 in late nineteenth-century Trieste. This was never completed and published posthumously in 1975.

life in all its forms which, under the name of *umorismo*, humor, he once called—speaking of his friend Svevo—"the supreme form of goodness."[12] Such goodness can be found in all but the last of the poems he wrote, poems celebrating birds either wild or—particularly dear—caged. The bitterness which made him to the very end a notoriously "difficult" man sounds through the epitaphs he was pleased to compose for himself. For example, in one of his last books:

> In questo libro tredici poesie,
> che il nome hanno dall'ultima,
> sono, me vivo, mie.
> Poi le avrò scritte come l'altre invano,
> per gli uccelli e un amico, al tempo triste,
> nel mio triste italiano.

In this book the thirteen poems, / that take their title from the last, / are mine—while I'm alive. / Still, like all the others, they will have been written in vain, / for the birds and a friend, in a sad time, / in my sad Italian.

That thirteenth poem was called "Epigrafe":

> Parlavo vivo a un popolo di morti.
> Morto alloro rifiuto e chiedo oblio.

Alive I spoke to a dead people. / Dead I refuse the laurel and ask oblivion.

In 1928, at the request of the widowed Livia Svevo, Saba had composed an epitaph for his friend, whose life had had certain aspects similar to his own. But the inscription he submitted reveals a Saba brooding over the disparities:

> Fortune / as much as it can for any man / smiled upon him / He had / his studies and tranquillity in childhood / in his youth hope and love / love and wealth in his industrious maturity / and in old age glory / . . . From his consciousness of his race / from the ambiance that disregarded him / he drew his materials / . . . He lived / the Thousand and One Days in his last years / as in a dream within a sunset / all of gold.[13]

Svevo had found himself to be a Lazarus, raised from the death of neglect in the final years of his life. For Saba, on the other hand, even if he acknowledged his glory it was too little and too late. His life, with all its joys and sorrows, continues its troubled course permanently in the pages of the *Canzoniere*.

The completed *Canzoniere*, published by Einaudi in 1961, is divided into three "volumes" roughly corresponding to the poet's youth, middle, and old age. Each volume contains approximately eight books or sequences, most of these previously published separately before their incorporation, with revision, into the *Canzoniere*.* The second volume covers the period extending from the late thirties to the threshold of fifty, a decade of self-torment and "breakdown" forecast in the final sequences of the first volume, and transcended (the verb is Saba's) in the last through the happy intervention of a psychoanalyst.

The first two volumes show Saba working mainly with the received forms of the Italian literary tradition; his working line is the hendecasyllable and its normal subdivisions; lines are disposed in "closed" arrangements such as sonnet, canzonetta, and so on. The last volume is more responsive to the "freer" metric and stanzaic patterns of twentieth-century modernism. We shall have occasion to refer frequently to the relations of biography and form in the pages to follow.

The *Canzoniere* is very uneven. Each volume has its great sequences and single poems as well as its weak ones. The book as a whole lends itself to anthological culling and weeding, no doubt, and Carlo Muscetta's recent *Antologia del «Canzoniere»* not only makes a generous portion of the poetry available in a reasonably inexpensive format, but is also a fair demonstration of the best of Saba.**

Another of the poet's originalities is his power to involve his reader in his life so that even the relatively inferior verses fascinate as variations, preparations, or echoes of poetically better times. Despite his exorbitant ego, Saba himself was aware of his unevenness. His *envoi* to *Cose leggere e vaganti* (Light and Airy Things) says:

---

* The *Canzoniere* itself has had three major installments. Its first appearance was in 1921, published by Saba himself. The second edition, greatly amplified, was put out by Einaudi at the war's end in 1945. All editions issued after 1957 (the year of Saba's death) are virtually complete, though the poet revised and suppressed continuously, making a variorum *Canzoniere* most desirable.

** This anthology was one of Saba's "last cards" played for the public recognition he felt he lacked; his correspondence with Muscetta on this score, quoted in the latter's introduction, is very sad. The *Storia* was written in order to rectify what Saba felt to be the failure of his admirers to express their feelings in print. The fact of the matter is that Saba was psychologically incapable of feeling himself sufficiently lovable, and therefore loved; hence the perpetual yearning for official laurels.

Voi lo sapete, amici, ed io lo so.
Anche i versi somigliano alle bolle
di sapone; una sale e un'altra no.

You know it, friends, and so do I. / Even poems are like soap /
bubbles; one goes up, another not.

Speaking to his friend Nora Baldi, he likened the failures, the *non-
poesia* of parts of the *Canzoniere,* to the "zum-pai-pai" or musical
fillings in the work of Verdi, concluding that "no one can stay on
the heights forever without lying."[14] And in the *Storia,* he offers his
work as very much a "natural phenomenon," wholly dependent on the
inspiration of the moment: "when inspiration fails him, or is thin,
Saba is worth little or nothing. And nothing can be done about it.
'Literature' was never a valid support for him. In terms of his
particular poetics, literature is to poetry as lie to truth. Such a man
had to be born in Italy, precisely in the land of *letterati!*"[15]

There is something of the mucker pose in this assertion. As part
of his long guerilla war against what he felt to be the modish in-
tellectualism of most modern verse, Saba at times exaggerated his
self-made, *naïf* proletarian side, priding himself on the largeness
and "naturalness" of his vein. Yet he revised and rearranged his
work incessantly, for all his naturalness, and "literature" most certainly
sustained and nourished his muse and him in the long course of
their life together, as even the general title for his collected poems
indicates. He was not remotely *maudit* (expressively and spontane-
ously "damned" like Rimbaud or Campana), but rather a hard
working, well-read storekeeper (specializing in antiquarian books!)
who was poor, insufficiently encouraged, often most unhappy, and
who wrote poems about it all.

Of course all poets must in the first instance depend on inspiration
or some sort of exceptional grace, and perhaps he was merely less
nervous or conscience-stricken about living up to or filling out the
given afflatus. He wrote more poems than most and discarded fewer;
thus there is a greater fluctuation in quality. And he sometimes
confused the mental anguish or pain or exultation attendant upon
the writing of poetry with poetry itself, experiencing an intensity
there that never really got transcribed. But such is his charm, or the
fascination of his egotism, that the reader is often seduced into
accepting lesser work simply because it is part of Saba's life. This
is not a contemptible achievement. In other words, a good case can
be made for reading all of Saba.

✿   ✿   ✿

The first chapter of the *Canzoniere*—that is, the poems included in what Saba came to call *Poesie dell'adolescenza e giovanili* (Poems of Adolescence and Youth), written between his seventeenth and twenty-fourth years—does not offer a completely authentic portrait of the artist as a young man. Composed not only in Trieste but in the course of his *vagabondaggio* in Pisa and Florence when Umberto Poli was still Umberto da Montereale and giving public readings of his work, many of the poems of this phase were literally fugitive, copied out by memory for friends and then either lost or misplaced. In 1921, when Saba came to compile his first *Canzoniere* for self-publication by his Libreria Antica e Moderna, he had already two volumes of verse on his record: the *Poesie* of 1911 (poems 1900–1910) and *Coi miei occhi* (With My Own Eyes) issued by *La Voce* in 1912 (poems 1910–1912, later to be called *Trieste e una donna*: Trieste and a Lady). The latter, written when Saba had completed his apprenticeship and was proudly conscious of the ends and means of his poetic vocation, could take its place with minor changes as a central chapter of the *Canzoniere*. On the other hand the *Poesie* presented him with problems of a moral as well as aesthetic kind. As far as the poems in that first book were concerned Saba wrote in 1921 that

> they appeared there not only in an order that was chronologically false, thus robbing my work of its main lines, but many—for example the poems of adolescence and young manhood, or those written in Florence: all necessary in order to comprehend the genesis and gradual developments, the releases from bondage and returns to origins of my work—were omitted. Still worse, others were so altered from their primitive form that they had become a wholly other thing, and not at all a better one.[16]

The stubborn confidence in his vocation which permitted the all but unknown Saba to issue under his own imprint a collected poems at the age of thirty-eight and to title it *Canzoniere* shows up clearly in his assumption that readers would be concerned with the genesis and development of his muse even if this meant admitting inferior or derivative work to the canon. In the preface to the first *Canzoniere* he speaks of his two years' labor to recover or recollect lost lines or lost poems, to reconstruct already published—and therefore effectively stabilized—poems in their "primitive form." In a sense this was a labor that was to occupy him all his life. For if on the one hand he was committed from at least 1911 onwards to "making poetry honest" (see above, pp. 14–18) and therefore to keeping as close to the original terms of expression as possible, on the other hand he recognized that an original verse could be untrue to its occasion and that an honesty of the spirit, as opposed to the letter, might demand revision.

In the *Storia* Saba writes of a certain poem of this early period that "it had been like a fixation to him" for over thirty years. He felt, he said, that "he had said something fundamental, something that it was impossible for him not to say, but he had said it in part poorly; hence the continual retouchings. . . . Yet, if it is still possible to correct while the state of mind, the constellation beneath which a poem was born lasts, how can it be done when everything inside and outside of us has changed?"[17] In the event, despite the fact that he found it "muddied over with either extraneous or imperfectly assimilated elements," Saba finally chose to print it in its original imperfect form for the second *Canzoniere* of 1945. But at other times he felt his post facto alterations actually fulfilled his original intentions. Thus in a new edition of his early poems published in 1932 he wrote of "how opportune" his latest revisions (that is, made since the 1921 *Canzoniere*) were. "My experience of the present moment and the memory I keep of how my poems, even the very oldest, were born, has enabled me to complete—in a moment of grace—this difficult and delicate task. . . ."[18]

Whether he retouched his work or not, the governing principle of his poetic maturity was his *coscienza* of whether or not a given poem reflected the "constellation" of its nativity. The stifled manifesto of 1911, "Quello che resta da fare ai poeti," provides an uncomplicated instance of this ethical check in action.[19] One night Saba had had what sounds like a "wet" dream in which he had gladly given himself over to desires which, awake, he was capable of resisting. Arising the following morning he saw himself in the mirror as quite different from his customarily edited impression of himself. These two successive shocks fused, "and from the parallel between what the dream had revealed of my inmost being and what the mirror had shown I was moved to write a short poem." The first stanza came in a rush:

> Credevo sia un gioco sognare;
> ma il sogno è un temibile Iddio
> è il solo che sa smascherare
> l'animo mio.

I thought that dreaming was play, / but the dream is a fearful God, / who alone can unmask / my soul.

Rereading the poem a few days later he noticed a discrepancy between original experience and expression centered in the image of the God. "Whenever had I conceived of comparing my dream with a vengeful divinity? It was certainly a literary reminiscence which had quietly crept in through some subtle association of thought or rhythm." He tried an alternate, "ma un giudice è il sogno" (but the dream is a judge), and found this worse. Then followed an impassioned solicitation of memory "to rediscover the psychological process out of which the poem had been born," and at length he recovered the primitive mirror which had given rise to the original comparison.

> Credevo sia dolce sognare;
> ma il sogno è uno specchio, che intero
> mi rende, che sa smascherare
> l'intimo vero.

> I thought it sweet to dream / but dream is a mirror that shows / me whole, that can unmask / my intimate truth.

"I breathed at last," he concludes.

> It was as if a mote had fallen from my eye or a dislocated nerve had returned to place. And yet, rereading the three stanzas with their different metaphors I don't know which is most effective from the point of view of literature. But it is an example. And if it does not establish as principle that one must not, even for the most beautiful line of one's literary lifetime, either wittingly or unwittingly falsify one's own vision, making a mirror into a judge or dreadful Deity, then for that possibly more beautiful line a hundred will be inferior, and the total result the death of the personality.

Although this particular poem never made any of the *Canzonieri*, the principle which it illustrates assuredly has, and is undoubtedly responsible for a number of revisions of a more or less documentary rather than aesthetic nature.* In some cases such a principle brings one finally face to face with an ultimate or Ur-falsehood which cannot in all conscience be denied. To his credit, Saba does not try to, but simply and retroactively calls himself hypocrite.

A second source for what Saba in 1921 felt to be the "impiety" of his first *Poesie* was his early and very natural fear of being found

---

* Though hard and fast distinctions on this order are all but impossible to make. Take for example the first quatrain of a very early sonnet ("Da un colle": From a Hill) in which Saba recalls a view of Peppa's cottage as seen from a hill. The original version (recovered and printed for the first time in the *Canzoniere*

derivative, unoriginal. The relevant passage in "Quello che resta da fare ai poeti," meant to introduce his second book, is fundamentally a key sequence in the self-examination which brought him at length to a true sense of his genuine vocation, a discovery symbolized by the assumption of common bread and rejection of the exclusive Royal Mount ("Montereale") in the matter of his pen name.

> Although *to be original* and *to find oneself* are used synonymously, whoever does not know in practice that the first is the effect and the second the cause, whoever begins not from the need to discover himself but from an uncontrollable desire to be original, whoever cannot resign himself when necessary to say what others have said . . . such a one will never find his true nature and will never say anything unexpected. It is necessary . . . to be original in spite of ourselves.

Now many of the omissions or major alterations made when publishing *Poesie* were intended to cover or disguise his debts from critical eyes. A decade later he could acknowledge them proudly, even to the point of trying to recover the unoriginalities of his originals. "How could I have committed this impiety towards myself?" he inquires in the preface to the first *Canzoniere*. "Was it an eclipse of *coscienza*?"

> Or was I perhaps still too young to take any pleasure—as I take pleasure today—in the unarguable Petrarchan and Leopardian deriva-

---

of 1957) is given below; italicized words or phrases refer to alternate wordings used in the 1945 *Canzoniere*.

(Original and 1957)	(1945)
Era d'ottobre; l'ora *vespertina*	. . . mattutina
di pace empiva e di dolcezza il cuore.	
Solitario il sentier della collina	Con me l'aspro . . .
salivo dietro un bue e un agricoltore.	saliva, dietro ai buoi, l'agricoltore.

It was October; the *evening* (morning) hour / with peace and sweetness filled my heart. / *Solitary, the* (With me, the rough) path of the hill / *I climbed behind an ox and a farmer.* (was climbing, behind his oxen, the farmer.)

Certainly the point of changing the time of day from morning to evening may have been in the interests of documentary accuracy, but just as certainly the latter hour (*vespertina*) is laden with habitual emotional associations, reenforced by the other adjective, *solitaria*, which build more efficiently the quiet, contemplative and somewhat valitudinarian tone of the sonnet as a whole. For the mood adjective *solitaria* (which can refer to both path and climber), Saba can easily renounce the generic naturalistic detail of the path's rough texture; simultaneously he gets rid of a fairly prosaic second sentence (including an inversion and a too-emphatically caesuraed last line), and regains the proper grammatical subject for a nostalgic poem of this type: "I" the climber-poet, rather than an anonymous farmer who is never mentioned again. Certainly "honesty" is a weak or simplistic word to describe the rationale governing these changes or reconstitutions.

tion of those first sonnets and canzoni . . . almost as though I had found, all by myself in my little room in Trieste, so blessedly removed from every artistic influence, at a time when no one had discoursed to me of good or bad authors, the golden thread of the Italian tradition—as if this were not the greatest title of nobility, the best testament that one could have to not being a common and misguided versifier.

Such echoes, then, came to seem to him a patent of his vocation, symptoms of a spiritual community from which he found he was not excluded.

Saba's practical relations with Italian literary tradition, with Leopardi in particular, are important and worth considering. All of the poems of *Poesie dell'adolescenza e giovanili* are cast in conventional lyric forms, sonnets, canzoni, canzonette. In most of them, syntactical inversions and poetical archaisms abound (*duolo* for *dolore, aura* for *aria,* etc.); and certain almost word-for-word appropriations from Leopardi are touchingly evident;* "Rather an amorous merging than a banal imitation," commented Saba some forty years later, and I am inclined to agree with him.[20]

He writes in the *Storia* that, perusing the *Canti* for the first time, he had had the sensation of rereading them, as if he had a vocation for the most unhappy world of Giacomo Leopardi. Certainly their characteristic responses to experience were broadly similar in many ways, particularly their common tendency to contrast sad present realities with blissful ignorance of the past, and the consequent disposition to idealize childhood—a mechanism, by the way, from which Saba is more or less "freed" through psychoanalysis. Obviously such thematic concerns are the common property of many poets; it is the particular *tone* with which they are voiced, the magisterial tact with which an easily sentimentalized material is expressed with a controlled intimacy that avoids any sort of condescension or self pity, that distinguishes and to an extent links Leopardi and Saba at his best.

Saba, in certain ways the most parochial and particularistic of

---

* E.g. such phrases as "vuoti inganni," "care immagini sì ma menzognere"; "inganno soave," and so forth; the debt will only be apparent to those who know Leopardi's *Canti* fairly well. The best way of observing Saba's youthful process of innutrition would be to compare certain of his early poems with their models in the *Canti:* "Lettura ad un amico pianista" with "A Silvia," "Così passo i miei giorni" with "L'infinito," "La sera" with "Ai patriarchi," certain passages of "A Mamma" with "Il Sabato del villaggio." The most flagrant imitations were of course already dropped from the canon by the time of the first *Poesie,* and never recovered. One of them, "A mia stella," has been reprinted in the *Storia.*

poets, also learned from Leopardi certain methods of employing a generic neoclassical literary vocabulary for maximum emotional effect. Whoever has followed in his rough drafts and notebooks the infinitely patient labor of Leopardi to arrive at, say, the first three lines of the immortal "L'infinito" (The Infinite), will recall the ascetic way he sought to transform a particular and personal landscape into the objective emblem of human limitation.

> Sempre caro mi fu quest'ermo colle,
> E questa siepe, che da tanta parte
> Dell'ultimo orizzonte il guardo esclude. . . .

Dear to me always was this lonely hill, / and this hedge that from so much / of the ultimate horizon excludes the view. . . .

Those Italian commentators who, in their zeal, almost invariably note beneath *colle* "Mount Tabor, near Recanati," erroneously specify what the poet has taken great pains to transcend. It is the opening *caro*, the intimate demonstratives and the vague *tanta* which work to harmonize the personal and "universal" elements in these lines so that what was dear to Leopardi is cherished by his readers.

Something of the same sort of astringency can be found filtering Saba's early documentations of childhood. It is no great wonder that in many of them he falls into mere echoings of Leopardian idyll. But for the most part they are testament to "promise," to a sensitive ear and an extremely literary precocity that belies Saba's own claims to rough untutored genius. It was that "given" ear, that solitude compensated for by bookishness, which evidently made up for the defects of his schooling, And despite certain similarities in subject with the *crepuscolari* (nostalgia for childhood and responsiveness to "little things"), the mature strength of his tonal range, and the way in which his expression of present unhappiness and longing for the past is free of all self-indulgence, more than substantiate Saba's declarations of independence from Pascoli and his followers. His *maestro* and father, at least in poetry, was Leopardi, who remained untouched by any of the "Oedipal" hostilities Saba felt for his historical parent (the *assassino*), and elements of whose style became an authentic part of Saba's own when at its very best.*

---

* In one of the little prose fables written for his daughter in his old age ("Le polpette al pomodoro": Tomato Paste) Saba performs his final act of piety to Leopardi. Through a "miracle of love" he is enabled to invite the Count—dead for over 100 years—to dinner. The afternoon is spent in loving anxiety over the menu (Leopardi had a notoriously weak stomach and the Sabas very little money); at six precisely the celebrated guest arrives. "The deformity which

Of these early poems Saba was to write in 1953 that they all, "the beautiful as well as the ugly ones, have too large a foundation, indicate too many future developments, to be the work of anyone destined to die before the age of twenty."[21] And certainly some of the sacred figures or icons recurrent in the *Canzoniere* make their first quiet appearance in the lines of *Poesie dell'adolescenza e giovanili:* the land, sea and skyscapes of Trieste for example, Lina, certain youthful contemporaries and *ragazzi,* the burdened mother, Peppa's cottage where he spent his earliest years. Typical of both his "amorous merging" with Leopardi and his early problem of trying to be distinctive and original is a sonnet devoted to the latter, where "La casa della mia nutrice" (My Nurse's House) is evoked in pastoral-idyllic vein. According to the poet, it was written in 1900 when he was eighteen, and published for the first time twenty-one years later in the first *Canzoniere.* "But I didn't remember it all," he writes much later.[22] The version he could reconstruct in 1921 ran as follows:

> La casa della mia nutrice posa
> tacita in faccia alla Capella antica,
> ed al basso riguarda, e par pensosa,
> da una collina alle caprette amica.
>
> Da lei si va per torta via sassosa
> fin presso il chiostro che in vetta s'abbrica;
> anche hai la vista del mar dilettosa,
> di vasti campi, di chi in lor fatica.
>
> È il vespro amato. Su per l'erta ancora
> salgo alla casa, che uno strano affetto
> nella mestizia m'infonde dell'ora.
>
> Viver mi sembra in quell'età serena,
> quando sazio di giochi uscir dal tetto
> guardavo il fumo azzurro della cena.

---

had made him suffer so had almost completely disappeared—hardly a trace remained. He wore a grey traveller's suit, cut rather sportily. His face was the same as ever. A smile both sweet and sad wandered over his lips; his eyes showed at once great kindness and intolerable fatigue, as of a man too strong to die and too weak to go on living." The dinner goes beautifully; the finicky guest even has seconds of *gelato.* Finally, when Lina has gone to the kitchen to fetch the coffee, and Saba is preparing a long-meditated question as to how, in Leopardi's "Sabato del villaggio," it is possible for the young girl to carry a bouquet of roses and violets when, at least in the environs of Trieste, the two plants flower at different times of year, the guest vanishes "like a dream." "Le polpette al pomodoro" is one of the most beautiful of Saba's prose-pieces, enormously moving in the context of his filial relationship with Leopardi.

My nurse's house stands / quiet opposite the ancient chapel, / looking down as though in thought / from a little hill hospitable to young goats. /

From it one goes by a twisted stony route / up close to the cloister that bathes in the sun at the top; / also you have the delightful prospect of the sea, / of vast fields, of he who labors in them. /

It is beloved eventide. Up the slope I still / climb towards the house which infuses me with a strange emotion / in the hour's sadness. /

It seems to me that I am still living in that serene age / when, tired of play, I watched rise from the rooftop / the blue smoke of supper.

Speaking of his subsequent revisions, Saba wrote that, while the details of the climb given in the second quatrain were true—that is, the way *was* stoney and twisting, there *was* a cloister for Capucine friars at the top—nevertheless, "the verses were not true." Although the sonnet's topography was faithful to his experience of suburban Trieste, its primitive form exacted another sort of faithfulness which made the 1921 version "untrue." In reading an old anthology of nineteenth-century verse, Saba came across a line in a sonnet by Arturo Graf: "La città dove nacqui ha nome Atene" (The city where I was born has Athens for name), which, through an involuntary operation of memory, brought back to him the original first lines of the second quatrain, lines evidently "repressed" in 1921 through what Saba diagnoses as subsconscious shame at his youthful derivativeness.

La città dove nacqui popolosa
scopri da lei per la finestra aprica. . . .

The populous city where I was born / is revealed to you from it [the house] sun-bathed through the window [or through the sunny window]. . . .

Whether or not one goes along with Saba's self-analysis of his variants (and who, even in Italy, would have accused him of plagiarizing Graf?), he came to recognize that his work was saturated with tradition, with echoes of his readings in earlier poets, and that he found this just as moving, every bit as autobiographically honest, as the precise local details of his life in Trieste. Thus seen, the "quotation" from Graf becomes an attempt to escape solitude into community just as poignant to him and, I believe, to the reader of the *Canzoniere*, as the sight of Peppa's cottage. I also prefer the original as being simpler than the later one and more focused in effect though both are awkward in construction, with inversions and literary archaisms (*s'abbrica, aprica*) evidently forced by the exigencies of the rhyme scheme. The Saba of 1900 would not have found these latter to be liabilities at all; quite the contrary.

The tercets of "La casa della mia nutrice" in the definitive *Canzoniere* are also different from those of 1921, another case of recovery. In this case the original version involves an image that was a cliché of a certain minor mode of nineteenth-century romanticism:

> Qui—mi sovviene—nell'età primiera,
> del vecchio camposanto fra le croci,
> giocavo ignaro sul far della sera.
>
> A Dio innalzavo l'anima serena;
> e dalla casa un suon di care voci
> mi giungeva,e l'odore della cena.

Here, I remember, in my earliest days, / amid the crosses of the old cemetery, / I played in my innocence while the evening came on. / To God I raised my serene spirit; / and from the house a sound of dear voices / reached me, and the smell of supper.

In a first reconstruction of the imperfectly recollected original, Saba had written *m'inginocchiavo* (I knelt in prayer), but this was "too much," and he finally substituted innocent play for kneeling. "I have never that I know of prayed in that place in that way. Maybe when I wrote that poem for the first time I thought my good nurse who wished to raise me in the Catholic faith and argued with my mother on this point might have loved me more if she had discovered me, in infancy, in such an attitude." But even with the change in verb, the image was "hypocritical": "If I didn't pray, neither did I play in that cemetery which at any rate contained no crosses. Beside the cottage there was an unused Jewish cemetery. . . ."*

Saba has written of his sense that the *Canzoniere* is not only a big book of poems but, for himself at least, *un vasto cimitero*.[23] Obviously, the oldest part of that cemetery is the section inscribed *Poesie dell'adolescenza e giovanili*, and this is inevitably the section he has revisited most emotionally, most persistently and piously. That fragment of the past condensed in the image of his nurse's cottage will amount to an obsession as his life draws onward; witness not only its frequent recurrence in later poems but the tormented story we have been reviewing of the variant of its first version.

---

* See the second stanza of "Tre vie," a poem written some ten years later, for a mature and less mannered handling of the identical locale. See below, p. 76.

Even in its definitive state, "La casa della mia nutrice" is a distinctly derivative sonnet, *not* because it cribs from Graf, whom no one reads, but because of the stiffness of its literary etiquette, its self-consciously "classical" language and syntax, the quaint formality of its generalized imagery and stereotyped sentiments. Yet its unbending decorum functions so as to "contain" the sheer longing that the poem is "about" and so to preserve it from the usual vice of most *poesie dell'ado-lescenza:* a garrulous sentimentalism. The sonnet's little triumph is manifested in the two last lines of the final tercet, an image of "Leopardian" austerity-cum-intimacy (an oxymoran which that master made as natural as breathing), which works to redeem all the rest:

> e dalla casa un suon di care voci
> mi giungeva, e l'odore della cena.

These are lines of which Saba wrote in 1945 in the *Storia* that they were "already (in 1900) entirely his own," but they are lines resulting as well from his "amorous merging" with the dead master, reminding us of the remark he made eight years later, at the end of his life when he had almost ceased to write: "today [it is] my glory to say, with some slight exaggeration, that there is not in my *Canzoniere* a single line that is entirely my own."[24]

Apropos of this poem and others of this period Saba has written in the *Storia* that his main difficulty was "to sheath (*far entrare*) a very precise content within a predetermined form." The various formal conventions which attracted him at this phase, whether sonnet, canzonetta or some hendecasyllabled and variously-rhymed version of the "free" canzone perfected by Leopardi, were largely dictated by the special emotions he had for the great tradition of Italian lyricism extending from Petrarch to Manzoni. Within it, anticipating his commandeering of the title *Canzoniere* later on, he previously found an inspiring link with a stable and accomplished past, hence the psychological support of a spiritual *élite* with which he could relate himself.

But study of "form" does not confine itself to matters of rhyme incidence, number of syllables per line or strophic pattern. In his apprenticeship Saba also naturally appropriated the venerable lexicon, imagery repertoire, and decorous or official viewpoints of the anthologized literary past he knew. In other words he took over a good deal of already established "content" as well, and this sometimes obstructed or effectively throttled the expression of his own identity or, à la Croce, intuition. "La casa della mia nutrice" provides a splendid example of what he means by a "precise" content, a local terrain saturated with personal associations of a high emotional vibrato, obscured to some extent by the formal means at his disposal, though, as we have noted above, these means themselves were also fraught with emotion. On the one hand they could and did serve as a sort of "outside" aesthetic conscience, objective devices for controlling and containing a very fluid affective material. On the other hand they tended to precondition those particular feelings of his to their own traditional standards of decorum, so that despite the genuine skill the poem reveals, the experience expressed seems predictable and rather stereotyped. Although "La casa della mia nutrice" is an impressive performance for a young provincial of something like seventeen, while it illustrates how the example of Leopardi could help Saba towards his own "natural" voice, and while it acquires an enormous resonance through its initiatory position in the "narrative" of the *Canzoniere*, Saba's own verdict on it in the *Storia* ("suffused with an intimacy and candor rare in young poets") is surely excessive.

The need for some sort of "predetermined" formal support is negatively shown in the most ambitious piece in the *Poesia dell'adolescenza* as well as one of the longest poems in the whole *Canzoniere*, the "A Mamma" (To Mamma) mentioned earlier as having undergone continual revisions before Saba's final decision to leave it *imperfettissima* in its original form. Here the guilt-ridden son, alone on a gloomy Sunday in Florence, evokes his sad and white-haired mother alone in Trieste. Sunday melancholia and concomitant thoughts of childhood, mamma, and the banal present, often accompanied, though Saba manages to avoid this, by the strains of a barbary organ, were in this period a crepuscular *specialité,* and "A Mamma" suggests that Saba's reading in Florence was not confined to the classics. Certainly some of the introductory passages, full of veristic picturesqueness, are more reminiscent of Pascoli and his heirs than, say, the "Sabato del villaggio" of Leopardi:

> Ed è un giorno di festa, oggi. La via
> nera è tutta di gente, ben che il cielo
> sia coperto, ed un vento aspro allo stelo
> rubi il giovane fiore, e in onde gonfi
> le gialle acque del fiume.
> Passeggiano i borghesi lungo il fiume
> torbido, con violacee ombre di ponti.
> Sta la neve sui monti
> ceruli ancora. . . .

. . . And it's a holiday today. The street / is all black with people although the sky / is clouded and a harsh wind / snatches the young flower from its stalk and blows up waves / on the yellow waters of the river. / The merchants stroll along the roiled river / with the violet-tinted shadows of the bridges. / The snow still lies on the blue / mountains. . . .

This pleasant, rather loquacious impressionism is really not at all typical of Saba, whose austere cityscapes will be considered in some detail when we come to the great street poems of *Trieste e una donna.* What is mainly apparent in "A Mamma" however is "precise content," free associations of a guilty son, in search of a form and settling for a welter of metered apologia blocked into lubberly "verse" by end-rhyme and ruthless enjambing;

> Guardi le donne, gli operai (quel bene,
> mamma, non scordi) gli operai che i panni
> d'ogni giorno, pur tanto utili e belli,
> oggi a gara lasciati hanno per quelli
> delle feste, sí nuovi in vista e falsi.
> Ma tu, mamma, non sai che sono falsi.
> Tu non vedi la luce che io vedo.
> Altra fede ti regge, che non credo
> piú che credevo nella puerizia. . . .

You watch the women, the workers (that blessing [that is, regular work, with paycheck, which her vagabond son has given over] / Mamma, you don't forget) the workers who today have doffed their everyday / clothes, no matter how practical and handsome, to show off their holidays suits, / so new to the eye and so false. But you, Mamma, you don't know they're false. / You're ruled by a different faith, one I don't believe / any more, that I believed in my boyhood. . . .

If nothing else, "A Mamma" illustrates the rightness of Saba's predeliction for severe, brief, "closed" metric forms which help censor the talky mechanisms of his lacerated ego. The aspiration behind it however, his will to record a particular moment of ordinary, non-idyllic, subjective experience, is of the greatest importance to the world of the *Canzoniere.* The failed "A Mamma" has at least as much future to it as the failed "Casa della mia nutrice"; if "Casa" is overly bookish and derivative, "A Mamma" is too encumbered by its "real-life" neuroses to achieve adequate poetic form. Still, as Saba was to write of it in the *Storia,* "A Mamma" was the "first poem in which [he] had tried to express entirely his very own world," and the *Canzoniere* shows that he was correct in feeling that the poem represented some-thing "fundamental" for him.[25] This of course was why he returned to it again and again in decades to come, reluctant to take the will for the deed. In the end he had to, and "A Mamma" remains a symptom of potential vitality rather than a poem in its own right.

The two compositions discussed above (two out of a total of six-teen in the definitive *Canzoniere*, a reduction by twenty-eight from the forty-four in the equivalent chapter of the first edition*) give a fair notion of the range and quality of work included in *Poesia dell'adolescenza e giovanili*. In the *Bildungsroman* of collected Saba this section is of primarily thematic interest insofar as it touches upon a number of the figures, places, and problems which will recur in various forms later on. This no doubt is why Saba felt he could legitimately reduce its size. So conceived, it serves as a brief prelude. I also suggest that the more strictly literary or technical side of this chapter has its own special pathos and place in the story (as aptitudes, gropings, the desire to "belong" via style, the need to accommodate this desire to the requisitions of one's own individuality and integrity) though this dimension can be only registered when the whole *Canzoniere* is familiar. But this power to engage the reader's sym-pathetic interest in his *becoming*, his human story, is a primary aspect of Saba's poetic genius.

✿   ✿   ✿

The *Poesia dell'adolescenza e giovanili* closes with a poem written in 1907 which simultaneously provides a bridge to his next chapter, the *Versi militari* (Military Verses) of 1908, and expresses an ex-perience of tremendous importance for Saba's understanding of his vocation. He spent that year as a conscript in the twelfth infantry regiment at Salerno, far from the north Italian cities with which he was familiar. He was also a poet, Umberto da Montereale no less, among professional soldiers whose reading habits could hardly have extended further than the daily papers. Compared with that crepuscu-lar Sunday in Florence, this was an authentic isolation.

What happened is given in the lines of the last poem in *Poesie dell'adolescenza*, "Il sogno di un coscritto" (A Conscript's Dream), subtitled where it occurred, "the inn outside the gates" of Salerno. The poem begins in a barracks bunk where the dreamer, Saba, recollects the stunning event of earlier that day when he had been seated at a table in that inn with his new colleagues, lonely, sipping

---

* Properly, the equivalent chapters, for in that edition poems of the same period were divided into three: *Poesie dell'adolescenza*, *Voci dai luoghi e dalle cose* (Voices from Places and Things), *Poesie fiorentine* (Florentine Poems).

his "two cents worth of wine." Suddenly, he recalls, an encumbering shadow fell away from him and with it the block which had held apart, as wholly antithetical, his "faroff life" of Florence, Trieste and poetry, and this crude milieu, "evening tumult," in which he now sat separate. With the shadow's vanishing came the revelation:

> Non un poeta, ero uno sperduto
> che faceva il soldato,
> guatandosi all'intorno l'affollato
> mondo, stupido e muto;
>
> che come gli altri, in negro
> vino il suo poco rame barattava
> che coi baci la mamma a lui mandava,
> triste no, non allegro;
>
> con nella mente fitta
> sola un'idea, recata
> a un suon lontano: fosse la prescritta
> ora trascorsa della ritirata.

No poet, I was a poor wretch / acting the soldier, / gaping around him at the crowded / world, stupid and dumb; /
one like the others, who into black / wine changed the few coppers / his mamma sent him with her kisses, / one neither sad nor happy; /
one with only one / idea fixed in his mind, induced / by a faroff sound: had / the hour of return to barracks slipped past?

In a prose memoir of the same name written exactly a half century later, the conditions of revelation are more ecstatic. Still in civilian clothes, he accompanies his new companions to the movies; because they are soldiers they are admitted at half price. He is going to pay full, until one of them takes his arm and tells the cashier "è uno come noi," he's one of us. "Oh, Linuccia," he writes his daughter,

> . . . that was one of the shining moments of my difficult life. I felt undone, liquidated with love. I was not—I felt no longer—alone and abandoned . . . I was part of a community of men. . . . It goes without saying that no one had the least suspicion of what was happening at that moment in my soul. But I think that the *Versi militari,* beautiful or ugly as they may be, were born then in their entirety, on the threshold of that cinema, on the top of a steep hill in Salerno.[26]

It may well be that the filament of exaltation accreted in the old man's memoir is supererogatory and slightly sentimental, that the quality of the experience is better expressed in the verse "Sogno" and better summarized in the dry epigraphy of *Autobiografia*:

> Me stesso ritrovai tra i miei soldati.
> Nacqui tra essi la mia Musa schietta.

I recovered myself amid my soldiers. / Born amid them was my simple Muse.

I mean that, while still for the most part work of preliminary reconnaissance, lines of a poet still in search of his voice, *Versi militari* is notably free of the expansive socio-religio-humanitarianism the memoir may imply; *that* phase redolent of Carducci and Pascoli lay well behind him in poems ultimately suppressed from the canon. Experience brought Saba no mission of philanthropy or programmatic "love," and in this respect, the tonal wryness verging on sour self-irony in the verse "Sogno d'un coscritto" is absolutely adequate, in keeping with the experience. In other words, it is properly decorous.

Saba's wholly apolitical "communism" is an old story which begins for us with "Il sogno d'un coscritto," threads the entire *Canzoniere*, and finds its supreme general expression in "Il borgo" (The Town) written in the late 1920's. "Il borgo"'s refrain ritually formulates his recurrent desire:

> . . . d'immettere la mia dentro la calda
> vita di tutti,
> d'essere come tutti
> gli uomini di tutti
> i giorni.

. . . to fuse my life within the warm / life of everyone, / to be like all / men of every / day.

Actually "Il borgo" is a meditation on a recurrent but failed (even futile) aspiration. This man, insofar as he is poet, is not like other men, and the saving warmth anticipated in the merger is not forthcoming. Indeed, the *sogno* of "Il sogno d'un coscritto" implies the poet's *a posteriori* recognition of the elusive and chimerical nature of the revelation vouchsafed him; *a dream* of community is what is meant.

Such dreams as this are in fact the poignant experience of everybody, *tutti*, and manifest what Quasimodo would call "man's wish to leave his solitude." Poets, like Jews, "are just like other people only more so." And Saba's empathetic communism lies in his objective consciousness of men's unhappy loneliness, his respect for the frail, compensatory dreams and petty solaces with which men populate their wretchedness, his honoring of human suffering whether explicable or inexplicable. The moment of experiencing and writing "Il sogno d'un coscritto" is the moment that an ideal chronology would indicate as the point when da Montereale became Saba. If men are, profoundly, brothers, it is their helpless suffering which makes them so.

Significantly, the "content" of *Versi militari* has shifted from past to present, from childhood memories, old dreams, and Peppa's house to current life in barracks, bar, or field: aching feet, the weight of shouldered gear, a comrade talking in his sleep, rifle drill, and so on. The result is not, and seldom is in Saba's better work, descriptive or documentary. It is rather a poetry of warmth and moral perceptiveness based on the ordinary details of a lived life.

A main tendency indicated by *Versi militari,* then, is Saba's increased confidence in immediate personal materials as the stuff of his poetry, poems of "a wretch like the others." His strophic habits are still conservative; the chapter consists of twenty-seven sonnets arranged at times in narrative pairs or sequences that anticipate the sonnet collections of 1924: *Autobiografia* and *I prigioni.* Increased technical skill and the assurance mentioned above reveal Saba beginning to be the master rather than the slave of that preferred form. One sequence in particular, the first half of a double sonnet titled "Ordine sparso" (Broken File), will illustrate this development as well as serving to introduce a thematic corollary to the idea of a community in suffering. He is on maneuvres:

Se sparando mi appiatto entro il profondo
bosco, o sfuggo di corsa ove il sentiero
s'apre, è un gioco bellissimo che invero
la superficie m'innova del mondo.

Pensa: È un cespuglio, è un ciottolo rotondo
che nascondere deve il corpo intero.
Quel che piú pesa diventa leggero,
dico il soldato col suo grave pondo.

Il volo che nel grano entra e poi scatta,
la pecora ricorda che i ginocchi
piega, indi pare che tutta s'abbatta.

E vedono il terreno oggi i miei occhi
come artista non mai, credo, lo scorse.
Cosí le bestie lo vedono forse.

If, firing, I lie low within the deep / wood, or flee headlong when the path / widens out, it's all a lovely game I play that really / makes the world's face new for me. /
You think: there's a bush, there's a fat rock / that has to hide my whole body. / And what weighs most grows light / —I mean the soldier with his heavy gear. /
You remember the bird's quick start up out of the cornfield, / or the sheep on bent / knees that seems self-abased. /
And today my eyes see the earth / in a way I think no artist has known it. / So beasts see it maybe.

Here he has achieved his voice: the curious mixture of intimate and almost impromptu speech—speech, as it were, without ulterior motives —and a rather formal, schematic eye (the deep wood, a bush, a rock, a bird and so forth), the classic reticence and simplicity of the great conclusion that locates a kind of Genesis in military manoeuvres, in the sublime plainness of the last line.

That line, "Cosí le bestie lo vedono forse," is thematically important and well annotated elsewhere in the poems of Saba. For example, in the opening quatrain of the inferior second sonnet-half of "Ordine sparso" itself:

> Le bestie per cui esso è casa, è letto,
> è talamo, è podere, è mensa, è tutto.
> Vi godono la vita, ogni suo frutto,
> vi dànno e vi ricevono la morte. . . .

The beasts for whom it [earth] is home, is bed, / is nuptial couch, is farm, is food, is everything. / There they take joy in life and all its fruits, / there they give and receive death. . . .

or in a short poem, "L'uomo e gli animali" (Man and the Animals), written at the end of his life:

> Uomo, la tua sventura è senza fondo.
> Sei troppo e troppo poco. Con invidia
> (tu pensi invece con disprezzo) guardi
> gli animali, che immuni di riguardi
> e di pudori, dicono la vita
> e le sue leggi. (Ne dicono il fondo.)

Man, your wretchedness is bottomless. / You are too much and too little. With envy—you think instead with contempt—you watch / the animals who immune from self-consciousness / and modesty express life / and life's laws. (They express the essence of it.)

He writes in the *Storia:* "The poet, like the child, loves animals, who by the simplicity and nakedness of their lives, far more than men who are obligated by social duties and continual pretences, are 'close to God,' that is, to the truth that can be read in the open book of creation."[27]

For Saba, life and its legible laws, "God's truth," amount to the abiding vision of the suffering and bewildered creature, Lear's "unaccommodated" man, the "poor, bare, forked animal" without veneer of acquired needs and manners. For Saba this vision bears with it the experience of brotherhood, a real cognition of community below apparent difference, indifference and isolation.

This community is based on a creaturely recognition of mutual impotence and suffering, as expressed by grief, anger, the quest for pastime, for love, the occasional exchanges of dismayed tendernesses. We know that once in the little hill town of Gubbio, St. Francis shook the right paw of a ravening wolf in friendship; that celebrating Christmas mass in a stable at Greccio he bleated the word "Bethlehem" like a lamb; that he called the dumb beasts brother and sister, *fratello e sorella,* "forasmuch"—to quote the *Fioretti*—"as he recognized in them the same origin as in himself." *Ne dicono il fondo.* In this respect as foolish and unworldly as the simpleton of Assisi, though by no stretch of even the unorthodox imagination a "saint," Saba found among animals not that fancied absence of anguish that can bring a fatuous king to look at a cat with envy, but, as in a miraculous mirror, his quintessential creatureliness, a consciousness of a common ground of elemental life shared with the whole creation. Men, like the beasts, are creatures, therefore *fratelli*. Hence too Saba's subsequent obsession with children which, though it has its morbidly erotic aspect, was also and perhaps primarily prompted by "the simplicity and nakedness of their lives."

Out of his memory of crawling on his belly in the woods near Salerno, of his sensations of the hunted hunter, reduced to staying alive and consequently thankful for the protection of a rock or brush, Saba produced quite unself-consciously his first *ars poetica*, the oddly "Franciscan" first half of "Ordine sparso." In Italy it is customary to adduce a few lines from a slightly earlier poem ("Meditazione" [Meditation] in the *Poesie dell'adolescenza e giovanili*) as the initial statement of his characteristic poetics. For example:

> Sfuma il turchino in un azzurro tutto
> stelle. Io siedo alla finestra, e guardo.
> Guardo e ascolto; però che in questo è tutta
> la mia forza: guardare ed ascoltare.

The deep blue fades within a starry / heaven. I sit at the window and watch. / I watch and listen, for in this is all / my strength: to watch and to listen.

This promises a poetry loyal to things as they are, a sort of voyeuristic *verismo*. It presumes an objective observer, as it were "outside" what is observed, and in my opinion it omits the vital element of affective participation formulated at the conclusion of "Ordine sparso":

> E vedono il terreno oggi i miei occhi
> come artista non mai, credo, lo scorse.
> Così le bestie lo vedono forse.

Interpreting this as above all an *aspiration*, it is clear that to realize it in poetry will require extraordinary self-perception and technical mastery to prevent its softening into either sentimental pantheism or humanitarianism. Saba is fond of regarding his poetry as "evidence of a natural phenomenon." If this ascription is at all viable, if it is to mean more than a poet's self-congratulation on being "self-made" and abundant, it must refer to those moments in the *Canzoniere* when he "sees" with a beastly directness and says it with a radical simplicity, *come artista non mai.* Most would agree that it is in his next collection, the *Casa e campagna* (House and Countryside) of 1909–1910, that he most movingly achieves this natural vision.

We have already noted the biographical facts, the recent marriage to Lina, the birth of Linuccia, that constitute the occasion for this little collection of five poems; a chapter for which a "kind of gratitude to life" rather than "the need to find relief from suffering" is the dominant motivation. Two of these poems, "A mia moglie" (To My Wife) and "La capra" (The Goat) will be found in any responsible anthology of modern Italian verse. Among the others, the most notable is the very first, "L'arboscello" (The Little Tree).

> Oggi il tempo è di pioggia.
> Sembra il giorno una sera,
> sembra la primavera
> un autunno, ed un gran vento devasta
> l'arboscello che sta—e non pare—saldo;
> par tra le piante un giovanetto alto
> troppo per la sua troppo verde età.
> Tu lo guardi. Hai pietà
> forse di tutti quei candidi fiori
> che la bora gli toglie; e sono frutta,
> sono dolci conserve

per l'inverno quei fiori che tra l'erbe
cadono. E se ne duole la tua vasta
maternità.

Today is rainy weather. / Day seems evening, / spring seems / autumn, and a great wind rips / the little tree that stands—so frail—firm: / among other plants it looks a youth too tall / for his too green years. / You watch it. You have perhaps pity / for all those white flowers / that the north wind strips from it; they are the fruit, / sweet conserves / for the winter, those flowers that fall / in the grass. And grieves for them your vast / maternity.

Formally, this poem, like the others in this collection, is far freer than anything attempted before. His acknowledged debt to the example of Ungaretti in his poems of the 1930's may be not disputed but qualified by recollecting the relative formal "openness" of *Casa e campagna*.* It could be the fourteen lines of "L'arboscello" are a reminiscence of the sonnet as frequently used up to this point, but certainly much more important is the evidence the poem provides of Saba's technical mastery.

Apparently belying the literal sense of rain and gloom at the beginning is the airy musicality of the three initial *settenari* (verses of seven syllables), the first two quickened by the elisions of juxtaposed vowels, the second and third by the *sera-primavera* rhyme (kin to our *moon-June*) as of some lilting canzonetta. In these rhythms we can catch the contrapuntal leitmotif of that *verde età* for which Lina and the mothering-poet are grieving. The four hendecasyllables that follow, adagio, appropriately introduce the central theme of maternal *pietà*: the brilliant use of enjambmental "irrational pauses" (*primavera/un autunno, devasta/l'arboscello, alto/troppo*) dramatically enforce the literal sense of youth's categorical ruination. The subsequent broken *settenario* now presents the griever implicit from the start, the mother (*tu:* Lina, Saba, whoever reads) in the starkest syntax possible ("Tu lo guardi. Hai pietà . . .) for whom the fall of lovely innocence, beginning with the exquisitely tactful "forse," is registered in its complexity. Saba is an adept at the emotive use of such ambivalent modes. These fallen flowers had to fall; they are the year's first fruits, their sweetness to be perpetuated in the jams of the winter to come. And so their fall is natural, part of terrestrial process rather than symptom, as Leopardi might have had it, of cosmic

---

* It is notable that metric and strophic "freedom" occurs in those moments of his life when his personal torments seem most in abeyance, as in the few years of harmony following his marriage or the precarious serenity won through psychoanalysis.

malice or, worse, indifference. Like the beasts of "Ordine sparso" who participate in "every fruit" of life, death included, so we ourselves, in our own lives or through the window of a poem like "L'arboscello," come to see that fruit involves a fallen flower, that fruitfulness is inevitably linked to change and that change, new life for old, is a consequence of dying. The clichéd wisdom of the poem is that this is so; its piety and humanity emerge with the fact that even so, accepting this, you grieve. And even its terminals chime such grief: maternity *vasta* rhymes across over half the poem with boreal *devasta; verde età* rhymes with *pietà* and the secret title *maternità,* implicit in the tenderly diminutive *-ello* of the printed title, stressed by enjambment at the very end as the other was by space at the very beginning. The risk of pretentiousness or sentimentality incurred by the final adjective (*vasta*) is triumphantly faced and vindicated; in its context, the common condition of all created things, it is the only possible word.

The famous "La capra" is related in theme:

> Ho parlato a una capra.
> Era sola sul prato, era legata.
> Sazia d'erba, bagnata
> dalla pioggia, belava.
>
> Quell'uguale belato era fraterno
> al mio dolore. Ed io risposi, prima
> per celia, poi perché il dolore è eterno,
> ha una voce e non varia.
> Questa voce sentiva
> gemere in una capra solitaria.
>
> In una capra dal viso semita
> sentiva querelarsi ogni altro male,
> ogni altra vita.

I have talked with a goat. / She was alone in the field, she was tethered. / Sated with grass, soaked / by the rain, she was bleating./ That flat-pitched bleat was brother / to my sadness. And I answered it, first / in jest, then because sadness is eternal, / has one voice and does not vary. / This voice I heard / shuddering out of that solitary goat./

From a goat's semitic face / I heard lamenting every other trouble, / every other life.

The community of *dolore* is the kingdom blatantly disclosed by this captive animal. She is no scapegoat if the function of such is to draw

off and concentrate in a single being the troubles of the rest, fr‹
them a while from their sorrows. Here her function is quite lit‹
choral, a communal expression which invites, and in the narrative
event gets, participation. "La capra" is a moment of eccentric auto-
biography transfigured into a parable of captivity, recognition and
fraternity.* The whys or wherefores of *dolore* lie outside the province
of the poem (and indeed outside of the poet's characteristic interests,
never analytic). It is simply that the goat is alone, tied, so full as
to have no desire for more, and drenched: the expression of her
condition, if not particularly happy, certainly not particularly wretched
either, is her bleating, and this, quite as much her "fault" as life's, is
doleful. Quite as simply the speaker walks in the field with his "given"
and unexplained sorrow, finds that bleating *fraterno* and, first play-
fully and then with dead seriousness, joins in. The unison links him
chorally with "every other life" and we may be properly reminded of
the obsessive aspiration to be voiced in "Il borgo": "d'immettere la
mia dentro la calda/vita di tutti . . .," though in the present instance
the adjective would be *dolorosa* rather than *calda.* (It is certain that
Saba would say that they expressed no antithesis.)

Subsequent Italian and European history has given the detail of
the goat's semitic nose a vibratory energy beyond what Saba in the
Storia notes as its primarily "visual" origin: such is the luck of the
poem. While assuredly this detail establishes a further personal con-
nection between the animal and the poet, it is not their shared
"Jewishness" which is at point here but the human and nonexclusive
associations of timeless humiliation and ancient suffering, "ogni altro
male," which give that extraordinary adjective its affective reso-
nance.** The poem's simplicity and transparency may divert us from
the shrewdness of the ear behind it; the *uguale belato,* for instance,
achieved before the letter through the high incidence of flat a's (23
of them) in the first stanza. Despite the comic potential of its plot,
"La capra" remains as inevitable and anonymous as a proverb.

But the central poem in *Casa e campagna,* one of the affective
centers of the whole *Canzoniere,* is Saba's great celebration of Lina in
"A mia moglie." This suburban idyllic bestiary hymn in which his
wife is compared to various small quasi-domestic creatures in and
about a farmyard, the yard about the *casa* where the Sabas first lived,

* It is reasonable to assume it is a parable which reverberated in the imagina-
tion of another Triestine Jew, Italo Svevo, whose Zeno stands a few years later
on a hill above the city and brays with an ass.
** Vittorini uses " "Chinaman" in just the same way in *Conversazione in Sicilia.*
Chinese solitude, in rural Sicily, is said to make him *piú uomo,* symbolically
"more human" than the natives. Likewise, as said above, "Jews are just like
other people, only more so."

the *campagna* the hill Montebello overlooking Trieste, is too long to be quoted in its entirety in these pages. It is, however, the most frequently translated of all Saba's poems. The first stanza goes as follows:

Tu sei come una giovane,
una bianca pollastra.
Le si arruffano al vento
le piume, il collo china
per bere, e in terra raspa;
ma, nell'andare, ha il lento
tuo passo di regina,
e incede sull'erba
pettoruta e superba.
È migliore del maschio.
È come sono tutte
le femmine di tutti
i sereni animali
che avvicinano a Dio.
Cosí se l'occhio, se il giudizio mio
non m'inganna, fra queste hai le tue uguali,
e in nessun'altra donna.
Quando la sera assonna
le gallinelle,
mettono voci che ricordan quelle,
dolcissime, onde a volte dei tuoi mali,
ti quereli, e non sai
che la tua voce ha la soave e triste
musica dei pollai.

You are like a young, / white pullet. / Her feathers ruffle in the wind, / she bends her neck / to drink and scratches in the earth; / yet she moves with your slow / majestic step / when she parades over the grass, / breast high and haughty. / She is better than the male. / So are all / the females of all / the serene animals / who are close to God. / Thus if my eyes, my judgment, / do not deceive me, among such as these you have your equals / and in no other woman. / When evening makes / the little hens drowsy / they utter sounds that remind me of yours / —so sweet—when now and then you complain / of your troubles, and do not know / that your voice has the gentle and sad / music of the henhouse.

This catalogue of praising comparisons continues for five more stanzas, sixty-three more lines of freely rhymed *settenari* interspersed with an occasional hendecasyllable or smaller phrasal unit like the sixth from last line above. A pregnant heifer, a faithful and protective bitch, a timid rabbit, the graceful swallow who returns in spring (and departs in autumn, but "you have not this art"), the prudent ant, the bee—such are "the females of the serene animals close to God" to whom Lina is likened. Saba has recounted amusingly in the *Storia* how her first reaction to this poem, composed "in an almost unconscious state" while she was off shopping, was one of profound annoyance rather than the loving gratitude he had expected; and how only a tender *explication de texte* prevented his offended wife from embarking on a major quarrel. But while Lina and others first found the mixture of amorous praise and local fauna a rather startling novelty within the Italian tradition (Saba says that Borgese linked "A mia moglie" to Futurism, but this must have been a joke), we can easily find a precedent to "place" it by recalling the poem that customarily opens most anthologies of Italian verse, the "Laudes creaturarum" of St. Francis of Assisi:

> . . . Laudato si, mi Signore, per sora luna e le stelle;
> in celo l'ài formate clarite et pretiose et belle.
>   Laudato si, mi Signore, per frate vento
> et per aere et nubilo et sereno et onne tempo,
> per lo quale a le tue creature dai sustentamento.
>   Laudato si, mi Signore, per sor acqua,
> la quale e multo utile et humile et pretiosa et casta . . .

> . . . Be praised, my Lord, for sister moon and the stars; / in heaven you formed them clear and precious and beautiful. /
> Be praised, my Lord, for brother wind / and air, cloudy and serene and enduring, / by which you give sustenance to your creatures. /
> Be praised, my Lord, for sister water, / who is very useful and humble and precious and chaste.

According to Saba, "A mia moglie" was written "as others would recite a prayer," and certainly its accretive vision of creaturely communion plus the simplicity and directness of its syntax and diction are reminiscent of the "Laudes." Apart from their common atmosphere of intimate domestic celebration, the two poems are also similar in their use of an elementary rhetorical device: a repeated initial governing phrase ("Tu sei come . . . ," "Si laudato, mi Signore, per . . .") followed by a loosely constructed, more or less discursive object phrase of varying length. In each case the effect is one of an "artless" spontaneity in which an exalted and intimate emotion is built up by repetition and accumulation rather than through that *ascesis* of reduction and concentration usually predicated of lyric poetry. Both poems perhaps derive from a popular mode observable in pulpit

oratory, based upon the rhythms of the psalms. Both thus fall out-
side the main line of Italian literary tradition which, from the *dolce
stil nuovo* and Petrarch onwards, is notable for its "aristocratic" and
fastidious self-collectedness. And the wonder is that at this genuinely
idyllic juncture of Saba's life, his literary preoccupation with the
"predeterminations" of fixed forms seems momentarily to evaporate,
leaving "content" free to determine its own expressive needs, as it
does in a miracle of musing tenderness. It is a rare moment for not
only Saba but for Italian lyricism.

❖   ❖   ❖

"A mia moglie" is also an epithalamium of sorts, a love idyll of
the married life. But it is a peculiar sort of love poem. Saba himself
calls it "infantile" in the *Storia:* "if a child could marry and write a
poem for his wife, he would write this." Of course such a precocious
marriage is quite unnecessary even in metaphor; what is being cele-
brated here above all is Lina the mother, the carrier of Linuccia,
the mothering spouse of Saba himself. Nothing could be further
from the erotic or sensual than "Alla mia moglie." There is no real
reason within the poem itself why it could not just as well be called
"A Mamma."

I do not make this point in order to inaugurate a facetious "psy-
choanalysis" of Umberto Saba, smartly anticipating conclusions ar-
rived at in treatment some twenty years later. But erotic desire, the
brama or yen of the senses for their sensual complement, is another
main thematic strand running through the entire *Canzoniere* and it
seems important to note its remove from this moment of honeymoon.
It is in fact worth breaking chronology at this point to record Saba's
own reflections on these matters much later on in his life.

In the summer of 1945, for example, we find the following entry
made among his *scorciatoie:*

> Poets—I mean lyric poets in particular—are either children who sing
> of their mothers (Petrarch), or mothers who sing of their children
> [he gives as example his friend Sandro Penna] or both (this is
> altogether more rare—perhaps the Shakespeare of the sonnets). I would
> say that, despite appearances to the contrary, the lyric cannot break
> out of this magic circle and that here, ultimately, we grasp the
> nucleus of poetic inspiration.[28]

From this viewpoint, "A mia moglie" would undoubtedly qualify as
"Petrarchan" in the species of its inspiration; in it a protective, loving
son sings of his young and vulnerable mother. And of Petrarch's
relation to Laura Saba wrote in another *scorciatoia:*

Certainly Laura existed; she was, in the light of every day, a blonde signora. In the inaccessible and infantile depths of the poet's soul however she was his mother: she was *the lady one can never possess*. All the fascinating, somewhat monotonous story of Petrarch's *Canzoniere*, of the over twenty years of unsuccessful (*willfully* unsuccessful) courtship is here. . . .

Laura absorbed all the poet's tenderness. He kept his sensuality for others . . . who didn't subconsciously remind him of his mother. But love, real and whole love, requires . . . a perfect fusion of sensuality and tenderness; thus it is rare. Consequently in all his long *Canzoniere* there is not one single line that can really be said to be written out of love. Much there is, but not "La bocca mi baciò tutto tremante" [*Inferno*, V, 136: Francesca's memory of Paolo's first kiss]—the most beautiful love-line ever written.[29]

But such an amorous "wholeness" will not be found in the younger *Canzoniere* either, although within it is stored a much greater variety of experience than can be found in Petrarch. Saba's poetry will certainly have its erotic, sensual side, but always compartmentalized from what he calls "tenderness," meaning by this a fraternal or human reverence devoid of all lust. The Dante verse, for instance, adduced as an expression of "real and whole love," is surely echoed in this passage from a canzonetta of the early 1920's:

> Dietro ad un muricciolo
> per man ti trassi, e sulla bocca ardente
> ti baciai, ti baciai lungamente. . . .

Behind a little wall / I drew you by the hand, and on your burning mouth / I kissed you, kissed you such a long time. . . .

But the "you" in this case is not Lina, but the bewitching young shop-assistant Chiaretta with whom he is having a brief affair. The same chiefly erotic function will be assumed, at least in his imagination, by Paolina and other girls (*ragazze, fanciulle*), who populate his postwar poems. They are the objects of the exacerbated sexual hankerings that are notably absent in his emotional set towards Lina.

Yet she is the woman in his life, the major "other" presence in his *Canzoniere*. And though her symbolic aura is not sexual (nor asexual), she could by no means be conceived of as Saba's "Laura"; she expresses a wholly different sort of ideality than that remote and Botticellian ancestress of the Marquis de Sade. For Lina is experienced and expressed as "woman" in something like the Old Testament or "Jewish" sense: companion, mother, keeper of the house and home, sharer in the joys, sorrows, and monotonies of day-to-day existence.

Very simply, *she is subject to time and change,* whereas the erotic fascination exercised by *fanciulle* like Chiaretta and Paolina lies precisely in their being the creatures of an imaginatively isolated moment, forever young, blooming, animally innocent. Such as these disappear or are replaced when the magic moment is over. Lina stays, which is to say, the idyll ends. It cedes to pathos and psychological complexities, not to say "complexes," of deep human interest. It involves, I would say, a love of a richness which Saba's doctrinaire and schematic Freudianism is inadequate to define, but which is amply expressed in the *Canzoniere.*

Thus, "A mia moglie" is not only celebration but prophecy. The industry, the trustfulness, the fierce loyalty, the mothering grace that place her in community with God's "serene animals" are those qualities of hers which endure, surviving physical alteration and mental suffering. This is proven by the *Canzoniere* in its entirety. And *Casa e campagna,* with its young bride and mother, its poet-husband-son-father, its infant, trees, and animals in and about the little house on Montebello, is the crystallization of Saba's own moment of idyll, the *paradiso di Saba* in which *dolore* is neither ignored nor forgotten, but acknowledged and accepted as precondition to everything else. This is despite the fact that Saba himself will continue to think of Peppa's house on Via del Monte as his paradise, obsessively returning there again and again as the sanctuary of his early felicity. But the *casa* on Via del Monte is already legendary, a paradise of nostalgia and longing for the womb; that on Montebello was, for a year or two at any rate, and forever in the *Canzoniere,* an earthly paradise where a man could live.

❖   ❖   ❖

In the chapters immediately following *Casa e campagna,* this paradise is lost; the poetry charts its course with great lucidity and frequent beauty. It is a poetry of harsh discords and oppositions, bitter moral quandaries, momentary respites, doomed resolutions.

The main installment of this poetry of fall is *Trieste e una donna* (Trieste and a Lady), written between 1910 and 1912.* It includes forty-five poems and is Saba's largest single collection. He writes in the *Storia* of its making:

---

* According to *Autobiografia,* "my book of most passionate sincerity." Called originally when published by *La Voce, Coi miei occhi* (With My Own Eyes). "Quello che resta da fare ai poeti" was written to be its annunciation and "manifesto."

At a certain point, through his persistence in digging in the depths, never letting go of a feeling no matter how (and especially if) painful before having exhausted or overcome it in his song; and in adding, like a mason building his house, stone unto stone, perhaps inwardly convinced that each poem would be the last of the series, if not of his life; he found himself—as at other times but never quite like this—with a book on his hands, completely done. And the book, born from life, from the "novel" of his life, was itself something like a short novel. It was enough to leave the poems in their chronological order so as not to disturb, by importunate transpositions, the spontaneous flow and transfiguration of life into poetry. For others perhaps this would have constituted a weakness. For Saba it was a strength.

There are three great presences in the "novelette" (*quasi un racconto,* almost a tale, as Saba entitled a very late sequence) of *Trieste e una donna:* Lina, the ambiance of Trieste, and the "I"—Umberto Saba—who experiences and records his experiences of all three. The story is a love story: an open-ended action involving the amorous tensions between the poet and the other two joints of the "triangle." Precisely how a city could become a love object has been suggested already and will be discussed more fully below. Our first attention will be given to the marriage plot.

To adapt a line by Montale, hymn has turned to elegy:

> Che succede di te, della tua vita,
> mio solo amico, mia pallida sposa?
> La tua bellezza si fa dolorosa,
> E più non assomigli a Carmençita.

What is happening to you and to your life, / my only friend, my pale bride? / Your beauty has become mournful, / no longer do you resemble my Carmencita.

Such are the first lines of the first poem, significantly titled "L'autunno" (Autumn). It is soon made clear what has happened to Lina: it is her own huband's increasing desperation at what seems to be the captivity of his life condition, his renewed conviction that he is unlovable and quite possibly unloved, his guilt at the unhappiness (refracted from her dolorous features) his unhappiness is causing, his anger at himself flaring outwards at her.

So in "Nuovi versi alla Lina" (New Lines to Lina) he at one moment chokes with bitter remorse at the lines his own senseless writhings have stricken on her face, at the next rages at her for betraying him by mental reservations: "But tell me now . . . how could you not be mine in your thought, living beside me?" He recol-

lects intermittently that these suspicions of betrayal, at the brink of
clinical paranoia, are by no means factually based. They have been
animated in his own sick imagination. In moments of clarity he can
hear a voice like Lina's crying,

> . . . ma tu stesso hai murata la tua cella,
> ti sei spinto tu stesso nel profondo.

> . . . but you have built your cell yourself, / have cast yourself into
> its depths.

"I don't know why," she continues: "Pride? Jealousy perhaps?" The
admonitory interview concludes: "Thus we shall lose one another in
your madness."

Or if not madness, a dream, but a "dream of which perhaps I shall
die." Dream or madness, a life filled with contagious anguish. "To be
born, to procreate, to grow old and die," so Saba describes the normal
lineaments of the life story of any man, the story he will try to write
much later in his effort at epic, *L'uomo* (The Man). But this abstract
omits the despair man feels as his horizons contract, his options wither
away.

> Né, come di vantarsi egli era usato,
> seppe di un colpo le catene frangere,
> con cui l'aveva il destino servile
> legato. . . .

> Nor, as he had been used to boast, / did he know how to break with
> a blow the chains / with which destiny had bound him servile. . . .

Thus runs a passage in *L'uomo* which deals with its "average" pro-
tagonist at something like the stage of life which Saba expresses in
far greater detail in *Trieste e una donna*. It is precisely this confining
of life which Saba now registers and strikes out against from the
claustrophobia pervading so many of these pages. We may recall his
family's agony, the father:

> . . . gaio e leggero; mia madre
> tutti sentiva della vita i pesi.
> Di mano ei gli sfuggí. . . .

and how he later diagnosed his lacerated and ambivalent character as
the incarnation of their ancient and irreconcilable quarrel within a
single heir: himself. Vagabond and child that he was, his father re-

solved the quarrel by desertion. No such solution was available to Saba, who seems like his mother literally to hoard his suffering. In "New Lines to Lina" we overhear fragments of the couple's conversation:

> Dico: «Son vile . . .»; e tu: «Se m'ami tanto
> sia benedetta la *nostra* viltà». . . .

> . . . I say: "I'm vile . . ." and you: "If you love me so, blessed be *our* vileness. . . ."

But we are also made privy to his pride in his pain, as though it were, as it may have been, an integral part of his vocation:

> Come farà il mio angelo a capire
> che non v'ha cosa al mondo che partire
> con essa io non vorrei, tranne quest'una,
> questa muta tristezza; e che i miei mali
> sono miei, sono all'anima mia sola;
> non li cedo per moglie e per figliola,
> non ne faccio ai miei cari parti uguali.
> ("La moglie")

> How shall I make my angel understand / there's nothing in the world I would not share / with her, except this single thing, / this dumb sadness—and that my troubles / are my own, are for my spirit only; / I cede them neither to wife nor daughter, / to my beloved ones I give no equal shares.

He feels he has a destiny, to suffer and express his suffering. If there is another woman in this phase it is his Muse, and their love-child, the *Canzoniere*, can also be regarded in such graphic chapters as this as the logbook of a precocious psychoanalysis conducted by the poet on himself before Freud was more than a name to him. (This helps explain why Freudianism, like Leopardi-ism earlier, will have in Umberto Saba what weirdly amounts to a "born" convert.)

The story, then, of a severely taxed and troubled love, whose ravages permeate the little household even unto the domestic cat of these famous lines:

> La tua gattina è diventata magra.
> Altro male non è il suo che d'amore:
> male che alle tue cure la consacra.

> Your kitten has grown thin. / No other illness, this, than love, / an illness that consecrates her to your cares.

Among other things love promised an escape from the weight and bondage of self, an exhilarating impression of *risorgimento* and enlargement through the chemistry of another, the snapping of the chains that held one slave.

> Io non so piú dolce cosa
> dell'amore in giovanezza
> di due amanti lieta ebbrezza,
> di cui l'un nell'altro muore.

I don't know a sweeter thing / than love in youth, than two lovers in joyous intoxication / each dying one into the other.

Thus the first voluptuous voice from one of the "fugues" Saba was to compose in the late 1920's in order to articulate his inner divisions. So conceived, love is a liberation that is bound to be short-lived: its conditions of youthfulness, sensual excitement and ecstatic swooning are fugitive. And of course it is either longed for or regretted for a far longer period than it is possessed. As such, this poignant joy and intermission in the prevailing human condition is a continuing source of unhappiness, a bright dream that plagues more than it consoles.

And so the kitten becomes thin and in "Dopo una passeggiata" (After a Stroll) Umberto and Lina out on their evening walk seem merely "two good, tranquil citizens out for a glass of wine," the perennial "husband who already shows regret for his liberty, a jealous wife." The true drama, the battle of the sexes joined, is wholly inward—

> Solo nei cuori rispondono squilli,
> si spiegano al vento bandiere. . . .

Only in our hearts bell answers bell, / flags unfurl in the wind. . . .

But if this hidden torment is true for the Sabas, it is also true for the citizenry of their community and city, their Trieste. This larger note is struck in the beautiful "La malinconia amorosa" (Amorous Melancholy) where the erotic malady that afflicts the poet also binds him in secret fellowship with—say—an anguished bank clerk, an insomniac prowler of the city streets, the living suffering body of Trieste itself within whose thoroughfares like veins the erotic virus courses—

> . . . come una cura secreta o un fervore
> solitario, piú sempre intima e cara. . . .

. . . like a secret care or solitary passion, ever more intimate and dear. . . .*

The Trieste of *Trieste e una donna* is composed not merely of earth and stone but of living beings, is itself alive—*come un ragaz-zaccio aspro e vorace,* like a rough and greedy kid, as he phrases it in the poem "Trieste." It teems with its various joys and sorrows, ennuis and furtive gratifications, a great and complex objectification of the single citizen's daily affective existence. Countless Linas and Umbertos live out their private jostling hells, purgatories and paradises no doubt, micro-worlds accruing to a world whose torments and respites, shames and ecstasies are no less poignantly real for being, on occasion, to its ruminative poet at any rate, chorally or threnodically "one."

And the reader of *Trieste e una donna* is enfranchised to follow the poet in his restlessness, to become accomplice to his delinquent wanderings through Trieste, enviously tracking the freighters as they move out into the Adriatic from the breakwater of San Carlo, sipping sour beer in a workers' *osteria,* gauging the progress of a construction gang raising a new building, watching a hen scratch in the dirt outside a public hospital. The *flâneur's* rationale is given in a poem like "Città vecchia" (The Old Town):

> Qui tra la gente che viene che va
> dall'osteria alla casa o al lupanare,
> dove son merci ed uomini il detrito
> di un gran porto di mare,
> io ritrovo, passando, l'infinito
> nell'umiltà.
> Qui prostituta e marinaio, il vecchio
> che bestemmia, la femmina che bega,
> il dragone che siede alla bottega
> del friggitore,
> la tumultuante giovane impazzita
> d'amore,
> sono tutte creature della vita
> e del dolore;
> s'agita in esse, come in me, il Signore.

Here amid people who come and go / from cafe to home or brothel, / where both merchandise and men are by-products / of a

---

* Saba's great, Lucretian statement of erotic longing as fundamental human energy—approximating libido—will be found in "La brama" in the collection *Cuor morituro.* He calls "La malinconia amorosa" "a youthful first draft" for that later visionary generalization, but it is better than that.

great seaport, / I find again, passing through, in lowliness / the infinite. / Here prostitute and sailor, the blaspheming / old man, the foul-mouthed hag, / the soldier seated / at the fishfry stand, / the reckless girl maddened / with love— / they are all the creatures of life / and of sorrow; / there stirs in them, as in myself, the Lord.

The curious "infinito/nell'umiltà" is of course another way of saying what he says of the animals: "Ne dicono il fondo." The dregs, the insulted and injured of this world, most nakedly manifest the laws governing suffering creation.

So the Trieste of this chapter's triangle is not just place or setting but an affective synthesis through which the common lot is made sensible and the pariah poet regains community. Its streets can work as lenses through which single sorrows are seen as part of an organic whole, an instance of the universal. The great street poems in *Trieste e una donna*, like "Città vecchia," "Tre vie" (Three Ways), or "Via della Pietà" function exactly in this manner. Here, from "Tre Vie," is the Via del Monte we have already encountered in "La casa della mia nutrice":

A Trieste ove son tristezze molte,
e bellezze di cielo e di contrada,
C'è un'erta che si chiama Via del Monte.
Incomincia con una sinagoga,
e termina ad un chiostro; a mezza strada
ha una cappella; indi la nera foga
della vita scoprire puoi da un prato,
e il mare con le navi e il promontorio,
e la folla e le tende del mercato.
Pure, a fianco dell'erta, è un camposanto
abandonato, ove nessun mortorio
entra, non si sotterra piú, per quanto
io mi ricordi: il vecchio cimitero
degli ebrei, cosí caro al mio pensiero
se vi penso i miei vecchi, dopo tanto
penare e mercatare, là sepolti,
simili tutti d'animo e di volti.

In Trieste where there are many sorrows / as well as many beauties of sky and landscape, / there is a rise called Via del Monte. / It begins with a synagogue / and ends with a cloister; halfway up / is a chapel, and there, from a field, / you can discover life's black passion, / the sea with its ships and promontory, / the crowds and the market awnings. / Also along that rise there is an abandoned / cemetery, entered by no funerals, / where for as long as I can recall no one / has been buried—the old cemetery / of the Jews, so dear to my

thought / when I think of my ancestors, after so much / suffering
and buying and selling, buried there, / all alike in heart and faces.

Ten years before the composition of "Tre vie," this rocky Via del
Monte, twisting up the hill past the old chapel by Peppa's cottage,
had been one element in a poetry where life experience was redistrib-
uted or redesigned through the poet's deep need to feel himself
part of a literary lineage. Hence the conventional pathos and pic-
turesqueness of a sonnet like "La casa della mia nutrice" with its fine
sunset, "vast fields," "delightful prospect" of the sea, cemetery re-
vels. The present revisitation in "Tre vie" is evidence of Saba's new
respect for his own materials as well as his ability to infer a timeless
human landscape residing in their local colors.

His Trieste is never programatic, never reduced to illustrating
general ideas. It is too big, too fluid, has too many streets for that. In
the same "Tre vie" the blue Adriatic glimmers between the shops on
Via del Lazzaretto Vecchio, Via Domenico Rossetti is bright with
leaves, a "street of joy and love." Even Via della Pietà, site of the
public hospital and persistent suffering, is gloriously metamorphosed
by the bright resisting red—"come in campo una bandiera," as a
banner on the field, of a grubbing hen's comb:

> . . . dietro la sua cresta
> tutta una fattoria piena di sole.

. . . behind whose crest, / a whole farmyard filled with sun.

Dolore is dominant, no doubt, and joy recessive. Still, it exists from
moment to moment, as vivid and fragile as that tiny bobbing bit of
red against the hospital's black gates, transforming temporarily even
Via della Pietà into a street of joyous defiance, a joy made all the
more exalted by its dark and difficult ground.

Saba's vision of Trieste is consoling not merely because misery
loves company—though this natural motive should not be ruled out
of any estimate of his "Franciscanism"—but because it fleetingly seems
to suspend his "complexes," frees him to see his suffering not as a
penalty for his inferiority or as a betrayal by his enemies but as a
"given" and impersonal condition of creaturely existence, the cate-
gorical *dolore* established in the earliest chapters of the book of
Genesis.

So the tormented Umberto, with his highly specialized burden of
trauma, wounds and anticipations which wall him off from others,
envisages a human complex that can include and "place" him, a man

among men. The open-ended action of *Trieste e una donna* is precisely this hapless oscillation between his personal wretchedness—anxiety, suspicion, self-revilement, erotic restlessness—and blessed moments of Old Testament communism which such tribulations are seen as human and acceptable.

✻   ✻   ✻

"Non un poeta, ero uno sperduto": No poet I, but a poor devil—such, we recall, was the conscript's dream. Yet he returned from *osteria* to barracks in order to write it down, and while he made a song of his experience he also called it *sogno*, dream. There is a certain pathos as well as egotism in a dream of being "ordinary."

Take a little poem written in 1930 when Saba was having psychoanalytic treatment and writing poetry about his childhood and the child—*il piccolo* Berto—that he had been, and in part still found himself to be. It offers notes, *appunti*, towards one of the most fundamental of all his "affective ambivalences." A piazza in Trieste, the noon-cannon booms, a flock of pigeons shrugs into flight, and a man corrects his watch with "jealous care" before resuming his grave perusal of his paper:

> . . . Io l'odio;
> l'odia in me il piccolo Berto. E ad un tempo
> di non assomigliargli mi fa onta,
> d'essere solo e diverso. . . .

> . . . I hate him; / the little Berto in me hates him. And at the same time / I am ashamed not to be like him, / to be alone and different. . . .

This self-styled pariah both covets and repudiates his fellows, is simultaneously aloof, *au-dessus de la mêlée* and yearning, amorously aching to be part of it. The dilemma is not unfamiliar, especially when conceived in terms of vocation. In "Il borgo" for instance, where his characteristic aspiration to "uscire/di me stesso, di vivere la vita di tutti" (get out of myself, to live the life of everyone) is perhaps most definitively articulated, a passage in the fifth stanza raises the problem of self-consciousness which Saba, as artist, must persist in, perhaps to the detriment of the man and his happiness. For in the passionate tide of that aspiration there is one reservation:

> . . . Ma un cantuccio,
> ahimè, lasciavo al desiderio, azzurro
> spiraglio,
> per contemplarmi da quello, godere

l'alta gioia ottenuta
di non esser più io,
d'essere questo soltanto: fra gli uomini
un uomo.

. . . But a hiding-place, / alas, I kept aside for my desire / —a
little chink of heaven-blue / —that I might contemplate myself from
it, savor / the lofty joy attained / by being no longer me, / by being
only this: among men, / a man.

Strictly speaking, the opposition here is between several sorts of
happiness, one solitary and self-aware, the other gregarious and ele-
mentary. The basic problem is, *he wants them both;* paraphrase the
passage cited and you get: "I proposed to myself the happiness of
becoming conscious of myself as a wholly ordinary and unself-
conscious being."

It is of course precisely this perennial need *to see himself living,* this
exorbitant and unmitigated egocentrism, which sets him finally apart,
poeta fra gli uomini rather than *uomo* (or, not to be too categorical
about it, a certain sort of man one part of whose temperament, exact-
ing his vocation, rules out any final surrender to and immersion in
that *calda vita di tutti* which another part of him longs for and com-
poses myths of regeneration about). There is a distinctly voyeuristic
element in Saba's "communism," something that must stay a bit apart
observing the community it aches for. Vision is solitary; one must be
alone in order to see and then to say what one saw. In the lovely
title poem to the collection *Parole,* written in the early 1930's, he
addresses his "words" (*parole*) with something of the same reservation
as we have found in his attitude towards his part in the human com-
munity:

. . . un angolo
cerco nel mondo, l'oasi propizia
a detergere voi con il mio pianto
dalla menzogna che vi acceca . . .

. . . I seek a corner / in the world, the propitious oasis / where I
might cleanse you with my tears / of the lie that blinds you. . . .

Un angolo, spiraglio, cantuccio—places apart, little corners, spots
with a chink or view—such solitary blinds or coverts are preconditions
for a poetry that aspires above all to be honest ("quello che resta ai
poeti") as well as for a poet jealously possessive of his world ("mine
because I was born there, more than others' mine, who as a boy dis-
covered it and as an adult forever to Italy wedded it with song").

These materials provide the basic action for the last poem that we shall consider from *Trieste e una donna*, "Trieste."

> Ho attraversata tutta la città.
> Poi ho salita un'erta,
> popolosa in principio, in là deserta,
> chiusa da un muricciolo:
> un cantuccio in cui solo
> siedo; e mi pare che dove esso termina
> termini la città.

I've traversed the whole city. / After, I climbed a slope, / crowded at the outset, deserted on top, / closed off by a low wall / —a hideaway in which I sit / alone; and it seems to me that where it ends / the city ends as well.

The first stanza, placing what will follow it, gives his view from the hill. How radical these lines were in the Italy of 1912 is probably not properly appreciated by an English-speaking audience, long used to a tradition of poetry involving "ordinary" speech. For Italians, with their motions of verbal decorum crystallized from the courts of medieval Sicily onwards, such verses nicely qualified for what Croce had called "nonpoetry"—mere prose-narrative, devoid of intensity, arbitrarily parceled out into hendecasyllables and *settenari*. Why not, they might legitimately inquire, economically and tastefully eliminate the first stanza entirely, begin with the second (that is, the "vision") and call the whole "Veduta da un colle" (View from a Hill)?

Oddly enough the *topographical* situation presented by this stanza is reminiscent of Leopardi's "L'infinito."

> Sempre caro mi fu quest'ermo colle,
> E questa siepe, cha da tanta parte
> Dell'ultimo orizzonte il guardo esclude.
> Ma sedendo e mirando. . . .

It is a hill, a solitude, a view delimited to some extent by an obstruction (Leopardi's hedge, Saba's little wall). I am reminded of Quasimodo's words that every poet in effect has his own Leopardian *siepe*, his peculiar hedge or frame which functions as the "confines of his world, limit within which his gaze can manoeuvre most distinctly."[30] Perhaps we can extend the metaphor to include not only the edge or focus of a given world, but its affective characteristics as well. Leopardi's is saturated with intimate emotion from the very start—"sempre caro mi fu," and so on. Saba's, at any rate in this stanza, is emotionally neutral. What we get is the bald itinerary of a walk, a climb, a resting: an aseptic account, above all, of *an act of possession*. It seems to me that the poetic "justification" for this stanza lies in its dramatic function as a laconic narrative of the conditions of Saba's vision. We track him, that is, from the "prose" of an ordinary day in the city to his withdrawal from it (the ascent of the lonely hill), to a commanding height and perspective where he can see it whole. It is at this point, as a consequence of the experience related in these obligatory and "expository" lines, that the vision can declare itself. We move into the second and central stanza:

> Trieste ha una scontrosa*
> grazia. Se piace,
> è come un ragazzaccio aspro e vorace,
> con gli occhi azzurri e mani troppo grandi
> per regalare un fiore;
> come un amore
> con gelosia.
> Da quest'erta ogni chiesa, ogni sua via
> scopro, se mena all'ingombrata spiaggia,
> o alla collina cui, sulla sassosa
> cima, una casa, l'ultima, s'aggrappa.
> Intorno
> circola ad ogni cosa
> un'aria strana, un'aria tormentosa,
> l'aria natia.

Trieste has a prickly (captious) / grace. When it pleases / it's like a rough and greedy kid, / with blue eyes and hands too big / to give a flower with, / like jealousy / in love. / From this point I discover every church, every street, / whether it lead to the crowded shore / or to that hill on which, at the rocky / summit, one house, the last, is grappled. / All about / and through everything there circulates / a strange air, a tormenting air, / the air of home.

"It is enough," says Debenedetti, "for Saba to name Trieste for a crowd of vibrant and yearning memories to possess him; one notes this wholly through the passionate affection with which he pronounces it. . . ."[31] Some such epiphanaic suffusion seems to take place *between* the first and second stanzas of "Trieste." From the perspective of

---

* One of Saba's self-styled *felici varianti*, arrived at years later. Originally, in the first *Canzoniere*, Trieste's grace was *selvaggia*, savage, wild. The variant, as he points out in the *Storia*, not only enriches the poem with a ground-bass rhyme (*scontrosa-sassosa-cosa-tormentosa*) but better accords with the intimate tenderness of the personification Trieste/*ragazzaccio*.

line twenty-two, the bar of white separating the last word of the first stanza, *città*, from the first word of the second, *Trieste*, seems to imply an enchanted inhalation or inspiration, through which the poet, surveying beneath him the world he customarily inhabits, is momentarily endowed with the voice to express his love for it in its entirety. Trieste is alive, he says, graceful and awkward, innocent and sly, aspiring, tenacious—all things to most men, perhaps, but to its elected poet, the City of Man, desirable, troubling, holy.

And for the moment, he has risen out of his day to possess it. The brief last stanza with its "city" says as much as it loops back to the source of vision, the transfigured poet on his hilltop:

> La mia città che in ogni parte è viva,
> ha il cantuccio a me fatto, alla mia vita
> pensosa e schiva.

My city, in every part alive, / has the hideout made for me, for my / moody and secretive life.

Subsequently, he must emerge and descend, to resume his life as an infinitesimal part of that city, to suffer and despair again. For above all, as we have noted above, *Trieste e una donna* is the story of an unhappy lover, plagued by his sense of confinement and failure. In the seventh fugue of *Preludio e fughe* (Prelude and Fugues: 1928–1929) the two voices concur in their love of life no matter how painful and uncertain; the second one concludes:

> Restiamo,
> per meglio amarla, in questo ascoso porto. . . .

Let us stay, / that we may love it [life] better, in this hidden refuge. . . .

However, there is no such refuge in *Trieste e una donna*. With his city and his lady, the poet's moments of transport cede to something more ordinary: the sway of routine, disillusionment, fretfulness.

❊ ❊ ❊

The "persistence" Saba boasts of in the *Storia*, his vaunted "never letting go of a feeling . . . before having exhausted or overcome it in his song," may account for the fact that *Trieste e una donna*, while certainly one of the central chapters of the entire *Canzoniere* in terms of both its lyric triumphs—the street poems in particular—and the "story" it tells, is also one of the most uneven. Nearly half of the poems in this big collection seem to be diffuse, rather repetitive variations on themes and motifs more economically and movingly handled in the rest.

A paragraph in "Quello che resta da fare ai poeti" shows that Saba himself was at least theoretically aware of this intimate problem. "The fear," he wrote, precisely at the time that he was gathering the *Trieste e una donna* poems together for proximate publication, "the fear of repeating oneself seems to me to be a harmful one."

> When a feeling and the need to express it are innate, it is only natural that, unless a man can abandon his own identity, that feeling and expression will be repeated, repeated with all that obsessiveness that belongs to whoever feels something that words and sounds and all the arts and external methods can never render perfectly. Hence his sense of frustration after every work and his hope of saying it better the next time. The *Canzonieri* of Petrarch and Leopardi and the *Paradiso*, the most sublime section of the *Comedy*, are full of repetitions for the reason that these poets tried to manifest fully their great passions rather than to dazzle like jugglers (woe unto them if the same trick is twice repeated!). If inspiration is sincere, and subject therefore to the influence of the particular moment that gave birth to it, there is always, no matter how many times one goes over it, a something that sets it apart—an unexpected freshness or a deeper fatigue, some special vista or stroke of landscape, a different season or hour of day—something, in other words, that gives to the line its unique coloring and that only the vulgar eye can confound with previous impressions.

Trieste e una donna is rich in this sort of obsession, returning again and again to the nagging "complexes" we know of—his increasing sense of bondage, fear of betrayal, guilt at hurting those closest to him. The nicely named *La serena disperazione* (Serene Desperation) written between 1913 and 1915, just before the outbreak of war, is a sequel to the *Trieste* chapter—that is, it continues to document Saba's suffering and the alternate therapy (besides poetry itself) of long walks in the city—but it adds nothing new to either Saba's story line or his development as an artist. Further on, we shall note with the rich discrimination of hindsight certain formal modulations perceptible in *Serene disperazione*, but the main impression it gives is of an exploitation of the work immediately preceding it, further "digging in the depths" out of *vis inertiae* and emotional numbness rather than expressive necessity. The life-materials were indubitably urgent; that urgency did not find translation onto the printed page. Such, it may be, is the peril of literary "honesty," where "will" and indisputable sincerity can easily do duty for the poetic "deed."

The few war poems, mainly sonnet-vignettes, focus predictably enough on the man—hapless civilian—beneath the uniform. During this time Saba had worked as part of the labor force at the Milan airport. The brutal world of combat and violent death—or Ungarettian cosmic consciousness won through such forcing conditions, is far removed from these brief pastels of home-front blues, the homesickness of his innocents abroad.

"Testimony of a period of decadence from which the poet emerged only—and slowly—when the war ended and he returned to Trieste" —this is Saba's *Storia* verdict on his work of the years from 1913 to 1919. Only substituting "exhaustion" for the overly recriminatory "decadence," it is a verdict with which I see no reason to quarrel.

❖   ❖   ❖

War's end hardly meant *incipit vita nova* for Saba. Like his fellow citizen Svevo, he was obsessed with *senilità* (drastic growing-older, the emergent *senex*) as a presiding fact in his life. A poem from *La serena disperazione* catches it nicely:

> Passò la giovanezza. Assai dispersi
> le richezze del cuore, e spoglio invecchio.
> Sapessi almeno scriver dei bei versi,
>
> un po'troppo sonori, anche un po'vani,
> nulla più che una musica all'orecchio,
> come piacciono i versi agli italiani.
>
> Io sono . . . io sono appena un ciabattino.
> Vecchie suola s'affanna a rifar nuove.
> Un bimbo piange, pigola un pulcino
>
> sotto il desco; ogni tratto alza la testa,
> aspira l'aria che il bel verde muove
> ed i colori sulle antenne in festa.
>
> Lei, che un dí fu l'amore, oggi non canta,
> non sorride, non è la sua parola
> che una bestemmia; la fatica è tanta
>
> e non basta a nutrir la famigliola.

Youth is over. I've wasted enough / of my heart's riches; I grow old, a husk. / If at least I knew how to write pretty verses, /
a bit too sounding, a bit vain too, / nothing more than a music for the ear, / the kind of verses Italians like! /
I am . . . I am merely a cobbler. / He sweats to make old soles new again. / A baby cries, a chicken peeps /
beneath the table; now and again he / raises his head, / breathes

in that air that moves the lovely greens outdoors, / the holiday pennants on the flagpoles. /
She, who once upon a time was love, does not sing today, / doesn't smile, her word is / only a curse, such is her weariness, /
and not enough to feed the little family.

Reason enough, perhaps, to purchase the Libreria Antica e Moderna and settle into life as an antiquarian bookseller. By this means he was also able to take his publishing affairs into his own hands. The Libreria published two separate fascicles of his poems in 1920 and 1921, *Serena disperazione* and *L'amorosa spina* (The Loving Thorn) and above all, in 1921, his retrospective exhibit, as well as challenge to his contemporaries, of all the work he chose to keep from adolescence on. This original *Canzoniere* was issued in a single edition of six hundred copies, the slowly sold ancestor to what is now called volume one in the final version.

I shall discuss the poems written between war's end and 1925 as a more or less unified phase composed of seven related installments.*
It has already been suggested that the decade initiated the year of Italy's entry into the war was a very difficult period in Saba's life and its crystallization into poems. Though the decade culminates with some of his very highest work—the great contemplative pieces of *Cuor morituro* like "La brama" and "Il borgo"—the bulk of his output during this period is less interesting in itself than for the indications it supplies of crisis reached in the poet's approach to his materials and of his gropings towards both psychic and aesthetic renewal. As part, that is, of his autobiographical novel-in-process.

The main life-events of this decade are soon told. First of all, the purchase of the Libreria provided him with a modest but stable means of livelihood which poetry obviously could not. The Libreria itself seldom makes an appearance in his poems; when it does, as it does

---

* E.g., 1) *Cose leggere e vaganti* (Light and Airy Things): 1920, 2) *L'amorosa spina*: 1920, 3) *Preludio e canzonette* (*Prelude and Canzonettas*): 1922–1923, 4) *Autobiografia*: 1924, 5) *I prigioni* (Prisons) 1924, 6) *Fanciulle* (Girls): 1925, 7) the main portion of *Cuor morituro* (Dying Heart): 1925. The collections of 1922–1924 were first published under the auspices of the short-lived literary periodical *Primo tempo*, directed by Giacomo Debenedetti with the aid of two young poets, Sergio Solmi and Eugenio Montale. (These three were later associated with *Solaria*, which in 1928 devoted an entire issue to critical discussions of Saba's poetry and sponsored the publication of his *Preludio e fughe*.) The first two chapters cited above were written in time to become the concluding sections of the first *Canzoniere*. The remaining five were collected in a single volume and published in 1926 by Treves of Milan under one of Saba's "alternate" titles for his complete poems: *Figure e canti* (Figures and Songs).

in the fifteenth and final sonnet of *Autobiografia,* it is clearly as a terminus, an obscure but dignified ending.

> Una strana bottega d'antiquario
> s'apre, a Trieste, in una via secreta.
> D'antiche legature un oro vario
> l'occhio per gli scaffali errante allieta.
>
> Vive in quell'aria tranquillo un poeta.
> Dei morti in quel vivente lapidario
> la sua opera compie, onesta e lieta,
> d'Amor pensoso, ignoto e solitario.
>
> Morir spezzato dal chiuso fervore
> vorebbe un giorno; sulle amate carte
> chiudere gli occhi che han veduto tanto.
>
> E quel che del suo tempo restò fuore
> e del suo spazio, ancor piú bello l'arte
> gli pinse, ancor piú dolce gli fe'il canto.

An antiquarian's strange shop / opens, in Trieste, in an obscure sidestreet. / Various golds of ancient bindings / charm the eye wandering through the shelves. /

A poet lives, tranquil, in that atmosphere. / In that vibrant monument to the dead / he completes his honest, willing work, / pondering Love, unknown and solitary. /

He would like some day to die broken / by his secret fervor, above his beloved papers / to close those eyes that have seen so much. /

And whatever remained beyond him in his time / and place, art depicted it to him as more beautiful still, / still sweeter song made it for him.

We can consider this excellent sonnet as the first of a long line of epitaphs. The entire *Autobiografia* is of course the brief recapitulation of a life that is felt to be nearly over, while the title *Cuor morituro* constitutes an express reference to his wretched *senilità.* (From this point of view even the publication of the *Canzoniere* in 1921 can be regarded as the putting of his papers [*amate carte*] in final order, a last will and testament.) In fact he has lived only a little over half of his life. His morbidity is not merely the token of *crise de quarante;* by 1924 his depression over his life conditions has grown imperious.

D'Amor pensoso: pondering Love—this phrase from *Autobiografia* refers to a development charted through the three preceding collections. Amor, or as he puts it in the *Storia,* "the fatality of Eros," had given him plenty to meditate upon if we judge from evidence compiled in *Cose leggere e vaganti,* the appropriately named *Amorosa spina* and the *Canzonette.* We have moved from the marital restlessness and *malinconia amorosa* of *Trieste e una donna* and *Serena disperazione* to an attempted liberation or renewal via adultery. That is, the main "figures" of these newest installments are not strictly domestic: are neither Lina nor Linuccia but, in the first, a certain Paolina, *fanciulla* or "girl" of Trieste, and in the other two Chiaretta, assistant for a short period at the Libreria counter. Whether Saba slept with them, whether he technically had a mistress, or whether his sensuality remained wholly imaginative, finding its sole release in these poems, I do not know. Many of the poems deal with specific erotic occasions: jealousies, assignations, and so on, while others contain a sort of hectic, panting imagery which makes them seem products of masturbatory fantasy. In any case it is what he subjectively found in or made of his *fanciulle* that is of main importance for the poems, and in the poems they live as fascinating sources or centers or targets for his "anti-Petrarchan" erotic yearnings.

We first encounter Paolina as a sort of local deity, *spiritus loci triestini* and thereby delicate sister to the *ragazzaccio* of "Trieste":

> Paolina, frutto
> natio,
> fatta di cose le piú aeree e insieme
> le piú terrene,
> nata ove solo nascere potevi,
> nella città benedetta ove nacqui,
> su cui vagano a sera i bei colori,
> i piú divini colori, e ahimè! sono
> nulla: acquei vapori.

Paolina, native / fruit, / made at once of the airiest and / earthiest things, born where you had to be born, / in the blessed city where I was born, / over which wander in the evenings beautiful colors, / the most divine colors, and alas! they are / nothing—water vapors.

Thus aureoled by her elemental *semblables, cose leggere e vaganti,* Paolina is ranged with what the poet calls in the *Storia* those "things that by their lightness wander to and fro, like happy apparitions, through and above life's heaviness." Such images are rife within these pages: not only the city nymphs, *fanciulle,* and *ragazze* (kids) like his own Linuccia, but birds, bubbles, balloons, the seafoam whitening on waves, the wind-dispersed smoke rising from Triestine hearths, the clouds

> . . . insensibili nubi
> che si fanno e disfanno in chiaro cielo . . .

. . . the unfeeling clouds / that compose and decompose them-
selves in the clear sky. . . .

or the tiny, bright and buoyant yellow sail that constitutes the final
image of the last poem ("In riva del mare": By the Seashore) of the
original *Canzoniere:*

> Passò una barca con la vela gialla,
> che di giallo tingeva il mare sotto;
> e il silenzio era estremo. Io della morte
> non desiderio provai, ma vergogna
> di non averla ancora unica eletta,
> d'amare piú di lei io qualche cosa
> che sulla superficie della terra
> si muove, e illude col soave viso.

A boat passed with a yellow sail / that tinged the sea beneath with
yellow; / and the silence was extreme. I for death / felt no desire,
but shame / at not yet having chosen her [that is, death] alone, / at
loving more than her some thing / moving on the surface of the
earth, / that deceives with gentle guise.

The thoughtless gaiety and lightness permanently associated with
his roving father, who bounded from the mother's restraining grip
like a brightly colored ball; the "Vagabondaggio, evasione, poesia,/
cari prodigi sul tardi!" (Vagabondage, evasion, poetry, /dear prodi-
gies when it grows late!) saluted in a later poem like "Felicità"—these
permanently draw the man who, like his mother and his wife, feels
all the weight of existence.

The very first poem of the entire *Canzoniere* is an "admonition"
deciphered by the youthful poet in a cloud made radiant by a rosy-
fingered dawn:

> Cangi tue forme e perdi
> quel fuoco veleggiando;
> ti spezzi e, dileguando,
> ammonisci. . . .

You change your forms and lose / that floating fire; / you break
up and, disappearing, / you admonish. . . .

Light and airy things: clouds, birds, *fanciulle,* are subject to the same
law as the heavier things of this earth: they alter and break up,
spezzarsi. If the fate of the former strikes us as specially poignant
and tragic, it is because of the illusion ("happy apparition," "dear

prodigy") they momentarily offer of seeming to suspend the law gov-
erning all matter, of transcending gravity through "thoughtless" joy
and instinctual grace.

I think of Yeats' girl dancing by the shore, or Ungaretti's cry to
his dead child in "Tu ti spezzasti" (You Broke Up),

> Grazia felice,
> Non avresti potuto non spezzarti . . .
> Tu semplice soffio e cristallo. . . .

Happy grace, / how could you not have shattered / . . . you simple
breath and crystal. . . .

where the very inevitability of his destruction goes to prove the
angelic essence of what seemed once a lively boy. For Saba as well,
such miracles are fugitive and doomed; what remains, as he puts it in
the first of the *Canzonette,* are "sad presentiments in the grieving
heart."

L'amorosa spina is dedicated to Chiaretta. Its first poem begins
with a picture of her as a little child, running to the store on an
errand for her mother; it closes with her present image as a
giovanetta, a young girl with a purse (containing a mirror) on her
arm, young breasts as "limpid" and calm and cool as a mountain
pool:

> . . . E c'è lí dentro,
> c'è quasi un cuore. . . .

. . . And within, / there's almost a heart. . . .

Compare his evocation of the "unfeeling clouds" or of the divine
indifference of *fanciulle* in the last poem of that sequence:

> Ah, che la vita è solo ancora un gioco
> generoso per esse
> con levità connesse
> con gli dèi, tutte simili un poco.

Ah, how life is still a munificent / game for them / joined in levity /
like the gods, all a bit alike.

These are not condemnations. By definition those "things that by
their lightness wander to and fro . . . through and above life's

heaviness" are self-absorbed, insensitive to others, *heartless.** In Saba's view *cuore* is not a "given" organ but a capacity for feeling and sympathy. It takes time to have a heart, to suffer, to feel the "weight" of things. "Quale angoscia non hai viva abbracciata,/vivo restando?": What live anguish have you not embraced, remaining alive? Such is the question with which he confronts his own heart in *Parole.* The heart is alive precisely through its capacity for *dolore,* fellow-feeling. At last it fails, *morituro* or "disheartened," worn out. But before all this, before it is developed by time and gravity, it is embryonically "light," linked to the gods in levity, of a purity and innocence which is at once, for Saba, both terrible and heartbreakingly lovely.

"Heartbreakingly," of course, because such lightness cannot last. Chiaretta too will alter, sustain weight and a human heart:

>. . . l'aerea una moglie
>sarà, la madre dura negli affanni. . . .
>
>   (Fanciulle, #4)

>. . . The airy one will be / a wife, the mother hardened by anxieties. . . .

The first half of the "Finale" to the *Canzonette* traces the same law, the common lot of not only Paolina, Chiaretta and the other *fanciulle* who populate this area of the *Canzoniere,* but the silent one, "Rebecca without amphora," the heartworn Lina who long ago was "Carmencita," *donna* of the red shawl.

>L'umana vita è oscura e dolorosa,
>e non è ferma in lei nessuna cosa.
>
>Solo il passo del Tempo è sempre uguale.
>Amor fa un anno come un giorno breve;
>il tedio accoglier numerosi gli anni
>può in una sola giornata; ma il passo
>suo non sosta né muta. Era Chiaretta
>una fanciulla, ed ora è giovanetta,
>sarà donna domani. E si riceve,
>queste cose pensando, un colpo in mezzo
>del cuore. . . .

° Cf., Chiaretta's pocket mirror, or her response when the poet calls her "Narcissus" in *Fanciulle* #4: "Si specchia nell'ingiuria ella, e ne gode" (She mirrors herself in the reproach, and takes joy in it). One of Saba's very last poems ("Vecchio e giovane" [Old Man and Youth] in *Epigrafe*) characterizes the youth as "Oblioso, insensibile, parvenza d'angelo ancora" (Oblivious, insensible, of angel aspect still).

Human life is dark and full of sorrows, / and nothing in it stands still. /

Only the step of Time is forever the same. / Love makes a year like a brief day; / boredom can gather countless years / within a single day; only Time's step / does not pause, nor change. Chiaretta was / a child, now she is a girl, / she will be a woman tomorrow. And / thinking of these things, one takes a blow / in mid-heart. . . .

As presented thus far, the variety of Love pondered seems that of Prospero for Ariel, paternal, tragic, far from Eros or what I have called "liberation via adultery." But Saba's *fanciulle* are not only heartbreakingly lovely but desirable; his poems about them seem to divide evenly between those of "tenderness" (such as those I have quoted from above) and those of sensuality, which we have still to discuss. We remember his remark apropos Petrarch that "love, real and whole love, requires a perfect fusion of sensuality and tenderness; thus it is rare." It is as rare in Saba as in Petrarch, although in Saba's *Canzoniere*, the two elements at least alternate in successive poems.

Whoever is familiar with the Botticellian Paolina aureoled with *cose leggere e vaganti* as cited above, for instance, will be struck by another poem in the same collection where Saba teases her by imagining his being asked in the future just who she was and replying she was much the same as other local girls "E non aveva che la sua cosetta" (And all she had was her little so-and-so). He will note the heavy breathing under Saba's avuncular or roguish-papa role, as when he chides the pubescent Paolina for nervousness:

> La mia fanciullo snella e polposetta
> è come un arboscello con le poma:
> una ne mangi ed un'altra t'alletta.
>
> La mia piccola cara è una bambina.
> Teme, se tardi rincasa, legnate,
> suo castigo di quando era piccina.
>
> E quando fa quella proibita cosa
> si volge, e manda sospettose occhiate,
> per veder se la mamma è là nascosa. . . .

My lithe and luscious girl / is like a little tree with apples / —one of which you eat, the other is for charming. /

My little darling is a baby. / When she gets home late she fears a spanking, / her punishment from when she was a tiny thing.

And when she does that forbidden thing, / she twists and peers about suspiciously / to see if mamma's hidden near.

The gloating archness of *cosetta* and *quella proibita cosa* are one with the sickly cosseting by diminutives which is a feature of Saba's address to *fanciulle* during this phase—more glutinous than Pascoli.*

Besides the baby talk there are little fables (*favolette*) ostensibly invented to amuse his favorites while at the same time working out fantasies of power in which he is able to possess and master the airy miracles which elude him. Here is a stanza from a *favoletta* composed for Linuccia:

> Tu sei la nuvoletta, io sono il vento;
>   ti porto ove a me piace;
>   qua e là ti porto per il firmamento,
>   e non ti do mai pace.

> You're the cloudlet, I'm the wind; / I carry you where I want; / hither and thither through the firmament I carry you, / and I never give you peace.

That last "teasing" insistancy of the wind easily develops into another sort of story where the fabulist reveals his erotic hunger. We have noted above his image of Paolina as a lithe and toothsome apple tree. In a subsequent *favoletta* it turns up again, with Saba as little goat—shades of the grieving *capra!*—reared on hind legs to nibble her high-hung breast-fruits. Elsewhere he is a falcon, swooping upon the "shivering and wretched" dove who is Paolina:

> Alte strida . . . ma poi chi piú diletto
>   ne avesse io non so piú.

> . . . Piercing screams . . . but who had greater pleasure / from it I forget.

In the first of the *Fanciulle* the girl in question stands naked as though a bound victim asking for "kindly punishment." "You're my thing—I could beat you" is the burden of another tale where he is a young sultan, the *fanciulla* his slave, Saba's dream-version of what she thinks: "How lovely it is for a slave to have a kind master!"

"Tra il sonno e la veglia è paradiso,/ma breve": between sleep and waking is paradise, but short-lived—so runs a passage in *L'uomo.*

---

* And not just girls—whether *fanciullette, ragazze, monelle, figliole, giovanette, piccine*—but the world they are projected into, full of the *ine*'s, *ello*'s, *ino*'s and *etto*'s of his sexual idolatry—*favolette, nuvolette, tazzine, testine, falchetti, caprette*, etc. The attributes of Saba's sensual dotage—his affective phantasmagoria—verge on the pornographic.

Such a paradise he dedicates to Chiaretta, who makes her appearance in it as the *cosina*, the little nothing, secreted in its depths.

> Come ho goduto tra la veglia e il sonno
> questa mattina!
> Uomo ero ancora, ed ero la marina
> libera ed infinita.
>
> Con le calme dorate e gli orizzonti
> lontani il mare.
> Nel fondo ove non occhio può arrivare,
> e non può lo scandaglio,
>
> una pietruzza per me, una cosina
> da nulla aveva.
> Per lei sola fremeva ed arrideva
> l'azzurra immensità.

What joy I found between waking and sleeping / this morning! / I was a man still, and I was / the free and boundless ocean. / The ocean—with golden calms and / distant horizons. / In the deeps where eye cannot reach, / which lead cannot fathom, / was a little pebble, a little / nothing, all mine. / For this alone shivered and smiled / my blue immensity.

Here are the dream-specifications for Saba's amorous relations: a prospect of limitless power whose miraculous condescension or grace it is to single out for special tenderness the minute grain of sand or crystal it anyway contains. The stupendous contrasts between infinite ocean and finite pebble, between the utter fluidity of the saline medium and the attendant still of its denizens, between grandiose nominatives like *immensità* and easy familiarities like *pietruzza* and *cosina da nulla,* between absolute freedom and absolute dependency—such are the polarizations of the compensatory fantasia composed by this harassed "antiquarian," poor, married with a child, who philanders with *fanciulle* and writes poetry "on the side." By means of *favolette* he can possess those light and airy beings who escape him in the flesh; within them he becomes their *sine qua non,* the precondition of that pure potentiality and liberating levity that they mean to him, their element, the residual Neptune-cum-Boreas who composes and decomposes the glittering spray and rosy clouds they so poignantly amount to. Pondering Amor, composing his fables of it, he locates the *vagabondaggio, evasione, poesia* life denies him:

> . . . Se tutti i succhi della primavera
> fossero entrati nel mio vecchio tronco,

per farlo rifiorire anche una volta,
non tutto il bene sentirei che sento
solo a guardarti, ad aver te vicina,
a seguire ogni tuo gesto, ogni modo
tuo di essere, ogni tuo piccolo atto.
E se vicina non t'ho, se a te in alta
solitudine penso, piú infuocato
serpeggia nelle mie vene il pensiero
della carne, il presagio

dell'amara dolcezza,
che so che ti farà i begli occhi chiudere
come la morte.

   . . . If all the saps of spring / had entered my old trunk, / to make it flower one more time, / I wouldn't feel the good I feel / just watching you, having you near, / following your every gesture, every way / you have of being, every little act of yours. / And if I do not have you near, if I think of you in my high / solitude, then still more inflamed / there snakes in my veins the thought / of flesh, the foretaste /
of that bitter sweetness / that I know of which will make you close your lovely eyes / like death.

❉   ❉   ❉

In the "Finale" to the *Canzonette* the first half of which is quoted above, his meditations on Time and its inevitable effect on Chiaretta had made him, as he says, heartsick. How that poem concludes must be of interest to us now:

   . . . Appena, a non pensarle, l'arte
mi giova; fare in me di molte e sparse
cose una sola e bella. E d'ogni male
mi guarisce un bel verso. Oh quante volte
—e questa ancora—per lui che nessuno
piú sa, né intende, sopra l'onte e i danni,

sono partito da Malinconia
e giunto a Beatitudine per via.

   . . . Thinking of them, even art scarcely / solaces me—the making within me of many separate / things into one, whole and beautiful. And a lovely line / cures me of every ill. Oh, how many times / —and this time too—in the service of this art [my gloss of *per lui*] which no one / any longer knows or understands, amidst shames and hurts, /
I have departed from Melancholy, / and reached Blessedness on the way.

His rather darker paraphrase in the *Storia* is also relevant: "For this, that is to say in order to conquer through the torment of art, in the illusion of art's immortality, torments still more sterile and illusions still more fallacious, his hard labor 'carving *canzonette*' was of use to him." The paraphrase of one who *tutti sentiva della vita i pesi*.

He is speaking of a therapy through form. One of the fascinating subplots of the poems of the period we are discussing is the evidence they provide of Saba's conscious and stubborn effort to resolve what he calls his "affective ambivalence" towards life, his "schizoid" tendencies whose master pattern he located in the warring temperaments of his parents, primarily by formal means.

From the start—it is his adult pride to say so—he was drawn to traditional closed stanzaic arrangements, most of all the sonnet, followed by canzonetta. And in the *Storia* he generously supplies a variety of reasons why, ranging from the geographical to the psychological. As a Triestine he was at least forty years behind the times, wholly out of touch with "modern" innovations. As a Triestine of Italian descent, living in an Austrian possession, he was emotionally irredentist with a special passion for *cose italiane*. As a ghetto Jew, he was "naturally" attracted to the older more enduring forms, forms with a persisting life behind them. As a neurotic and a product of a broken family, he psychologically required a tradition, a literary ancestry at least by adoption, that he could grow up in. And certainly anyone at the age of twelve who makes a bonfire of his school editions of the classics in frustration at their difficulty reveals an impassioned, if odd, classicism precociously far removed from the contempts of indifference or respect.

At the beginning these inclinations resulted in work of a certain rigidity. His problem, as he says, was to make his very idiosyncratic content fit a "predetermined form," and the eloquent "Quello che resta da fare ai poeti" shows the intensive scrutiny and self-examination he found he needed in order to keep good faith with his materials. The 1921 *Canzoniere* offers dramatic evidence of his progressive confidence in them as legitimate matter for poetry as well as an increasingly sophisticated skill in adapting the cut of his repertoire of received forms to suit his particular cloth. The line from the earliest work through *Trieste e una donna* is characterized by a growing flexibility in his employment of traditional stanzaic forms, and this development partly resulted in and partly is conditioned by a greater frankness and intimacy of tone. Form loses its absolute or "predetermining" function, becomes an ally rather than an emperor.

It should go without saying that Saba's little liberties are profoundly conservative. He never abandons the hendecasyllable as his basic measure and never—at least not until much later—gives over his relish for the stimulating symmetries incurred by rhyming. Neither "L'arboscello" nor "Trieste" for example are very "free" poems—both work out of and stay fairly close to a hendecasyllabic swell, both have a high frequency of rhyme. But the occasional contraction of a line of verse to a single word (as in, the climactic *maternità* of "L'arboscello") or the articulation of an especially emotional passage by the brakings and prolongations of radical enjambment and phrasal blocking ("Intorno / circola ad ogni cosa / un'aria strana, un'aria tormentosa / l'aria natia") are, along with a more colloquial lexicon and grammar, evidence of his greater openness to his own expressive needs. Technique is no longer "given" but is governed by dramatic urgencies or the expediencies of voice.

But in the poetry we have been discussing, written in the decade extending from *La serena disperazione* through *Fanciulle* and beyond, Saba's tendency is to work once more in tight strophic units. As noted, *Serena disperazione* is an inferior follow-up to *Trieste e una donna*. Formally, however, it marks a return to the old symmetries. Its heavy-duty stanza is the space-framed hendecasyllabic couplet (visual neatness infrequently blurred by run on lines), followed by a variant of *terza rima* (aba, cbc, ded, fef, etc.—see "Il ciabattino") more static than Dante's owing to the relative autonomy of each tercet. A very large proportion of the lyrics in *Preludio e canzonette*, *Cose leggere e vaganti* and *L'amorosa spina* are—as the titles infer—composed in that buoyant, lilting dispensation of short lines and strong, regular rhymes known as songlet or canzonetta, and if not this then a variety of rhymed quatrains, alternating hendecasyllabics with seven- or five-syllable lines, that achieves an equivalent brightness. *Autobiografia* and *I prigioni* are sequences of fifteen sonnets apiece; *Fanciulle* contains twelve identically modelled lyrics, each of four regularly rhymed quatrains.

In the case of the canzonetta and its derivatives the form is traditionally associated with a spècific content. It was popularized by the Arcadian clubs or circles of the eighteenth century as an appropriately light vehicle for hymning Eros with all possible elegance, suavity and charm—serious plaint or too audible suffering ruled out as coarse and in bad taste. For the Saba concerned with not only light and airy things but the fatality of Eros in his life of this period, canzonetta stood ready to hand as providentially applicable to the "levity" he yearned for. He also employed it as a wry music for the expression of his *malinconia amorosa*, a lesson in formal irony he might have learned from Leopardi's sardonic "Risorgimento."

But not all closed forms have such an incremented halo of associative content as the canzonetta. If one tries to describe their general effect on his increasingly intimate materials, I think the correct impression would be that they—such forms—seem to function as a sort of artifically-induced *perspective,* a cooling device which lets him get outside of or "see around" a very fluid and inflammable mass of affective experience. Via the perhaps arbitrary but blessedly impersonal rules of prosody, he submits this experience to a discipline which temporarily removes him from his pain, objectifies it for him. To wit: *I suffer, but my moan must be of a certain specific duration and timbre, must rhyme precisely with that memory or desire which preceded it—and already I hear my moan become something else; perhaps a song.*

Thus, he conceives and executes an essentialistic *Autobiografia* in terms of fifteen sonnets, and it seems to me that the presiding form, the sonnet, is a major accessory to its success, contributing to that chapter's extraordinary dignity and lucidity. Elsewhere, as in the sequence *Il piccolo Berto* written 1929–1931 during psychoanalysis, he does not always escape the sentimental and/or valedictorian pitfalls common to such a subject. This is not to say that a sonnet is somehow more "influential-for-objectivity" than is a blank verse arrangement, but since it contains a built-in cutoff point (line fourteen), it tends to discourage expansiveness, and as it traditionally involves some sort of crescendo and climax, it encourages awareness of overall shape and pattern. And this suggests a degree of objectivity.

The effort at perspective through form has a corollary in *favoletta,* the sub-genre that Saba was fond of working in from the 1920's on. Fable is, in fact, the genre made for *senilità,* a way of talking to children which incorporates brevity, drama, levity and moral seriousness, as well as a mode of contemplating and finding inclusive pattern in experience. Svevo and his heroes loved it, so did Saba. "My little girl is like an appletree," "You are the cloud, I am the wind," the catalogue of light and airy things—all are manifestations of Saba's attempt to fabulize experience, to make it elemental and common. So are the prisoners in *I prigioni*—creatures caught or caged by ruling passion, obsession, psychic mechanism; so are the various females in *Fanciulle,* the girls in Saba's life presented as moral-temperamental types or emblems; the narcissist, the self-willed, the mother, etc. These sequences are rather frigid and contrived, exempla or "humors" that one would take as dull "neoclassical" exercises if one were not aware of the desperate motive behind them: an attempt through poetry to see experience clear of its subjective and affective claims, to contemplate it rather than suffer it. An impossible effort which marks all the verse of *Figure e canti* with a special pathos and tension.

One recalls that removed *cantuccio* above Trieste from which he was able to take possession of his city, to see it whole. Such things as fables, sonnets and *canzonette* might be conceived as other removes, placements for contemplative vision. They relate to the healing virtue he finds in *un bel verso:*

> . . . fare in me di molte e sparse
> cose una sola. . . .

❋   ❋   ❋

Cuor morituro, an expiring or moribund heart, is the title of the final section of poems contained in *Figure e canti*. An appendix to it also figures in Saba's next large collection, the *Tre composizioni** published in 1933. In the *Canzoniere* its span is given as 1925–1930; my guess would be that the "1925" refers to the date of first publication and that a compositional dating would move it up to 1924 or 1923. At any rate it would seem that *Cuor morituro* is the poetic expression of a larger time span than any other chapter in the *Canzoniere* with the single exception of *Ultime cose* (Last Things: 1935–1943), where the reason was political. In my opinion *Cuor morituro* would be more fittingly placed at the end of what Saba later came to call "volume two (1921–1932)" of the *Canzoniere* rather than where it now "definitively" is, between *Fanciulle* and *L'uomo*. It provides a capsule version of the story of that volume (increasing depression climaxed by "treatment" and renewal) and because of this I propose to consider it after the three compositions that follow it in the *Canzoniere*.

L'uomo is one of Saba's fascinating failures. Along with the *I prigioni* sequence with which it has a certain affinity, it offers a good example of the liabilities involved in his effort to generalize and objectify his experience. The underlying conception of *I prigioni*— that one is the "captive" of the psychological disposition one is given at birth—is certainly intimately involved with Saba's understanding of his own difficulties, but he invents his illustrative examples rather than relying on his own experience, and the result is the gallery of statues he does too much honor to by calling *michelangelesco*. *Autobiografia* and *I prigioni* are both sequences of fifteen sonnets, and this parallelism—as Saba points out in the *Storia*—is

---

* E.g., 1) *L'uomo* (The Man): 1928, 2) *Preludio e fughe* (Prelude and Fugues): first published by *Solaria* in 1928, 3) *Il piccolo Berto* (Little Berto): 1929–1931. The additions to *Cuor morituro* were not, then, designated in the title.

quite deliberate: "It is as though Saba meant to say: I treat the external world even as I have treated myself." But one is a triumph, the other not, and the moral one is tempted to draw is that the peculiar muse of Umberto Saba thrives on self-centeredness as a precondition for her descent; less floridly, that he is a poor inventor.

L'uomo is not only Saba's longest (487 lines) but most ambitious single poem, and in this case the length is a measure of the ambition. It aims to be no less than a "natural history of man" as reflected in the life vicissitudes of the title *uomo*. The melancholy Jacques in his similar but far shorter and more trenchant version remarks how "one man in his time plays many parts." So Saba's protagonist—and, patently, "hero"—assumes a number of parts in his progress from cradle to grave: infant, son, adolescent, adult, friend, laborer, lover, husband, provider, neighbor, truant, dreamer, ultimately dotard. In a sense, *L'uomo* tells the same story as the *Canzoniere* will in its entirety. But it is too self-conscious; it is a special strength of Saba's imagination to make the local color and palpability of his own existence quietly implicate *ogni altra vita* rather than "just" one man's life; he aims directly at nothing less than the life of all mankind.

For this reason, Saba ill-advisedly cultivates an extreme genericism in his narrative. The poem contains no proper names. Its entire cast is invariably nominated by summary substantives with definite articles: not only "the man" but "the father," "the wife," "the children," and so forth. The single exception to this rule actually reenforces it; at one point the hero's youthful slumber is likened to "Adam's, at the world's beginning." Clearly Saba's *uomo* is meant to suggest an Adam, someone residual and enduring, living out the dolorous life of *tutti*. But he never comes clear, he is faceless and abstract, a monumental proposition whose vicissitudes remain schematic.

This strange metabiography has certain parallels with the poet's life. The nameless subject has a grieving mother, a brutal father (armed with a cane rather than those absentee blue eyes). He seeks freedom from the weight of his responsibilities by intermittent wandering, and imbibes the guilt of his delinquency through the "mute rancor" in the eyes of his aging wife. And *L'uomo* as a whole can be read as the slightly garrulous fable of man as prisoner, his wisdom the gradual perception and acceptance of the fact of his captivity. The poem begins with the infant besieged in his cradle by night terrors. Slightly older he begins to see the normal condition of life as "squalid" and "narrow"; his first job seems a "dark prison." Through the length of the poem, in marriage, paternity and breadwinning, the images of chains and imprisonment multiply. In the end he submits, *gigante sommesso* (a bound giant), as the wearisome frictions of his experience erode his subjective capacity for dream and aspiration, closer to Faulkner's enduring meek than any titanic and Aeschylean ancestor that Saba may have had in mind.

To give some shape to this composition, to engage some limits beyond the merely biological ones of birth and death, Saba invented an elaborate stanzaic system. The nearly five hundred lines of *L'uomo* are divided into fifty-seven stanzas of two alternating kinds, one eleven-lined, the other six-lined, both composed of regularly rhymed hendecasyllables or their normal subdivisions. The general effect is to create a pervading systaltic rhythm; frequently Saba reserves the longer stanza to carry the narrative burden, the shorter for illustrative or even "epic" simile, reflective comment, lyric coloring. These structural innovations, while they provide a sort of external scaffolding for his imagination to work against, often force him into the literary artifices, archaisms, contractions, inversions, that he had outgrown twenty years earlier. In general, *L'uomo* is an attempt at epic fable, *favola* rather than *favoletta*, that illustrates the boundaries of Saba's shortbreathed and localized genius.

In the despondent mood of this period, Saba found that even his intimations of proximate recognition—"my glory is coming; I sense its kiss, though late," as he writes in "La vetrina"—could not prevent him, *cuor morituro*, from dreaming of his death. That ending, or "release" as he would call it in this mood, was still well over a quarter of a century away. But Saba's reputation as an important poet (always, as far as he was concerned, too little and too late, and soon to be stifled by the silence forced upon him by political developments), was indeed beginning to declare itself. He was, as we have noted, featured in *Primo tempo* in the early 1920's. The volume of 1925, *Figure e canti*, was the first of Saba's books to be noticed generally and on the whole favorably throughout the whole of literary Italy. But 1928 was the real year of his arrival. That May, *Solaria* brought out an entire issue devoted to all of his work to date (important articles by Debenedetti, Solmi, Benco, Montale). It also published one of his central chapters, *Preludio e fughe*, which immediately earned him the enthusiastic recognition of his literary peers.

The lovely prelude establishes the program for the series of twelve related "fugues" to follow. It is an invocation or entreaty to what the poet calls his "voices" to become present to him once more now as his life moves towards its end:

Oh, ritornate a me voci d'un tempo,

care voci discordi!
Chi sa che in nuovi dolcissimi accordi
io non vi faccia risuonare ancora?

Oh, return to me, voices of a former time, / my dear discordant voices! / Who knows whether I might not even now make you resound / in new chords of utmost sweetness?

The nature of these voices is quickly revealed in the fugues proper: they are Saba's basic affective positions, inner attitudes towards life, "disembodied" utterances precipitated out of his contemplated experience. The two basic "sides" of his ambivalence are familiar by now, as expressed in the psychological geneology of the third sonnet of *Autobiografia*: he is the ground of a "racial" quarrel between his father's idyllic levity and his mother's sense of life's dolorous gravity. These are the root or Ur-voices out of which the voices in his fugues develop, voices of a creature who cannot in all honesty say "I," but must be content with an unresolved pluralism, "we," "me,"[1] "me,"[2] "me,"[3] etc.

These are "psychic" voices, then, voices of Psyche, but with nothing of that Freudian "drama for three characters" for which Saba will proselytize in his post-psychoanalytic *Scorciatoie*.* *That* drama postulates a perpetual civil war, whereas Saba's prelude profers at least the possibility of a sweet new style, a novel harmony to be fashioned out of what were once upon a time jarring sounds:

. . . in pace
vi componete negli estremi accordi,
voci invano discordi. . . .

. . . peacefully you compose yourself into ultimate harmonies, vainly discordant voices. . . .

Of course the very notion of fugue is predicated upon some such choral eventuality, for if it literally means a flight or chase—hence an original rivalry of melodic strands ("voices"), it also means a building contrapuntal situation wherein each voice is gradually and satisfyingly revealed as a vital accessory to the emergent condition of choir. Out of what seemed contrasting claims, then, emerges an

---

* E.g., #54 (*Prose*, p. 284): "DRAMA FOR 3 CHARACTERS" alive in us all. The Id—from the depths, dark, organic, still unexplored—screams, "Go do that terrible thing." "If you do," Superego quickly intervenes. "I'll punish you until you die, and even—one never knows—if possible, even beyond. But if you don't dare do it you're a vile creature." And the wretched Ego cries, like Faust, "Why was I ever born?"

ultimate chorus or integrated community; out of an agon of com-
peting melodies comes that *finale della commedia* called harmony.

> La luce e l'ombra, la goia e il dolore
> s'amano in voi. . . .

> Light and shadow, joy and sorrow / love one another within you. . . .

In the fugues themselves these imagistic oppositions are multiplied:
a black coal cellar against the azure sky and many-masted sea, an
April garden against a haunted slaughterhouse, the shining world
and a prison, dawn and dusk, spring and fall, fabulous islands and
interminable deserts, impassioned youths and weary old men, a
budding leaf attached to its branch and the fresh varnish (manu-
factured by Italo Svevo?) on a departing liner, man and his sinister
companions, echo and shadow; all, in short, variations and nuances
based on Saba's simple and familiar dualism; "the expression," as
he writes in the *Storia*, "of the yes and no he says to life, to that
calda vita, loved, detested and feared at the same time by the same
person."

Despite its inherent presumption of conflict, *Preludio e fughe* is the
most "organically" unified chapter in the whole *Canzoniere*. With or
without misgivings, one could suppress a poem or two from any of
the others, even several strophes from *L'uomo;* it may be that such
is the virtue of a poetry of occasions. But the fugues vibrate beyond
their single selves to increment a twelve-part ensemble or Gross
Fugue. Imagistically and prosodically each one is distinct;* each is
itself ("intramurally") fugal, with its own local contestation leading
to some sort of climactic provisional resolution. But each fugue also
serves to comment upon and illuminate the others. The fundamental
polarities, positive and negative, are perpetually shifting and ex-
tending themselves, sometimes to the fantastic verge of changing
places. Nothing is settled, everything moves, the dance of displace-
ments and disclosures illuminates old stands as well as those to come.

And so the "blanket" depression of the first voice in the first fugue—

---

* E.g., each has its own basic key images and each its own pacing and
visual/auditory shape, ranging from "blank" hendecasyllables to rhymed quat-
rains which approximate a canzonetta, to a condensed version of the *Uomo*
stanzas, to the unusual eight-syllable quatrains of the famous sixth fugue (for
three voices). Voices define themselves in the course of their fugue; they are
distinguished one from another by contrasted typesettings (italic or roman),
with the single exception of the sixth, where each of the three voices is given
a number.

> La vita, la mia vita, ha la tristezza
> del nero magazzino di carbone
> che vedo ancora in questa strada. . . .

Life, my life, has the sadness / of the black coalcellar / I still see in this street. . . .

—is modified in the course of its colloquy with its affirming counter-voice to the admission that it is prompted by a fear of painful losses to come rather than actual despair, and then to an indirect, imagistic confession that the vision of loveliness that it has "realistically" denied may actually exist. *Se puoi, taci . . . voce che dalla mia sei nata:* Be still if you can . . . voice born of my own—so the first voice responds to the affirmatives of the second, and the trouble in its tone testifies to the change. What was originally a categorical declaration of black fact has altered gradually to allow a wistful awareness of the "other" reality its earlier intransigence had blocked. The azure sea and skies with which the second voice had countered the black cellar from the beginning, now became this fugue's climaxing last words, articulated longingly by the very voice that from the first rejected them.

Simultaneously the second and affirming voice has, in the ordeal by counterpoint, disclosed the generating source of its vital joy. It is not the simplistic "animal" and Mediterranean sensuality that its emblematic seascape might imply, the happy hedonism of living for the moment without thought for the morrow. It is rather its delight and sensuous feel *for process* above and beyond the particular fortune, its gift for experiencing whatever fortune befalls, in terms of the continuing and "immortal" story of the species, the creation (rather than the single creature) which moves at the heart of its levity.

It is not a belief or philosophy; it is not to be confused with any brand of biological evolutionism or humanitarianism. It is a vital sense or instinct. If the first voice adduces life's brevity as a reasonable cause for despair, the second can grant the premise and *still* affirm:

> . . . Oggi i tuoi occhi,
> del nero magazzino di carbone,
> vedono il cielo ed il mare, al contrasto,
> piú luminosi: pensa che saranno
> chiusi domani. Ed *altri s'apriranno,*
> *simili ai miei, simili ai tuoi.* . . .

Today your eyes / see the sky and sea more luminous, / by contrast, than the black coalcellar. / Think that they shall be shut tomorrow. / *And others will open, like mine, like yours.*

If the first adduces its fear of loss as a reason for calling the unborn happy, the second can respond:

> . . . *I non nati*
> *non sono, i morti non sono, vi è solo*
> *la vita viva eternamente.* . . .

. . . *The unborn / do not exist, nor do the dead, there is only / life eternally alive.* . . .

And as such, as testimony of vital process, even the suffering expressed by the first voice is valued and affirmed as value by the second; not only the blue sky and sea and the anchored or departing vessels, but the black coal cellar as well that, like an archway, "frames" the vision and sets off its contrasting joys:

> . . . *il nero magazzino di carbone,*
> *che il quadro, come per caso, incornicia*
> *stupendamente, e quelle più soavi*
> *cose che in te, del dolore al contrasto,*
> *senti—accese delizie.* . . .

. . . *the black coal cellar / that, stupendously, as though by chance, frames / the picture, and those more gracious / things inside you that, contrasting with sorrow, / you feel as intense* [burning] *delight.* . . .

So too, at the conclusion of the brief second fugue, which expresses the "courtship" of the first voice by the second, of *dolore* by joy, the latter cries out ecstatically for the sorrow of the other, and as the other tenderly, ruefully accedes ("take of me what you can . . . "), sings exultantly

> *Io prendo tutto: la dolcezza, e poi,*
> *che più mi piace, la tua essenza amara.*

. . . *I take everything: your sweetness, and then / what pleases me more, your bitter essence.*

It is in the nature of fugue that its various component voices never crystallize, never grow "definitive." Thus, even these victories of the second and affirming voice, as it cajoles and woos its opposite, are impermanent, melodic "rests" that subsequently become points of departure for further alterations. As the first fugue, for example, was imagistically inaugurated with the vision of life as grim as a coal cellar, so the third begins with the triumphant song of the second voice:

> *Mi levo come in un giardino ameno*
> *un gioco d'acque.* . . .

I arise as in a pleasant garden, / a play of waters. . . .

And as in that first fugue where despair was checked and "converted" to an explicit consciousness of at least the coexistence of an azure world, so here, upon the negative admission that life is a good beyond even present sorrow, the affirmative instantly offers to dress itself in black, to be *triste,* to assume the other's just-abandoned place.

> Ascolta, Eco gentile, ascolta il vero
> che viene dietro,
> che viene in fondo ad ogni mio pensiero
> piú tetro.
>
> Io lo so che la vita, oltre il dolore,
> è piú che un bene.
> *Le angosce allora io ne dirò, il furore,*
> *le pene;*
>
> *che sono la tua Eco, ed il segreto*
> *è in me delle tue paci.*
> *Del tuo pensiero quello ti ripeto*
> *che taci.*

Listen, gentle Echo, listen to the truth / that arises within, / that arises in the depth of each of my darkest / thoughts. /
I know well that life, beyond sorrow, / is more than a good. / *Then I shall speak its anguishes, its frenzy, / its pains;*
for I am your Echo, and the secret / of your calms is within me. / Of all your thought I repeat to you that one / about which you remain silent.

No position is final, each gives way to converse, contradiction or contrary in what seems an infinite series of struggles and embraces. The condition of fugue obtains.

We should recall the promise made in the prelude:

> Come i parenti m'han dato due vite,
> e di fonderle in una io fui capace,
>
> in pace
> vi componete negli estremi accordi,
> voci invano discordi. . . .

Even as my parents gave me two lives / and I was capable of fusing them into one /
so peacefully / you compose yourselves into ultimate harmonies, / vainly disharmonious voices. . . .

Yet the final *congedo* or envoi rejects this happy ending for something far more problematical:

O mio cuore dal nascere in due scisso,
quante pene durai per uno farne!
Quante rose a nascondere un abisso!

O my heart split into two from birth, / how many pains I endured to make you into one! / How many roses to conceal an abyss! /

Is the heart healed and unified, or only lyrically, idyllically masked? The two successive exclamations are of course contradictory; if he is now "integrated," then there is no abyss; if the roses of poetry conceal the deep fracture within him, then the poet is not whole. But in fact, his division has never been concealed, and the little tercet of *congedo* is yet another self-lacerating expression of the abiding ambivalence towards life that neither poetry nor the analyst's couch will ever cure.

Yet, the lasting impression given by *Preludio e fughe*, this chapter of inner contrasts, is of a transfiguring harmony and serenity. Saba writes in the *Storia* that "these contrasts are only *apparent* even as life with its struggles will seem univocal to whomever can contemplate it from a sufficient height." To rise, to see life whole but not remotely, may be an ironic blessing derived from *senilità*, the bequest of a heart somewhat detached or *morituro*. The hour, as indicated in the prelude, is propitious:

L'aurora
è lontana da me, la notte viene. . . .

Dawn / is far from me, night comes. . . .

But the "sufficient height" should not imply any stratospheric coldness or cerebral monism. In his essay *"L'umorismo"* Pirandello defines humor as as artist's ability to entertain simultaneously all the various sides or aspects of any question, to preserve them in suspension without suppressing any in the interests of common sense or certainty. Pirandello's exemplary masters here were Cervantes and Manzoni; his own variety, it seems to me, is not always exempt from witty parodox-mongering. But a concept like *umorismo* seems to be of use in understanding Saba's achievement in *Preludio e fughe.*

Apropos of his friend Svevo who, after a lifetime spent in fear of dying, found dying easier than writing a novel, Saba wrote, *"umorismo* is the supreme form of goodness."[32] It is also a harmonic mode, conducive to serenity. In the fugues, the dance of theses and antitheses ("light and shadow, joy and sorrow," and so on) is not ironed into synthesis; much more miraculously, they *s'amano in voi,* love one another by means of the voices he has given them. As the title tells us, *Preludio e fughe* is a musical interlude, a translation of struggle into song whereby the struggle itself provides the harmonic impetus. Its affective components are not cancelled but contained or compassed in a humorous acceptance, a capacious music. Even in the play of rhyme, ostensible contraries link and mutually support one another; *cara* (dear), rhymes with *amara* (bitter), *amore* with *dolore, cuore* with *errore,* and so forth, and these contraries audibly come "to love one another" as part of the *canzone* of a man's life. Much more truly than in the *Canzonette* (where one could really say that inner chasms were provisionally bridged with cables of roses) *Preludio e fughe* achieves the dancing lightness or almost-divine levity that he cherished in so many of the forms about him.

The longest fugue of all, the sixth, is a lilting debate upon the nature of joy carried on through an intricate concert of echoing refrains and interlinking rhymes by three voices singing their varying visions of the sweetest things in life. Writing in the Saba issue of *Solaria,* Sergio Solmi brilliantly summarized the three approaches, two active, the third contemplative. The first voice is familiar to us: the sensualist, the "voluptuous lover of life." The second, he writes, belongs to "he who attests the joy of sacrifice and sorrow," and the important location of a possible joy in *dolore* would seem to show Saba's growth in self-knowledge.* The third is "Poetry, which conjoins and resolves the other two in the mirror of contemplation."[33]

Surely that third voice is the muse of these fugues. Light, shadow, joy and pain are reflections in its azure eye. Yet, its last words, addressed to its companions, tell of the amorous dependency of poetry on the *calda vita* it reflects:

---

* In a late letter to Nora Baldi Saba frankly calls the second voice "masochistic": ". . . the second voice is, psychologically speaking, masochistic, as adolescence usually is—or at least was; when the ego is 'devoured' by the object love" (*Lettere a un'amica,* p. 63). This is interesting but in my opinion a good example of Saba's post-analysis intemperance, resulting in a certain loss of "humor." His analysis omits the notion of "legitimate" sacrifice and joy in it which Solmi's note rightly points up.

Nata son dal suo disgusto,
nata son dal tuo tormento:
tanto viva esser mi sento
quanto amate il viver mio.

Ma se voi tacete, anch'io,
ecco, in aere mi risolvo;
con voi libera m'evolvo,
muoio libera con voi.

I am born from his disgust, / I am born from your torment; / I
feel myself alive / in measure as you love my living.
But if you grow silent, see how I too / resolve myself into air; /
with you I freely grow, / freely die with you.

The original "Congedo" to *Preludio e fughe* ran:

Dalla marea che un popolo ha sommerso,
e me con esso, ancora
levo la testa? Ancora
ascolto? Ancora non è tutto perso?

From the tide that has submerged a whole people, / and me with
it, still / do I raise my head? Am I still / listening? Still is not all lost?

When *Solaria* published the book in 1928 it was not possible for
political reasons to publish this envoi; hence the substitution of the
second one (appropriately enough more "inward") cited above.
These last years of the 1920's were extremely difficult ones in Italy,
and despite the censorship that made any more or less direct refer-
ence to the regime impossible (the censor would have stuck on the
word *popolo* above) the bulk of the poems of the period are full of
inquietude and a pervading sense of personal helplessness. 1928 is
the year, for instance, in which Ungaretti's growing anguish finds
expression in the despair of "Pietà," where man is seen as a "mo-
notonous universe" affixed to the void by spider's thread. 1928 is the
year of the second edition of Montale's *Ossi di seppia*, augmented by
the great poems of stifled or strangled life like "Arsenio," "I morti,"
and the concluding *ora pro nobis* of the magnificent "Incontro":
"Pray for me while I descend . . . through the dark air . . . that I
may descend without vileness."
I believe that "the times" constrained a poetic approach to the
crisis in inward and personal rather than public or Carduccian terms;
I also believe that the poets we are concerned with would have
freely chosen this approach even if the censor hadn't existed. Certainly

there is nothing obscure or evasive about these masterpieces. Oddly enough, if any of them had to be categorized "hermetic" it would be perhaps the *Fughe,* and this simply on the strength of Saba's remarks on them in the *Storia.* He points out "vague" references, for example, to Mussolini and Matteotti in the sixth fugue, but while these men may have been "on his mind," as he says, during its composition, knowledge of this is unavailable in—and nonessential to—the poem itself. That certain lines from the same fugue referring to the joy of "inward liberty" were found, as Saba says, written on the walls of a Florentine torture cell during the German occupation means not that the "Canto a tre voci" was an anti-Fascist code in verse but that it is a great human statement, continually relevant. Along with Montale's new conclusions to the *Ossi* and Ungaretti's *Inni* (Hymns), *Preludio e fughe* is a statement of "man's feelings, his thirst for liberty and wish to leave his solitude" as humanly committed as even the late-developing Quasimodo could desire.

In order to drown out the official loudspeakers, we recall, Saba had literally stopped up his ears, "hearing instead, with more concentrated attention, other 'voices' that quarreled in his own heart." In effect, *Preludio e fughe* could be considered an unorthodox psychoanalysis *avant la lettre,* and the serene harmony it achieves would seem an auspicious sign of Saba's resolution of at least his internal problems. But in fact, by the end of the 1920's, Saba was undergoing genuine Freudian analysis and the poems written in the course of this experience (1929–1931) are brought together in *Il piccolo Berto,* dedicated to Dr. Edoardo Weiss, a former student of Freud's and one of the earliest practitioners in Italy.* We shall have something to say about the effect of psychoanalysis on Saba's later poetry; there is not much to say about the sixteen poems it directly occasioned. Perhaps the title intimates the problem: it was Peppa's pet name for him. Peppa, Mamma, his Paduan relations Cousin Elvira and Aunt Stellina to whom his mother sent him in order to make him forget his "eternal Peppa"—such is the gallery of competing mothers among whom little Berto, closely and sentimentally tracked by Umberto, makes his traumatic way. Notwithstanding the gossipy background material it provides for the "novel" of the life of Saba, *Il piccolo Berto* seems an authentic decadence following so closely on *Preludio e fughe,* and constitutes the sole chapter in the *Can-*

---

* We are told that Weiss, a friend of Svevo's, was once troubled by rumors that *La coscienza di Zeno* was a *sottisier* of modish Freudianism, with himself as model for the complacent "Dr. S." He was (correctly) relieved when he read it. Saba's course lasted for two years, was broken off when Weiss transferred to Rome. After the Fascist "racial" edicts he emigrated to Chicago.

zoniere with an irredeemably soft and prosey center.* The *Storia* judgment is fair enough: "In some sense there was inspiration, but it was born in solitude—destined, therefore, never to become poetry, or to become so for the author alone." His memories, volatile anyway in a regimen of psychoanalysis, simply swamped him.

❀   ❀   ❀

Contrasting with the plain and reticent titles on either side of it (*Autobiografia, I prigioni, Fanciulle, L'uomo, Preludio e fughe*) the sense of *Cuor morituro* sounds with a special urgency. If, as we have said, to have a heart is to experience *dolore*, to sustain the weight of things, a dying heart indicates a gutted survivor, he who remains after the wrack of regrets and longing, he whose life is petering out, he for whom things are "over."

One could say that *Cuor morituro* is a revisitation of the sacred figures and landscapes of Saba's youth and so constitutes, from a radically altered angle of vision, a reworking of the contents of the *Poesie dell'adolescenza e giovanili*. He himself, his mother, his young friend Glauco who, in that earliest collection, had expressed an anxious and prophetic concern over Berto's moodiness, Peppa and her husband on Via del Monte, the view of the harbor, the cemetery and the old chapel—all are reinvoked, no longer in the yearning past definites and lingering imperfects of those early poems, nor with the mawkishness of most of *Piccolo Berto,* but in the present, as residual dreams, known to be such, that haunt his suffering mind. Or *favolette:* stories based upon something that is over.

Thus, in the "Sonetto di paradiso" that inaugurates this chapter, the familiar shrine once more bears its benediction, but *in sogno,* in dream only:

> Mi viene in sogno una bianca casetta,
> sull'erto colle, dentro un'aria affatto
> tranquilla; e il verde del colle è compatto
> e solitario, e l'ora è benedetta.

There comes to me in dream a small white house / on a steep hill,

* No doubt such an assertion will stimulate a curiosity in the reader more than would the most impassioned praise. I therefore append a literal translation of one of the emotional peaks of the sequence, when Berto first sees Peppa after his return from Padua. "'Oh Berto! oh Berto!' she exclaimed, happily pouring me my milk and coffee. I told / her of all that had happened. Then when / as a secret between the two of us, she asked me / if I'd been happy at Padua, if I was / happier down there or with my mother, 'It was lovely / with Elvira,' I told her; 'but with you' / and I begged her to bend down, since I wished / to whisper this in her ear, 'it's even / lovelier.'"

enveloped by an air of utter / peace; and the hill's green is dense /
and solitary, and the hour is blessed.

As the quatrains quicken into tercets, other iconic objects from that
fable declare themselves: the *dolce capretta*, sweet young goat,
cropping her grass on the hill "squints up at me with human calm,
as if a tacit treaty bound us"; and the old twilight from "Da un colle"
once more brings the sinking sun to strike flame from Peppa's
window:

> E tutto il dolce che c'è nella vita
> in quel sol punto, in quel solo fulgore
> s'era congiunto, in quell'ultimo addio.

And all there is that is sweet in life / within that single point, that
single flash, / that last goodbye, has converged.

In the governing tense of the sonnet all of this *is*, but *is as in a
dream;* this is reiterated in the "mi viene in sogno" that initiates
each quatrain. Another "Casa della mia nutrice" in *Cuor morituro*
beautifully evokes the cottage and its inhabitants in an extended *ubi
sunt* whose very first lines fatally give the game away:

> O immaginata a lungo come un mito,
> o quasi inesistente,
> dove sei . . . ?

O imagined from afar like a myth, / O nearly nonexistent, / where
are you?

The eventual answer echoes in *un sogno dall'adolescenza uscito,*
a dream issued from my youth, a dream which, unlike those
of youth, the dreamer accepts as not having a chance of being realized.
This acceptance is one of the stoic strengths of a *cuor morituro.*

In "La vetrina" (The Glass-doored Cupboard), the poet lies in
a sickbed contemplating where the little collection of English bone-
china teacups, purchased by his grandparents in the "divino per me
milleottocento" (for me divine nineteenth century), hangs in a
corner cupboard. But the ripples of friendliness emanating from
them are cancelled by his deep recognition that the feelings they
give off have to do with a life that is over and done with, that the
consolation afforded him by these fragile relics of family history
is weaker than his desire for oblivion:

> . . . ed oh quale
> ho nostalgia di lasciarvi! Nel buio,
> tornar nel buio dell'alvo materno,
> nel duro sonno, onde piú nulla smuove,
> non pur l'amore, soave tormento. . . .

> . . . and oh what / nostalgia I have to leave you! Into the dark, / to return into the dark of the mothering womb, / into fast sleep, where nothing moves more, / not even love, suave torment. . . .

Thirty years before, in the stammeringly honest "A Mamma," a weaned and vagabond Saba in Florence had thought of his mother home in Trieste and written out his homesickness. Another nostalgia pervades the pages of *Cuor morituro,* this time no longer for the iconic figures and places of childhood (they, like the tea set, are kindly but impotent phantoms) but for the *alvo materno,* the sourcing earth that offers the perfect peace of total annihilation. His mother is dead and under ground:

> . . . farmi, o madre,
> come una macchia dalla terra nata,
> che in sé la terra riassorbe ed annulla.

> . . . make me, O mother, / like a stain born of earth / that unto itself earth reabsorbs and nullifies.

In her last, dark nihility, she has become his saint and intermediary. The last poem of *Cuor morituro* (ideally at least the last poem of volume two of the *Canzoniere,* since the composition of "Preghiera alla madre" postdates *Il piccolo Berto*) is his prayer to join her.

❁   ❁   ❁

In a 1933 essay on Saba, Sergio Solmi remarks on his "attempts to condense within a great synthesis the fatalities of flesh and the pre-destined cycle of human life."[34] Solmi is specifically referring to *I prigioni* and *L'uomo,* but surely the loftiest of all Saba's efforts at synthesis, less inclusive and more specialized than the fugues but possibly more intense and poignant, is the great *canzone* "La brama" at the center of *Cuor morituro.*

"Brama" can be understood "clinically" as libido, more loosely as that erotic hungering which, disguised or openly, consciously or not, Saba has come to recognize as fundamental life-energy, *élan vital, anima mundi.* "La brama" therefore is an almost Lucretian expression of Saba's most urgent fable and credo, half-celebration and half-ritual propitiation of what he calls in the *Storia* "the ancient Eros who unifies the world." Its position in almost the exact center of the completed *Canzoniere* constitutes an odd spatial confirmation of the centrality of the god's presence that he acknowledged in all his work:

> Altro che te che ho detto
> io nei modi dell'arte, che ho nascosto
> altro che te, o svelato?

. . . Other than thou of what have I spoken / in the modalities of my art? what have I hidden, / other than thou, or veiled?

Being a hymn, "La brama" contains a variable refrain, a recurrent or obsessional epithetic bloc which regulates the pulse of the andante with which the poem unfolds. This bloc is first proposed, as a direct ritual invocation, as the brief first stanza:

> O nell'antica carne
> dell'uomo addentro infitta
> antica brama!

O deep-fixed / within the ancient heart of man, / ancient hunger!

Brama is now celebrated for the gift of supreme pleasure it confers directly upon our lives, "as much sweetness as the creation holds, unified through flesh." As Freud teaches, flesh cheated or frustrated of its fleshly desire may console or compensate itself through "spiritual" displacements, sublimations. The hymn adduces "the departure of tall ships" in quest of new worlds, a religious passion to "conquer the tomb." In this creative aspect, *brama* is hailed by two adjectival epithets: *assidua*, (assiduous, diligent, perpetual), and *generante*, (generative, fructifying).

But the image evoked by the initial participle (*infitta*) forecasts a darker note of pain and *dolore*. From the young boy's innocent virility sickening to guilt and self-abuse to the old man's torment leading to his wish to die, life is threaded by anguish. In its role as punisher and nemesis, *brama* accrues two other adjectives: *cupa* (dark, mysterious, inscrutable), and *feroce* (ferocious and ravening).

"La brama" is evoked as the dynamic source and condition of all animate life, "cause of my ills and also—yes—my good." To deny it would be blasphemy, a denial of life itself. Hence the recurring qualifier, ANTICA *brama*, repeated six times above and beyond the more specialized others, modifying and deepening the phrase *antica carne* inexorably linked to it.

> Ti riconosce colui che alla sera,
> con lotta e pena, della vita è giunto;
> ti riconosce e, per sfuggirti, morte
> s'invoca. . . .

. . . he recognizes you, he who has arrived, / with struggle and pain, at the evening of life; / he recognizes you and, to flee you, invokes / his death. . . .

"He" is plausibly Umberto Saba, but here the "documentary" specificity of a given life is dissolved into the larger synthesis or fable, or present only as a special overtone to the reader familiar with his story. Perhaps the most moving example of this sort of transformation in the poem occurs in the final stanza, where the plight of Vittorio Bolaffio, the Triestine painter who was painting Saba's portrait almost simultaneously with the composition of "La brama," is evoked:

> Devotamente egli la mano stende,
> che d'ansia trema, a colorir sue tele.
> Sopra vi pinge vele
> nel sole, accesi incontri
> di figure, tramonti sulle rive
> del mare e a bordo, e su ogni cosa un lume
> di santità. . . .

. . . Devotedly he extends his hand, / which trembles with inquietude, to color his canvases. / Upon them he paints sails / in the sun, vivid encounters / of figures, sunsets above shores / of the sea and from a ship's railing, and over everything a light, / of holiness. . . .

But this image of the artist—Bolaffio but also Saba—as the celebrant of *cose leggere e vaganti* culminates inevitably in disaster: a man "not yet old but bent," a dreamer of terrible dreams, crippled by desire. Like the cat of *Trieste e una donna* or the goat of *Casa e campagna* whose absurd plaint recapitulates the pain of *ogni altra vita,* so Saba and Bolaffio become figures in a fabulous landscape, elements in the continuous present of a master fable.

"La brama" is one of the great examples of Saba's piety towards the Italian literary tradition, and proof of that tradition's viability in the present. "La brama" could not have been made without the nourishment Saba received from his masters from Petrarch to Leopardi. But influence is inevitable; what counts is what can be made of it, and what Saba makes of it here is something profoundly his own. With the grave deliberateness of its periods, the deep plangency of its stern music, "La brama" stands as the latest of the great Italian *canzoni,* last of the line begun with the *stilnovisti* and Cavalcanti's "Donna mi prega." And despite the fact that the world view it espouses is highly specialized, it rises above its obsessive and doctrinaire originating impulses to become in the end a truly noble exposition of the epistemology of joy and sorrow.

✲   ✲   ✲

Immediately following "La brama" in *Cuor morituro* is another very different major poem: "Il borgo" ("The town": the title refers not to Trieste but to one of its hillside and now suburban adjuncts where Saba lived at the turn of the century). Like "La capra" or "La brama," "Il borgo" constitutes one of the moments in the *Canzoniere* to which one returns again and again as to the definitive utterance of a crucial experience. We have quoted from it several times already when referring to Saba's perennial ache for community.

Like the majority of *Cuor morituro* poems, "Il borgo" relates to an early poem of adolescence, in this case an identically named piece which, though included in the first, was dropped from the 1945 second edition of the *Canzoniere.* "It was a poem of little or no value," comments Saba in the *Storia,* "with touches of 'civic' verse—Carduccian and socialistically slanted in the manner fashionable in the very first years of the twentieth century." The occasion of the Ur-"Borgo" had been an illness ("more of spirit than body," a note in the *Storia* elaborates) during which a suicidally depressed Saba observed from a *cantuccio* the crowd of workers returning from various jobs through the streets of his *borgo* and found himself suddenly and ecstatically filled with the passion to break out of the prison of self, his wretched and self-serving conviction of solitude and "difference," in order to become *uomo,* a man of every day, one like the others. A later, wryer Saba might have remarked that the first thing to be done would be to abandon not only the writing of but the aspiration towards poetry. The young man conceived of himself becoming a sort of Béranger or Guest; he would be a people's poet:

> . . . E vorrei che dal mio povero verso . . .
> nascesse, ma per tutti, un pane. . . .

. . . and I would wish that from my poor verse / . . . might be
born, for everyone, bread. . . .

"Saba," as we know, equals "bread." The title "Borgo" could thus be
spiritually rendered as "community." A source of at least a part of the
sense of solidarity which Saba experienced here presumably came
from the "youth" of this *borgo*, its budding like a human flower
fervente d'umano lavoro (fervent with human labor), on one of the
previously bare hills overlooking Trieste. So he linked his expec-
tations, youthfully "great" as they were, to the life of that district.

If this first "Borgo" had been kept, it would have been the first
sounding of that theme of aspiration towards human community
which is touched so many time in the *Canzoniere*, the complex af-
fective counterpoint to those many other poems that express Saba's
sense of isolation and pariahdom. The "Borgo" of *Cuor morituro* is not
a rewrite of that old experience but a palinode or revision of it in
the light of experience. So it begins, its aspirational refrain (lines
6–11 below) made pathetic and futile by the verb tense (*passato
remoto*) and simile announcing it:

> Fu nelle vie di questo
> Borgo che nuova cosa
> m'avvenne.
>
> Fu come un vano
> sospiro
> il desiderio improvviso d'uscire
> di me stesso, di vivere la vita
> di tutti
> d'essere come tutti
> gli uomini di tutti
> i giorni.

It was in the streets of this / town that something new befell me.
It was like a vain / sigh, / the sudden desire to come out / of
myself, to live the life / of all, to be like all / the men of all / days.

It is impossible to translate this. The language is as ascetic and
spare as it can be, as "transparent" as a Sophoclean chorus. Rhyme is
irregular and scarce, though there are a few in the old synthetical
style: for example, the wide-gapped *vano-umano* coupling which
capsulizes a main tenet. Functioning rhythmically are chunks or para-
graphs of repeated material. The most obvious of these is the refrain,
"di vivere la vita/ di tutti," and so on, with its parcels of recurring
words and phrases: *essere come, giorni, vita, uomini* and above all

the enjambment-accented *tutti . . . tutti . . . tutti.** There are other keying nuclei, notably those linked with the vanity of his old desire, which articulate his ambivalences:

> lines 4–6: come un vano / sospiro / il desiderio
> "   16–17 il desiderio vano / come un sospiro
> "   26–27 il desiderio dolce / e vano
> "   50–51 il desiderio, appena un breve / sospiro
> "   67–68 il mio sospiro dolce / e vile.

The canzonetta briskness of the short seven-syllable lines, balanced against fives and elevens, with threes used mainly for emphasis, is consistently retarded beyond the sombre sense by the brilliantly deployed enjambments which persistently create a break or catch in what would normally be simple noun-adjective phrasal units (*questo/ Borgo, vano / sospiro, tutti / gli uomini, umano / lavoro,* and so on). We are made to syllable this threnody.

The first five stanzas of "Il borgo" tell the old story in lines of extraordinary limpidity. The occasion, setting and nature of his desire are accompanied throughout by the bleak tolling of the *vano* terminal and the reductive apposition of *desiderio* with *sospiro,* the vibrance of the first belied by the impotent regret of the second. The sixth stanza moves from this disconsolate retrospect to the diminished present:

> Nato d'oscure
> vicende,
> poco fu il desiderio, appena un breve
> sospiro. Lo ritrovo
> —eco perduta
> di giovanezza—per la vie del Borgo
> mutate
> più che mutato non sia io. Sui muri
> dell'alte case,
> sugli uomini e i lavori, su ogni cosa,
> è sceso il velo che avvolge le cose
> finite.

Born of dark / conditions, / how short-lived was that desire, hardly a brief / sigh. I find it again / —lost echo / of my youth—[note the comparable "sogno dall'adolescenza uscito" of the contemporary "Casa

---

* Oddly, the procedure here echoes the famous refrain of a poem from another world, "Alla mia moglia" with its "come sono tutte/le femmine di tutti/i sereni animali."

della mia nutrice"]—in the streets of the Town, / changed / even more than I have changed. Over the walls / of the tall houses, / over men and their works, over everything, / the veil has descended that envelopes finite / things.

So the original parallel linking the futures of *borgo* and poet is traced out to its ultimate bankruptcy; awaiting his deliverance by death, *solo con i mio duro/patire* (alone with my hard suffering), the poet lives incarcerated in himself in a *mondo/finito* (finished world) that mirrors him.

❖   ❖   ❖

The lucid desolation of "Il borgo" perfectly fulfills the skeletal specifications of a *cuor morituro;* it is the supreme articulation of Saba's second or negative voice. That it is not his last word will not surprise anyone familiar with the ambivalences of his temperament; a window in "the black coal cellar" opens onto azure vistas.

Back-to-back, at the heart of *Cuor morituro,* stand two masterpieces, "La brama" and "Il borgo." The first diagnoses all animate life in terms of one vital disease, sexual desire. The second recapitulates one particular life in terms of the phantom that broke its heart, the dream of human community. Between the two of them, perhaps supplemented by the great prayer for death addressed to his mother as predecessor and intercessor, they constitute the epitaph to the dolorous "middle" age contained in volume two of the *Canzoniere.*

But "La brama" and "Il borgo" are between them also symptomatic of a change which will have an enormous effect on the future volume three. "La brama," as we have noted, is rich in literary resonance. It marks the loftiest manifestation that I know of Saba's piety to the Italian tradition, a superb tribute to the masters of *bel canto* who fed him. It is also a *vale* or farewell.

In its rigorous spareness, the rareness of its rhyme, its focus on the single, drastic word rather than the hendecasyllable or period, "Il borgo" signals the beginning of a new prosodic adventure. Technical matters, we know, are never unrelated to matters of the spirit; Saba himself connects the increased clarity and objectivity of his self-knowledge (achieved through the anguished self-study we have been tracing and, above all, through his experience of psychoanalysis) with what he feels to be the greater clarity and objectivity of his poems written from 1925 onward. "The process," he comments in the *Storia,* "starts in *Cuor morituro* (we can pinpoint it in "Il borgo") . . . it will accelerate in the work of his last years—that is, that work of clarification and excavation (*illimpidimento e scavo*) which will bear its fruits to complete maturation in *Parole,* in *Ultime cose,* in *Mediter-ranee"* . . . in effect, the poems of volume three.

The antonyms to "limpidness" are turbidity, roiling, muddiness; none of these even remotely characterize Saba's earlier work. He has always been clear, even clear about his confusion. Obscurity would be the last charge one could make against him. It is not, then, that volume three is somehow "clearer" than volumes one and two; the banner *Chiarezza* (Clarity) which he considers as a "polemic" title for the whole *Canzoniere* is perfectly accurate.[35]

More specifically, Saba asserts that "from *Cuor morituro* on, the reader will find fewer archaic words, fewer words artificially elided or truncated in order to make up the line . . . Words will be increasingly taken from common speech." However, this was a "reform" already well under way by the time of *Trieste e una donna;* with the single exception of *L'uomo* there has been no noticeable relaxation in this effort at expressive naturalness. His reference to the line (*il verso*) —in effect the hendecasyllable and its standard subdivisions—is more pertinent; we have seen how in "Il borgo," the line is frequently and very effectively reduced to a single word or brief phrase. This in itself of course is not a new procedure; witness the last line of "L'arboscello" in *Casa e campagna,* passages in the street poems of *Trieste e una donna.* But the frequency of this accentual device is greater in the late poems. "Already in *Cuor morituro,*" he writes in the *Storia,* "the word *taken in itself* is more highly valued. . . . If, previously, the song [*canto*] taken in its entirety was of exclusive interest to him, now he increasingly places attention on the value and color of single words . . . he isolates them in order to give to each of them its full value."

> Fu come un vano
> sospiro. . . .

With its "isolation" as the second line, the sigh expired by "Il borgo" is gathered to its full weight in the poem. It is not that Saba ever writes "free" verse. His working line will always be the hendecasyll-able,* with the isolating device we are discussing employed for *ritardo,* prolongation, stress or magnification.

The post-1925 "appendix" to *Cuor morituro* is full of it: for instance, this masterly opening invocation from the "Preghiera alla madre":

---

* He would be in absolute accord with the remark made in 1929 by no less an experimentalist than Giuseppe Ungaretti: "The hendecasyllable—with its components the *settenario,* the *quinario,* the *novenario* (the seven-, five- and nine-syllable line)—is the natural poetic instrument of our language."[36]

Madre che ho fatto
soffrire
(cantava un merlo alla finestra, il giorno
abbassava, sí acuta era la pena
che morte a entrambi io m'invocavo)
                                    madre
ieri in tomba obliata, oggi rinata
presenza. . . .

   Mother that I made / suffer / (a blackbird was singing at the
window, day / was lowering, the pain was so sharp / I prayed to
both for death) / mother / yesterday forgotten in the grave, today
reborn / presence. . . .

where in a rhythmic context of hendecasyllables (plus a *novenario*
and *quinario*) the key words of major emotional resonance, *soffrire,
madre, presenza,* are given each a line, and with it a weight, an em-
phasis, an appropriate valuation. Other "modernisms" include the
flashback device indicated by the parentheses, the internal rather than
terminal rhyming, the unorthodox spacing of the second *madre* in
order to regulate stress and pitch (softer, lower).
   In the *Cuor morituro* chapter of the *Storia*, Saba makes generous
acknowledgment to the work of a famous contemporary. "We know
that roughly in this period he was reading Ungaretti attentively. . . .
The little graft applied to this old tree resulted in a flowering some-
what different from what it would have been if Saba had not been
reading *Allegria di naufragi* (Ungaretti's first widely circulated book).
To the very jealous Ungaretti he was always grateful for the gift."
   Certainly the little poems in the appendix which Saba calls "dry-
points" seem exercises in Ungarettian manner. For example the con-
clusion to "Colloquio":

Si sta
fragile foglia
nella mia spoglia
umana.

   I discover myself / fragile leaf / within my human / husk.

—is reminiscent in both sound and sense of "Militari" in *Allegria di
naufragi:*

Si sta
come d'autunno
sugli alberi
le foglie.

We are/as in autumn/on the trees/the leaves.*

But such echoes are temporary and in the long run superficial. The little genre of "drypoint"—engraving by needle on bare copper plate—suggests what Saba made of early Ungaretti; the essentials of this metaphor are repeated in the *Storia:* "One is not speaking here, of course, of an 'imitation,' for Saba did not imitate . . . but something impressed him in the dry incisive manner, corrosive of superfluity, proper to Ungaretti's technique."

Now while Ungaretti is the very opposite of a colloquial or chatty poet—criticism loves to speak of his *essenzialità*—he is neither dry nor acid. We shall see how his "isolated" *parola* is kin to Leopardi's in the sense of being a dense secretion of historical and cultural and situational vibrations, fraught with powerful associative overtones. The famous "fragment"

> M'illumino
> d'immenso

. . . I illuminate me / with the immense . . .

is *all* connotative energy, at the farthest possible remove from trenchancy or "dryness."

Of course what this all means is that in Ungaretti, Saba found what he needed for use in his own work. Saba found Ungaretti suggestive; it was of no matter that that suggestion derived from a partial reading.** In his trouble Saba sought for coolness and objective clarity, *limpidezza*. He found a way to it through what he made of *Allegria di naufragi*. Essentially what he learned from Ungaretti was a technique for abstinence.

In general, from 1933 until he stopped writing verse in 1954, he gave up rhythmetic symmetry, accustomed shapelinesses like sonnet and canzonetta, the well-loved patterns through which he had married

---

* "Militari" is a first version of the "Soldati" in *L'allegria* (Ungaretti's revision of *Allegria di naufragi*). Of course there are distinctive differences between "Colloquio" and "Militari": not just the more reticent yet more insinuating rhyme effects in the Ungaretti, but the fact that its four lines constitute the whole poem, as opposed to twelve stanzas of "Colloquio."

** Or "misreading." Saba's remarks made in 1950 on *Allegria di naufragi* are an extraordinary interpretation of that book as an objective correlative for the military virtues of the "stiff upper lip" and disciplined response: ". . . in some brief poems . . . he [Ungaretti] rendered the feeling of dedication, of renunciation, of self-sacrifice . . . with which . . . the spiritual 'élite' among our soldiers confronted the risks and nausea of trench life."[37]

his peripherality to the *canto italiano* of tradition. He also, for the most part, gave up rhyming.

> Amai trite parole che non uno
> osava. M'incantò la rima fiore
> amore,
> la piú antica difficile del mondo.

I loved trite words that no one / dared. The rhyme *fiore /amore* enchanted me, / the most ancient and difficult in the world.

Almost from the beginning, Saba was a master not only of the poignant manipulation of stock rhymes of the moon-June variety, but of what I have called synthesizing rhymes: rhymes linking either oppositions, as in the *Fughe,* or specific with general, as the *semita-vita* pairing in "La capra," or even capsulating the drift of a meditation, as in "Città vecchia," where the fryer of eels (*friggatore*) chimes with a young girl's erotic impatience (*amore*), and both of them participate in a suffering creation: *dolore-Signore.* He gave this up, however.

He gave up the relatively neat inductions of fable or apologue for more inscrutable epiphanies or "designs" caught on the wing without comment. Thus, a man and a young girl enter a dairy-bar; the man orders for them both; another girl smiles secretly as she serves them:

> Però un apologo questo non dico;
> non c'è nessuna morale nascosta.
> Forse è solo un disegno. . . .

But I don't call this a fable. / It has no moral hidden in it. / Perhaps it's only a design. . . .

He gave up what he sardonically called his "prosaicism," by which he meant what remained of his old and unfashionable disposition to *verismo,* to circumstantial description and narrative. He gave up all discursiveness; he contracted and simplified. One of the grosser distinctions between the first two volumes and the third is the high proportion of white on the pages of the latter.

He gave up a great deal—a veritable *ascesis.* What he gained was not honesty or clarity (two of his abiding virtues) but concentration and speed, an effect of spontaneity and directness, laconic, edgy, shrewd. It should be clear that these are not characteristically Ungarettian features; if I must select an influential modern master here it would be Eugenio Montale, whose forceful and dramatic middle style leaves traces in the pages of *Parole*.* But there is little doubt that the main factor behind this transformation was his experience of psychoanalysis which, while it did not rid him of his "complexes" (Saba always said that a real cure would have stopped him from writing poetry), led him to a greater understanding and therefore tolerance of them.

The final volume of the *Canzoniere* consists of the following installments: *Parole* (Words: 1933–1934), *Ultime cose* (Last things: 1935–1943, published in Lugano, Switzerland during the Resistance), two brief appendices (*1944* and *Varie*) which ended the second edition of the *Canzoniere* when it was published in 1945, *Mediterranee* (Mediterranean Things: 1946), *Uccelli* (Birds: 1948), *Quasi un racconto* (Almost a Story: 1951), *Sei poesie della vecchiaia* (Six Poems of Old Age: 1953–1954), and *Epigrafe* (Epigraphs: 1947–1948 but now standing as conclusion to the definitive *Canzoniere*). Neither form nor content is complex and the entire volume can be treated together.

The times it spans are hard: increasing erosion of freedom and prologue to world war in Ethiopia and Spain, the German alliance and promulgation of the edicts against the Jews, world war and hiding (first in France, then in Rome and Florence), cold war and exhaustion, illness *passim*. The conventional image of "wintry" old age finds terrible confirmation in the political climate. "Brilla come un ghiacciuolo l'odio" (Hate gleams like an icicle) he writes in one of the *Ultime cose* and finds in the boreal weather of another the annunciation of his doom:

> Tutto si muove contro te. Il maltempo,
> le luci che si spengono, la vecchia
> casa scossa a una raffica. . . .
> Ti pare il sopravivere un rifiuto
> d'obbedienza alle cose.
>   E nello schianto
> del vetro alla finestra è la condanna.

* I think particularly of the unspecified but directly addressed *tu* which Montale uses to plunge his reader *in media res*, as though "coming to" in an intimate conversation already begun. There are specific verbal mementoes of Montale's "Portovenere" in both the title poem and "Felicità" of *Parole*. The younger Montale knew and admired Saba from the days of *Primo tempo*. Later they were further united by their common anti-Fascism. The opening lines from Saba's "Firenze" in part refer to this:

> Per abbracciare il poeta Montale
> —generosa è la sua tristezza—sono
> nella città che mi fu cara. . . .

In order to embrace the poet Montale /—generous in his sadness—I am / in the city that once was dear to me. . . .

The Montales helped conceal Saba during the occupation.

> Everything moves against you. The foul weather, / the doused
> lights, the old / house shaken in the blast. . . . / Survival seems to
> you a refusal / of obedience to things. /
> And in the cracking / of the window pane is your condemnation.

Loneliness in the 1930's is no longer wholly attributable to his tem-
perament or neurosis—"*Everything* moves against you." Long ago, in
the honeymoon of *Casa e campagna*, a great wind had buffeted a
little tree, stripping it of its flowers. But through the cottage window
a compassionate eye was watching.

> . . . E se ne duole la tua vasta
> maternità.

The haunting "Inverno" (Winter) of *Parole* is a grim companion-
piece to "L'arboscello":

> È notte, inverno rovinoso. Un poco
> sollevi le tendine, e guardi. Vibrano
> i tuoi capelli selvaggi, la gioia
> ti dilata improvvisa l'occhio nero;
> che quello che hai veduto—era un'immagine
> della fine del mondo—ti conforta
> l'intimo cuore, lo fa caldo e pago.
>
> Un uomo si avventura per un lago
> di ghiaccio, sotto una lampada storta.

> Nighttime, ruinous winter. / You lift the blinds a bit, and you look
> out. Your / savage hair stirs, joy suddenly / dilates your dark eye. /
> For what you saw—it was an image / of the world's end—comforts /
> your heart of hearts, makes it warm and satisfied. /
> A man ventures out upon a lake / of ice, beneath a crooked lamp.

The frozen solitude of hell has replaced the old pieties of that faroff
spring "that seemed an autumn" but was not. "L'inverno" is a good
example of the *implacability* of Saba's last manner, its nudity and
rude force culminating in the nightmare image of the ill-starred and
unaccountable pilgrim. The *lampada storta* is a brilliant detail. Who-
ever "you" is—"myself," or the reader, the voluptuous malice increas-
ingly characteristic of our era has been incisively caught, *punta secca*.

> O tu che sei sí triste ed hai presagi
> d'orrore—Ulisse al declino—nessuna
> dentro l'anima tua dolcezza aduna

la Brama
per una
pallida sognatrice di naufragi
che t'ama?

O you who are so sad and have premonitions / of horror—Ulysses
in decline / —does within your soul no sweetness distil / Desire / for
a / pale dreamer of shipwrecks / who loves you?

So, in *Parole's* loveliest poem Saba imagines some Nausicaa-*fanciulla*
addressing him as, removed from her emotion, he contemplates his
bleak future. Indeed we are told in the *Storia* that the book's projected
title had been *Distacco* (removal, separation, severance). The refer-
ence was not to any foreseen physical uprooting, though the man on
the frozen lake is a premonition of exile to come, but to the "objective"
understanding of his life that Saba felt he had gained through suffer-
ing and psychoanalysis. The *parole* of the actual title retain the
property of *distacco*:

Parole,
dove il cuore dell'uomo si specchiava
—nudo e sorpreso—alle origini; un angolo
cerco nel mondo, l'oasi propizia
a detergere voi con il mio pianto
dalla menzogna che vi acceca. . . .

Words, / where the heart of man was mirrored / —naked and aston-
ished—at the origins; I seek / a corner of the world, the propitious
oasis / where I may cleanse you with my tears / of the lie that blinds
you. . . .

The brief title poem proposes a return to Edenic conditions where
words were not just "expressive," vehicles of partial interpretation
of what one feels about or makes of things—but a true reflection of
things as they are. The "lie," then, is what we may legitimately be-
lieve to be that inevitable subjectivity which filters and colors all our
conscious experiencing; the "tears" are the poet's impossible struggle
to "recover" transparency. Such is the aspiration, at least, announced
at the threshold of this volume, and the title poem concludes in a
metaphor of the objective paradise that might be regained . . .

. . . Insieme
delle memorie spaventose il cumulo
si scioglierebbe, come neve al sole.

. . . Together / with frightful memories the weight / of things would disperse, like snow in the sun.

So far we have stressed the dolorous presence of Saba's "second voice" rising out of these final pages. Yet, despite the times and the misfortunes accumulating in the external biography, the major impression is of resilience and affirmation.

> La giovanezza cupida di pesi
> porge spontanea al carico le spalle.
> Non regge. Piange di malinconia.
>
> Vagabondaggio, evasione, poesia,
> cari prodigi sul tardi! Sul tardi
> l'aria si affina ed i passi si fanno
> leggeri.
> Oggi è il meglio di ieri,
> se non è ancora la felicità.
>
> Assumeremo un giorno la bontà
> del suo volto, vedremo alcuno sciogliere
> come un fumo il suo inutile dolore.

Desirous of burdens youth / spontaneously puts its shoulders to the load. / It fails. Cries with melancholy. /
Vagabondage, escaping, poetry / —dear prodigies when it gets late! When it gets late / the air grows pure and steps become / light. / Today is better than yesterday, / even though it is not yet happiness. /
One day we shall take on the goodness / of its face, shall witness someone dissolve / his useless sorrowing like smoke.

As "Parole" so "Felicità" concludes with the image of matter immaterializing, weight grown light and airy as it rises in the smiling azure, like Dante's expiated souls soaring from the purgatorial mountain. "*Dolore,* where are you?" the poet queries; "here everything moves joyously, as though everything were happy to exist." Certainly one cannot neglect the problematical nature of this happiness, governed as it invariably is by future and conditional tenses, wishful subjunctives. Still,

> Oggi è il meglio di ieri,
> se non è ancora la felicità . . .

and still the positive "first voice" persists, an integral part of the affective fugue which is the source and condition of his vitality.

At the time of the "racial" edicts, when his shop was under surveillance and his work could no longer be published, Saba had found a special solace in observing and even studying the lives of the almost-domestic animals and birds about him:

> Da quando la mia bocca è quasi muta
> amo le vite che quasi non parlano. . . .

Since my mouth has grown almost dumb / I love those lives which almost cannot speak. . . .

Memories of Salerno and the "sacred bestiary" of Montebello are a reminder that this is not a novelty but an old and persisting affection. The attraction of these elemental lives was particularly poignant in the times of his greatest trouble. The sickness in the postwar air as well as that racking his exhausted body made him consider even poetry as "almost an insult to the world's sorrow," at best a sort of morphine. "The sadness, the anguish, the uncertainty, the anxiety . . . the relativity of everything . . . have become un-bearable ills," he wrote to the publisher Alfredo Rizzardi in 1951. But at the same time he enclosed his retouchings of a little poem he had found among Leopardi's juvenilia, the fable of a bird who, despite the loving care it enjoyed in its cage, abandoned all for the open fields when the chance came.[38] Almost a century and a half before, in Recanati, the twelve-year-old Leopardi had concluded with this generalizing couplet:

> Di libertà l'amore
> regna in un giovin core.

The love of liberty / reigns in a young heart.

Nearly seventy, in Trieste, Saba made this emendation:

> Di libertà l'amore
> regna ai fringuelli in cuore.

Bird-hearted: the song and soaring articulated by the first voice of the fugues and embodied in the birds that populate his last poems are not a matter of chronology but a perennial disposition, the affirming energy in his ambivalence. And that letter to Rizzardi with its "inconsistent" enclosure is the essence of the man.

Uccelli and *Quasi un racconto* are poems from Saba's aviary. In the war-games in the Salerno woods and the fraternal bleat of the tethered goat, he had found inspiration for a bestiary through which the hard laws implicit in "the open book of creation" could be given form. *Ne dicono il fondo* he writes in one of his very last poems. But birds are something else, "the sublimation of the reptile," and for all his well-documented illness in those last years, the aviary dominates the closing pages of the *Canzoniere*. He writes in the preface to *Uccelli* how observing and studying birds seemed like discovering a paradise on earth. "Since one had to be born, the one enviable destiny was to be born a bird. . . . To feel light and to fly by one's own power seemed to me, during that last gasp that life was giving me, to be the height of happiness."

These are words written by a bedridden old man, *fringuello in cuore* or partly so. Not being born a bird, at least he could contemplate them. Long ago he had gazed at *fanciulle* and other light and airy things—they were, we recall, heartbreakingly desirable. Now in their sheer *mobilità* the creatures visiting his window-ledge or inhabiting his cages appeal to his senses of wonder, gratitude and humor.

The female of his two canaries is brooding. Since she needs to be left in peace and her mate gives her none, Saba separates them. In the male's eyes he is both tyrant and sexual rival. The poet has recourse to music . . .

> Per divertirti apro una scatoletta
> musicale. Il dolor del mondo n'esce
> in un suono cosí mite che riesce
> a commuovermi quasi. Ascolti. Un poco
> tenti imitarla sopraffarla. O i vostri
> sono cuori volubili e leggeri!

To divert you I open up a music / box. The world's sadness rises from it / with such a gentle sound that it almost / succeeds in moving me to tears. You listen. You try a bit / to copy it while drowning it out. O how / your hearts are changeable and light!

In the affectionate reproach, envy and admiring tenderness integrated in the music-man's expostulation I find a harmonious and characteristically two-minded conclusion to his story—more true to his spirit, certainly, than the stunningly deep-vowelled epigraph which brings his *Canzoniere* to its actual close:

> Parlavo vivo a un popolo di morti.
> Morto alloro rifiuto e chiedo oblio.

❀   ❀   ❀

In a letter to Saba written in 1946, soon after the publication of the *Canzoniere* and the poems gathered in *Mediterranee*, the novelist

Pierantonio Quarantotti Gambini offered his impression that the book as a whole was "more than a canzoniere or book of songs, [but rather] a type of *Odyssey* of man in our times."[39] He even suggested that Saba change his general title to something that would underline this aspect.

There are indications, certainly, that Saba himself had given the matter some thought. In two fleeting occasions in the course of *Il piccolo Berto* he refers to himself as a Ulysses, first comparing that hero's joy at reaching Ithaca to his own at returning to Peppa's house, then calling himself "esperto di molti beni e molti mali."* We have cited above the *Parole* poem on "Ulisse al declino." The book of *Mediterranee*—best translated "Mediterraneana," Mediterranean poems or things—is full of allusions to the *antico mare perduto* (ancient lost sea) of epic antiquity. Three poems addressed to his friend the young poet Federico Almansi are titled "Poems to Telemachus." The brief "Mediterranea" compares his momentary exultation in 1946 (over the publication of the *Canzoniere* and its enthusiastic reception) with Ulysses' mastering of Circe and its sad post-coital aftermath:

> penso cupa sirena
> —baci ebbrezza delirio—; penso Ulisse
> che si leva laggiú da un triste letto.

. . . I think of that deep siren / —kisses intoxication delirium—; I think of Ulysses / who rises down there from a sad bed.

The final poem of *Mediterranee* is titled "Ulisse" and recapitulates the poet's lifetime by means of a Ulysses-fable with a specially Italian aura—Dante's, that is to say, rather than Homer's.

> Nella mia giovanezza ho navigato
> lungo le coste dalmate. Isolotti
> a fior d'onda emergevano, ove raro
> un uccello sostava intento a prede,
> coperti d'alghe, scivolosi, al sole
> belli come smeraldi. Quando l'alta
> marea e la notte li annullava, vele
> sottovento sbandavano piú al largo,
> per fuggirne l'insidia. Oggi il mio regno
> è quella terra di nessuno. Il porto
> accende ad altri i suoi lumi; me al largo
> sospinge ancora il non domato spirito,
> e della vita il doloroso amore.

* His comment in the *Storia*: "But Ulysses was going to converse with the goddess Circe, not with his nurse."

In my youth I navigated / along the Dalmatian coasts. Little islands, / where rarely a bird paused intent on its prey, / covered with slippery seaweeds, rose from the sea at wave-level, / lovely as emeralds in the sun. When high / seas and the night obliterated them, my sails / spread out against the wind towards the open sea, / fleeing that covert peril. Today my kingdom / is no man's land. The harbor / lights its lamps for others; for myself, on high seas, / an indomitable spirit still sustains me, / and a dolorous love of life.

Ulysses *did* converse with his nurse, in fact, as well as with Circe, and Joyce did no more than follow leads in Homer when he made uxorious and domesticated Bloom the hero of his *Odyssey*. The protagonist of the *Canzoniere* is Ulyssean insofar as he struggles through and up to death survives the "perilous seas" that life has allotted him. But, then, who is not?

The Homeric allusions are too casual and Saba's life in poetry too local, *sui generis*, to encourage any specific comparison of this sort. Words like "Ulysses" are similar to words like "canzoniere" for Saba; their magic lies in their common *mediterraneità*, their share in a world as old as man himself.

> Ebbri canti si levano e bestemmie
> nell'osteria suburbana. Qui pure
> —penso—è Mediterraneo. E il mio pensiero
> all'azzurro s'inebbria di quel nome.
>
> Materna calma imprendibile è Roma.
> S'innamora la Grecia alle sue sponde
> come un'adoloscenza. Oscura il mondo
> e lo rinnova la Giudea. Non altro
> a me vecchio sorride sotto il sole. . . .

Drunken songs and curses rise upwards / in the suburban inn. Yet here, / I think, is what is Mediterranean. And my thought / grows drunken on the azure of that name.

Impalpable mothering calm is Rome. / Greece falls in love with her own shores / like an adolescent maiden. Judea darkens / and renews the world. For me / an old man, nothing else smiles beneath the sun. . . .

But "epic" suggests something of a central quality of the *Canzoniere* taken as a whole, and for this reason it is worth pursuing.

Throughout the *Storia*, Saba is fond of speaking of his *epicità* as that feature of his work which excludes it from conventional "modernism." His "epicness" refers to his willingness—at least up to his "conversion to modernity" in *Parole*—to deal with setting, character, narrative events as well as feelings in his verses. If one prime modernist trend during the first third of this century was to "purify" a lyric emotion of its *gestalt*, it was Saba's satisfaction to be impure, to purvey *sentimento* with all its "contingent" and conditioning ganglia. His careless synonym for epic was "psychological novel." Either way he claims a poetry with a horizontal as well as vertical dimension.

"The peculiar *largeness* of Saba . . . is more than ever evident when we compare him (let us say) with Ungaretti, our most illustrious modern example of a poet who has developed primarily in a vertical direction." So (as cited in the *Storia*) writes Pierantonio Quarantotti Gambini, the critic we have already quoted as having misgivings over Saba's title for the collected poems. "Canzoniere" implies a songbook, a collection of individual lyrics on the Petrarchan model. Quarantotti Gambini feels that such a title is misleading for the simple reason that (italics his) *"the poetry of Saba is not only lyric."* "From this point of view the entire work of Saba will appear to us as it really is, taking on its complete and highest value: a vast poetic production, closely interconnected and therefore a whole, occupying an intermediate position between what we understand as *canzoniere* and what we understand as *un poema*, one single poem."⁴⁰

Others have concurred. Critics like Giuseppe Ravegnani and Pietro Pancrazi have stressed that Saba needs to be read *en bloc*, that main attention should be fixed on the *Canzoniere* in its emergent richness rather than on the individual lyric. This is easier to agree with now than it was once, for once upon a time a reviewer had only a fascicle or "slender volume" to base his verdict on. What would be one's view of Saba if one had only *L'uomo* to go on? In his story there are exceptional moments that can and do stand by themselves as anthological star-turns. But even poems like "A mia moglie," "Trieste," "La brama" or "Il borgo" are deprived when detached from their context; whoever knows them only in isolation knows only a part of their resonance. The same thing is true of the slighter poems. The *poesie dell'adolescenza*, the little fables, sketches and *variora*, inherit special pathos from the company they keep. This has only been obvious since 1945, since there has been a *Canzoniere* conveniently available.

Finally, it takes more than critics' instructions to make us care to read all of Saba. This, I think, is the miracle, and it is all his doing. The Umberto that he offers is really no Ulysses; he is, proudly and wretchedly, himself. He has a demanding body as well as an aspiring spirit, a lengthening history, and a diminishing future, wife, child, and *fanciulle*, shop and shop-assistant, particular complaints and particular compensations. He lives through a number of wars and uneasy peaces, dictatorship and persecution, exile and, at the end, the sort of affectionate public recognition he had always longed for.

And this in itself is nothing extraordinary; take away the fame, which he finds too late anyway, and much the same could be written of most Italians of his generation. His distinction is to have written a poem about it all, about not only his own life and times but others' as well, insofar as all are linked in the community of *dolore* that it was his genius and misfortune to perceive. I think of this inclusive vision as something epical. It underlies everything that Saba ever wrote and integrates his poetry of occasions into *poema*. And in the pages of the *Canzoniere* it is preserved as that *calda vita di tutti* that he so often despaired of grasping in his life.

Notes

(Unless otherwise indicated all references to Saba's prose will be found in the volume *Prose* [Milan, 1964] edited by Linuccia Saba.)

1. "Come di un vecchio che sogna," *Prose*, pp. 226–30.

2. "Profilo autobiografico," in Livia Veneziani Svevo, *Vita di mio marito con altri inediti di Italo Svevo*, ed. Anita Pittoni (Trieste, 1958), p. 209.

3. *Storia* ("Conclusione"), *Prose*, p. 629.

4. *Uomini visti* (Milan, 1955), vol. I, p. 207.

5. *Storia* (chapter on *Piccolo Berto*), *Prose*, p. 575.

6. "La poesia di Saba," *Saggi critici* (Milan, 1952), p. 140.

7. "Per Saba, ancora," *ibid.*, p. 146.

8. *Scorciatoie e raccontini*, #68: *Prose*, p. 290.

9. "Discorso della laurea," *Prose*, pp. 737–42.

10. *Storia*, first two chapters: *Prose*, esp. pp. 407, 420, 489.

11. *Storia*, chapter on *Piccolo Berto*: *Prose*, p. 563.

12. "Italo Svevo all'Ammiragliato britannico," *Prose*, p. 154.

13. *Vita di mio marito*, p. 255.

14. Nora Baldi, *Il Paradiso di Saba* (Florence, 1958), p. 49.

15. *Storia*, ch. 1: *Prose*, p. 412.

16. "Ai miei lettori: prefazione al *Canzoniere* 1921," *Prose*, pp. 664–65.

17. *Storia*, ch. 2: *Prose* p. 422. The poem in question is "A Mamma."

18. "Premessa ad *Ammonizione ed altre poesie*," *Prose*, p. 668.

19. For what follows, see *Prose*, pp. 756–57.

20. *Storia*, ch. 2: *Prose*, pp. 418–20.

21. "Prefazione per *Poesie dell'adolescenza*," *Prose*, p. 735.

22. For materials on "La casa della mia nutrice," see not only the *Canzoniere* but the relevant chapter in the *Storia* (*Prose*, p. 415), the "Prefazione per *Poesie dell'adolescenza*" (*Prose*, pp. 732–34), and the version published in *Canzoniere* 1921.

23. "Prefazione per *Poesie dell'adolescenza*," *Prose*, p. 731.

24. *Ibid.*, p. 734.

25. *Storia*, ch. 2: *Prose*, pp. 421–22.

26. "Il sogno di un coscritto," *Prose*, pp. 231–35.

27. *Storia*, ch. 4: *Prose*, p. 436.

28. *Scorciatoie e raccontini*, #137, *Prose*, p. 322.

29. *Ibid.*, #12, *Prose*, pp. 264–65.

30. "Una poetica" in *Il poeta e il politico e altri saggi*, p. 23. Quasimodo's *siepe* was Sicily.

31. See above, n. 6.

32. "Italo Svevo all'Ammiragliato britannico," *Prose*, pp. 152–54.

33. "Umberto Saba: *Preludio e fughe*" (1928). Collected in *Scrittori negli anni*, pp. 72–76.

34. "Umberto Saba: *Tre composizioni*," *Scrittori negli anni*, p. 138.

35. *Storia*, ch. on *Varie: Prose*, p. 628.

36. Interview with G. B. Angiolotti, cit. in Luciano Anceschi, *Lirici nuovi* (Milan, 1943), p. 107.

37. "Di questo libro e di un altro mondo," *Prose*, p. 698.

38. "Poesia in tre stati," *Prose*, pp. 849–55.

39. *Il vecchio e il giovane*, p. 12.

40. *Storia*, "Conclusione": *Prose*, p. 636.

III GIUSEPPE UNGARETTI

Cerco un paese
innocente

"This old book is a diary. Its author has no other ambition, and he believes that not even the great poets had any other, than to leave behind a beautiful biography." *Diario: una sua bella biografia*—these are the attributes and aims proposed for himself by Ungaretti in 1931.[1] Some ten years later, when the Milanese publisher Mondadori undertook to bring out Ungaretti's complete works, the general title chosen for the whole was, consistently enough, *Vita d'un uomo:* the Life of a Man. To date (1968), the number of volumes in this enterprise runs to twelve; there will almost certainly be more forthcoming.[*]

[*] The numeration and arrangement of this *Vita* in process has varied. At present it works as follows:
A. 7 volumes of poetry.
  I   *L'Allegria* (The Joy): poems 1914–19.
  II   *Sentimento del tempo* (Feeling of Time): poems 1919–35.
  III *Poesie disperse* (Scattered Poems) 1914–27. This includes 23 poems either not included, for aesthetic reasons, in the preceding 2 volumes, or included but radically revised. It also includes a complete listing of all published variants for the poems of these first 3 books plus an essay on the "formation of Ungaretti's poetry" by Giuseppe De Robertis.
  IV   *Il Dolore* (The Grief): poems 1937–46.
  V   *La terra promessa* (The Promised Land): fragments of a long poem employing the myth of the *Aeneid.* Begun in 1935, it is still "in process." An appendix of 27 last choruses to it can be found in vol. VII below. A critical essay by Leone Piccioni and variants is included.
  VI   *Un grido e paesaggi* (A Cry and Landscapes): poems 1949–52 (with one exception which dates from 1940). Critical essay by Piero Bigongiari and variants.
  VII *Il taccuino del vecchio* (The Old Man's Notebook): poems 1952–60.
B. 4 volumes of translations.
  I   40 *sonnetti di Shakespeare:* written approx. 1931–43.
  II   *Da Góngora e da Mallarmé:* 40 sonnets plus passages from the fables of Góngora, translated 1932–42; from Mallarmé, translations of *Monologue d'un Faune* and *L'Après-midi d'un Faune* plus some of Mallarmé's personal inscriptions (*offrandes*), translated 1946–47.
  III *Fedra di Jean Racine* (*Phèdre*): translated 1948–50.
  IV   *I visioni di William Blake:* a copious selection from the *Songs* and prophetical works translated 1930–65.
C. One volume of prose in a category designated as "Essays and Travel

Is there any significance in Ungaretti's calling his work *biografia*
rather than *autobiografia?* Surely it is intended to emphasize an as-
piration toward "third-person" objectivity, an attempt to qualify
drastically the usual associations of *diario* with egocentricity and
impressionism. In the preface to *La terra promessa* Ungaretti has
characterized the main "direction" of his work as that of "elevating"
personal experience into "ideas and myths." The (incomplete) manu-
script and complete textual variants which he has wished published
with his "finished" poems are witness to his struggle against the merely
historical or circumstantial. His revisionary trend is *always* ascetic,
reductive, suppressing whatever seems anecdotal or documentary.

When Poe or Baudelaire spoke of cosmetics, of the "cock's feathers,
red paint and black patches" constituting the *charlatanisme indispen-
sable* involved in making a poem, they meant wittily to instruct the
reader in the artificiality of art, to remind him of the craft connected
with most effective expression. They aspired to an unearthly Beauty,
and it is not surprising therefore that, on aesthetic grounds, they
never dreamt of revealing their more mundane strategies to the
public.* For Ungaretti, on the other hand, even his variants are a
relevant part of his story—on moral grounds. In his preface to
L'Allegria he speaks of his inveterate habit of revising:

> . . . His poems represent his formal torments, but he would
> appreciate it if once and for all it were recognized that form torments
> him solely because he insists that it adhere to the variations of his
> soul; and if he has made some progress as an artist, he would wish
> that this indicated some perfection achieved as a man.

So that the tendency indicated by Ungaretti and his variants is, at
least in intention, one of *approfondissement,* a voyage from contin-
gency to quintessence, a slow and difficult recognition (re-vision) of
what was deeply meant in the first place, more a progress than a
process. And hence the inclusion of variants in the *Vita.*

Such an intention is the subject of an early (1916) piece about the

---

Prose."
    I *Il deserto e dopo* (The Desert and After): a series of essays written
       for the Turinese *Gazzetta del Popolo,* based on travels in Egypt, Corsica, Holland
       and Italy during 1931–34; plus a collection of translations of and notes on some
       Brazilian poets, made approx. 1940–46.
  See headnote to Notes for a description of the current status of *Vita d'un uomo.*

    * Unless polished out of all plausibility, as in Poe's best tale of ratiocination, the "Philosophy
of Composition."

making of a poem, the "Commiato" or *envoi* addressed to his editor
with which he concluded his first published volume:

> Gentile
> Ettore Serra
> poesia
> é il mondo l'umanità
> la propria vita
> fioriti dalla parola
> la limpida meraviglia
> di un delirante fermento
>
> Quando trovo
> in questo mio silenzio
> una parola
> scavata è nella mia vita
> come un abisso

Gentle / Ettore Serra / poetry / is the world humanity / life itself /
flowered from the word / the limpid marvel / of a delirious ferment /
   When I find / in this my silence / a word / it is dug out of my
life / like an abyss

Here first is expressed the poet's affirmation of the miracle of the
poetic word. Secondly, the creative act is likened to the act of ex-
cavation, complete with sensations of muscular strain and racking
which involve both pain and loss (*un abisso*). But the "experimental"
absence of punctuation in "Commiato," derived in part from the
precedents of Futurism and Apollinaire's *Alcools,* may obscure the
fundamental point made in the first stanza: that is, that the apparently
romantic equation of the third and fourth lines becomes a trans-
formation or metamorphosis by line six; that the world and humanity
and Ungaretti's very life *are not* poetry but *become* poetry only when
elevated by the word; that it is only via the word that the inchoate
and fluxive fermentation of experience becomes available as idea or
myth . . . becomes, that is, thinkable, or real. This brings us to
Alexandria-born Ungaretti's "platonic" verticality, or what he would
call his "Egyptian nominalism."

In the great third chapter to *Seven Pillars of Wisdom* T. E. Law-
rence writes of the extremism and ascetic strain in the Arab mentality
which, as he puts it, "oscillate(s) from asymptote to asymptote." He
relates an illustrative story which in my opinion could with a shade
more syntactical convolution be taken as composed by Stéphane
Mallarmé:

But at last Dahoum drew me: "Come and smell the very sweetest scent of all," and we went into the main lodging, to the gaping window sockets of its eastern face, and there drank with open mouths of the effortless, empty, eddyless wind of the desert, throbbing past. That slow breath had been born elsewhere beyond the distant Euphrates and had dragged its way across many days and nights of dead grass, to its first obstacle, the manmade walls of our broken palace. About them it seemed to fret and linger, murmuring in baby-speech. "This," they told me, "is the best: it has no taste."

Lawrence's Arabs, then, are nature's *symbolistes*, haunted by some pre-literary version of the Azure that enflamed and mocked that exclusive French circle. For the Arabs the result is a certain coolness towards the phenomenal and worldly, an epistemological skepticism regarding the pleasure-pain syndrome which finds expression in a "brutal" shrug. Lawrence accounts for this by references to environment and climate, the man-abolishing perennials of blaring sun and shifting sand which enforce, he feels, a *contemptu mundi*.

For Ungaretti as well, the self-styled "nomad" from Alexandria, the vision of the ephemerality and ghostliness of things below is constant.

> Ti vidi, Alessandria,
> Friabile sulle tue basi spettrali. . . .

I saw you, Alexandria, / crumbling on your spectral foundations. . . .

Thus begins one of the "legends" of his life, written in the 1930's. His poems are full of imagery drawn from his experience of the African desert: intense heat, brilliant sand, the cruel sun that "rapes" the swarming metropolis beneath it, a physical terrain cooked into metaphysics: friable, spectral, occult.

The imagery of desolation was obsessive within me from my very first poems. It was the desert that defined it in me: out of the desert were born, in my faroff infancy and youth, the notion and feeling of the infinite, of the primal, of the fall of all things into nothingness. . . . As is well known, the desert together with the sea surrounds Alexandria, Egypt, my native city. There desert and sea are in continuous contact and contrast. The first is static and seems immobile, the other is in perpetual agitation. The first represents . . . that which ceaselessly wears away; without pause the other furiously manifests renewal. Between them they constitute my first vision of reality.[2]

One might observe that the element of renewal for Ungaretti is literally unearthly; one departs—nomad, pilgrim—from the land one knows in order to seek it. And the luck of life gave Ungaretti from birth the vistas correlative to his mature "vision of reality." Alexandria, we understand, is a city with a past, not merely "Alexandrian" but Homeric as well. In the fourth book of the *Odyssey* Menelaus reminisces to Telemachus of his Egyptian sojourn en route home from Troy—

> There is an island washed about by swelling waves of sea.
> Its name is Pharos, and it lies in front of Egypt's land,
> As far away as in a day a hollow ship would sail
> With a shrill following wind behind to help her on her way.
> It has a harbour, a good place to anchor. Here men take
> Aboard black water, then set sail across the open sea.
> And in this place the gods detained me twenty days.
> (translation by Rex Warner)

Traditionally this is interpreted to be the site of what was to become Alexandria. Pharos is now a promontory, an island no longer, off the northwestern coastline of the city. The harbor—certainly prehistoric: it has been linked to Ptolemaic and Minoan culture, while theosophists have annexed it to the lost world of Atlantis—lies from four to twenty-five feet beneath the surface, accessible only to divers and, as we shall see, dreamers. In Ungaretti's youth, the submarine presence of the ancient harbor was dramatized by archeological investigations carried out by Gaston Jondet (aided by the poet's close friend Jean Thiule). In his memoirs of life in Alexandria, Enrico Pea recalls Ungaretti's "bizarre" claim to be able to land at that buried port (*porto sepolto*) when the waters were clear and unroiled. As it turned out, he was not talking about diving: his first published volume was entitled *Il porto sepolto* and we shall see when we examine this book the precise nature of the "landing" he made there. But that submerged harbor was an image to hand of a deep and abiding reality, a "promised land," sought for under various guises throughout the *Vita d'un uomo.*

The actual land, the desert or the mirage of Alexandria, manifests the decimation and obliteration of matter. Here is the suburb of Mex, described as Ungaretti experienced it during his revisitation of 1931:

> Already the sun falls perpendicular. Now everything hovers, disturbed; every motion is concealed, every slightest sound suffocated. It is not an hour of shade nor an hour of light: it is the hour of utter monotony. . . . No more can one make out the worm-eaten rocks, a whitish outcropping in sand. Even the fine undulations of

the sand are abolished in the fixed web of rays that beats down from all directions. No longer is there sky or earth. Everything has a ruined, same yellow-grey color, through which you move with difficulty, as though within a cloud. Ah, if there were not the whipped man who from the very soles of his feet lets loose his blood in song—hoarse, melancholy, accursed—you would say that this was the void. It enters the blood like the experience of this absolute light that consumes itself above this aridity.[3]

Out of such experiences emerges, in the same year, his meditation upon ancient Egypt and what he calls the "nominalism" of the Egyptian mentality:

. . . all the energy of the Egyptians is directed towards insuring the eternity of the tomb. And that nominalism of theirs—by which perhaps Plato was struck and Greek metaphysics given life—surely has no other end in view (placing as it does all its care in the resistance of a carved name and its evocative duration among the live) than death, threshold to eternity. In this nominalism of theirs those Egyptians must have thought: a person or a thing incarnates and materializes an eternal idea, and is thus the particular name or fleeting symbol of an eternal idea. By making this particular name imperishable, a person or a thing is made forever evocable. An immense value is given to the power of the word, its magic.[4]

Egyptian or not, such a nominalism is intimately related to the idea of poetry articulated in "Commiato," translated above:

> . . poesia
> è il mondo l'umanità
> la propria vita
> fioriti dalla parola
> la limpida meraviglia
> di un delirante fermento . . .

The wrestling proudly attested to by the variants can be viewed as part of the search for the "magic" or evocative word that seems to arrest time and preserve what, unuttered, perishes, even as the carved name on the pyramid or tomb raises the living presence in the dust it "really" contains.

But a tomb (and, following the analogy, a poem) also marks a term or mortality. Hence, as Ungaretti remarks in the preface to *Terra promessa*, the rock memorializing the drowned Palinurus in both *Aeneid* and the *Terra* confers only an "ironic immortality." The bust survives the emperor and the sonnet the lady no doubt, but what sort of consolation does print or marble offer doomed flesh? "Ripara il logorio alzando tombe": He, Man, mends or repairs or in any case compensates for the wasting away of things by raising tombs—such is the conclusion to "La pietà," Ungaretti's famous hymn of total despair. But in the context what a weight of wretched sarcasm is centered in the verb *riparare!* What has a tomb or word to do with immortality? And yet, absurdly—this is the final irony—in our mortal need such things bear a kind of consolation.

> And since only abstraction can give us some vain simulacrum of essence—of the unreachable purity we aspire toward—mortal existence has always been a flaming fury to reach some sense of an order. I wonder whether everything that touches the soul, all our purifying actions, are not, like a *terzina* by Dante, a music hurled and prisoned within a geometry. It is our glory, it is our damnation, to have to employ conventional forms in order to render human things less transitory, superior to individual destinies.[5]

Ungaretti's "nominalism" will oscillate through the years between despair and hope, curse and carol,* Mallarmé and the Roman Catholic Church, but the vertical thrust, the need to see the temporal *sub specie aeternitatis*, is constant and, whether or not we choose to invoke Taine's race, moment, and milieu, as good as biological. It begets and develops a poetics and a characteristic thematic repertoire, and, as the poet wished, an intense and beautiful spiritual *biografia*.

❂   ❂   ❂

Giuseppe Ungaretti was born in Alexandria on the eighth of February 1888, as "peripherally" as Saba. His parents had left Lucca and had decided on Egypt rather than the more usual America so that the father might find remunerative work in the heavy program of public works construction taking place at that time. With the father's death in 1890, the poet's mother became wholly responsible for the material welfare of her small family. They lived in a poor workers' quarter of the city inhabited mainly by Arabs, Jews and migrant laborers from Europe. The mother baked and sold bread for a living. The actual economic facts are obscure, but the mobility possible in cosmopolitan Alexandria is best shown by the fact that Ungaretti was able to attend one of its finest schools, the École Suisse Jacot.

---

* ". . . poetry is witness to the existence of the divine, even when poetry is merely blasphemy. Today's poet knows that one must see the invisible in the visible." A useful compendium of Ungaretti's various attitudes on the relations of poetry and "reality" may be found in "Reflessioni sullo stile" [1946] and "Ragioni di una poesia" [1949], both in *SI*.

The poet was bilingual at an early age; although Italian was spoken at home and around the quarter, students at the École conversed, were taught, and wrote in French.[6]

Ungaretti lived in Alexandria until he was 24. His world until his departure in 1912 was triple: he was an Italian citizen with familial and patriotic loyalties to that unknown country, a dweller in a largely Arab and migrant quarter of a large city, a French scholar who wrote his first poems in that language. It is not surprising, then, that when he left Alexandria to seek his fortune in Europe he went to Paris. His interests were literary from the start and his closest associates as a young man were either French or admirers of French letters—such as the cultured Thiule brothers (Henri was a protegé of Francis Jammes) who were particularly acquainted with French poets of the symbolist persuasion, possessed a sumptuous library devoted mainly to that school, and formed a literary circle at their house in the Mex suburb. "I knew of Baudelaire and Nietzsche, of Mallarmé and Rimbaud, of Laforgue and so many others," he later wrote of those days, "when in Italy there was only ignorance of them. Italians without the name of Leopardi have taught me very little. . . ."[7]

Above all, Ungaretti was drawn to Paris because of its attractions as a center of literary vitality (nothing in Italy could match it in this regard), because of the educational opportunities it afforded (his professors at the Collège de France and the Sorbonne included Lanson, Bédier and Bergson), because he was at ease with the language and had friends from Alexandria who now lived the life of artists and students there. In this milieu he inevitably became friendly with members of the French art avant-garde, Braque and Picasso, Salmon, Jacob, Cendrars, Breton and Apollinaire, as well as loosely affiliated members of the Italian Futurist movement such as Papini, Soffici and Palazzeschi in whose short-lived periodical, *Lacerba*, Ungaretti in 1915 published his first poems.

The *Poesie disperse* provides the full texts of the poems written by Ungaretti during his *Lacerba* phase. By the time they appeared in book form in 1919 they had been radically condensed and revised. The *Lacerba* versions were composed in Italian (not all of Ungaretti's work in these prewar years was), full of verve and rather derivative. Current experimentalist touches abound—*vers libres*, abolition of capitals and punctuation; there is a good measure of "tough" documentary detail thrown in to scandalize the conventional lovers of poetry; language is slangy and determinedly laconic. Such a poetry finds its poetics in the various manifestoes of Marinetti, the related polemics of the *Lacerba* editors, and Apollinaire's engaging speciality of the "draft" or talk-poem (*poème-brouillon, poème-conversation*), a resolutely antipoetical poetry, sometimes exhilarating and often exhibitionist, whose desired effect is a naive spontaneity and immediacy.

Ungaretti's poems of the *Lacerba* period are of interest primarily as evidence of where he started from and the company he kept; they are fascinating when, reading *Poesie disperse*, we follow their "reformation" over the years into utterances definitively his own. It is worth looking at a few of them from this angle as an aid towards defining his voice.

One such utterance revolves about what Ungaretti was later to call the "metaphysical tragedy" of rootlessness,[8] a theme particularly poignant to him because of his own *déraciné* early life and his peculiar sense of being a nomad in search of his own *paese*. An old friend of his at the École Suisse Jacot, the Arab Mohammed Sceab, had also left Alexandria to continue his studies in Paris; the two "Africans" had roomed together in a boarding house in the Latin Quarter where, in the summer of 1913, Sceab shot himself dead with a pistol. Ungaretti's first treatment of this episode occurs as part of a very early poem, "Roman cinéma" (Movie Novel) composed in French and dated from Paris, March 11, 1914. The Sceab material runs as follows:

> il était étendu dans son lit
> tout habillé
> sa sigarette tombée
> de sa bouche
> quelques secondes avant
> seulement le temps
> de se dire
> va-t-en
> éteinte
> bien éteinte maintenant
> était là
> posée doucement
> près d'un peu de cendre
> quelques gouttes de sang
> à la tempe
>
> un fil de sang
> à la bouche
>
> c'etait un roi de désert
> il ne pouvait pas vivre
> en Occident
>
> il avait perdu
> ses domaines

        tout à coup
        il est rentré chez lui

        il souriait
        à qui voulait le voir

        pour retenir une pareille paix au sourire
        il faut bien être un mort

    he was stretched out in his bed / all dressed / his cigarette fallen /
    from his mouth / a few seconds before / just time enough / to tell
    himself / time to go / well put out now / was there / gently put
    down / close to a bit of ash / a few drops of blood / at his temple /
    a thread of blood / at his mouth /
    he was a king of the desert / he could not live / in the West /
    he had lost / his dominions /
    suddenly / he has returned to his own /
    he was smiling / at whoever wished to see him /
    to keep such a peace in the smile / it is most necessary to
    be a dead man*

In the initial response, the "tragedy," let alone the metaphysical
dimension, is drowned in mannerisms learned from *Alcools* or
Cendrars' "Panama" or "Poèmes élastiques"; it is probably significant
that "Roman cinéma" is in fact dedicated to Blaise Cendrars. Well
over half of the material quoted above is given over to a modishly
hardboiled "ashcan" painting of the body, with "cinematic" closeups
of the cigarette *qua* significant detail whose stubbing yields an amal-
gam of pathos and wisecrackery clearly attractive to the Ungaretti of
this phase; the "bien éteinte maintenant" apropos Sceab's last cigarette
links up with the last two lines to make a sour comment at life's
expense. But life is indifferent, and the poet himself seems more
impressed with his own panache, the tough front and the just per-
ceptible heart of gold, than with the meaning of Mohammed Sceab.

    The sole exception to this might be found in the single attempt
at diagnosis embedded in the journalism ("c' était un roi . . . chez
lui") where the treatment is nonsensational, the language relatively
general, the tone sober and meditative. These are the qualities gov-
erning the emergent myth of Sceab to be found in "In memoria,"
composed over two years later in the trenches of the Carso, the first
poem—we shall examine why—in *Il porto sepolto*. It is at once a
burial service and epigraph:

    * "Roman cinéma" was printed for the first and only time not in *Lacerba*
(which took only his work in Italian) but in the *Allegria di naufragi* of 1919.
Stylistically, however, it belongs with the *Lacerba* work.

Si chiamava
Moammed Sceab

Discendente
di emiri di nomadi
suicida
perché non aveva piú
Patria

Amò la Francia
e mutò nome

Fu Marcel
ma non era Francese
e non sapeva piú
vivere
nella tenda dei suoi . . .

His name was / Mohammed Sceab /
Descendent / of emirs of nomads / suicide / because he no longer
had / a Country /
He loved France / and changed his name /
He was Marcel / but was not French / and knew no longer how /
to dwell / in the tents of his own people . . .

"In memoria" contemplates the tragedy of a man without a country,
without a sustaining culture and tradition. The poem's dateline,
"Locvizza [in the Carso] il 30 settembre 1916," works as a re-
minder that the occasion for this memorial is war, that Ungaretti, an
ardent interventionist in 1914, an Italian infantry officer in 1915, had
found his *Patria* and bound himself to it under life and death condi-
tions. Sceab "loved France . . . but was not French"; in France he
had lost touch with the ways of his fathers and lost but unable to
return, had killed himself. Up to a point the parallels with the poet's
life are clear. The difference lies in the fact that Ungaretti left Africa
eventually to discover the land of his fathers; to that extent the dif-
ference is a happy one. He survives Sceab:

E forse io solo
so ancora
che visse

And maybe I alone / still know / that he lived . . .

and as the ancient Egyptians resisted death by carving names, so
the poet composes his friend's memorial, granting him at least an

ironic immortality. The original last stanza of the poem (following those cited above; it has now been definitively suppressed) ran

> Saprò
> fino al mio turno
> di morire

I shall know / until my turn / to die . . .

Here, while a common end is touched upon, the distinctive conditions leading to it are much more intimately related with the poem's deepest concerns: there is death by suicide at number 5, Rue des Carmes, Paris (as the poem informs us) and there is death *pro Patria,* perhaps at Locvizza on September thirtieth. The first is tragic; the second, for the poet-memorialist meditating on the several deaths, is in harmony, an acknowledgement of and repayment due to one's origins. And for this meditation the poet has fashioned a language devoid of all stylishness, ironizing, and journalistic sensationalism (cf. "Roman cinéma"), direct as the epitaph it is, moving in a solemn and deliberate cadence. Personal experience has been translated here into something as transparent and catholic as "myth."

The *L'Allegria* version of another poem on the Sceab story, "Chiaroscuro," can be contrasted with the original *Lacerba* version of April 1915 in order to clarify the direction of Ungaretti's self-discovery by revision:

> *Lacerba*
>
> Il bianco delle tombe se lo è sorbito la notte
> Spazio nero infinito calato
> da questo balcone
> al cimitero
>
> Mi è venuto a ritrovare il mio campagno arabo
> che si è suicidato
> che quando m'incontrava negli occhi
> parlandomi con quelle sue frasi pure e frastagliate
>
> era un cupo navigare nel mansueto blu
> È stato sotterrato a Ivry
> con gli splendidi suoi sogni
> e ne porto l'ombra
>
> Rifà giorno
> Le tombe ricompariscono
> appiattate nél verde tetro della ultime oscurità
> nel verde torbido del primo chiaro

Le annate dopo le annate
trovatelle a passeggio
in uniforme
accompagnate da suore di carità

Ma ora mi reggo tra le braccia
le nuvole che il mio sole mantiene
e all'alba non voglio sapere di piú

L'Allegria

Anche le tombe sono scomparse

Spazio nero infinito calato
da questo balcone
al cimitero

Mi è venuto a ritrovare
il mio compagno arabo
che s'è ucciso l'altra sera

Rifà giorno

Tornano le tombe
appiattate nei verde tetro
delle ultime obscurità
nel verde torbido
del primo chiaro

Lacerba: Night has absorbed the white of the tombs / Infinite black space fallen / from this balcony to the cemetery /
My Arab companion has come to find me / who committed suicide / who when he used to meet my eyes / speaking to me with those pure and carven phrases of his / there was a dark voyaging in the gentle blue / He has been buried at Ivry / with his splendid dreams / and I bear his shade /
Day comes again / The tombs reappear / flattened out in the gloomy green of the last obscurities / in the turbid green of the first clearing /
Whole years after years / foundlings passing by / in uniform / accompanied by sisters of mercy /
But now I support within my arms / the clouds that my sun maintains / and in the dawn I have no wish to know more

L'Allegria: Even the tombs have vanished
Infinite black space fallen / from this balcony / to the cemetery /
My Arab companion / has come to find me / who killed himself the other evening /
Day comes again /
The tombs return / flattened out in the gloomy green / of the last obscurities / in the turbid green / of the first clearing

The radical contraction in the *Allegria* version eliminates the original's descriptive discursiveness and crepuscular imagery (that is, Sceab's questing eyes and the bathetic analogy of the years' passing in stanza five). It also suppresses the note of weary self-pity characteristic, incidentally, of many of the *Lacerba* contributions—which makes the first version just another rendering of the *Weltschmerz* of a melancholy young man with insomnia. And out of the debris of the *Lacerba* poem rises an evocative chiaroscuro composed of shadowed greens and fluctuating light, of a kind of immortality wrested from the night-abolished tombs when, freed by "infinite black" from the weight of dust and marble, a dead "companion" may walk again in the *illusion of an eternity*—as the first returning rays of day remind—which is nonetheless desirable for being apparition. Again, a characteristic Ungarettian theme, expressed in a language at once simple and suggestive, a moody memory become something like an objective account of the pathos of human hope.

A final *Lacerba* poem is worth citing and briefly commenting upon for two reasons: it eventually will come to be the opening—and therefore directional—poem in *L'Allegria,* and it constitutes a kind of *ars*—or *fides*—*poetica.* As published first in 1915 it is titled "Eternità":

> Tra un fiore colto e l'altro donato
> l'inesprimibile vanità
>
> Fiore doppio
> nato in grembo alla madonna
> della gioia

Between a flower gathered and the other given / the inexpressible vanity /
Double flower / born of the womb of our lady / of joy

The "eternity" of the title refers at least in part to the immeasurable gap separating two major moments in the lifetime of a flower: the flower when taken or plucked (gathered, that is, through a conscious act involving will and muscle) and the flower as proposed and given by nature. Humanly speaking, the attempt to measure, connect or relate these two moments—the moments, we may say, of true creation and mere appropriation or expression—is, as the second line says, an "inexpressible vanity." And so even the nominal assertion of a single, underlying identity in the flower in both of its moments is fallacious: the poem informs us that at each moment the flower is *altro,* other. Hence the first stanza is cautionary, drastically limiting.

In the second stanza however this view gives way to another

wherein the flower is not "two" but "double" (one with two aspects rather than plural and disjunctive), born of an eternal—this is the second and affirmative point of the title—and creative cosmic love (*madonna della goia*). So that if we choose to consider "Eternità" as applicable to poetry, and if we choose to understand the flower as the poem seen in terms of its original inspiration and the inevitably reductive translation of inspiration into verbal structures, then Ungaretti can be seen to be defining poetry as a visionary act and an "impossible" capture which nevertheless participates, in its own degree, in what he feels to be a cosmic pattern of joyful creativity. The general titles of *Allegria di naufragi* and *L'Allegria* no doubt echo this. And a comment written as late as 1957 as part of a preface to a selection of his poems seems to offer us a perfect paraphrase of this early composition. Even an organic metaphor is employed (fruit), and surely the "patient, desperate solicitation" corresponds to the "gathering" of the flower:

> I'm not sure that poetry can be defined. I believe and profess that it is indefinable: that it manifests itself in that moment of our expression when the things we have most at heart, that have most shaken and tormented our thoughts, that most deeply belong to the very meaning of our life, appear to us as profoundly human truth. *And this must occur in a vibration that seems almost to go beyond a man's strength, that can never be won by immersion in traditions or by study, though both of those are substantial aids to self nourishment. Poetry then, as is usually agreed, is indeed a gift; or better, it is the fruit of a moment of grace—towards which a patient, desperate solicitation, particularly among the older, cultivated languages, is never out of place.*[9] (Italics mine.)

It is interesting to note that in 1919, with the publication of *Allegria di naufragi*, Ungaretti drops the entire second stanza for good; now the poem concludes with "vanità," and the problematic or limiting side is given dominance. Without the reconciling phrase, *fiore doppio*, the deep identity of the "two" flowers in line one is obscured or even rejected, while the poem as a whole is made darker, more inscrutable, and gnomic. The final version of 1943 has further alterations. It is now called "Eterno" (Eternal):

> Tra un fiore colto e l'altro donato
> l'inesprimibile nulla

Between a flower gathered and the other given / the inexpressible null

The new adjectival title suggests a repeated process rather than a visionary "idea"; the substitution of *nulla* for *vanità* removes the cautionary or what might be called anti-hybristic note and adds (contrary to the affirmative spirit of the first version) a disquieting glimpse of Pascalian void or gulf. So read, the poem now becomes a dark evocation of the utter impossibility of poetic expression, and might be explained biographically by the "dark" time in which this last revision was made, the time of both public and personal tragedies in the late 1930's and 1940's when Ungaretti was writing the counter book to *L'Allegria—Il dolore*. In terms of idiosyncratic usage, however, one may note that Ungaretti most often employs *nulla* or *nonulla* (less than nothing) to stand for a materially considered "mere nothing" which amounts to everything on a spiritual scale.* Bearing this in mind, "Eterno" would be about ineffability or, put positively, the miracle of apperception.

❂   ❂   ❂

In May, 1915, Italy entered the war on the side of the Allies against its old enemy Austria. In the same month *Lacerba* permanently discontinued publication and Ungaretti volunteered for military service. He was posted to the front on the Carso tableland beyond the River Isonzo, a rough Alpine terrain well to the north of Trieste where he lived mainly under combat conditions until his infantry regiment was transferred to the western front at Champagne, France, in the spring of 1918. It was under such conditions that his first book, *Il porto sepolto*, was written and published—eighty copies, at Udine, December 1916.

Possibly as a last influence from Blaise Cendrars, all of the thirty-three poems were accompanied by a notation as to the place and date of origin. The effect of course is to suggest a journal or diary; it also serves to remind us of the conditions of creation. While two of the *Porto* poems were composed in the December of 1915, the real composition of the book did not begin until the end of April of the next year; twenty-eight of them are dated between April and September, 1916. With the exception of the two opening poems ("In memoria" and the title poem which will be discussed further on) and the two concluding ("Italia" in which he dedicates himself and his poetry to his newfound *patria* and the "Commiato" dedicated to his first editor, the *gentile* Ettore Serra**), the poems of *Il porto sepolto* are arranged

---

* See, for example, the poem "Il porto sepolto," or the exquisite poem on the inscrutable passage of time in *La terra promessa*, "Variazioni su nulla."

** In 1932 the poet recounted the story of his meeting with Serra and how the book came to be published: "I found myself at Versa. From Versa I left for Udine. At the last moment they had lent me a breadbasket into which I'd put all my poems written on any old scraps of paper. One fine day I met a com-

chronologically, as "given," with the four exceptions providing a sort of personal patriotic frame for the whole.

Despite its genesis in the trenches *Il porto sepolto* contains very few allusions (beyond the implications of "Locvizza il 30 settembre 1916" etc.) to the well-known phenomena of that war—mud, barbed wire, screaming shells and so forth. "*Il porto sepolto*," the poet has recollected recently,

> was the poetry of a soldier, the poetry of a man exposed to death in the midst of death. It was also perhaps the poetry of a man who accepted suffering with resignation as a necessity—it certainly was not a book exalting heroism. It was a book of the poet's compassion for himself, for his companions, for human destiny. It was a cry, an offering, an invocation of fraternity.[11]

Certainly the very placing of the poem to the memory of Mohammed Sceab at the beginning of the little volume suggests a concern with quite another sort of casualty than that produced by military combat. Sceab died not "in action" but in extreme isolation:

> E forse io solo
> so ancora
> che visse . . .

The book begins then with an evocation of terrible alienation, a *paese* irrecoverably lost, a nomadship only terminated by self-destruction: a lost soul surviving precariously in the memory of an embattled friend. But as we have noted, this friend's very presence in the Carso bespeaks his discovery of *paese*, not only a land but a fraternity, not only Italy but Italians. In the climactic "Italia" he defines a poet—his sort of poet at any rate—as "un grido unanime" (a unanimous outcry) and concludes, addressing Italy:

> E in questa uniforme
> di tuo soldato
> mi riposo
> come fosse la culla
> di mio padre

---

missary officer, Ettore Serra. He was about ten years older than I. 'Why don't you salute your superior? Who are you?' I hadn't noticed him, I'd missed the point. 'I'm a writer.' He took my papers, looked them over. He was my first editor. . . . The book contained only the last poems remaining in the breadbasket that this famous lieutenant of the Quartermaster Corps had laid his hands on. . . ."[10]

And in this uniform / of your soldier / I repose myself / as though it were the cradle / of my father

Frequently in the *Porto* this spiritual co-presence is invoked (rather than "affirmed") as something infinitely fragile and tenuous—as in the beautiful "Fratelli" (Brothers) where that bonding word is likened to a budding leaf:

> Di che reggimento siete,
> fratelli?
>
> Parola tremante
> nella notte
>
> Foglia appena nata
>
> Nell'aria spasimante
> involontaria rivolta
> dell'uomo presente alla sua
> fragilità
>
> Fratelli

To what regiment do you belong, / brothers? /
Trembling word / in the night /
Leaf scarcely born /
In the shuddering air / involuntary turn / of the man present to his own / fragility /
Brothers /

Mortal frailty, the precariousness of simple contact, finds a completely appropriate imagistic expression with the young leaf quivering in the shell-convulsed night air; this is seconded by the simplicity of the language and the effect of delicate intimacy suggested by the typographical deployment of the slender lines against the main whiteness of the page.*

The prosodic strategy governing the so-called free verse of "Fratelli" as other *Porto* poems rests upon the primacy given the

---

* The initial (that is, the *Porto*) version was somewhat more garrulous. A *come* (like) joined "word" and "leaf" reminded the reader that he was in the presence of a literary comparison. The last stanza but one was (by comparison with the miraculous tact achieved in the revision) rather aggressively "pathetic." As regards whiteness, here are remarks made during the poet's travels in 1932, prompted by a snowy landscape in Corsica. "I have always felt that great painters ought to be thought of as those who know how to use white. It is a color that contains all the voices. . . . It is not the absence of color. . . . When, in a picture or a poem, the white succeeds in clarifying the profound sense of the words, then, poet or painter, one has nothing more to learn."[12]

single, crucial word (e.g. *fratelli* . . . *Fragilità* . . . *Fratelli*) or, at most, the grammatically unified short phrase. (It might be noted in this regard that there are no genuine "run-on" lines at all in "Fratelli," with the single exception of lines 8–9, where *fragilità* is separated from its possessive pronoun for purposes of surprise and emphasis.) The first stanza of "Fratelli" could make up a perfect hendeca-syllable:

> Di che reggimento siete, fratelli?

but the gain in dismantling it comes in the greater control Ungaretti gets over his pauses, the greater intensity given the vocative and the slower pacing in the movement of the question. Again, a prepositional phrase like "nella notte" would lose much of its vaguely ominous vibrato if it were to appear on the line before, joining the adjective *tremante* that it modifies. The general suppression of punctuation—an old Latin Quarter device—also tends to heighten the focus on the key components of the sentence rather than on the sentence itself. Generally speaking, such a prosody—conditioned of course by the "seriousness" of the content—enjoins a slow and deliberate method of reading, a meditative mode in which word or brief phrase seems to gather in upon itself its full expressive weight, connotative above all.

Of course, the conditions of composition offer alternate explanations for the brevity and fragmented effect of the *Porto* poems: "Confronting death in the trenches. . ." Ungaretti has said, "it was necessary to write with agility, to write the essential."[13] But we should not take this *essenzialità* to mean a hasty shorthand prompted by violent conditions. We have noted above (see page 11) how Ungaretti's experience of war brought him a spiritual revelation, how he found in these con-ditions what he later called "a spontaneous and disquieting immedia-tization with the cosmic essence of things," a direct and sensuous perception of man's fragility and solitude and renovating love for his fellows. The famous "Mattina" (Morning), consisting simply of

> M'illumino
> d'immenso

is one attempt to utter his ecstasy.

When Ungaretti speaks of "writing the essential" we can be very sure that that essential will be "nominalist" or vertical in character. The aesthetic problem he faced was to find a means to express or suggest his extraordinary experience. The answer lay first in aban-doning all tries at statement or description for a poetry of pure evocation, secondly in attempting this evocation by means of single word or brief phrase presented so that it could be seen, heard, sensed and understood in all the slow unfolding of its various meanings. Who could say that the last "stanza" of the poem "Fratelli"—that is,

Fratelli

—meant just "brothers" or "comrades"? In the context of what has gone before it (including two previous appearances of that very word) its resonances are considerable: it has become, like one of Fenollosa's ideograms, food for meditation.

Here is Ungaretti's own description of the genesis of his method. One should note his insistence on its intimate connection with his radical experience of war, its roots in *coscienza* rather than any literary modernism.

> Without presuming too much on the importance of my early energies, nor discrediting my contemporaries—whether Futurists, Crepusculars or Voceans, in the midst of whom I took my first steps—I don't think that what the critics have recognized can be contradicted. That is, it suddenly dawned upon me how the word (*parola*) ought to be called to birth through an expressive tension that loaded it to over-flowing with the fullness of its meaning. . . . If the word were made naked, if one stopped at each cadence of rhythm, each beat of the heart, if one isolated moment after moment each word in its own verity, this was because in the first place one felt oneself a man, religiously a man, and it seemed that this was the revolution which under these historical circumstances [the war] necessarily had to be initiated by and from the words themselves. . . . The word [as ordi-narily employed]—whether enlisted in the pompous vacuities of oratory, or trifled with in the expression of decorative and "artistic" longings, or perverted in picturesque sketches or sensual melancholia or rising from aims not purely intimate and universal—such a word seemed to me to fail in its poetic purpose. . . . The conditions of our poetry and the poetry of other countries at that period required no other reform if not this fundamental one.[14]

*   *   *

As for characteristic *Porto* themes, we have already touched upon most of them. There is the central sense of solitude and isolation of which Mohammed Sceab, friend transfigured into myth, is the threshold emblem. There are the poems, like "Fratelli" or even "In memoria," where a bond stretching via memory beyond the grave is quietly affirmed, where, for a moment, solitude seems bridged or broken. In "Nostalgia," the pre-war Paris of Ungaretti's apprentice-ship is evoked:

Quando
la notte è a svanire
poco prima di primavera
e di rado
qualcuno passa

Su Parigi s'addensa
un oscuro colore
di pianto

In un canto
di ponte
contemplo
l'illimitato silenzio
di una ragazza
tenue

Le nostre
malattie
si fondono

E come portati via
si rimane

When / night is about to vanish / a little before spring / and
seldom / does someone pass /
Over Paris condenses / an obscure color / of weeping
In a corner / of a bridge / I contemplate / the limitless silence / of
a slender / girl/
Our / troubles / mingle /
And we stay / as if carried away

Nostalgia is another mode, of course, of coping with solitude; a
related theme deals with the bittersweet consolations of fantasy or,
to put it in Saharan terms, mirage. Hence such elegant "fragments"
evoking projected reveries, as "Stasera" (This Evening)—

Balaustrata di brezza
per appoggiare stasera
la mia malinconia

Balustrade of breeze / whereon to lean this evening / my melancholy

or the concluding two stanzas of "Pellegrinaggio" (Pilgrimage) where,
after calling up the mud and psychic pulverization of the trenches, he
declares the transcendency in his life of transforming imagination or,
put more caustically, "illusion":

Ungaretti
uomo di pena
ti basta un'illusione
per farti coraggio

Un riflettore
di là
mette un mare
nella nebbia

Ungaretti / man of pain / an illusion suffices / to give you courage /
A searchlight / out there / puts a sea / into the fog

This is of course a theme we have already met in "Chiaroscuro"
where night's black temporarily blots out the tombs at Ivry and per-
mits a resurrected Sceab.

But the main thematic tide of *Il porto sepolto* deals with the poet's
ecstatic sense of unity with all things above and below. The sense
of human cohension, *paese*, celebrated in "Italia" sometimes heightens
into genuine cosmic drunkenness (sponsored, surely, by the imman-
ence of death, the great simplifier). Samples of this Dionysian pastoral
can be found in "La notte bella" (Beautiful Night):

. . . Sono stato
un stagno di buio

Ora mordo
come un bambino la mammella
lo spazio

Or son ubriaco
d'universo

I have been / a tarn of dark / Now I suck / on space / like a baby
at the breast / Now I'm drunk / with universe

or in the middle of "Annientamento" (Obliteration):

M'ama non m'ama
mi sono smaltato
di margherite
mi sono radicato
nella terra marcita . . .

She loves me loves me not / I have plastered myself / with daisies /
I have rooted / in the marshy ground . . .

The beautiful "I fiumi" (Rivers) "tells" and celebrates the rivers in
his life: the Serchio (flowing near his ancestral Lucca), the Nile,

the Seine, but most of all the Isonzo cutting through the wartorn present landscape:

> —qui meglio
> mi sono riconosciuto
> un docile fibra
> dell 'universo

. . . here have I best / recognized myself / a docile fibre / of the universe . . .

In this stanza he hymns, in the baptismal image of the running water in which he strips himself of uniform and bathes, floats and reposes, the miraculous unity he perceives in all his times and places, the joyous harmony he experiences in these ecstatic and stolen moments.

Such moments pass of course: in a moment one "goes dark" and holistic ecstasy cedes to a sense of impotent solitude. Still, such moments return: *Il porto sepolto* is bright with them. The title-poem (pairing with "Commiato" as poems about poetic vision even as "In memoria" pairs with "Italia" as poems about *Patria*) is about both this alternation between vision and darkness and the expressive dilemma confronting the returned visionary.

> Il porto sepolto
>
> Vi arriva il poeta
> e poi torna alla luce con i suoi canti
> e li disperde
>
> Di questa poesia
> mi resta
> quel nulla
> d'inesauribile segreto

The poet arrives there / and then returns to the light with his songs / and scatters them /
Of such poetry / remains to me / this nothing / of the inexhaustible secret*

Here we can recollect Pea's account of the bizarre boast by the young Ungaretti to the effect that he would land (*approdare*) at

---

* A useful gloss for this poem, pointed out by many critics, is the voyage described in the "voyant" letter from Rimbaud to Paul Demeny of 15 May 1871 in which the poet, by drastic strategies involving love, suffering and madness, wins through to the *Inconnu*: "when, driven mad, he ends by losing the understanding of his visions, still he has seen them." Cf. also Claudel's parable—written apropos Rimbaud—of Animus and Anima in his essay on French verse in *Positions et propositions*. Such literature was of course very familiar to Ungaretti from early on through his browsings in the Thiule library.

the submerged harbor off Alexandria when the waters were sufficiently limpid. It is clear that such waters as Ungaretti had in mind are as substantial as the waters of the sea suggested by the play of an army searchlight in the fog ("Pellegrinaggio"); his trip, that is, will be interior, psychic or spiritual in nature.

As for the *porto sepolto* itself, it is worth offering here a passage by Pierre Reverdy which Ungaretti used to quote with approval:

> The image is a pure creation of the intelligence.
> It cannot be born of a comparison but from the bringing together of two more or less widely separated realities. The more the *rapports* between the two realities brought together are mutually distant and at the same time precise (*lointains et justes*), the stronger the image will be, the more it will possess of emotive power and poetic reality. . . .[15]

Lointains et justes might fairly characterize the several realities that compose the meaning of the buried harbor. "Autobiographically" it would include: associations with a personal past, an early home, a fabled antiquity, the excitement occasioned by Jondet's heroic explorations. But this is private magic, with which the reader, if aware of it all, can sympathize but never use. And Ungaretti is careful to make his port as abstract and therefore as accessible as possible. *Porto:* a harbor, a place that receives, shelters, sustains and conserves. But *sepolto:* buried—some sort of journey, a descent or dive, is necessary if the goods it holds are to be found. The diver, we are told immediately, will be a poet; he alone can arrive at this mysterious cache, descending from the *connu* into what, by comparison, is dark. But on issuing from it, "returning to the light" of common day, he will have songs to sing. It is suggested he has momentarily "fathomed"—touched upon some source of harmony and joy.

But in effect "Il porto sepolto" is a memory poem written after the poet has surfaced. From this viewpoint it laments the loss of the miraculous power now dispersed or spent in lyric song *at the same time* as it recognizes in the syllables of that song—no matter (*quel nulla*) how inadequate—at least an echo or phosphorescent trace of the ineffable music of its source. In other words the poem conceives the poet as a voyant or seer and views him in that role as at once wretched and exalted: wretched because expression invariably mocks inspiration, exalted because "he has seen" and because even that *nulla* he is able to produce is—however removed from the source— at least a witness to its actuality.

"Il porto sepolto" as the title poem of Ungaretti's first book there-
fore makes a commitment: the book will deal with a reality very
different from that historically represented by the dates and places
appended to each of its poems. This reality will be both "secret"
and "inexhaustible." Its presence, ecstatically found, lost and longed
for, pervades the pages of the little wartime edition, the source of its
mysterious *allegria*.

❀   ❀   ❀

In the spring of 1918 Ungaretti's regiment left Italy for the French
front near Champagne. At the war's end he was discharged and took
up residence in Paris as correspondent for Mussolini's *Popolo d'Italia*.
In 1918 his second book was published in Paris in an edition of
eighty copies. This was *La guerre* and consisted of eighteen poems
in French: eleven translated from the original Italian, seven written
directly in that language. *La guerre* was dedicated to the recently
dead Guillaume Apollinaire "en souvenir de la mort que nous avons
accompagnée . . . en souvenir des fleurs enterrées."*

In 1919 the publishing house of Vallecchi in Florence brought out
Allegria di naufragi (Joy of Shipwrecks), the work that first brought
Ungaretti's name to the attention of a large group of readers, in-
corporating as it did, in a relatively large printing as opposed
to the grand total of one hundred-forty copies of his previous
books), the body of his poetry written between 1914 and 1919,
scrupulously revised.

Allegria di naufragi itself is not an integral part of the *definitive
Vita d'un uomo*. Most of its poems have been further pruned and
revised and now, in a completely new sequence devised in 1931,
comprise the first volume of the *Vita*, simply titled *L'Allegria*.** In
these pages we shall mainly use the *L'Allegria* text as the basis for our
remarks. Still, it is of considerable interest to examine briefly the

---

* " . . . in memory of Death that we accompanied . . . in memory of buried flowers": the
phrases are from Ungaretti's dedicatory poem. In a letter to Soffici written in 1918 Ungaretti
compared the two war-books just published by Apollinaire and himself: "*Calligrammes* is a book
of poems, the greater part written in time of combat. Kin to my *Porto* but in another mode—
less dryness and oppression of soul and less of the liberating participation in nature, but with a
more lively, dislocated, acrobatic sense of the mechanism of war."[16]

** Ungaretti's French poems include *La guerre* and a sequence from *Allegria di naufragi*
entitled *P-L-M 1914–1919* (capitals stand for the Paris-Lyon-Mediterranée, French north–
south express train) which gathers poems dedicated to André Breton, Cendrars, and André
Salmon. They are brought together under the title *Derniers jours* in TP.

grosser differences between *Allegria di naufragi* and *L'Allegria,* particularly in terms of general organization—the groupings and sequences of poems in terms of *capitoli* or chapters. The poet himself has made much of the importance of chapters in his work: "Each different section of these two books [*L'Allegria* and *Sentimento del tempo*]," he writes in a preface to the latter, "forms a canto or song with its own organic complexity—with its own dialogues, dramas and choruses—each unique and indivisible." It is true that in the various *capitoli* there is a certain community, thematic and also chronological, which gives a sort of narrative shape to what otherwise might appear to be a casual deployment of diversified lyrical moods.

Allegria di naufragi is divided into eleven chapters which work mainly from the present (postwar 1919) into the past (various phases of the war—including *Il porto sepolto* which now constitutes the largest chapter—climaxing with a heavily revised selection of the prewar *Lacerba* poems). There is a coda of very recent poems in French and Italian, *La guerre* and *P-L-M* included. Chapter titles are sprightly (a debt here perhaps to *Calligrammes*); they include the names of the seasons and months, a *Cycle of 24 Hours,* and the *Lacerba* work arranged in two more or less self-explanatory divisions—*The Panorama of Alexandria Egypt* and *Babel* (Milan poems). The volume closes with a set of five prose poems, heavily titled *Finali di Commedia* (Finales to the Comedy) and dedicated to the *Ronda* chief Vincenzo Cardarelli. The *Ronda* of course was pushing poetic prose at this time.

Paralleling the chastening tendency of the revisions of particular poems (e.g., the difference between "Roman cinéma" and "In memoria"), the chapterization of *L'Allegria* is far more sober, less "Apollinairian." Chapters have been reduced in number to five and they are strictly chronological, moving from pre- to postwar, in their order. The titles are appropriately more reserved: *Ultime:* the last poems before the war, written 1914–15 for *Lacerba, Il porto sepolto*: the central chapter, *Naufragi* (Shipwrecks): written following the *Porto* in the Carso area from December 1916 through August 1917, *Girovago* (Wandering), mainly from the French front in spring to summer 1918, and *Prime:* first poems of the postwar period written in Paris and Milan in 1919.* This new arrangement better suits the

* By *Prime,* Ungaretti has written to his French translator Jean Lescure, he meant "*first* steps of an experience which is . . . completely different, strangely different. . . . *Premières:* time which opens with all of its unknownness."[17] Lescure intelligently translated *Prime* as *Nouveaux commencements.* The first chapter of *Sentimento del tempo* is also called *Prime.*

conventional form of a *Vita d'un uomo*. It sacrifices, however, something of the ebullience of that man's beginnings.

The same drive toward simplification and abstraction can be found in the book's new title, though I prefer the first—*Allegria di naufragi*—as best expressing the oxymoron or paradox upon which the book as a whole is founded. The poem of that title (called until 1923 "The Poet's Philosophy") doesn't strike me as living up to it:

> E subito riprende
> il viaggio
> come
> dopo il naufragio
> un superstite
> lupo di mare

And quickly he resumes / the voyage / as, / after shipwreck, / a surviving / seawolf . . .

This expresses stubbornness or tenacity but hardly *allegria*. Something closer to the title's meaning will be found in the poem which once began *Allegria di naufragi* (hence tending from pride of position to modify or define the title) and now ends *L'Allegria*. It is called "Preghiera" (Prayer) and ran in its first published version as follows:

> Allorchè dal barbaglio
> delle promiscuità
> mi destero in attonita
> sfera di limpidità
> e porterò sui flutti
> il peso mio
> leggero
>
> Concedimi Signore
> di naufragare
> a quel baccio
> troppo forte
> del giovine giorno

At that moment when from the vertigo / of promiscuity / I shall raise myself into astonished / sphere of limpidity / and bear above the waves / my light / weight /

Grant me Lord / to shipwreck / at that too strong / kiss / of the young day*

---

* Later, by 1931, Ungaretti will rewrite this poem in traditional hendecasyllables for the most part; this is in line with the reconstitution of traditional metrics which is one of the features of *Sentimento del tempo*. The following is

Here *naufragio* is seen as the ecstatic obliteration of the sensual man and the commencement of a new life, a yearned-for release into spirit related to that "cosmic immediatization" which informs all the *Porto* chapter. For an Italian, another *naufragio*, connected with a perception of the flow and perishing of all created things, would suggest itself; for example, that sweet wreck proposed at the conclusion to Leopardi's terrible masterpiece, "L'infinito":

> . . . e mi sovvien l'eterno,
> E le morte stagioni, e la presente
> E viva, e il suon di lei. Cosè tra questa
> Immensità s'annega il pensier mio:
> E il naufragar m'è dolce in questo mare.

. . . and I remember the eternal, / and the dead seasons, and the present / and living one, and the sound of it. Thus within this / immensity my thought annuls itself: / and the shipwreck is sweet within this sea.

We shall see that, starting in 1919, Ungaretti begins a long and intensely personal quest for a viable tradition, a quest which in many ways is conducted under the leadership of Leopardi. The title *Allegria di naufragi* then is at once an index to a supernatural order of reality encountered during the five year's history that the book encloses, and a homage *cum* fraternal salute to a master of a century before.*

But the ecstatic communion which is the dominating vision of the *Porto sepolto* is damped or seriously qualified in the context of the

---

the final version of "Preghiera"; it seems to me a definite advance in its graver cadences and greater clarity:

> Quando mi desterò
> dal barbaglio della promiscuità
> in un limpida e attonita sfera
>
> Quando il mio peso mi sarà leggero
>
> Il naufragio concedimi Signore
> di qual giovane giorno al primo grido

When I raise myself / from the vertigo of promiscuity / into a limpid and astonished sphere /
When my weight is light on me /
Grant me shipwreck Lord / at the first cry of that young day

* In a lecture on "L'infinito" written in 1944, Ungaretti meditates anew on Leopardi's use of *naufragar*, finding it "ironic": at once referring to annihilation *and* "immediatization, ecstasy in the infinite."[18] "Naufrage" is also a key word, aligned with "circonstances éternelles," in the *Coup de dés* of Ungaretti's other master, Mallarmé.

total experience offered by *Allegria di naufragi and L'Allegria.* True that in the poems immediately succeeding those of the *Porto* period there are some—like "Transfigurazione" or "Godimento" (Delight) or the ejaculatory morning poem in which he becomes a filament of cosmic light—where the vision is ecstatically reaffirmed. Still, the experience of "immensity" can be reductive as well as expanding, as in "Vanità" where a soldier sees his image reflected in a standing pool, then fractured into shadowed ripples beneath "the limpid stupor of immensity." The prevailing mood in the final and post-*Porto* chapters of *L'Allegria* is one of fatigue, nostalgic melancholy and a recurrence of that sense of terrestial homelessness originally associated with the history of Mohammed Sceab. Thus the spring poem written in March 1918:

> Si porta
> l'infinita
> stanchezza
> dello sforzo
> occulto
> di questo principio
> che ogni anno
> scatena la terra

One carries / the infinite / fatigue / of the occult / force / of this beginning / that yearly / unchains the earth . . .

where one feels only the weariness involved in the effort toward release and renewal—an exhaustion that finds its appropriate autumnal simile in the beautiful "Soldati" (Soldiers) which closes *Girovago:*

> Si sta come
> d'autunno
> sugli alberi
> le foglie*

* Literally: "One is like / in autumn / on the trees / the leaves." A good example by the way of the untranslatable quality of much of Ungaretti. In *La guerre* he himself translates it into an approximate alexandrine which is flat and unwieldy: "nous sommes telle en automme sur l'arbre la feuille." Two of his French translators—Jean Chuzeville: *Vie d'un homme* (Paris, 1939) and Jean Lescure, *Les cinq livres* (Paris, 1953)—have made better tries:

Chuzeville:	Lescure:
On est là	On est là come
Dans l'attente de son sort	sur les arbres
Telles sur l'arbre en automne	les feuilles
Les feuilles	d'automne

Chuzeville glosses and localizes Ungaretti's simile: his title for "Soldati" is "Vie des tranchées," so giving his "là" a meticulousness which injures the "meta-

The *girovago*, the roaming or wandering about as if one were a "fleeting image taken in a timeless whirling," has not the remotest connection with problems of where to live (Paris, Rome, Alexandria, etc.) or how to settle down—job, marriage and the rest. It is clearly the symptom of spiritual crisis:

> In nessuna
> parte
> di terra
> mi posso
> accasare . . .
>
> Godere un solo
> minuto di vita
> iniziale
>
> Cerco un paese
> innocente

In no / part of the earth / can I / find my home . . .
To joyously savor one single / instant of initial / life
I seek an innocent / country . . .

This *paese*, the realm of the buried port, the profound terrain touched at during the war years, has been lost; with our hindsight we may add "permanently." That miraculous immanence and sense of immediate contact with the joyous source at the heart of all things is now a memory; so too is that direct perception of the confraternity of all men—*fratelli* in their solitude and "fragility"—that had been born in the forcing conditions of combat. With the cessation of these conditions combined with the exhaustion of the veteran-poet (now over thirty), life has suddenly grown old. In Paris, as he writes in one of the concluding prose-poems, "space is finite," all things "tend to chaos." In Lucca, the *paese* of his ancestors, he can find in himself but a tired wish to "adjust," to compromise: "Nothing remains but to resign myself to dying./I shall therefore tranquilly raise my offspring."

---

physical" point of the original. He also explicitly moralizes that which is left indeterminate and suggestive in "Soldati." Lescure is much better. Nothing much can be done with the verb *stare* with its medleyed associations of "staying," "standing," "living," "being," etc. "Si sta" is not tonally the same as "Si é" which is still more or less the only way to paraphrase it in Italian. The inversion in the last three lines of the original (moving from large to small, from agent to patient, from condition to symptom) so fraught with pathos and so natural in Italian, is a poetic vice in modern French or English . . . neither we nor Lescure can do anything about it without losing, as my crib has done, the transparency and simplicity of the original.

And so, with that prayer to the Lord we have already discussed, the experience of *L'Allegria* concludes. And with it concludes that part of *Vita d'un uomo* that centers on a "religion" of ecstasy, the spontaneous "immediatization with the cosmic essence of things." The accompanying *allegria* is subdued to *sentimento del tempo*, the feeling of time. And memory, the ultimately tragic attempt to re-create and resurrect the past through an act of imaginative recollection, replaces ecstasy. The "religion" becomes progressively tormented, almost desperately (or baroquely) Roman Catholic—the religion of his infancy and ancestors.

❋   ❋   ❋

In the years following the other [First World] war a strange theory circulated and was widely credited. It was promulgated by my friends, the writers who were associated with the review *La Ronda*. For them verse was dead and buried, and modern poetry could only find its proper form in a rhythmed prose (*prosa numerosa*). I remained alone for almost ten years, showing polemically and with the testimony of my own work that song (*il canto*) continued to have metrical exigences that were much more pertinent.[19]

The *Prime* chapters in both *L'Allegria* and *Sentimento del tempo* show that this statement is not quite accurate; the final chapter of *Allegria di naufragi* was even more freighted with Cardarelli's conception of the prose-poem.* One might say that the closing rhythms of *L'Allegria* have become appropriately heavy, the prosody mirroring the despondency and exhaustion of this particular phase of the poet's life. To a certain extent this is true, but the real significance of Ungaretti's brief (1919–20) alliance with the *Ronda* lies not in his experiments with *prosa d'arte* (whose heritage will be found not in his poems but in the elaborate periodic structures of *Il deserto e dopo*) but in the testimony it provides of his new and intense concern with Italian literary tradition.

"My preoccupations in those first postwar years . . . all tended toward the necessity of recovering an order—and since my *métier* was to be poet, of recovering an order in that domain in which my profession directly engaged me."[20] *L'Allegria* too had had its order, of course, but in the years following the war, Ungaretti felt increasingly that its prosody centered on the *parola* was at best a

---

* *Allegria di naufragi* for instance included two versions of "Girovago," three stanzas of which are cited above (p. 164). In *Finali di commedia* these became:

Non mi posso accasare.
Ad ogni nuovo clima, mi ritrovo di averne già saputo . . .
Cerco un paese innocente.

temporary and makeshift solution—"a brief detour"[21]—to the problems confronting him as poet. The prosody of *L'Allegria* had been a highly specialized instrument, an expressive means for an ineffable experience. The traditional vehicle for poetry—"the natural poetic order . . . that every true Italian poet has in his blood,"[22] the hendecasyllable with all the "infinite resources that it has achieved during its long life,"[23] had been sacrificed (he now judged) to a part or component, the word. With this, rightly enough at the time and under the circumstances, the poetry of meditated experience, of sequence or *durée*, of man considered as an historical and self-conscious creature living in and modified by time, had been "neglected" for a poetry of ecstasy, a poetry focused on the extraordinary timeless or pure moment wherein man seems to leap free of his atmospheric conditions, of his fleshly weight and temporal identity.

Sentimento del tempo is governed and bound by the emotional focus indicated by the title—e.g., the feeling of time, its passing, the heavy sense of mortal transience within it. In *L'Allegria* perspectives in space and time are for the most part abolished in an overwhelming sensation of the here and now; the whole of creation seems to be luminously present in the atomized *moment*. Most of the moments in *L'Allegria* occur in a pure present that casts no shadow on past or future, innocent of any taint of cause or consequence. So, of a morning, the poet simply catches light (*M'illumino/d'immenso*) and existence, in the jargon of our days, seems consumed by sheer intensity of essence. Nothing else exists but the subject ("I") and its ecstatic consciousness of the co-presence of "its" cosmos.

Moving from this to the *Sentimento*, the impression will be one of—to put it mildly—enormous complication. Pure presence has given way to a poignant sense of existence in time, with all the darker ramifications that this implies: the related sensations of aging, of loss, of fear of what is to come, of futility. Concomitantly, a desperate desire for *paese innocente*, for renewed experience of the harmonious wholeness of all things, and (above all) a turning towards the past—personal, cultural, human—for what it may yield of such innocence and integrity. The characteristic mode of cognition is either memory or that aspect of memory which has lost its self-consciousness: dream.

Ungaretti had in common with Cardarelli and the *rondisti* a passionate conviction that the health of invalid Italian letters was to be found in its glorious past, that the new order would be discovered through an arduous study and cultivation of the literary tradition. For Cardarelli, as we know, the preferred territory for exploration was art-prose as practiced by masters from Boccaccio to Leopardi. For Ungaretti, the answer lay in the tradition of *canto italiano,* and it was here that he split with the *Ronda* to pursue his own course.

They (the *rondisti*) wanted prose, poems in prose. And on the contrary I felt, deep within me, memory like an anchor of health. With humility I reread the poets, the poets who sing. In the verses of Jacopone, or those of Dante, or Petrarch, or Guittone, or Tasso, or those of Cavalcanti or Giacomo Leopardi, I searched for song. It was not the hendecasyllable of such-and-such a poet, nor the lines of nine or seven of some other, it was Italian song (*canto italiano*), the song of the Italian tongue that I sought in its constancy through the centuries, through voices so numerous and so different in timbre, each so jealous of its own novelty, each so singular in the expression of thoughts and feelings. It was the beating of my heart that I wanted to hear in harmony with the heartbeats of my ancestors, with my desperately beloved land. Thus were born, from 1919 to 1925, "The Seasons," "The End of Chronos," "Sirens," "Hymn to Death" and other poems in which, supporting myself as much as possible by ear and soul, I attempted to tune into harmony with our modern tastes an ancient musical instrument which was, as a result, for good or ill, taken up by everyone in Italy.[24]

✿   ✿   ✿

Paralleling the *Ronda* example certainly, the nature of the legends in *Sentimento del tempo* has become intensely literary. The tersely noted personal landscapes of the Carso, Paris, Milan and Alexandria are replaced by a more elegant and traditional *paesaggio* drawn partly no doubt from Mediterranean littoral and grove* but mainly from the dream fictions of the golden age or Arcadian idyll. And the focal "I" of *L'Allegria* now works out its salvation in the company of an ampler *dramatis personae* drawn like the landscape itself from ancient myths—besides unnamed shepherds and nymphs we encounter Iris, Diana, the Sirens, Chronos, Apollo, Juno and Leda.

No doubt one of the reasons for this development is the poet's study of the poetry of tradition, as well as his need to find his work in harmony with it. But this is no cool neoclassic Parnassianism born

---

* In recent years the poet has connected the mythic landscapes of the *Sentimento* with the landscapes of the Lazio district where he lived, after the war, in an old Roman castle in Marino. "Thus," he remarks, "when I penetrated the wood at Marino, or came to a lake at Albano or Nemi, I found myself in the midst of a landscape that was full of history, with such seductions in its nature and so many distances in time that it seemed to take on the prodigious lineaments of fable. From the atrociously despoiled nature of *L'Allegria* I had therefore reached a world in which history in its immediacy and in the passage of millenia assumed mythic form."[25] As this intimates the Latian landscapes never function as elements of a descriptive or "nature" poetry. Here as elsewhere in Ungaretti (qua "nominalist") the spatial dimension is mainly employed as analogy, correspondence or correlative for states of mind or emotion.

of aesthetic admiration for the literary past, as *La Ronda's* mythicism was. The *paesaggi* and figures Ungaretti draws from mythical antiquity are hostages, survivors, emblems of the *paese innocente,* and as such, as the creatures of a fabulous illusion (since the *paese* no longer exists, since we no longer credit these deities), they become the personifications of a personal and cultural memory, nodes of joy and pathos animated by the *sentimento del tempo.* "Jove and Venus and Mars are divinities who have perished, who contests that?. . . We are no longer dealing with a wisdom or ritual but with the primordial movement of our feeling (*sentimento*) and imagination towards recovering those times in which such grace existed. Art persuades us because, laden with our memories, it moves our imaginations to the point of enabling us to rediscover our innocent eyes."[26]

In an article written for the *Ronda* in 1922 Ungaretti meditated on the *donnée obscure,* the "mystery" that he feels at the heart of all life, the "mystery" and the human mode of coping with it which he calls "measure": "not the measure of the mystery, which is humanly absurd, but the measure of something which is in a certain sense opposed to the mystery while at the same time constituting for us its highest manifestation, the terrestial world considered as man's continual invention."[27] We are familiar with this sense of the mystery of things in Ungaretti's work from almost the very beginning. The *porto sepolto* was his first famous analogue for it, and what he calls the "measure" would be his attempt to objectify his experience of it by means of the poetic *parola—quel nulla.* "Ti basta un'illusione," he wrote in *L'Allegria,* and he concludes the *Ronda* essay with this query: "Is there, through an effect of metamorphosis, an order of images that deliberately defy death, induced in our mind by the natural inclination of the living to seek their own well-being?"

At any rate he finds such an order of images in the legendary forms of antiquity, not because the ancients may have believed, say, Apollo immortal but because *he* finds that this god once constituted a purely human "measure" for our fabulous sense of the mystery of grace and harmony. On Ungaretti's reckoning, Apollo still appeals to the human need for such a measure: hence our desire finds both aesthetic and spiritual satisfaction ("well-being") in what that name evokes. It need hardly be said that this is a satisfaction with its accompaniment of melancholy: Apollo is a dead god, an echo registered by memory in its incessant ranging through time. Ancient myth, then, is an illusion akin to poetry—*bella menzogna,* a sweet lie. This means: sweet, but a lie, as well as: a lie, but how sweet!

And so in a key essay, "Innocence et mémoire" written for the

Nouvelle revue française in 1926, he speaks of the return of poets to pagan mythology as not simply a cultural mechanism but a "piety without hope manifested in the thirst for beauty." The poet is no longer, he says, the spokesman for divinity; he is merely the operator of "un jeu de reflets" a manipulation of reflected images. "It has been given unto him alone to make surge forth, out of a contemplated nature, the apparitions of memory. Memory—man's profundity."[28] *Mémoire, profondeur de l'homme.* And such profundity as he has gropes "back" to the idea or myth of initial innocence and purity, the same myth that wooed and plagued the symbolistes, from Poe to Mallarmé.

❂   ❂   ❂

> Leopardi recognizes—and he is the sole Italian to recognize it clearly until contemporary poetry—that a fracture has occurred within the human spirit. The acceptance of the human condition with its temporal and spatial limitations . . . is henceforth considered to form the antithesis to man's innate aspiration towards liberty and poetry. We know . . . what a predominance time's passing assumes in the *canzoni*, that is, at the very beginning of Leopardi's work. This is *durée* as Vico understood it in his interpretation of historical time and as, two centuries later, Bergson will understand it in his interpretation of psychological time. Leopardi wonders whether we are not reduced—since time exists no longer, or only consumed or defunct time—to no longer being able to evoke the reality of our being, to no longer being able to set it in motion, save through the efforts of memory. . . .[29]

The *rondisti* had revered Leopardi as a master of classical literary style, *lo bello scrivere.* Ungaretti certainly shared their veneration, but, as the passage above indicates, he looked upon the older poet not only as an artist but, and above all, as a man who pioneered in the perception and expression of peculiarly "modern" experiences. In the peroration to his "second discourse" on Leopardi at the University of Rome in 1944 he made this extraordinary claim regarding his relations with his master:

> Whatever my poetry is worth, I believe it to have one merit. In order to recover the traditions of our poetry and to perpetuate them, in order to reunite our poetry with history, it was necessary to return to Leopardi, and to understand him. . . . Critics will come to see, and the dates are there to prove it, that from 1914 to today there is no poetic work in Italy that does not carry the signs of this labor of mine, in metrics, in the dialectic of images, in the orientation of inspiration.[30]

Ungaretti has never been reticent about his admiration for—and obligations to—the French symbolistes of the nineteenth century, Mallarmé in particular. In the course of the remarks cited above, for example, he observes that since all Italian poets after Leopardi were "anachronistic"—that is, they evaded with varying degrees of success the poet's responsibility of creating a voice for his own times—"there was nothing for it but to turn to the French poets . . . after Poe and up to 1900" for inspiration and guidance. Nevertheless it is not at all excessive to say that Ungaretti views Mallarmé and French *symbolisme* in general as the unwitting heirs to the pioneer labors of the isolated poet from Recanati. And since this whole genealogical matter is important for a real understanding of "hermeticism" and its role in twentieth-century Italian poetry, it will be worth pausing here to review the issue and its background. The "hermetic" book par excellence is Ungaretti's *Sentimento del tempo*.[31]

❖   ❖   ❖

Ermetico as a pejorative adjective referring to an obscure and deliberately "closed" poetry was popularized in the early 1930's by the Crocean literary historian Francesco Flora. His volume of essays entitled *La poesia ermetica*, focusing mainly on what he felt to be the obscurantism of Giuseppe Ungaretti, was first published in 1936, thereby giving a name which has clung to a kind of poetry about which he, and Croce, and many other critics of the time, had serious misgivings. In the course of his book Flora remarks that "the adepts—hardly poets—of this New Muse, born of Hermes rather than Apollo, should be called *analogists*, since their true art is the art of analogy."[32] In context it is clear here that by "adept" Flora is referring to the damnable sorcerer's apprenticeship supposedly served by certain Italians to the infamous demon of Mallarmé as well as to the doctrine of occult *correspondances* celebrated in Baudelaire's sonnet. At the close of this review of what he conceives of as a poetry of subjective impressionism passing for cosmic vision, of moral confusion and formal breakdown, he concludes that Ungaretti's *analogismo* is a trans-Alpine import—"The real basis for his tendencies and their development is French, and nineteenth-century French at that . . . the poetics of French symbolism."[33]

As noted in chapter I, the "reformed" hermetic Salvatore Quasimodo basically agrees with Flora: "Ungaretti's hermeticism is of Mallarméan derivation . . ." (see p. 26 above). He views this interwar "movement" as one dominated by what he has called *una poetica della memoria* (a poetics of memory) and finds it wholly out of phase in articulating the social and ethical needs of the contemporary and particularly the postwar world. Through this suggestive phrase of Quasimodo's, one which in its context is offered as a common denominator linking Petrarch, Leopardi and the "poets between wars" (Quasimodo himself included), I find a clue as to how a twentieth-century Italian might legitimately honor Hermes without playing sedulous ape to French symbolism and while sustaining and developing the great lyric tradition of *canto italiano*. The link, originally discovered by Ungaretti, lies with Giacomo Leopardi and the *poetica della memoria* elaborated in his journals—the remarkable *Zibaldone*—and the *Canti*, especially as seen in the monumental Moroncini variorum edition published in 1927.

Certainly memory *as a theme* is a familiar one in the history of Italian literature, from the *lacrimae rerum* revealed to Father Aeneas when he sees the eight murals at Carthage depicting his and the Trojan past, through the great triad of Petrarch, Tasso and Leopardi, to the *grido* or scream of Ungaretti himself for his dead son Antonietto. But a poetics is different from a theme; pictures, flashbacks are one thing, Aeneas *lacrimans* is another, a man suddenly aware in his bones of the irreversible gap between what is and what has been, a man suddenly prey to *il sentimento del tempo;* and in tears. A *poetics* of memory should mean a program for the evocation of such a sentiment; not just the elegiac talking about the past or the episodic and more or less realistic presentation of its speciman days, but a poetry of extraordinary duplicity, creating in us by means of words the illusion of perpetual motion between present and past, a poetry of continuing loss and continuing aspiration to regain, a poetry like memory which hasn't quite mesmerized itself into the hallucination or *sogno* of the past regained. (And who better than Hermes as the patron of such poetry—Hermes Psychopompos, voyager through time as well as space, between here and there, now and then?)

No one who has read Leopardi's *Canti* will be surprised to hear that memory is a central theme of these lyrics, whether the memory of the past greatness of Italy (as in the early *canzoni*) or, as in the idylls, memory centered on the poet's own youth, figures and landscapes drawn from a personal past. Sickly, brilliant, geographically isolated from whatever peers he might have had, deformed, neurotic, and convinced by the suffering of the last twenty years of his life that he could die in agony at any moment, the present—which he called "il vero," the true—held no charms for Leopardi. Hence he lived, as he said, on the *via delle rimembranze,* turned toward a childhood and youth which gave him the pleasurable illusion (*errore beato*) of a better, happier time: better and happier because *not now,* because distant and therefore less ruthlessly defined than the present.

Writing of his travels he says he never felt content, never felt at home in any place until he had memories to attach to it; "memory," he says, "makes the least thing important and dear."[34] And so he lived on the infinite path of memory stretching between present and past definite, the ineffable tense of his poems.

He writes in the journals:

> To the sensitive, imaginative man, who lives—as I have lived for a long time—feeling and imagining continually, the world and its objects are in a certain sense double. With his eyes he will see a tower, a countryside; he will hear with his ears the sound of a steeple bell; and at the same time with his imagination he will see another tower, another countryside, he will hear another bell. In this second sort of objects is all the beauty and delight of things. Sad is that life that sees, hears, senses only simple objects. . . .[35]

This doubleness is due to memory. Between the "simple" object given by senses and ratified by common sense, and the "imagined" or unpresent simulacrum suggested by memory, is created a penumbral zone or vector of emotional density in which the poet locates maximum beauty and delight. The aim of the poetic of memory—wherein memory is not only a subject or theme but the Muse of formal innovation—is to recreate this experienced density, the *effect* of memory, by the choice and manipulation of words and rhythms.

Leopardi's first poetic efforts can be seen as exercises in the quest of the *eighteenth-century* sublime. Believing with Longinus that the end of poetry is "not persuasion but transport,"[36] and seeking to create an emotionally contagious style, he early inaugurates—curious prototype of Ungaretti's search for *canto italiano* a century later—a regime of studies in Italian lyric poetry in search of masters and models of sublimity. His admirations at this stage are Monti, Petrarch and the pindarizing, anti-marinistic poets of the *Seicento:* Filicaia, Testi and above all Chiabrera, whose verses he finds to be sublimity incarnate.

The electric moment in the *Zibaldone* occurs amid the entries for late 1818, when Leopardi, in the course of his reading of Chiabrera, literally stumbles upon a poetic effect offering the possibility of creating the doubling effect of memory by means of words.[37] Chancing upon a wholly unremarkable *canzone* in which the city of Florence appears personified as a grieving woman, he notes in bewilderment that he has misread the way the personification works: he has construed two distinct but mutually supporting images where, on reflection, he sees Chiabrera had intended only one. What impresses him about this is not that hasty reading can distort what in fact is very clear, but that, in the course of this experience, the two images of sorrow, each with its concomitant associations, have appeared to overlap simultaneously, thereby creating an illusion of doubleness. "It is good," he writes, "that the reader be always between images."

Such images, he continues, should not confuse or contradict one another. Nor should either be preferable to the other: that is, neither should be seen as the "right" one. The effect of the two together, one object experienced by the reader from two slightly different stances, would be stereoscopic: an illusion of space, of time, of depth and perspective hollowed out in the slender discrepancy between two views or denotations. He concludes in excitement: "this could be the source of a great art . . . and a supremely poetic effect."

His journal entries between 1818 and 1823 center on the various means of achieving this effect. D'Annunzio once wrote that "the hunchback Leopardi versified like a philologist,"[38] and if we can overlook the characteristic viciousness, the comment has something to it. His health had been ruined by the precocious and prodigious philological researches of his strange adolescence; he now makes use of these researches in realizing the potentials of his newly discovered "great art." Believing that language has its roots in metaphor, that it develops through the proliferation of metaphor, and that, deplorably but inevitably, words originally expressive of sensuous experience harden into neutrality or abstraction where the primitive image is forgotten or ignored, he proposes to achieve the desired double effect by playing the metaphoric etymology of a certain word (costringere: to tie or bind together; vago: the vibrato of yearning or desire) against its conceptual current sense (costringere: to force; vago: vagueness, imprecision). He feels that readers of poetry are more attentive to the historical overtones and values latent in words; still, to be able to respond adequately to his intention, the writer of Italian poetry must use words of Latin origin. Such words as these, which do "not merely offer the single idea of the object signified. . . but certain accessory images as well,"[39] Leopardi calls parole, words with layers of connotations secreted through time. To these he contrasts what he calls termini, terms, which, as the name implies, are words fixed and limited to their "single idea" or denotation. Greek-rooted and scientific vocabularies like French, he feels, abound in termini, hence are antipoetic. The more a language possesses parole, like Italian, and particularly an Italian rooted in the classical language of the Trecento and Quattrocento, uncontaminated by post-Renaissance French influence, the more it is adapted to poetry and to the poetic of memory.

Any reader of the Zibaldone for these years will recall the vast lists of *parole* Leopardi kept; any reader of the Moroncini critical edition of the *Canti* can review the strategic drama of their incorporation in the texture of the poems. (The Moroncini edition may have given Ungaretti the idea of the *Poesie disperse* as an integral part of his *Vita,* with Giuseppe De Robertis as *his* Moroncini.) Moving from the single *parola* to the phrase and period, Leopardi seeks to duplicate the same sense of movement through the dimension of time by the tactful placing of what he called the *pellegrino* (the archaic or antique word or word-form or syntactical turn of phrase) into the context of an unobtrusive plain-style. The despair of his translators, Leopardi's vocabulary is characteristically and deliberately generic: part of his effort to avoid stilling the reverberations of mythohistorical associations by a "terminal" specificity. As with Tasso, certain words or phrases become obsessions to him, felt to be "poetic in themselves." They are, predictably, "purely" Italian, rather general, and relevant to the theme of memory: *irrevocabile, lontano, antico, notturno, mai più* and the like, the sort of words that Valéry in his Teste-phase likened to trombones, for resonant sounding in poetry only.

All these modes are meant, in Leopardi's phrase, "to move the mind swiftly and, as it were, in one sole place from one idea to another."[40] They are intended to give poetry a temporal dimension in which the "meaning" of a word, phrase, period and, ultimately, poem is troubled and stirred by association and connotation toward a past evoked by memory, and in which the journey itself, rather than the arrival at a specific moment with a specific and terminal meaning, constitutes the main attraction, at once poignant and pleasurable. This is the poetics of memory, developed out of Leopardi's observation that "all the pleasures called poetical consist in the perception of similarities and rapports, and in remembering."[41]

The fortunes of Leopardi from his death in 1837 until the second decade of this century are not notable. Carducci, Pascoli and d'Annunzio found little in him that was usable. When, past the turn of the century, the examples and precedent as developed by these three were felt to be inadequate, the symptomatic Enrico Thovez (like a reformed rake ordering a glass of water) called for a return to Leopardi, but to a sentimentalized Leopardi radiating bucolic innocence and the simple life.[42] Elsewhere, as we know, the poet of Trieste, Saba, independently drew on the *Canti* for nourishment during his apprenticeship as poet, but remained for many years to come in isolation. Only with the *Voce* and the *Ronda* do we find a more consequential, and influential, attention paid to this poet who, most largely through the efforts of Giuseppe Ungaretti, was to become the most fruitful traditional influence on Italian poetry for the first half of this century.

Though the "joy" informing *L'Allegria*, the momentary "wreck" or dissolution of the finite in the infinite, is linked to the memory of Leopardi, its treatment by the Ungaretti of this phase is not; Leopardi is not a poet of ecstasy. In general, the poetic of memory does not apply to *L'Allegria*, which is basically concerned with the violent *abolition* of time. Properly speaking, then, and despite the fact that Flora does a great deal of contemptuous quoting from that volume, *L'Allegria* is not hermetic.

Still, in Ungaretti's early poetics of the *parola* where the word or phrase is isolated as though to assay its emotional, tonal weight, or specific gravity, there is a link to be found with the hermetic poetics of memory as derived from the "philological" tendencies of Leopardi. Speaking retrospectively of the period during which the *Sentimento* was composed, Ungaretti has underlined the connection:

> If in those days I meditated upon memory, it was . . . owing to the plenitude of meaning it gave the word (*parola*), endowing it with weight, enlarging it and rendering its prospects profound. A word that has lived for centuries, that through so much history reflects so many different things, that returns us to the presence of so many people whose bodies have disappeared from earth but whose spiritual presence remains when their words are operative within us—a word that, to our joy or sorrow, can make us feel into the live history of that industrious, dramatic people to which we belong—such a word, that a Leopardi had seized upon with such truth and beauty of effect, could still suggest to a poet of today the best means of enriching himself both morally and in his lyric expansiveness. And so it was that I felt my poetry had increasingly to infuse itself (*compenetrarsi*) with memory as its substantial theme.[43]

Like the traditional hendecasyllable—"the natural poetic order" with its "infinite resources"—the literary *parola* also reverberates with its great historical occasions, its aureole of traditional associations. In the *Sentimento*, the *parola* will occupy once more its contributory place in the classic line, that "ancient musical instrument" he had dismantled, scrutinized, and now recreated for his own times.*

In his critical pronouncements during the 1920's, it is clear that Ungaretti is intent on forging a programmatic poetics that will serve

---

* *Vide* his remark in the Angioletti interview (1929): "The difficulty is not to disturb the harmony of our hendecasyllable, not to renounce any of the infinite resources it has achieved during its long life *and at the same time* to be second to none in boldness and adherence to one's own times. . . . "[44]

as rationale and theoretical basis for approaching the considerable difficulties of the *Sentimento* lyrics. Essentially, this poetics integrates his two fields of literary "scholarship," that of French *symbolisme,* centering on Mallarmé (his specialty from Alexandrian days), and that of *canto italiano,* centering on Leopardi. We have already seen how Ungaretti conceives of Leopardi's views on subjective memory and psychological time as profoundly anticipatory of Bergsonian *durée,* and how he continually describes Leopardi's *sentimento del tempo* in positively Bergsonian terms: time, for Leopardi, is "relative and inward," a mobile mode of consciousness "moving between present and past," a "fluid symbol," a "mirror of psychological life," etc.[45] In the important "Innocence et mémoire" written for the *NRF* in 1926, he asserts that there is an intimate connection between Leopardi and Mallarmé in their "unappeasable thirst for innocence" and the fact that they are *deux philologues:* ". . . two philologists, drawn above all to that which is indefinable in the word, to the musical power of the word, to that substance of the word which seems least perishable to them, and most universal. . . ." Their mutual theme and evocative concern is his own: ". . . to make surge forth, out of a contemplated nature, the apparitions of memory. Memory, man's profundity."[46]

Mallarmé's basic prosodic conservatism, as described in his meditations on *vers libre* and that "definitive jewel" the alexandrine in his "Crise de vers," provided one important model for Ungaretti's own "return" to traditional measures. Another, of course, was Leopardi, whose formal experiments and innovations always occurred in a traditional metric context: ". . . the hendecasyllables that are most contemporary and most *ours* are . . . those of Giacomo Leopardi . . . Leopardi has removed from the hendecasyllable all bombast, all slickness, all externality. He has left it, I should say, silent. This is poetry to dream on, not for declaimers."[47]

Again, the deliberate elusiveness characteristic of Ungaretti's language during this phase has its ancestry not only in Leopardi's cultivation of the *vago,* the indeterminate and therefore suggestive effect, but in Mallarmé's self-styled *vague littérature* where mystical effects are built by means of oblique allusions and precisely blurred evocations. The "demon" of analogy who haunted Mallarmé and his imagistic repertoire found another voluntary victim in Ungaretti, who spoke enthusiastically of his own ellipses in an interview of 1929:

> I mobilize brusque transpositions from reality to dream; ambiguous usage of words in their concrete and abstract senses; *unexpected* switching of a subject so that it functions as object, or vice versa;

constant and split-second interchanges of grammatical properties of various parts of discourse. I don't recall any longer who, but someone [Reverdy] said—and said well—that modern poetry proposes to put the most distant things in touch with one another. The greater the distance, the more superior the poetry. When such contacts give light, poetry is achieved. In short, I use and perhaps abuse elliptical forms.[48]

But such strategies as detailed here are also beholden to Leopardi's conception of the supreme poetic effect: to keep the reader "between images," "to move the mind swiftly and, as it were, in one sole place from one idea to another."

When the controversy for and against "hermeticism" broke out in the 1930's, one of the main accusations levelled against it was its lack of *italianità*. Ungaretti's main response* was to point out the example of *his* Leopardi. In 1936, he began his association with universities, lecturing primarily on Leopardi first in São Paolo, Brazil, and then, from 1942 on, at the University of Rome. Ungaretti's extraordinary readings of Leopardi's "L'infinito" and "Alla primavera" stress the *poetica della memoria* and the "hermetic" strategies threading both lyrics. In another discourse he praises the *indefinitezza*, the suggestivity and musical evocativeness of Leopardi's language, connecting "Alla primavera" to Mallarmé's "Après-midi d'un Faune" on the grounds of their both being moving expressions of "that uncertain state between dream and memory." And his lecture on "Alla primavera" concludes: "Siamo arrivati all'ermetismo, sisignori." (Yes gentlemen, we've arrived at hermeticism!) It is in the epilogue to this discourse that he makes his boast, cited above, regarding his crucial recovery of Leopardi. Those few Leopardi lectures that have been thus far published[50] make an ideal model for a methodology of reading the suave complexities of Ungaretti's own work, beginning with *Sentimento del tempo*.

❉   ❉   ❉

Dall'ampia ansia dell'alba
Svelata alberatura.

Dolorosi risvegli.

Foglie, sorelle foglie,
Vi ascolto nel lamento.

Autunni,
Moribonde dolcezze.

* Others were: to laugh the title off as a mere academic invention; to assert all "high" poetry "difficult" and in that sense "hermetic" or closed to the crowd.[49]

O gioventú,
Passata è appena l'ora del distacco.

Cieli alti della gioventú,
Libero slancio.

E già sono deserto.

Perso in questa curva malinconia.

Ma la notte sperde le lontananze.

Oceanici silenzi,
Astrali nidi d'illusione,

O notte.

By the ample yearnings of the dawn / unveiled orchards. / Dolorous awakenings. / Leaves, sister leaves, / I listen to you in the lament. / Autumns, / dying sweetnesses. / O youth, / the hour of leavetaking is scarcely past. / High skies of youth, / free thrust. / And already I am desert. / Lost in this curved melancholy. / But the night disperses distances. / Oceanic silences, / astral nests of illusion, / O night.

This is the first lyric in *Prime,* the first chapter of the *Sentimento.* The poem is dated 1919, although the capitals and punctuation only appear in 1933; the *Poesie disperse* also tells us that an occasional use of italics for emotional emphasis and a handful of supplementary lines have been suppressed over the years. But through the sparse details of an awakening in an autumnal dawn, the central theme of the coming of age and the loss of youth's vitality unveils itself like the apparitional verticals of the treetrunks in the agitated light of dawn so elegantly and hypnotically assonanced in the first stanza.

In its concluding stanzas, the poem also involves a kind of *naufragio* akin to that of Leopardi's "L'Infinito."* Thus the overpowering thought of the infinite—urged by massive elemental adjectives like "oceanic" and "astral"—is, when set against the barren *paesaggio* of middle age, intimately consoling. Hence the "nests" of illusion, where the tragic vector of personal time is swamped in what seems to be endless space. It is interesting to note that the hendecasyllabled third stanza from the end ("Ma la notte sperde le lontananze") originally read, as a line of free verse, "la morte sperde le lontananze"; the poet's substitution of "night" for "death" of course advances the theme of

* Stanza three, of the leaves and lament, also recalls "L'Infinito"'s *cara siepe* and the wind heard rustling through its branches.

desperate illusion, as well as keying the final line ("O notte") with its mixture of evocation, prayer and sigh.*

Metrically the poem achieves a nice balance between the old poetics of the *parola* and the newly-reconstituted poetic line. Of its total of seventeen lines three (9, 13, 14) are hendecasyllables, eight are *settenari*, two others either *quinari* or *novenari;* all are natural subdivisions of the eleven-syllable master verse. All of these ten shorter lines group themselves about the hendecasyllables, of which they constitute what may be thought of as caesural rests. Three of the remaining lines are fragmented, or isolated *parole* (*Autunni, O gioventú, O notte*) of particular dramatic-affective importance. Hence the general rhythmic effect of the poem is systaltic, an oscillation between *parola* and traditionally measured line, between a maximal tension and a dispersion or relaxing; an oscillation sensuously equivalent to the interplay of despair and consoling illusion that makes up the subject. The use of alliteration (l's) and "deepening" assonance (a's to o's) particularly in the opening lines seems to reenforce through linked sound values the compounded despair of that overture. Thus an elaborate "musical" effect is created which unlike, say, d'Annunzio's or Quasimodo's, is put at the service of a something (an experience, a feeling) beyond its own suave self.

Prime, as its position and dates (1919–24) indicate, is a transitional chapter. Rebay has documented in detail the Mallarmean reminiscences that are rife in it[51]—sometimes, as in the four-part "Le stagioni" (The Seasons), to the detriment of Ungaretti's own voice. Its final poem ("Ricordo d'Affrica": Memory of Africa) is worth considering in its first and final versions as illustrative of the problems and tentative solutions occupying Ungaretti over this period. It first appeared in the magazine *Il Convegno* in 1924 with the title "Sera" (Evening):

> Ora non piú tra la valle sterminata
> e il mare calmo m'apparterò, né umili,
> di remote età, udrò piú sciogliersi, piano,
> nell'aere limpido, squilli. Né miro
> piú Diana agile che la luce nuda

---

* This first poem in the *Sentimento* appears to be alluded to and, in a sense, recapitulated in the volume's last poem, dated in 1932 and titled "Silenzio stellato" (Starred Silence):

> E gli alberi e la notte
> Non si muovono piú
> Se non da nidi.

And the trees and the night/move no more/if not from nests.
Surely here again the nests are star-clusters which *seem* to lovingly control and console the night-enveloped earth.

(nelle speglio di gelo s'abbaglia, ove
lascia cadere il guardo arroventa
la brama, e un'infinita ombra rimane).
Torno da lontano, ed eccomi umano.
Il mare m'è una linea evanescente,
e un nappo di miele che piú non gusto,
per non morire di sete, mi pare
la valle, e Diana com'una collana
d'opali, e su un seno nemmeno palpita.
Ah! quest'è l'ora che annuvola e smemora.

Now no more between the interminable valley / and the calm sea
will I withdraw, nor, / from remote ages hear any longer dissolving,
humble, / in the limpid air, gently, the sound of bells. Nor wonder /
I any longer at agile Diana whom the light strips naked / (in the
icy mirror she dazzles, where / she lets her gaze fall / desire sears and
an infinite shadow remains). / I return from afar, and here am I
human. / The sea is an evanescent line for me, / and a goblet of
honey that I taste no more / —so that I may not die of thirst—seems
to me / the valley, and Diana, like a necklace / of opals on a breast
throbs not at all. / Ah! this is the hour that clouds and disremembers.

In this approximately hendecasyllabled, unrhymed, fifteen-lined ghost
of a sonnet, the critical ninth line ("Torno da lontano, ed eccomi
umano") baldly serves as hinge or turn between the fabulous African
past—where an Acteon-like youth can spy on bathing goddesses and
catch mythic syllables in the luminous air over sea and desert—and
his deflated "humanity" where such magic is only a memory. In these
lines we catch a glimpse of what could be a tendency towards an
aesthetic neoclassicism of the *Ronda* variety: Diana in particular
seems a conventional literary "grace" with no personal resonance
involved. The rhythmic patterns are perfunctory and frigid.

The final (1943) version—now "Ricordo d'Affrica"—runs as follows:

Non piú ora tra la piana sterminata
E il largo mare m'apparterò, né umìli
Di remote età, udrò piú sciogliersi, chiari,
Nell'aria limpida, squilli; né piú
Le grazie acerbe andrà nudando
E in forme favolose esalterà
Folle la fantasia,
Né dal rado palmeto Diana apparsa
In agile abito di luce,
Rincorrerò
(In un suo gelo altiera s'abbagliava,

Ma le seguiva gli occhi nel posarli
Arroventando disgraziate brame,
Per sempre *Torna da lontano ed eccomi uma...*
Infinito velluto).

È solo linea vaporosa il mare
Che un giorno germogliò rapace,
E nappe d'un miele, non piú gustato
Per non morire di sete, mi pare
La piana, e a un seno casto, Diana vezzo
D'opàli, ma nemmeno d'invisibile
Non palpita.

Ah! questa è l'ora che annùvola e smemóra.

No more between the interminable plain / and the spacious sea
will I withdraw, nor, / from remote ages, hear any longer dissolving,
humble, / in the limpid air, clear, the sound of bells; nor any more /
will go stripping naked the unripe, young, immature, bitter-tasting
[all senses of *acerbe*] graces / nor will exalt them into fabulous
forms / my mad fantasy, / nor from the sparse palm-grove Diana
appearing / in agile habit of light / will I pursue / (in her chill,
haughty, she dazzled, / but there followed her eyes when she stilled
them, / searing unlucky desires, / for always, / infinite velvet.) /
It is only vaporous line the sea / that once upon a time blossomed
lustily, / and goblet of a honey, no more tasted / in order not to die
of thirst, seems to me / the plain, and at a chaste breast, Diana a
necklace / of opals, but not even with the invisible / does it throb.
Ah! this is the hour that clouds and disremembers.

In "Ricordo d'Affrica" can be found one of the rare examples of an
Ungarettian revision by amplification rather than condensation: there
are now twenty-three lines rather than fifteen (though some of them
are extremely brief phrases isolated for focus). What have been
elaborated are the "fabulous forms," the quasi-erotic dream-visions of
the sylphlike graces and Diana. The final effect is similar in kind, as
Rebay points out, to kindred visions in "Alla primavera" and the
"Après-midi." The flat *"miro,"* wondering-at Diana of the original has
been replaced by a sequence altogether more sensual and passionate.
He now "pursues" her: the ambivalence of the pursuit, its double
character as curse and blessing is pointed up by adjectives like *acerbe*
and *disgraziate* and, above all, by the hesitance and erotic suggestive-
ness of lines like "Per sempre/Infinito velluto" which replace the
perfunctory and chilly "un 'infinita ombra rimane."

The field of the poem is "that uncertain state between dream and
memory" which he has called characteristic Leopardi-Mallarmé terri-

tory. The element of dream which was only implicit in a verb like *miro* is now made elegantly explicit in letter-linked sequences like *"forme favolose. . . . Folle la fantasia"* where the withholding of the clause's subject (now "fantasia" rather than "I") until the end of the clause underlines the subjective pathos not only of the stripping and exulting but of the pursuit itself. We experience the evocation of a subjectivity moving through time rather than a show of slides on the topic of the antique past.

Particular word substitutions are of some auxiliary importance. The "valley" has become a "plain" and the waterline "vaporous" rather than "evanescent"* probably in the interests of Afro-biographical accuracy. The heard bells of remote antiquity are now vivid and "clear" instead of swooning in a conventional *piano*. The original confrontation with a wretched present reality (the old line 9) has now become an interstrophic bar of white, so that the present seems continually to dissolve (up to the final line: "Ah! questa è l'ora . . ." into the aching memory of another (hallucinatory) order of experience. But above all, Diana herself has been metamorphosed from a bookish allusion into an authentic embodiment of an impossible sensual hankering for the past. The stock epithet for her prowess ("Diana agile"), in the circumstances overly athletic, has become an elaborately cadenced and assonanced evocation of an aureole of supple light (". . . dal rádo palméto Diána appársa/In ágile abito di lúce.") The original Ovidian mirrorlike pool where she bathed ("speglio di gelo") as at Gargaphie is now contracted into an analogue for her divine distance and otherness ("un suo gelo") paradoxically arousing phantoms of passional heat and thick sensual longing ("infinite velvet") in her stricken pursuer. Finally, all these elements (her icy brilliance, remoteness, erotic influence) are fused in the last image— no longer distanced as a simile—of an opalescent necklace on a *chaste breast* that no longer sensuously responds (*palpita*) to the invisible presence of divinity—an extraordinarily complex image of metaphysical absence leading inevitably to the *grido* of the now-isolated last line.

Stylistically, the final version is notable for its augmented elegance. The heightened sonic interlinkings effected through alliteration and assonance, the elaborate periodic structure and Latinate inversions (generally the verbs are placed early and their governing subjects only towards the end of clauses) are instances of what Leopardi called

---

* This adjective also occurs in a contemporarily revised version of an old *Allegria di naufragi* poem ("Levante") whose first three lines now read "La linea/vaporosa muore/al lontano cerchio del cielo" (The vaporous/line dies/at the distant circle of the sky).

the *pellegrino,* that stylistic sumptuosity of which his "Primavera" is a prime example and whose function is not only to "match" the subject and so provide a kind of memory-saturated articulation, but also, through its very reconditeness (which can only be clarified by a scrupulous attention to syntax over large stretches), to provide an aura of remoteness and strangeness which Ungaretti, like his two masters, finds increasingly necessary in order to express the poetic blur of longing memory and dream.

Finally we can note the heightened pathetic irony of "Ricordo d'Affrica" in the way in which it so to speak revives and emotionally reconstructs what grammatically it writes off. The entire poem is built on a skeleton of negatives—*non piú ora, né, né piú, Né non piú, non, nemmeno, non*—which dwell upon what ("really") was and is no more. Yet, as it happens in the course of negation, memory is stirred. The result is that recollection connives with resurrected dreams to effect via poetry a momentary triumph over the barren terminus of "this hour."

✿ ✿ ✿

"La sera" was submitted to another reworking before it eventually became "Ricordo d'Affrica." In 1925, a year after its initial publication, Ungaretti elaborated it into a pastoral dialogue for two characters, Man and Echo. Man's speech stays very much as it was in the "Sera" stage, but in the dialogue it is preceded by two lines by Echo:

> Il battito d'ale d'una colomba
> d'altri diluvi ascolto.

The flutter of a dove's wings / from other floods I hear.

This observation, contracted to a single hendecasyllable ("D'altri diluvi una colomba ascolto."), was later detached entirely fróm the "Ricordo" to make up the opening poem of the next *capitolo* of the *Sentimento,* "La fine di Crono" (The End of Chronos).* This chapter and the one following ("Sogni e accordi" [Dreams and Accords])

---

* A precedent for such runic brevity (apart from Ungaretti's own "M'illumino / d'immenso") can be found in one of Apollinaire's *Alcools,* the self-sufficient alexandrine entitled "Chantre": "Et l'unique cordeau des trompettes marines." But the punning gaiety of this (see the Meridith-Steegmuller notes to Meridith's translation of *Alcools*) is entirely alien to the spirit of nostalgia and hope expressed in Ungaretti's line. "Una colomba" (as it is now called) ought to be read as an epigraph or motto for its chapter, a poem about surviving, if only via dream or memory. It is a poem by the way which threw Flora into paroxysms of outraged sarcasm (what dove from what other floods? and what on earth did it say? and so on.) over Ungaretti's capriciousness and refusal to "communicate." See *La poesia ermetica,* pp. 146–47.

seem to me, with the exception of the great "Inno alla morte" (Hymn to Death) which I want to discuss along with the "hymns" and "legends" written later, to focus on the consolations of dream, precarious and intermittent (but renewable) as they may be. That preliminary *colomba* whose flight is heard is one such *accordo* or harmony struck, and there are others, drawn largely from the mythic and pastoral conventions of antiquity. This vision, which incorporates both impermanence and persistence, is outlined very simply in "Stelle" (Stars):

> Tornano in alto ad ardere le favole.
>
> Cadranno colle foglie al primo vento.
>
> Ma venga un altro soffio,
> Ritornerà scintillamento nuovo.

Return to flame on high the fables. /
They will fall with the leaves at the first wind. /
But come another puff, / will return new scintillation.

Such a general title as the "End of Chronos" appears to suggest several things: a kind of stasis or pause in the eternality of myth (allegorically construed the end of that old god is equivalent to the end of time), and the beginning, according to myth-genealogy, of the Olympians. The *poem* of this title synaesthetically presents a strange *grido* or cry at the twilight hour* and hymeneally celebrates the coming of the starry night in which the Lord (*il Signore*)

> . . . riporge l'Olimpo,
> Fiore eterno di sonno.

. . . once more sets forth Olympus, eternal flower of sleep.

Thus is proposed a dream poetry with its roots in the Arcadian age of gold, but fevered, troubled, precarious, as with the consciousness that one is sleeping, consorting with the apparitions of wakening desires.

The most elaborate and beautiful of these dream-flowers is "L'isola" (The Island), a classic elaboration of the landing first presented ten years previously in "Il porto sepolto."

---

* Doubtless the cry of the failing light itself. In "Grido" (1928) Ungaretti writes of the "Grido torbido e alato/Che la luce quando muore trattiene" (The turbid and soaring cry/with which light resists as it dies).

A una proda ove sera era perenne
Di anziane selve assorte, scese,
E s'inoltrò
E lo richiamò rumore di penne
Ch'erasi sciolto dallo stridulo
Batticuore dell'acqua torrida,
E una larva (languiva
E rifioriva) vide;
Ritornato a salire vide
Ch'era una ninfa e dormiva
Ritta abbraciata a un olmo.

In sé da simulacro a fiamma vera
Errando, giunse a un prato ove
L'ombra negli occhi s'addensava
Delle vergini come
Sera appiè degli ulivi;
Distillavano i rami
Una pioggia pigra di dardi,
Qua pecore s'erano appisolate
Sotto il liscio tepore,
Altre brucavano
La coltre luminosa;
Le mani del pastore erano un vetro
Levigato da fioca febbre.

At a shore where evening was perpetual / with ancient thickening woods, he descended, / and went forth / and rumor of wings called to him / released from the shrill / heartbeat of the torrid water, / and an apparition (it was languishing, / reflowering) he saw; / turning to ascend he saw / it was a nymph and she was sleeping / upright, arms about an elm. /
Within himself from semblance to true flame / wandering, he reached a meadow where / the shadow thickened in the eyes / of virgins like / evening at the foot of olive trees; / the boughs distilled / a lazy rain of arrows, / here sheep were drowsing / beneath the suave warmth, / others browsed upon / the luminous cover; / the shepherd's hands were a glass / laved by faint fever.

This island, like Olympus and the fabulous starlight, has its source in a yearning for Arcadian innocence that can find its only conceivable satisfaction in the exfoliations of dream—the entire *paesaggio* with its inhabitants are the products of that ambiance. One of the wonders of "L'isola" is its evocation of the erotic atmosphere enveloping this land of heart's desire, close and sultry, Thus, alongside the brooding shadows of woods and eyes, the dim points of light, the postures of fatigue or sleep—the focusing on a single detail of the human figures (the virgins' eyes, the shepherd's hand) contributes to the odd air of suspension or spell—the sense of a hovering eroticism is promoted by investing the landscape with intimate details drawn from the dreamer's state. Torpor, the flush and throbbing pulsing of the waters, the pumping larva, the fever-worn hands, all dreamily develop the passive suggestiveness of the nymph's posture and the dark ambivalence of the virgins. All of this is entirely alien to what can only be called the "healthy sexuality"—all bites and wrestling—of Mallarmé's faun.

But "L'isola" is more than the evocation, via analogy, of a passive state. It is also a narrative involving a landing, an exploration, and discovery of a sort; the direction is away from shadow and blurred synaesthesia towards great light and distinction. Thus from woods, perennial evening and the "rumor" of wings rising from the water the voyager arrives at a meadow with virgins, sheep, a shepherd: light pencils through the interstices of the branches and soon the entire prospect is luminous (even the shepherd's hands are transparent, flesh eaten away by desire). And the diaphramic throbbing of the *larva* becomes, on second sight, a nymph embracing an elm.* The character of exploration and discovery is presented directly at the start of the second stanza, ("In sé da simulacro a fiamma vera/Errando"), where a progress from unreality to reality is affirmed and the degree of reality is related to deepening absorption in fantasy or dream—the "true flame".** Does the poem "say" then that only in dream is truth and illumination? Yes, but on one level only. "L'isola" partakes of the "irony" that Ungaretti admires in Leopardi and Mallarmé. Even as *il naufragar* in "L'infinito" is both a word of disaster

---

* *Larva* is a prime example of Leopardian *parola*, meaning both the immature form of any insect or animal and ghost or apparition.

** The line cited here is the only one in the entire poem which states the "inward" nature of the landscape and journey, though this is of course suggested *passim* by imagistic means. It "rescues" the original simile from what Flora might call the "hermetic" inscrutability of ellipsis or subjective analogizing. Interestingly, the progress was reversed in the original version of the poem. The second stanza began

> Errando il pensiero da quella
> fiamma vera al simulacro . . .

suggesting that the poet thought less of the poem's narrative dimension than of its function of conjuring a dream-state. I am reminded of the early version of a detail in Yeat's "Lake Isle of Innisfree" where "noontide there be all aglimmer, and midnight be a purple glow . . . " (in the definitive version these attributes are exactly reversed)—specific naturalistic description meant nowhere near as much to Yeats as exotic suggestiveness and "enchantment." The "Lake Isle" and "L'isola" belong to the same dream-terrain, though Yeats' region of it lacks the erotic strata of Ungaretti's.

signifying obliteration in the void and a word of joy signifying ecstatic union with the cosmos,[52] so the dreamed island is at once the home of a higher order of reality than that occupied by the "simulacra" of so-called waking life *and* the phantom-projection of an exorbitant and feverish desire, a desire that, as the dominant images of suspension and immobility suggest, takes solace solely in the subjective ramifications of its own fantasies. It is, in short, a sumptuous and rarefied *isola* of illusion, alluring and engrossing and ultimately as fatally misleading as the mirage to the wandering nomad.

✻   ✻   ✻

"L'isola": an uneasy dream, a siren song. Surely the siren is that "unappeasable thirst for innocence" Ungaretti reads in his masters and finds at the heart of his own "nominalism." In the beautiful "Sirene" of this period he invokes that thirst as the *funesto spirito* that leads him deeper into dream . . .

> Funesto spirito
> Che accendi e turbi amore,
> Affine io torni senza requie all'alto
> Con impazienza le apparenze muti,
> E già, prima ch'io giunga a qualche meta,
> Non ancora deluso
> M'avvinci ad altro sogno.
>
> Uguale a un mare che irrequieto e blando
> Da lungi porga e celi
> Un isola fatale,
> Con varietà d'inganni
> Accompagni chi non dispera, a morte.

Mournful spirit / who kindles and troubles love, / in order that I turn without rest towards on high / with impatience, you shift appearances, / and already, before I attain to any goal, / not yet deluded, / bind me to another dream. /
Comparable to a sea that restless and smooth / from afar puts forth and conceals / a fatal island, / with variety of deceptions / you accompany he who does not despair to death.

The second half of the *Sentimento del tempo* testifies to a crisis of despair which will eventually lead Ungaretti "back" to the Roman Catholicism of his early upbringing. In the terminology of the 1922 *Ronda* essay (see above, p. 168), it is not so much the "mystery" of things that plagues him as his shaken faith in the "measure"—that is to say, in "an order of (man-created) images that deliberately defy death," the expressive means through which man envisages and to a certain extent controls the world in which he finds himself. In 1922, we recall, Ungaretti could consider the terrestrial world with equanimity as "man's continual invention." And the word was "magical". . .

> . . . poesia
> è il mondo l'umanità
> la propria vita
> fioriti dalla parola . . .

In 1930, however, his view of the human measure and its efficacy had drastically altered: "Each man is indeed close to being locked up in the solitude of his own mind, walled within a prison of matter, that is to say in relativity, where a man like Pascal can find nothing better to offer human society than this scornful declaration: the world is the work of the imagination."[53] Of course he is quoting not only Pascal but himself—what was once a point of human pride now tastes of ashes. In the recent past he had rated "the primordial movement of feeling and imagination" above "wisdom or (religious) ritual" (see above, p. 168); in "L'isola," as we know, he had somewhat uneasily located "the true flame" in the splendid images bequeathed by cultural memory. By 1928 certainly this uneasiness had developed into a sickening awareness of solipsism, of the abysmal gap separating presumptive human knowledge from the unknowable truth of things that is its mocking goal, of the crushing irony of the mortal "measure"—scientific theory or religious belief, carven name or poetic word—when set against immortal mystery.

According to Ungaretti, it is from the second half of the *Sentimento* that all his subsequent books take their departure,

> a departure that stresses a man's dismay at finding himself involved in an increasingly complicated and fragmented process whose cause—during his earthly passage—he can never know. . . . Another war was starting to declare its proximity: at that moment (1928) one after another there burst from my soul, lacerating me, my "Pietà" and the other *Hymns*. The lack of communication between men, the developing political conditions laden with inevitable horrors, other personal factors—all placed me in a state of sheer desperation.[54]

In these years he began a series of brief retreats, "struggling to resolve my uncertainties before the idea of the Supernatural,"[55] to the monasteries at Subiaco and Montecassino. Returning from Subiaco to his

Marino home in 1928, for example, he speaks of how "I suddenly knew that the Word of the liturgical year had made itself close to my soul: in those times the *Hymns* would be born in me."[56]

The *Inni,* constituting the crucial chapter of *Sentimento del tempo,* are by no means the songs of thanksgiving to God that their name implies. They express severe crisis, more specialized than Ungaretti's own later description of it ("extreme disquietude, perplexity, anguish and fright over man's destiny"[57]) allows. What is in question is the relevance of the poetic word to any order of reality beyond a single individual's hopes and fears and projected imaginings; the whole matter of poetry and what it is to be a poet—egotistic entertainment, private pastime, *or* raid on the *Inconnu,* vision of some higher truth— is in the balance. Ungaretti's temperamental "nominalism" nourished by his scholarship under poet-seers like the *symbolistes* would make any lower conception of poetry meaningless. Yet this whole lofty idea of his calling has been thrown in doubt.

The first hymn, an inferior variant of "Sirene," is chiefly of interest for its symptomatic treatment of the dilemma of solipsism in orthodox "Pauline" terms. The mind's imaginative faculty is said to "corrupt" and even "damn" its possessor through radiating "untrue light" on its surroundings; its beguilements are a *felice colpa* (happy sin or fault) to the fallen creature who cheers his benighted existence by means of them. It is fascinating to note how even Ungaretti's interpretations of traditional artists are transformed by his personal preoccupations at this time. The atheist Leopardi for example is seen as the inventor of a "Christian psychology," as profoundly "a Christian who sees the trace of sin everywhere." Ungaretti's "La pietà," the longest and most tor- mented of the hymns, is clearly related to his experience of Michel- angelo who, "as incapable of renouncing Plato as Christ, taken with an equal love for the illusory flesh and the redeemed spirit, struggles vainly to discover the face of divinity in a world full of the germs of corruption. He will only be able to unleash his internal hell in the cry (*cri, grido*) of his *Pietà.*"[58]

In his own "Pietà" Ungaretti too cries out his torments and self- doubts:

> . . . Ho popolato di nomi il silenzio.
>
> Ho fatto a pezzi cuore e mente
> Per cadere in servitú di parole?
>
> Regno sopra fantasmi. . . .

I have peopled the silence with names.

Have I shattered heart and mind / only to fall into servitude of words?
I reign over phantoms. . . .

In this desolate vision God is "only a dream," another name. The poem closes in the despair of absolute metaphysical solitude:

> L'uomo, monotono universo,
> Crede allargarsi i beni
> E dalle sue mani febbrili
> Non escono senza fine che limiti.
>
> Attaccato sul vuoto
> Al suo filo di ragno,
> Non teme e non seduce
> Se non il proprio grido.
>
> Ripara il logorio alzando tombe,
> E per pensarti, Eterno,
> Non ha che le bestemmie.

Man, monotonous universe, / thinks to increase his goods, / and from his fevered hands / endlessly issue only limits. /
Fastened above the void / on his spider's thread / he fears and is tempted / by his own cry alone. /
He repairs decay by raising tombs, / and to think of you, O Eternal, / has only blasphemies. /

So much for "nominalism," the scratching of shallow, solipsistic incantations against a ruthless weathering upon frail stone, as pathetic a bid for immortality as the tumulus of his Palinurus "which shows the vanity of everything—struggling, pleading—*everything* that depends upon the wretched earthly vicissitudes of man."[59]

The other major hymn is "Caino" (Cain) which, appropriately employing Old Testament rather than pagan mythology, invokes that fabulous outlaw as "the image of the heart," passionate, dangerous, ultimately unsoundable. It is the memory's addition to such images (phantasmal counterpart to the Dianas and fatal islands of earlier poems) which blocks—like Michelangelo's love for the "illusory flesh" —the soul's hunger for innocence:

> Figlia indiscreta della noia,
> Memoria, memoria incessante,
> Le nuvole della tua polvere,
> Non c'è vento che se le porti via?

> Gli occhi mi tornerebbero innocenti,
> Vedrei la primavera eterna
>
> E, finalmente nuova,
> O memoria, saresti onesta.

Indiscreet daughter of weary spleen, / memory, incessant memory, / the clouds of your dust, / is there no wind to bear them away? My eyes would turn innocent, / I would see eternal spring. / And new at last, / O memory, you would be honest.

Such paradise regained as the last two stanzas allow is couched in conditionals dependent upon an impossible development: the sublimation or spiritualization of memory. No such cleansing wind will blow; the image of the heart is the stained and raging Cain.

Yet juxtaposed to the *Inni* is a chapter which better deserves the name. These are the *Leggende*, "legends" preserved in the poet's memory of certain events (a first love affair, his "discovery" of Italy in 1914) and people he has known, his mother, an officer during the war, the Futurist poet Auro D'Alba's young daughter, who committed suicide. Together they make up a gallery of recollected innocence; this of course is why they are legendary. The times are over, the people are dead, yet their innocence "resists" oblivion (like, long ago, Mohammed Sceab) in the cherishing memory of their elegist.

Thus, in his memorial to Ophelia D'Alba, Ungaretti celebrates a transformation already wistfully touched upon in "Caino"—"Gli occhi mi tornerebbero innocenti. . . ." In his reflective memory Ophelia's remembered eyes grow increasingly unearthly—*pensosi . . . begli . . . sazi . . . immortali* (pensive, beautiful, surfeited—that is, with the illusions of this world—immortal) and now gaze upon only deathless things,

> Emblemi eterni, nomi,
> Evocazioni pure. . . .

Eternal emblems and names, pure evocations. . . .

The beautiful "La madre" evokes the simple piety of his dead mother "kneeling, as in life, like a statue before the Eternal," conducting him "when (his) heart with its last beat will have made the wall of shadow fall" before the Lord for pardon. In "Il Capitano" the officer first invoked against the "crushing humility" of war is purified by his serene death into the emblem of innocence:

> Parve di piume.

He seemed made of feathers.

This image of becoming light, angelically weightless and winged, is recurrent in Ungaretti. The loss of gravity is implicit, of course, in the ecstatic moments of illumination threading *L'Allegria*—it will be recalled that its final poem was a prayer to rise ("weight become light on me") and shipwreck in a "limpid . . . sphere." The closed and inward-gazing eyes of Ophelia D'Alba are, with her death, "henceforth deprived of weight"; later his dead son Antonietto will be seen as so light and graceful in his life *that in the nature of things below he had to be crushed*—"Non avresti potuto non spezzarti": How could you *not* be broken? Such images and memories provide a counterpoint to the anguish and despair of the *Inni*.

But the hope permeating Ungaretti's legends is rooted in the conception of death as precondition to release: a *sentimento del tempo* must logically involve the *sentimento della morte*. Death's gift may be oblivion or "innocence"—perhaps these two words are ironic synonyms; at any rate it is desirable, and the closing *capitoli* of the volume (*Leggende, Inni* and the six songs comprising the appropriately named *finale*,* *La morte meditata* [Death Meditated]) are obsessed with its approach.

> Ti odo nel fluire della mente
> Approfondire lontananze. . . .

I hear you in the flowing of my mind / deepening distances. . . .

so the poet addresses death in the first *canto* of *La morte meditata;* in the second,

> Ti odo cantare come una cicala
> Nella rosa abbrunata dei riflessi. . . .

I hear you singing like a locust / in the dew-glistening mourning of the rose. . . .**

In the earlier "Inno alla morte" (Hymn to Death) from *La Fine di Crono* Ungaretti had bid his "youthful emblem," Love, farewell ("mi pesano gli anni venturi" [My coming years weigh on me]), turning to death as an ironic paramour whose embrace gives blessed oblivion:

---

* At least in the first (1933) edition; the definitive closing chapter *L'Amore*, was added in 1936.

** It was in this period that Ungaretti began his study and translating of William Blake. Surely these lines are a reminiscence and transposition of the "Sick Rose" where no locust but an "invisible worm . . . Has found out they bed/Of crimson joy,/And his dark secret love/Does thy life destroy."

. . . Immemore sorella, morte,
L'uguale mi farai del sogno
Baciandomi.

Avrò il tuo passo,
Andrò senza lasciare impronta.

Mi darai il cuore immobile
D'un iddio, sarò innocente,
Non avrò piú pensieri né bontà.

Colla mente murata,
Cogli occhi caduti in oblio,
Farò da guida alla felicità.

. . . Immemorial sister, death, / dream's equal you will make of
me / by kissing me. /
    I shall have your step, / I shall go without leaving trace. /
    You will give me the immobile heart / of a god, I shall be inno-
cent, / I shall have no longer thoughts nor goodness. /
    With my mind walled up, / with my eyes sunken into oblivion, /
I shall be as guide unto felicity.

The stately movement of the hendecasyllables, the slightly abstract
elegance of the diction and imagery, may hood the total nihilism
carried in these terrible lines, where innocence is equated to nonbeing
and the void is christened *felicità*. "Inno alla morte" marks an early,
desperate stage of Ungaretti's preoccupation with death as, along with
memory which records its claims and the sense of passing time which
acknowledges its nearing, his chosen "field" and theme. Death had
been present during the war of course, but had functioned to inten-
sify his feeling for life, a curious source for *allegria*. In the *Morte
meditata* series of 1932 the sardonic despair of the "Inno" has been
tempered, through contemplation and "retreat," to a more than
notional acceptance. Death is a *gentildonna*, canto five tells us, who
passes like a leaf and leaves the fire of autumn on the trees.
    The title poem "Sentimento del tempo" was composed originally
as part of the *Morte meditata* sequence and has been placed in the
volume as the last of the *Inni*, providing a note of reconciliation to
that tormented chapter.

E per la luce giusta,
Cadendo solo un'ombra viola
Sopra il giogo meno alto,
La lontananza aperta alla misura,

> Ogni mio palpito, come usa il cuore,
> Ma ora l'ascolto,
> T'affreta, tempo, a pormi sulle labbra
> Le tue labbra ultime.

And through the just light, / only a violet shadow falling / upon the lesser peak, / the distance open to measure / —my every heartbeat, as is the heart's wont; / but now I hear it / —O hasten, time, to place upon my lips / your final lips.

This too is a "hymn" to death—time's last caress—though nothing like the earlier poem of that name. Here terrestrial existence in space and time is pastorally reviewed as a mobile proportion of light to shadow which is accepted as "giusta," both precise and equitable, mensurable against the scale of the calmly beating heart. (Compare its desperate and erratic pounding in "Caino.") Momentarily at least a truce has been struck between the mortal measure pulsing in the wrist and the mystery surrounding it—like an offered embrace rather than a siege. There is a temporary solace in the reflection that that fragile pulse "times" the slow turn of the globe beneath the "just light" of the heavens, until it too, inevitably and naturally, is covered by shadow and seems still. Although "Sentimento del tempo" is not the final poem in the volume,* it offers a satisfying postlude to the experience of erosion which permeates these pages.

✽   ✽   ✽

By the early 1930's, thanks in part to hostile critics like Flora, Ungaretti was generally accepted in Italy as the major practitioner of and spokesman for the "new" poetry. He was also a figure of some European reputation, contributing to French as well as Italian literary journals, participating frequently in international conferences on some aspect of the state of letters, poems translated (by himself, Chuzeville, Pierre Jean Jouve) in the pages of the *NRF*. He has never been retiring about the importance of his work for Italy. Sending a presentation copy of *Sentimento del tempo* to the critic Lorenzo Gigli in 1933 he wrote: "Put it beside the *Allegria*, look at the date of the poems. It will tell you clearly that in nineteen years I have done everything for the New Italian Poetry. Feeling, tone, rhythm, imagery, the musical syntax of the line . . . everything has come from my obstinate and desperate effort."[60] Though overly absolutistic this is broadly true. It lurks behind Quasimodo's jealousy. It is humorously acknowledged in Saba's demonstration of what he called a "small

---

* These others, written toward the mid-1930's, will be discussed below as transitional to *La terra promessa*.

grafting" from *Allegria di naufragi* effecting his own final style. ("To
the fiercely jealous [*gelossissimo*] Ungaretti," Saba adds, "he was
always grateful for the gift."[61]) "He alone," Montale has written, "in
his own time, succeeded in profiting by the freedom already in the
air. The others didn't know what to do with it."[62] In my opinion Mon-
tale himself has considerable right to a position of centrality such as
Ungaretti assigns himself, though it may well be that Montale's main
influence in Italian letters has been moral rather than stylistic. At any
rate Ungaretti's claim is not a ridiculous one.

From 1921 to 1935 Ungaretti lived and worked in Rome and its
vicinity. The importance of the Latian landscape to him has already
been noted; the emergent importance of baroque Rome itself will be
discussed below. In 1936 he was invited by the Argentinian govern-
ment to participate in the PEN Club Congress at Buenos Aires; while
there he was offered the chair of Italian language and literature at
the University of São Paulo, Brazil. For the six years from 1936 to
the end of 1942 Ungaretti settled with his family in São Paulo, teach-
ing and writing; he returned to Rome to take the chair of contem-
porary Italian literature at the University in 1942, working there
through the days of the various invasions, "open city," the various
occupations, and thereafter.

Il dolore—surely the title is deliberate antonym to the book of the
first World War—expresses the *vita* for the calamitous years 1937–
1946. The tragedy haunting its pages is in fact triple. The first chapter
consists of poems in memory of his recently deceased brother; the
following two (*Giorno per giorno* [Day by Day] and *Il tempo è
muto* [Time is Silent]) evoke the last days and persisting presence
of his son Antonietto who died of an illness in 1939 at the age of nine.
The remainder has to do with the catastrophe that has overtaken his
country.

Ideally, the first major sequence, the *Giorno per giorno* centering
on the death of Antonietto and its emergent meaning for the bereaved
father, should be read with "Gridasti: Soffoco . . ." (You Cried: I'm
Choking), a poem in fact written immediately before the sequence
(1939–1940) but only published in 1949.* It was to become the
grido (cry) of his penultimate volume *Un grido e paesaggi*. In these
pages we shall reinstate the original order and consider "Gridasti:
suffoco . . ." as the beginning of the *canto*.

---

* See Ungaretti's note to it in *Un grido e paesaggi*: "These are the beginning
stanzas of the *canto Giorno per giorno* of *Il dolore*. . . . I did not collect
them in that book with the others because they seemed to me to contain motifs
that were intimately my own. This was still egoism. One can reserve nothing
wholly for oneself of human experience without presumption."

The chapter took shape between the years 1939 and 1946—that is, in Brazil in the period immediately following Antonietto's death, through the return to Rome, the occupation, war's end and after. But these external and public matters are almost entirely muffled. At most, the spirit or apparition of place is quietly and fleetingly evoked as in "Gridasti . . ." when the poet, by the bedside of the dying son, overhears himself bemoan their isolation in an exotic world:

> È troppo azzurro questo cielo australe,
> Troppi astri lo gremiscono,
> Troppi e, per noi, non uno familiare. . . .

This southern sky is too blue, / too many stars crowd it / —too many and, for us, not one familiar. . . .

or, in the beginning of the ninth section of *Giorno per giorno*, where the pain of a hemisphere's separation from Antonietto's grave suggests a violently obstructive nature that may incorporate something of the war:

> Inferocita terra, immane mare
> Mi separa dal luogo della tomba
> Dove ora si disperde
> Il martoriato corpo. . . .

Ravening earth, monstrous sea, / you separate me from the place of the tomb / where now is scattered / the tormented body. . . .

or the whole of section ten, where the poet's return to Lazio contains reminiscences of Petrarch's revisitations of Vaucluse, Laura dead ("Zefiro torno e'l bel tempo rimena . . ." etc.):

> Sono tornato ai colli, ai pini amati
> E del ritmo dell'aria il patrio accento
> Che non riudrò con te,
> Mi spezza ad ogni soffio. . . .

I have returned to the hills, the beloved pines / and the fathering accent of the rhythm of the air / that I shall not hear again with you, / I'm broken with every breath. . . .

But as these citations show, the drama is almost entirely internal. What elements of the outer world there are serve mainly as reflectors of the world within.

The action is the survivor's feelings, then and now. They begin with the coming of death—objective and gross enough now, rather than an intuition or *sentimento*. The "Soffoco" (I'm choking) of the first poem are the words of Antonietto, the *tu* addressed throughout the entire sequence. And it opens, so "intimately" that the poet at first withdrew it from circulation, with the boy's last agonies:

> Non potevi dormire, non dormivi . . .
> Gridasti: Soffoco . . .
> Nel viso tuo scomparso già nel teschio,
> Gli occhi, che erano ancora luminosi
> Solo un attimo fa,
> Gli occhi si dilatarono . . . Si persero. . . .
>
> Poi la bocca, la bocca
> Che una volta pareva, lungo i giorni,
> Lampo di grazia e gioia,
> La bocca si contorse in lotta muta. . . .
> Un bimbo è morto. . . .

You couldn't sleep, you didn't sleep / . . . You cried: I'm choking / . . . In your face already faded into skull, / your eyes, still luminous / only a moment past, / your eyes grow wide . . . They're lost. . . . /
Then the mouth, the mouth / that once seemed through the days / a flare of grace and joy, / your mouth was twisted in dumb struggle. . . .
A child is dead. . . .

These poems can really be thought of as a drama for two characters, one of them dead and existing wholly in the memory—gradually the hope—of the other.* The drama is rooted in the anguished *pietà* of the speaker, "Ungaretti"; it oscillates between despair and a wild hope in some sort of survival or afterlife, between the destruction of his world and the poignant recollection of the dead one's "grace" which serves as his sole and tenuous light among the ruins. There is little precedent in *Vita d'un uomo* for this genuinely diaristic sort of poetry, with its declarative directness, its "naturalism" (as in the use of dots to represent the shifts and discontinuities of mind and memory), or its obsessional repetitiveness—in the passage cited the drumming on Antonietto's eyes and mouth or, threading and linking the entire poem, the memory of his hands, trusting and grasping as a

* Long ago, in 1926, in his article on Mallarmé and Leopardi for the *NRF* ("Innocence et mémoire") Ungaretti had judged that "for artists of the first quarter of the twentieth century, the characters in our (human) drama are memory and innocence." The Antonietto poems are the terrible realization of this prophecy.

baby, growing dry and pale and still, finally warding off the succubal oppression of dying breathlessness and the coffinlid of the southern hemisphere's unfamiliar stars:

> Cielo sordo, che scende senza un soffio,
> Sordo che udrò continuamente opprimere
> Mani tese a scansarlo. . . .

> Deaf sky, falling without a breath, / deaf sky I'll hear continually press / on hands held up to fend. . . .

Or if there is a precedent it is not in the ecstatic nakedness of *L'Allegria* but in the crisis-hymn "La pietà" that we shall find it. Here there is a similar simplicity of diction, a similar absence of imagery, the same return time and time again to an obsessive word or concept, the same hesitant or halting movement; above all, an almost identical relationship of two characters. In "La pietà" the "other" is God, absent like Antonietto, present—clearly not in memory —but as an old possibility made vibrant by need. As in "La pietà," "Gridasti . . ." ends in the dark, despairingly. The three lines cited above conclude in the same impotent and "blasphemous" resentment.

The period of the composition of *Giorno per giorno* corresponds to the period during which Ungaretti wrote his extraordinary discourses on Leopardi and Petrarch (published 1943–1944). Rebay has examined and demonstrated very brilliantly what he calls *riconoscimenti,* "recognitions" wherein Ungaretti finds analogues to his own experience in the experiences of certain great predecessors—Bergson or Mallarmé, above all Leopardi and Petrarch.[63]

Occasionally it is a question less of mutuality than of unwitting projection, as when, in the *Inni* period, Ungaretti tended to christianize Leopardi to match his own strong sense of religious despair. But the "Secondo discorso su Leopardi" is full of occult references—possibly quite unconscious—and parallels to *Giorno per giorno.* In the *discorso* Ungaretti speaks of Leopardi as "one for whom the dead are dead, and the living carry the weight of the centuries unlived by the dead"[64]; in "Gridasti . . .":

> Sconto, sopravvivendoti, l'orrore
> Degli anni che t'usurpo,
> E che ai tuoi anni aggiungo,
> Dimente di rimorso. . . .

> I expiate, surviving you, the horror / of the years I usurp from you, / that—mad with remorse / —I add to your years. . . .

In the *discorso* he cites a manuscript note written by Leopardi which is almost a scenario for the entire sequence: "If you must, in writing poetry, feign a dream wherein you or another see a loved one who is dead, especially just following his death, make sure that the dreamer struggles to show him the grief (*il dolore*) he has felt over his misfortune."* In the same *discorso* we might also note Ungaretti's close reading of Leopardi's "L'infinito" and in particular his remarks on the adjective *caro* (dear) which is affectively a central word in both that idyll and the "Gridasti . . .":

> . . . but *caro* is a turning to the affections, to the pathetic; to the affections that can be so rooted within us, can flower within us and become such a part of us as to make us forget that they had a beginning and can end, fatally, one day; to the affections that are unavoidably conditioned by the duration, brief or long, of the existence of a man, a mortal, a finite being.[66]

Leopardi here is conceived of as the *maestro* of the pathos surrounding absolute despair, as "one for whom the dead are dead" and for whom memory—like resurrection—is "blessed illusion." His position is crystallized at the conclusion of his elegy for Silvia:

> All'apparir del vero
> tu, misera, cadesti: e con la mano
> la fredda morte ed una tomba ignuda
> mostravi di lontano.

> At the appearance of truth [*that is, the fact of her having no future; an early grave for mortal Silvia*], / O wretched one, you fell; and with your hand / cold death and a bare tomb / you pointed in the distance.

But absolute despair is not the final station on the *via crucis* of *Giorno per giorno;* beside the heavy gravestone there is death *conceived of*—not "believed in" but desperately prayed for as the ghost of a chance—as threshold to a "limpid sphere" where spirit sheds its material encumbrances and becomes *senza più peso*, weightless, light at last, radiantly itself. Even in the nadir of "Gridasti . . ." this other possibility is at least fleetingly present:

> . . . Sei animo della mia anima, e la liberi.
> Ora meglio la liberi

---

* The remainder of the note as well as the variants and final version of Leopardi's elegy called "Il sogno" are all relevant to the psychology of such a situation and the artistic means of realizing it.[65]

> Che non sapesse il tuo sorriso vivo:
> Provala ancora, accrescile la forza,
> Se vuoi—sino a te, caro!—che m'innalzi
> Dove il vivere è calma, è senza morte. . . .

. . . You are the life of my soul, and you free it. / Now you free it better / than your live smile could. / Attempt it still, increase your strength, / if you wish to raise me—up to you, dear! / —where living is calm, is deathless.

Still intermittent and tenuous, the possibility develops in the post-mortem of the *Giorno* proper. Thus, in the fourth section:

> Mai, non saprete mai come m'illumina
> L'ombra che mi si pone a lato, timida,
> Quando non spero più. . . .

Never, you [the *voi* form is directed to us, the living; *tu* is reserved for Antonietto] will never know how the timid shade / illumines me that stays by my side, / when I hope no more. . . .

The eleventh involves a prayer—to whom, Antonietto or the Eternal, is left unstated, though prayer needn't bear an address:

> Passa la rondina e con essa estate,
> E anch'io, mi dico, passerò . . .
> Ma resti dell'amore che mi strazia
> Non solo segno un breve appannamento
> Se dall'inferno arrivo a qualche quiete. . . .

The swallow passes and with it summer, / and I too, I tell myself, shall pass / . . . but let there remain of the love that lacerates me / not just a brief darkening as sole sign / if out of hell I am to arrive at some quiet. . . .

The noun *appannamento*, the drawing-over or infolding or tucking in as with *panno* or woolen cloth is an appropriately simple, domestic and evocative word for the darkening that death brings for the survivor. But the context is a plea—"let this be not all"—and involves the hope of something more permanent than a fading grief or memory. In the fifteenth section of *Giorno per giorno*, the sufferer suffers not from the finality of his son's death as before but from the quickening into life of his own sense of sinfulness contrasted with what he now feels as Antonietto's immortal purity released through death. The last poem of the chapter finds words for the absentee in hendecasyllables of great simplicity and beauty:

Fa dolce e forse qui vicino passi
Dicendo: «Questo sole e tanto spazio
Ti calmino. Nel puro vento udire
Puoi il tempo camminare e la mia voce.
Ho in me raccolto a poco a poco e chiuso
Lo slancio muto della tua speranza.
Sono per te l'aurora e intatto giorno.»

Fair day, and maybe close by you pass, / saying: "May this sun and so much space / calm you. In the pure wind you can hear / time move on and my voice. / Little by little I have gathered myself within me and have encompassed / the mute thrust of your hope. / For you I am dawn and day intact."

Remember in the last days of his life Antonietto had cried out "Soffoco," or—as in the first of the Giorno poems—"Nessuno, mamma, ha mai sofferto tanto . . .": No one, Mamma, has ever suffered so. Now he speaks—or is spoken for—as to the spirit and no longer the ear. The agony of the flesh has fallen away; what remains at the end of this six-years' sequence of mourning moments is what, in the legend of Ophelia d'Alba, the poet called "pure evocation," the guiding presence of the released and beckoning spirit.

✿   ✿   ✿

This brings us to what the later Ungaretti calls his *petrarchismo*. For just as Leopardi provided a poetic precedent for despair, so Francesco Petrarch serves as Ungaretti's guide through the experience of bereavement resulting, after much pain and suffering, in the acknowledgement of a life beyond the grave. For Petrarch, the "triumph of death," the terrible sense that follows Laura's death, of the transience of all things—is at length succeeded by the "triumph of Eternity":

Dapoi che sotto 'l ciel cosa non vidi
stabile e ferma, tutto sbigottito
mi volsi al cor e dissi: «In che ti fidi?»
Rispose: «Nel Signor, che mai fallito
non à promessa a chi si fida in lui. . . .»

Since beneath the sky I saw nothing / stable and firm, all terrified / I turned to my heart and said, "In what do you have faith?"
It answered: "In the Lord, who has never broken / promise to whomever has faith in Him. . . ."

Ungaretti's faith in the Lord will never achieve anything close to this serenity; nevertheless what he calls the "thrust" of his hope parallels the Catholic verticality mapped in Petrarch's poems for Laura live and dead and the *Trionfi*. And even as the several *discorsi* reveal Ungaretti's sense of the parallel between certain aspects of his inwardness and Leopardi's, so his 1943 essay on Petrarch shows him meditating on a similar affinity discovered with the experience of that master. Rebay in fact goes so far as to evoke an Ungaretti "writing *Laura* but thinking *Antonietto!*"[67] But the discovery of Petrarch has ramifications on levels even more important than thematic congruity.

Long ago, in the postwar post-*Allegria* days, the beginning scholar of *canto italiano* had dreamed of consolidation with tradition: "It was the beating of my heart that I wanted to hear in harmony with the heartbeats of my ancestors. . . ." What gradually declares itself during this phase is what I would call a temperamental need for literary precedent, a passion to see his *vita* in a perspective of established literary values. His rehabilitation of the hendecasyllable is one symptom of this; it also constitutes a secret motive in his scholarship, implicit not only in the essays and *discorsi* but in the considerable bulk of his translations from the French, Spanish and English. In translating the *Anabase* of St. John Perse, for instance, he studied relationships between "traditional metric and the expressive needs of today"; he found Perse working for the same renewal-by-recovery in French poetry that he was striving for in Italian.[68] In a preface to an anthology of his translations (*Traduzioni*: 1936) he writes how he "confronted the *Songs of Innocence* of William Blake, the 'inspired' poet if there ever was one, in order to stimulate a similar response in myself in a period in which . . . I was too absorbed in problems of technique." The rationale of all his translations is stated in his preface to *40 sonetti di Shakespeare*:

> This is a labor over which I have meditated since 1931 when, in an exhaustive attempt at renewal, problems of either a technical or simple inspirational order brought me . . . to analyze *sul vivo*, as one can only do through translating, certain aspects of writers of varying moods and origins. . . . I dreamed of a poetry where the secret movements of the soul, neither betrayed nor falsified by impulsiveness, would be reconciled with an extreme sapience of discourse.

In a letter of the 1940's quoted by Giuseppe De Robertis,[69] Ungaretti describes the two main tendencies of his work as "the scholastic or Petrarchan current and the current of personal 'vein' or inspiration." The latter is clearly rare and probably best understood as the diaristic poetry written in periods of intense inner turmoil

("La pietà," "Gridasti . . ." and parts of *Griorno per giorno*) where the art grows transparent and seemingly subordinate to the cathartic urgency of expression. The "scholastic or Petrarchan" current is in effect the main current; it gets underway in the researches underlying *Sentimento del tempo* and grows more elaborate and "sapient" in the late 1930's and 1940's when he begins his long association with various universities.

Leopardi too had nourished himself on Petrarch, even publishing a school edition of the *Canzoniere*, and it is not surprising to find the following passage on the historical resonance of Petrarchan style at the very beginning of the second *discorso*:

> A language recovered from the grave—such is the miracle of the *Canzoniere*. A language recovered in the ingenuous pulsations of a new language, a new language . . . which . . . was augmented by a light, shed from thousands of years of human experience—by an ancient light. Through Petrarch's merit Italian suddenly became an ancient language, an efficient mode of speech that would serve as model for the tongues of adolescent Europe.

From Petrarch his interests quickly spread to *petrarchismo*: hence his studies in what he has recently called "the main line of Italian poetry" extending from Petrarch to Michelangelo, Tasso, Leopardi and (presumably) himself,[70] with extensions in other tongues in the work of Shakespeare, Góngora, Racine and Mallarmé.* "The Petrarchan tradition," he writes, "is linked forever to the development of every poetic language in Europe."[73]

Originally what appealed to Ungaretti in Petrarch's style was its antiquity, the memories it evoked not only of the national tradition inaugurated in the *Trecento*, but of silver Latinity preceding it. He loved it, therefore, for much the same reasons that Leopardi loved it: for its verbal elegance and richness, the suave complexities of its Latinate construction, its historical-cultural aureole. Increasingly, however, he gravitated towards its late Renaissance variety (exemplified, he finds, in the work of Shakespeare, Góngora, Racine, and above all, Michelangelo) characterized by the sense of extreme tension and barely contained conflict known broadly as "baroque."

Despite his birth and travels, Ungaretti was basically a naturalized Roman from the 1920's onward. "I lived in Rome," he reminisces,

---

* As early as 1929 Ungaretti dubbed the *elegantissimo* Mallarmé the best of the *petrarchisti*.[71] Quasimodo is taking a crack at this aspect of Ungaretti when he connects the "decadence" of much modern Italian poetry with "an involuted Petrarchan humming . . . an Alexandrian Petrarch moreover from the lifeless times . . . of Marinism or Gongorism or euphuism."[72]

"the city of Michelangelo and the baroque."[74] It was here that he experienced what he calls his "crisis of taste (*una mia crisi di gusto*) from which I would escape only when the naturalness and expressive power of the baroque—which was in the very air I breathed each moment—had finally been made immediate in the modes of my own poetry."[75] For Ungaretti *barocco* meant the style of titanic suffering discernible in the Sistine ceiling and the last Pietàs; it sprang

> not only from the will to combine dramatically contrary elements but also and especially from the need to manifest a feeling of the catastrophic. The baroque was born of the conviction that the experience of antiquity was over as was the experience of historical or temporal Christianity, the hour now striking being the hour of apocalypse. And isn't the feeling of catastrophe implicit in the feeling of nothingness and the horror of the void . . . ? These are all phantoms that tormented Michelangelo, while he only wished to affirm the Eternal.[76]

In short, another *riconoscimento*. The "baroque petrarchism" of Michelangelo, with its sense of gigantic strain and conflict, is found to be the adequate stylistic precedent for Ungaretti's own sense of catastrophe confronting the death throes of Antonietto and his poor broken country.

The first evidence of the "immediatization" of the baroque he mentions occurs in the second half of *Il dolore,* poems written mostly after his return to Rome in 1942 and during the occupation. The most remarkable of these are the two Antonietto pieces, "Amaro accordo" (Bitter Harmony) and "Tu ti spezzasti" (You Shattered Yourself) in which an apotheosis of a sort is involved. The *bimbo,* first conjured with images of joy, radiance and grace, is set in *paesaggi* of monstrous and primitive catastrophe, and by this juxtaposition is composed an almost bearable Necessity—weight must fall, crystal must shatter, grace be broken in the grinding shambles that is space and time. Antonietto's death, then, proves he was angelic.

In these two poems particularly one can observe the considerable dramatic effects of Ungaretti's version of *barocco*. It provides a contextual sense of weight, mass and tension which sets off Antonietto's frailty; not only the oblique and Latinated syntax, but the polysyllabic and aureate diction create an effect of massiveness at once exalted and threatening. In the "Tu ti spezzasti" the brief second and third sections of this three-part poem are couched in the wistful pastoral style of much of the *Sentimento*; these focus on Antonietto rather than the crushing *paesaggio,* and are intended to provide absolute contrast to the great baroque first stanzas which evoke the Brazilian coast, its rocks, sands, pines and marine life. The several styles recapitulate the tragedy.

Both poems, as we would expect, move in memory. The "amaro accordo" of the first is a recollective association made, presumably, by the poet as he walks near the Capitoline hill on a cloudy October noon. The poem begins with "Oppure . . .," (Or) as if we are to overhear a meditation that has been developing for some time previous to the start of the poem. It may well be that the poem "really" begins as the poet moves up the great stairs designed by Michelangelo towards the Piazza del Campidoglio that is flanked and guarded by the massive statues of the fabulous Dioscuri, Castor and Pollux, the miracle-working twin brothers of Helen, here with their horses, benevolent to old Roman destinies. But here they are seen not as statues but as elemental powers; one notes this in the fact that it is their horses that do the moving in this poem:

> Oppure in un meriggio d'un ottobre
> Dagli armoniosi colli
> In mezzo a dense discendenti nuvole
> I cavalli dei Dioscuri. . . .

Or in an October noon, / from the harmonious hills, / in the midst of dense lowering clouds, / the horses of the Dioscuri. . . .

The following two-lined limiting clause sketches *in nuce* the polar opposition that will structure the poem:

> . . . Alle cui zampe estatico
> S'era fermato un bimbo. . . .

. . . at whose hoofs / had stopped an ecstatic child. . . .

where the accumulated sense of massive movement, clouds and horses, dramatically confronts the still smallness of the remembered Antonietto, innocently "ecstatic" beneath the trampling hoofs. At this point, in a vast parenthesis that occupies a stanza, the octaves of memory resound bitterly: the recollected image of the child beneath the equestrian statues releases a Brazilian counterpart, and in the phantasmagoria of the grieving mind, the horses of the Dioscuri move westward to a beach scene where the *bimbo* is playing in an elemental landscape:

> . . . Sopra i flutti spiccavano

(Per un amaro accordo dei ricordi
Verso ombre di banani
E di giganti erranti
Tartarughe entro blocchi
D'enormi acque impassibili:
Sotto altro ordine d'astri
Tra insoliti gabbiani)

Volo sino alla piana dove il bimbo
Frugando nella sabbia,
Dalla luce dei fulmini infiammata
La transparaenza delle care dita
Bagnate dalla pioggia contro vento
Ghermiva tutti e quattro gli elementi.

. . . over the waves leapt /
(by a bitter harmony of memories / towards shadows of banana
palms / and giant roaming / tortoises amid blocks / of enormous im-
passable waters / under another order of stars / among unfamiliar
gulls)
    into flight unto the plain where the child, / delving in the sand /
—by the flaming light of lightning bolts / the transparence of his
dear fingers / bathed by the wind-tossed rain / —grasped all four of
the elements.

Obviously there are two sorts of strength involved here. This is not
just a poem about Antonietto as victim. The last line cited above
clearly expresses a triumph, wherein all four elements—the sandy
plain of the beach, the sea and the rain, the wind, the lightning—are,
with the horses, at the beck of innocence. Nevertheless, such a triumph
is doomed, of course, as indeed the building of the periods leading to
that victorious verb *ghermiva* indicates. Thus, if the syntactical skele-
ton of these three stanzas is ". . . the horses of the Dioscuri . . .
sprang over the waves . . . in flight to the plain where the child
. . . grasped all four of the elements," the continually interruptive
subordinate clauses, qualifiers and parenthetical material all tend to
undermine that victory with massed images of overwhelming physical
power and weight (even the water is coagulated into *blocks*) and
resurgent primitivism (the *cavalli* merge into the *giganti erranti Tar-
tarughe*). And of course the very complexity of the syntactical
ordering* obscures the precarious triumph of innocence when it at
least finds expression, even throwing it into violent question. This

---

* E.g., the main subject does not appear until line 4, and its verb, halved
by a parenthetical stanza, hangs fire between lines 7 and 15. Similarly, with
the adjectival clause modifying the object *piana*, where *bimbo* is kept from its
verb (*ghermiva*) by four lines of stormy auxiliary detail.

being so, the final stanza of "Amaro accordo" strikes me as being close to redundant, spelling out abstractly what has already been dramatically realized through the *paesaggi* and premonitory complexities of the massive three-stanza sentence preceding:

> Ma la morte è incolore e senza sensi
> E, ignara d'ogni legge, come sempre,
> Già lo sfiorava
> Coi denti impudichi.

But death is colorless and without senses / and, ignorant of all law, as always, / already was grazing him / with brazen teeth.

Such *sfioratura,* we know, had been present from the start, built into the most intimate tissues of the poem. Its *statement* here only contributes an extra and "bitter" irony with the thought that, if death is *always* ignorant of every law—specifically the law of respecting innocence which even the elements obey—then this murderous ignorance is itself the law of laws.

"Tu ti spezzasti" continues to employ the polar contraries evoked in "Amaro accordo," specifically the absolute contrasting of the coastal life of Brazil, in all its ominous volcanic and prehistoric massiveness (it is populated by giant "fabulous tortoises"), with the "temerario, musico" (rash, musical) Antonietto who, in his blithe ascent to the tip of a Brazilian pine, is likened to the fiery-crested *fiorrancino* or wren.* A conflict is set forth in terms of mutually exclusive images, with the tragic outcome hardly in doubt.

Like the *Giorno per giorno* sequence, "Tu ti spezzasti" is directly addressed to the dead Antonietto: *non rammenti*—do you not recall or bring to mind—is the verb which grammatically activates the first two stanzas. But subject (*tu*) and verb (*rammenti*) are—as in "Amaro accordo"—all but swamped in what is to be remembered:

> I molti, immani, sparsi, grigi sassi
> Frementi. . . .

The many, monstrous, scattered, grey stones / trembling. . . .

and so the stanza goes implacably on for twenty-seven more words until the end and the tender query («non rammenti?»). Thus, the impossible contrasts are evoked, the ponderous, gross, implacable

---

* "Smallest of the Italian birds," wrote Ungaretti in a note to the poem for its first publication in 1945, ". . . light in flight, most full of grace in all its actions, in motion from morning to evening."

and ancient stones and sands and trees and creatures of the deep framing the "wren," all grace and light and motion, *musico*. Despite the effortless ascent to the tip of the ancient pine, the eventual victor is clear, and so the poem, which has dramatized "law" in terms of textures, speed, weight and gradings of light and dark, concludes:

> Grazia felice,
> Non avresti potuto non spezzarti
> In una cecità tanto indurita
> Tu semplice soffio e cristallo,
>
> Troppo umano lampo per l'empio,
> Selvoso, accanito, ronzante
> Ruggito d'un sole ignudo.

Happy grace, / how could you not have shattered / in a blindness so rigid, / you simple breath and crystal, /
Too human blaze for the impious, / savage, hungering, droning / roar of a naked sun.

The poem, turning on a triumph of happy grace, wren's flight, the child's weightlessness, his dance and fragile transparency, must end where it began, in the blaring light of the natural world, with obsessed rhythms cataloguing an implacable nature through a chain of heavy adjectives. In both "Amaro accordo" and "Tu ti spezzasti," an affirmation (amounting to angelification) of Antonietto's purity and innocence is mounted in an extraordinary evocation of crude and majestic natural process; these opposing and irreconcilable "ideas" are yoked and definitively contained in the explosive and sumptuous *barocco* recovered by the poet through his passionate study.

Il dolore closes with a series of poems inspired by the human and national tragedy of the war. The penultimate chapter, *Roma occupata*, comprises the most concertedly Roman Catholic phase of the entire *Vita d'un uomo*.* The characteristic *paesaggio* is of course Rome, and its pines, streets and houses, the Tiber, Michelangelo's Vatican ceiling and cupola, a crucifixion attributed to Masaccio in the church of San Clemente, the Colosseum, are evoked by name. Yet as we would expect of such a nominalist as Ungaretti, this is by no means an

---

* A tendency among Italian fascists to embrace a mystical Catholicism towards the war's end has been noted, and it is sometimes cited to Ungaretti's disadvantage. (For a particularly virulent attack, see the review of *Il dolore* by Gino Raya in *Italica* for March 1964). But this implies an opportunism on the poet's part which is completely at odds with what we know of his inner life, beginning at the very latest with the crisis registered by the *Inni* of 1928.

historical or political poetry, nor a poetry of place. The real subject of *Roma occupata* is the poet's "Michelangelical" need for a faith in order to bear or accept the revelation of a world in ruins. The complicated and expansive style we have just examined is perfectly adapted for this anguished theme. It is even appropriate that such a style should be employed in poems whose main occasion is the contemplation of baroque Roman artifacts—buildings or paintings. Such contemplation is undertaken in a desperate quest for hope—the resonant word through the chapter is *speranza*.

Thus in "Folli i miei passi" (Mad My Steps) and "Defunti su montagne" (The Dead on Mountains) a certain inward or spiritual movement is described in terms of the present broken city and a Roman artist's heroic witness to Christian faith as these elements declare themselves to the desolated poet in the streets. In "Folli i miei passi" we first encounter him mechanically wandering ways which have become opaque, blankly two-dimensional, pure meaningless present:

> Le usate strade
> —Folli i miei passi come d'un automa—
> Che una volta d'incanto si muovevano
> Con la mia corsa,
> Ora più svolgersi non sanno in grazie
> Pieno di tempo. . . .

The trodden streets / —mad my steps like an automaton / —that once stirred with enchantment / with my passage, / now no longer can unfold in graces / rich with time. . . .

and even in the familiar objects of his personal life, when with night he returns to his rooms, no longer can give surcease or relief to his benumbed heart. In "Defunti su montagne" the pedestrians by the Colosseum have become grey ghosts, the city itself a void:

> Come nelle distanze
> Le apparizioni incerte trascorrenti . . .
> Da pochi passi apparsi
> I passanti alla base di quel muro
> Perdevano statura
> Dilatando il deserto dell'altezza,
> E la sorpresa se, ombre, parlavano.

As in distances / uncertain fleeting apparitions / . . . the passers-by appearing / a few steps away at the foot of that wall / were losing physicality / as the desert of height swelled, / and what a surprise if, shades, they were speaking.

Having presented this ghosted, zero landscape, both poems turn, prostrated, from the bleak Roman horizon to something higher. In the first, his "carnal eyes" and "absurd ear" are schooled by Christ's *braccia offerte*, the outstretched and offering arms of both crucifixion and loving entreaty. In the second the speaker somnambulistically follows a "strange drum," his heart "burning even while it seemed consumed away." And both poems end in a baroque vision which exemplifies and kindles *speranza*. In either case it is a vision of the crucified. In "Folli i miei passi," he experiences the agony of Michelangelo:

> . . . Quell'umile speranza
> Che travolgeva il teso Michelangelo
> A murare ogni spazio in un baleno
> Non concedendo all'anima
> Nemmeno la risorsa di spezzarsi.

> . . . that humble hope / that worked spreadeagled Michelangelo / to wall up every space with lightning, / not conceding to the soul / even the refuge of breaking itself.*

Here baroque is seen as a frantic immersion in one's burning thirst for God, a total plunging of spirit into matter in order that matter may take fire and spiritualize itself. The poem's last stanza locates the image of this transformation in the cupola of St. Peter's, an "arcane" and winged shape of spiritual longing given to Rome by the "desolate shudder" of the maker Michelangelo. That artist, *teso*, spread and nailed to his suffering, bears witness in his art to that "humble hope" which animated and tortured him, thus acting as guide and great brother to the desolate *io* who utters the poem.

In "Defunti su montagne" it is the fresco of the crucifixion ascribed to Masaccio in San Clemente that miraculously bears *speranza* (literally the poem's last word) to the poet. The eye moves from the turmoil and *pietà* at the fresco's base, the suffering women, the watchers, the centurions on horseback ("equestrian wrath"), up to the larger figures of the two thieves flanking a towering Christ on the cross, with behind all three, emergent from clouds and mountains, the absorbed and risen dead. So, in the poem, Ungaretti moves from the "clutching smokes" and mists of a spectral Rome, with pedestrians

---

* This evocation of the baroque attitude seems to anticipate his description of "Petrarchan baroque" in the preface to his translation of *Phédre*. There "memory has come to have a horror of itself as of a void" and the spirit desperately constructs a violent homage to God which does not permit "the least liberty or space for the mind to flee to other considerations."

experienced as suffering wraiths, to the mystery of faith and resurrection as articulated by Masaccio:

> Allora fu che, entrato in San Clemente,
> Dalla crocefissione di Masaccio
> M'accolsero, d'un alito staccati
> Mentre l'equestre rabbia
> Convertita giú in roccia ammutoliva,
> Desti dietro il biancore
> Delle tombe abolite,
> Defunti, su montagne
> Sbocciate lievi da leggere nuvole.

Then it was that, having entered San Clemente, / from the crucifixion by Masaccio, / *they* received me—by a breath removed, / while the equestrian rage / petrified below grew still, / awakening beyond the whiteness / of the abolished tombs / —the dead, on weightless / mountains unfolding from light clouds.

The last poems of *Il dolore* envisage a world permeated with the abiding presence of the dead—a world in which, within the soul, beyond the *equestre rabbia* of bereavement, guilt or politics, they mark a threshold and a call. In "Non gridate più" (Cry Out No More),

> Hanno l'impercettibile sussurro,
> Non fanno più rumore
> Del crescere dell'erba,
> Lieta dove non passa l'uomo.

They make imperceptible murmur, / they make no more sound / than growing grass, / happiest where man does not pass.

A decade later, a poet who had profited from the formal explorations of Ungaretti would write a book entitled *La terra impareggiabile* (Incomparable Earth). As epigraph Salvatore Quasimodo would use a line from his translation of Aeschylus' *Choephoroe*: "Dico che i morti uccidono i vivi," I tell you that the dead are killing the living. Surely his title is meant to provide a contentious alternative to Ungaretti's *Terra promessa*, to which we turn now; for in the epigraph is a choice for *terra* and that "equestrian rage" which Ungaretti's "nominalism" has found increasingly insubstantial. For Ungaretti's fundamental sense of reality is not only "nominalist" and fraught with an agonized *contemptu mundi* but perfectly Bergsonian—that is, his present is haunted, ghostly, saturated with memory, the thin edge of a stupendous past. Compared with the manifestations of human life on earth, "il grido dei morti è piú forte," the cry of the dead is stronger. Such is the very last line of *Il dolore* and in it is compressed what belief has crystallized out of the confrontation with death that its pages recount: the certainty that erosion and decline underlie all natural existence, the desperate hypothesis of some sort of supernatural survival. He feels his dead about him and, to a degree, takes heart.

❖   ❖   ❖

When Mondadori undertook to bring out *Vita d'un uomo* in 1942, its prospectus included the proximate publication of a volume called *Penultima stagione* (Penultimate Season). The title suggests Ungaretti's original conception of what was eventually (1950) to be *La terra promessa.*

"It was autumn that I meant to sing of in my poem, an advanced autumn from which the last sign of youth, of earthly youth, the last carnal appetite, detached itself forever . . ."[77] Autumn had not been far from the poet's thoughts from the early 1930's onward. It is present, as we have seen, as the *gentildonna* who passes "as a leaf" in the fifth canto of *La morte meditata*; it is also present in many moments of *Giorno per giorno,* where the death of Antonietto ironically raises the absurdity of his own continuing existence:

> Già m'è nelle ossa scesa
> L'autunnale secchezza. . . .

Already autumn dryness / has descended into my bones. . . .

The sense of an ending, then, already occupied Ungaretti well before the specific losses giving rise to *Il dolore* had occurred; as pointed out above, a *sentimento del tempo* is ultimately an experience of perishing. The chronologically last poem of *Sentimento del tempo* is a birthday greeting for himself ("Auguri per il proprio compleanno") written in 1935, before Brazil and the war, at the age of 47. It will be the nucleus for what he will later think of as his book of the *penultima stagione.*

> Dolce declina il sole.
> Dal giorno si distacca
> Un cielo troppo chiaro.
> Dirama solitudine
>
> Come da gran distanza
> Un muoversi di voci.
> Offesa se lusinga,
> Quest'ora ha l'arte strana.

Non è primo apparire
Dell'autunno già libero?
Con non altro mistero

Corre infatti a dorarsi
Il bel tempo che toglie
Il dono di follia.

Eppure, eppure griderei:
Veloce gioventú dei sensi
Che all'oscuro mi tieni di me stesso
E consenti le immagini all'eterno,

Non mi lasciare, resta, sofferenza!

Gently the sun goes down. / From the day departs / a too clear sky. / Solitude ramifies /
As from a great distance / a moving of voices. / Threatening and inviting, / this hour has strange art. /
Is this not the first appearance / of autumn already free? / With no other mystery /
Surely runs to bedeck itself / the beautiful season that takes away / the gift of madness. /
And yet, and yet I would cry out: / Swift youth of my senses / that keeps me in the darkness of myself / and yields images to the eternal, /
Leave me not, stay, my suffering!

One of his loveliest poems, the "Auguri" is also a transitional one. A passage from a letter quoted in Piccioni's essay on the origins of the *Terra promessa* published as an appendix to that book illustrates the poet's *post facto* view of its significance:

All my poetic activity from 1919 on developed in . . . a more objective direction than *L'Allegria,* that is, in the projection and contemplation of my feelings in [external] objects, in an attempt to elevate my own biographical experience to the level of ideas and myths. "Auguri per il proprio compleanno" in particular indicates this transition. . . .

Certainly this double tendency towards contemplation and abstraction is perceptible in the birthday-poem. The effort to "objectify" feeling by the use of analogues in space or time (as *paesaggio, tempo, stagione*) is of course one of the features of the first half of *Sentimento del tempo*; the effort to express ideas directly without recourse to images is characteristic of the second half, particularly in the *Inni* and parts of *La morte meditata.* "Auguri per il proprio compleanno" can thus be said to incorporate key developments of Ungaretti's "second season" as inscribed in *Sentimento del tempo.*

The letter continues:

> If, on the one hand, the poet (like his Palinurus in *La terra promessa*) declared in the "Auguri" his desperate faith in images [that is, the human "measure" built against superhuman "mystery"], even if these are only "illusions of our senses," so on the other hand he saluted in the image of an infant's laugh [in "Senza piu péso," 1934] the perennial beauty of life, even if this beauty . . . can only illuminate us momentarily . . . through a more or less ephemeral action. . . . Perennial beauty—but inexorably bound to perishing, to images, to earthly vicissitudes, to history, and therefore only *illusorily* perennial, as Palinurus will say—assumed in my mind the aspect of Aeneas.

The "Auguri" for his forty-seventh birthday still treated biography in terms of landscape and "idea"; the mythic projection of it in terms of Vergilian personae had not been clearly conceived at this point. Yet, with our hindsight, we can detect circumstances in his life during the early 1930's which may have encouraged it. There was, first of all, his translation of Saint-John Perse's *Anabase* in 1931, an experience which might have suggested the viability of an epic lyricism to him. In 1932 he travelled extensively in the Vergilian country of the *mezzogiorno* around Naples, writing a series of travel articles for the *Gazzetta del Popolo.** In one of them, he makes his first public *riconoscimento* with Vergil:

> But I am in places that were visited by Vergil, and he was so attentive, so sensitive, and so precise that it is difficult here not to borrow his eyes. They speak of the fineness of Vergil's ear, and I too would concede it, meaning that no one better rendered the soul's music than he. But one ought also to say what an unequalled painter he was. If, therefore, good clear sight can aid me now, it will all be thanks to Books V and VI of the *Aeneid.*[78]

This was written at Palinuro, site of the tumulus for the drowned pilot which will be found so pathetically "ironic" in the pages of *Terra promessa.* His visits during that year to Cape Palinurus, Paestum, Elea and Cumae led—as one might have guessed—less to visual description than to "nominalist" meditations on time and permanence, illusion and reality inspired not so much by Vergil but by the evoked presences of the masters of the Eleatic School, Xenophanes and Par-

---

* See *Il deserto e dopo*, particularly pp. 153–71. The essays entitled "Elea e la primavera," "La pesca miracolosa," and "La rosa di Pesto" are especially useful as collateral materials for a reading of *La terra promessa.*

menides. For instance: standing on a height surveying Elea, seeing ("like Parmenides") sea and sky in the heavy hazy light merge into a common grey and thus a visible "new proof" of the illusoriness of all things save the one unimaginable and unnameable reality, Ungaretti apostrophizes the exiled Greek founder of the School:

> Oh Xenophanes! . . . how bitter you were, man who had been upon the seas for so long, to discover that thought alone is immortal. You sought, oh voyager, Being rather than appearances, Unity rather than individualities, and for the first time in the western world, in this land of Italy, you—cruel poet!—you divested divinity of all images.[79]

Xenophanes, the radical skeptic who condemned all imagist "measures" as blasphemies upon the divine "mystery," stands of course for one pole of Ungaretti's own dilemma as a man and poet. Without images, no poetry can be made. "Divinity" remains inconceivable; hence the *"desperate* faith in images" (italics mine) of the "Auguri."

It is a dilemma that, short of utter silence, cannot be solved. Time, moreover, brought to Ungaretti an order of experience in which idea, myth, and philosophy had to give way to unmediated life itself, the catastrophic shocks of personal bereavement and national trauma that are registered in *Il dolore*. Until the war was over, myth had to be suspended.

❋   ❋   ❋

In 1948, the year following the publication of *Il dolore,* Ungaretti published in the Roman periodical *Alfabeto* a fragmentary sequence of five quatrains, appending a note which said that they had been conceived in 1935 immediately following the composition of the "Auguri," and that he had been unable to proceed any further with them during the entire period spent in Brazil. Accompanying them was a study by the critic Leone Piccioni (to whom the poet had given access to earlier manuscript version and variants) which traced the laborious evolution of even these unterminated quatrains and offered a close account of Ungaretti's extraordinarily conscientious, not to say baroque, methods of composition.

The outcome of this creative-critical activity was fortunate. Ungaretti had felt the "Frammenti" to be stillborn; their publication and analysis stimulated him to alter them radically and complete them, so that they eventually became the opening "Canzone describing the inner state of the poet" of the *Terra promessa* published just two years later. It was in the period of 1948–49, when so much of the volume as it now stands was composed, that Ungaretti confided to

Piccioni his vision of what the completed poem would be: an ambition, as its subtitle (*Frammenti*) tells us, so far unrealized.[80]

At the very beginning, the poem had had as its working title *Il Palinuro* (Palinurus). Already in 1932 during his travels in the Vergilian *mezzogiorno*, Ungaretti had meditated on that tragic *naufragato* as what he called an emblem of "desperate fidelity," meaning not only his selfless loyalty to the heroic and beautiful "image" of Aeneas but his faith unto death (earning him his "ironic immortality") in the idea of innocence. In a note in *Terra promessa* Ungaretti writes of Palinurus' "mad undertaking to reach an harmonious place, happy, peaceful: *un paese innocente* as I once said." I feel it is a pity that the poet decided not to make the drowned mariner the central objectification of the poem, since the figure as he conceived it seemed a dramatic embodiment of his own baroque and desperate faith. As we shall see, Ungaretti eventually chose Aeneas as his filtering and shaping inwardness.

In tune perhaps with "Vergilian music" the work was first thought of as a *melodrama,* an instrumentally accompanied text with *recitativi* and choruses.* Some of this nomenclature remains in the definitive version (the choruses of Dido, *recitativo* of Palinurus, last choruses etc.). Another index of Ungaretti's absorption with harmony in this work might be his unprecedented use of end-rhyme in two major sections of it—the opening "Canzone" that developed from the original quatrains and the "Recitativo" of Palinurus composed as a Petrarchan sestina (in which, of course, the terminal sound-chimings are over half the game).

The subsequent prospectus-scenario communicated to Piccioni ran as follows. *Terra promessa* was to begin with Aeneas' landing at Cumae, in the land promised him by the gods: an exultant *vita nuova.* But precisely at this initial moment of triumph, his memories of the past possess Aeneas. This corresponds to the visitation of the dead—the fundamental concept underlying the whole work; its Vergilian locus and *paesaggio* was to be the entry to the underworld by Lake Avernus near Cumae. Aeneas first remembers Carthage (Ungaretti's Africa) and, as in the *Aeneid,* Dido is solicited, appears and fades away: here follow the choruses lyrically expressing her passion and anguish and lonely death. Following this come the evocation, apparition and tale of Palinurus, the wrecked companion. Subsequently the souls of the dead children arise and are mourned in a (projected)

---

* Elsewhere the poet has spoken of the inspirational value to him to hearing some records of Tasso madrigals set by Monteverdi.[81] It is "poetic justice" perhaps that quite independently the composer Luigi Nono has set Ungaretti's Dido choruses to music.

threnody for Marcellus, the dead stepson of the emperor Augustus.*
So the *Terra* as originally planned was to have grouped itself
about four main points: the initial triumph at arrival in the promised
land and its subversion or drastic qualification by three visitations:
Dido, Palinurus, the emblematic Marcellus. Thus the preluding
rinascimento is revealed as being what Palinurus-Ungaretti would
doubtless call "ironic": the *grido* of the dead (upon which the present
is predicated) troubles and complicates the victory.

As it stands today, very little of this master plan has been realized.
Nineteen choruses "descriptive of Dido's inward state" and the
elaborate Palinurus sestinas are there as proof of original ambitions;
we are also told that certain "choruses of Aeneas" have been sketched.
Ungaretti's accompanying notes elequently assert a pattern that his
verses don't bear out.

> Aeneas is beauty, youth, ingenuousness forever in search of the
> promised land, where his own beauty creates a smile of enchantment
> in the contemplated and fugitive beauty about him. But this is not
> the myth of Narcissus: Aeneas is the vital union of the life of memory,
> imagination and speculation, of the life—that is to say—of the mind;
> he is also the fruitful union of carnal life in the long succession of
> generations . . . Many facts of my life and the life of my country
> have gone into and necessarily amplified the original project of the
> *Terra promessa*. At any rate, even today, the poem should develop
> from the point at which, Aeneas having reached the promised land,
> the figures of his previous experience arise to bear witness to him,
> in his memory, how his present experience—and all the experiences
> that may follow it—will end, until what time it is given to men, when
> time has consumed itself away, to know the true Promised Land.

The poem still, as originally projected, is intended to take place
"within" the inwardness of Aeneas; although Ungaretti doesn't say
so, it still seems to me that the old setting at Cumae or in the fields
of mourning beneath Lake Avernus constitute a sensible aid towards
placing the poem's occasion. But in fact except for the notes Aeneas
is absent from the poem. For example, there is no good reason in
the poems themselves why the reader of good will should experience

---

* This would have been patterned on Vergil's threnody in the closing lines
of Book VI. The theme of *i morti bimbi,* the young and innocent dead—so close
to *Giorno per giorno* and the great Roman-Brazilian elegies of *Il dolore*—is not
not an Ungarettian projection but a substantial Vergilian theme associated with
Aeneas' visit to the fields of mourning in Book VI: besides the Marcellus
passage there is Daedelus's grief for Icarus (VI, 30–33) and the section
beginning on VI, 426 where the thin crying voices of *animae infantum* are
terribly heard.

the choruses of Dido or sestinas of Palinurus as filtered through Aeneas' memories of the past: these sections *as written* stand as the first-person meditations of an aging woman and a man overtaken by catastrophe. Even the original "Canzone" which, as we shall see, involves an experience of "landing" and was originally undoubtedly meant to belong to Aeneas, lacks all sense of triumph and in fact now bears a subtitle which frankly abandons any claim to Vergilian myth: "descrive lo stato d'animo del poeta."

In short Vergil provided stimulus rather than structure. Even in the initial "Canzone" the sole proper name—apart from the crucial "Lethe"—is not "Troy" but "Ithaca," Homer's rather than Virgil's name for home and "promised land."* Of the four sections of the poem that have not been mentioned thus far, one was occasioned by the death of a friend of the poet (Ines Fila) and has no particularly Vergilian relevance; if anything, it belongs with Ungaretti's own *Leggende* of apotheosis-by-dying in the *Sentimento*. The beautiful "Variazioni su nulla" (Variations on Nul) is a superb musical-imagistic evocation of the *sentimento del tempo* and could be a postscript to that volume. The "Segreto del poeta" (Poet's Secret) is in fact a late adjunct to the experience of *Giorno per giorno*, the secret being the precarious faith that has arisen in the father in "the true Promised Land," an afterlife. The "Finale" was originally conceived of as a "chorus of undines."

My own belief is that *La terra promessa* must be read primarily as a roughly "penultimate" installment of a *Vita d'un uomo*, a book of late autumn and coming winter largely composed in the period the poet was moving into his seventh decade.** It hangs upon the idea

---

* "Ithaca" is used again (never "Troy" or "New Troy") in the fourth of the "Last Choruses to the *Terra promessa*" published in *Taccuino del vecchio;* even here the allusion is complicated by Biblical extensions:

> Non d'Itaca si sogna
> Smarriti in vario mare,
> Ma va la mira al Sinai sopra sabbie. . . .

Not of Ithaca they dream, wandering over various seas, but the gaze goes towards Sinai above the sands. . . .

Of course the very title *La terra promessa* immediately suggests Abraham rather than Aeneas, and certainly Ungaretti's remark cited above on the "true Promised Land" suggests a Catholic and unworldly level of intention. Still my point is that the mythic allusions are by no means consistent or controlled, providing no useful "key" for the reader.

** The poet's decision in 1967 to publish *La terra promessa* and *Il taccuino del vecchio* together under the new title *Morte delle stagioni* [The Seasons' Death] would seem to confirm this judgment. The title is also Ungaretti's latest homage to the abiding powers of Leopardi's "L'infinito"—

> . . . e mi sovvien l'eterno,
> E le morte stagioni. . . .

of dying—as indeed what work of Ungaretti from the second half of the *Sentimento* onward does not? The *dolore* of the experience in its most sensuous form is distilled in the nineteen choruses for the abandoned Dido, alone with her memories and premonitions, above all with her exacerbated *sentimento del tempo.* The obsession with some mode of "immortality" or survival—resurrection either via loving memory as in the elegy for Ines Fila or via memory and a "secret" faith in the indestructibility of the pure spirit as in the little Antonietto poem—provides another and by now familiar variant. The two most ambitious moments of the *Terra,* the opening "Canzone" and the "Recitativo di Palinuro," both deal with *naufragio* and descent-by-drowning (old themes) in a new manner—in effect, an intensification of the "Petrarchan and scholastic" vein combined with an arduous cultivation of the elaborate symmetries of traditional stanzaic vehicles. These extremely difficult and "Alexandrian" poems will occupy most of our attention.

As for the *Aeneid,* it should be treated as a suggestive precedent with no schematic function; Vergil is a ghost, an occult presence, who haunts this poem as completely and elusively as Petrarch, Michelangelo, Leopardi and Mallarmé haunted previous poems.

✿   ✿   ✿

It is Petrarch, rather than Vergil, who can provide us with a useful *approdo* to the "Canzone" with the opening quatrain to one of the sonnets to Laura *in morte:*

> Tornami a mente, anzi v'è dentro, quella
> ch'indi per Lete esser non po' sbandita,
> qual io la vidi in su l'età fiorita
> tutta accesa de' raggi di sua stella. . . .

Returns to my mind, and is there within me, she / who therefrom not by Lethe can be banished, / such as I saw her in her flowering time, / wholly radiant with the rays of her star. . . .*

Laura's bright presence, then, survives her physical death and obliteration ("Lethe") through its permanency in the poet's "mind" (and poems); the sonnet triumphantly affirms this immortality.

Ungaretti's "Canzone" opens with the following quatrain:

* This connection is not fortuitous. Piccioni points out in his essay the great number of citations from the *Canzoniere* Ungaretti scribbled in the margins of the "Canzone" mansucript. At one point, the "Canzone" bore the Petrarchan title of "Il trionfo della fama" (The Triumph of Fame).

Nude, le braccia di segreti sazie,
A nuoto hanno del Lete svolto il fondo,
Adagio sciolto le veementi grazie
E le stanchezze onde luce fu il mondo.

The naked arms, swimming, with secrets satiated, / have unveiled
the depths of Lethe, / have slowly released the vehement graces /
and wearinesses whence light was the world.

Here the mood is one of weariness and exhaustion, the quest oblivion.
The memories of "our" world, its flickering and impassioned images,
are willingly relinquished* by the archetypal Ungarettian diver,
now bent on extinction rather than—as in "Il porto sepolto"—"returning
to the light with his songs." Here the major nouns and adjectives
sketch a quiescent descent and self-negation, "arms" tired of con-
serving and bearing now relax and release the phosphorescent
emotions they once served. The poet deliberately places the adjective
nude as the clef of the poem, cupping it with a comma and so accent-
ing the primary thrust towards bareness, *ascesis*, the rejection of
those once blessed images which had obsessed and consoled him.

The single image that remains is Lethe itself, evoked with either
the most abstract and geometric touches—a "strange road," an "impal-
pable propagation of walls" within an iced silence—or, as in the
second quatrain, in terms of negatives or absences:

Nulla è muto piú della strana strada
Dove foglia non nasce o cade o sverna,
Dove nessuna cosa pena o aggrada,
Dove la veglia mai, mai il sonno alterna.

Nothing is more mute than the strange road / where leaf is not
born nor falls nor winters, / where nothing hurts or pleases, / where
waking never, never alternates with sleep.

This is the imperium of the exhausted *senex*, the man who has at
last arrived at the threshold of his death; it is viewed in terms of
quenched senses, passions spent, chill calm. Epistemologically it is a
kind of "nominalist" truth: the vision of the void, the cool nihilism
of the all-but-"pure" mind that can see nothing but shadowy ap-
paritions; "horrid cognizance," says Ungaretti in a note.

It is perhaps useful though not "required" here to recollect Vergil's
Lethe-region, that peaceful pastoral "great good place" where spirits

* In the original manuscripts, Ungaretti used *memorie* instead of the more
oblique and mysterious *segreti*.

drink "the peace-giving waters and long forgetfulness." Vergil's stoic vision of terrestial existence is such that his Aeneas can only wonder why anyone would ever leave the underworld, once more donning the "sluggish body" in the "wretched light" of our day. There is nothing of this pastoralism in Ungaretti's Lethe, whose peace is of the void rather than positive or paradisal. This, rather terrifyingly, is Ungaretti's version of Aenean triumph.

Yet there is suffering even in Vergil's underworld. Aeneas seeks to embrace his father, *tristis imago,* and three times that image dissolves like wind or dream. There is the image of Dido, of passionate love and suffering, as a silent reminder and reproach. In Vergil's cosmos these remnants of unhappy carnality can be placed and comprehended in the great epiphany of *Anima mundi* offered by the father to his son. If, as Anchises says, *Quisque suos patimur Manes* (Each suffers his own ghosts), such suffering purges and eventually frees the spirit for Elysium.

In the original scenario, the joy of Aeneas' arrival in the promised land had been immediately subverted by his memories of the dead. In the bleakly ironic parallel afforded by the "Canzone," the protagonist's (that is, the "poet's state of mind") prognostication of his lethal *terra promessa*—the peace of utter zero—is broken by his memory of life, now imaged as a mysterious *donna*, possibly suggested by Dido though Ungaretti is careful to keep this image as indeterminate, as "mental", as possible. ". . . a lampi, rompe il gelo e riconquide": in flashes there breaks through the ice and reconquers what he calls the first or primal image of love:

> . . . Roseo facendo il buio e, in quel colore,
> Piú d'ogni vita un arco, il sonno, teso.

> . . . making the darkness rosy and, in that hue, / an arch of sleep more taut than any life.

Two important verbs attached to this image are *trasalire* and *rifremire,* to start or tremble as with surprise, to shudder anew as with passion; they indicate the sudden and instinctual-sensual shock of recognition that overtakes the swimmer in the depths of Lethe. Love stands, then, *avversa al nulla, in breve salma,* in opposition to the void that surrounds her, in her mortal flesh.* In an attitude ironically reminiscent of Leopardi's Silvia, who stood pointing out her truth: "cold death and a bare tomb . . . in the distance," she stands and raises her arms in a counterpoint to the swimmer's *nude braccia:*

* It is worth recalling that *salma* is normally employed as a stoic-platonic noun for the flesh conceived as a burden or weight born by the spirit.

> Rivi indovina, suscita la palma:
> Dita dedale svela. . . .

She divines the shores, raises her palm: reveals a daedal finger. . . .

Her truth is mysterious. Are the shores she indicates those of what the poet will call "the true Promised Land"? The adjective modifying the finger that points is "daedal," and so associated with both the fabrication of and mastering of labyrinthine ways (and Lethe itself is called a "propagation of walls") Is her attitude one of prophecy, faith or simple hope? Whatever strengths may lie behind it are made complicated by her frailty and the halo of dream—the firm and roseate arch of sleep—surrounding her.

In effect this apparition concludes the poem. No concessions have been made, no answers given. On the verge of the void, a hint of moving color, a *nulla* in comparison with the abysmal context. But this, says the poem, is enough:

> Non distarrò da lei mai l'occhio fisso
> Sebbene, orribile da spoglio abisso,
> Non si conosca forma che da fama.

. . . Never will I turn from her my fixed eye / although, made horrible in the barren abyss, / form is known only by fame.

The lines from Petrarch vibrate here:

> Tornami a mente, anzi v'è dentro, quella
> ch'indi per Lete esser non po' sbandita . . .

Laura has returned "to mind," an idea that not even Lethe can eradicate. This was what Petrarch meant by what he called "The Triumph of Fame"—not worldly glory or renown but the "immortality" of forms by their metamorphosis into the idea (*fama*) through memory and intelligence. And this was what Ungaretti had in mind when he toyed with the idea of calling his "Canzone" "Il trionfo della fama." But triumph is too strong a word for this desperate vow, this anguished clinging to an image that may be totally illusory, ironic, that in any case recalls the drowning man to his fleshly suffering. Nor has the reality of the void, Lethe, been in any sense abrogated by this precarious resurgence of the "idea"—*that* horrible experience is no illusion. The poem concludes with a last evocation of the blank *strada* towards which all life imperceptibly moves

> . . . Dove lo spazio mai non si degrada
> Per la luce o per tenebra, o altro tempo.

> . . . where space is never reduced / by light or shade, or by some
> other time.

❋ ❋ ❋

The period spanned by the composition of the "Canzone" is something like fifteen years, from 1935 to 1950. The large number of variant versions (for the most part in the manuscripts, though two of them were published in periodicals before the definitive Mondadori edition of 1950) testify to the fact that the "Canzone" is one of the most tormented and self-conscious of Ungaretti's texts. This is a criticism: in my opinion its laborious genesis, conducted semi-publically, has resulted in a wholly scholastic poem. The drastic life experience that it was meant to express has been frozen into something monumental and remote in the classical style, less Carduccian than Palladian. The "Petarchan tendency" in later Ungaretti has produced some of his supreme poems, but these will be found in the later chapters of *Il dolore* rather than in *La terra promessa*. Here it results in a literature of the academy, so freighted with classical allusions and mannerisms as to become at certain points sealed ("hermetically") to anyone but a specialist. My reading makes it clearer than it is. The "Canzone" *needs* the accompanying notes and review of variants and the entire Piccioni apparatus to bring it into focus—consciously or not they are in fact designed to make us instant specialists.* The master-version of the experience underlying the "Canzone" will be found in the lovely birthday poem "Auguri" which suggested it in the first place.

The "Recitativo" of the *gubernator* Palinurus is like the "Canzone" in its stifling concern with literary pedigree and manner. Its plot is close to Vergil's. In *Aeneid* VI Aeneas meets the shade of the lost pilot Palinurus who, scapegoat for the wrath of Juno, was attacked and overcome by Somnus, god of sleep, while he watched the stars. Palinurus tells Aeneas of his end, how he swam, reached the Italian shore and there lost his life. He begs for proper burial and is informed

---

* One example is the key line,

Non si conosca forma che da fama.

Without access, via Piccioni, to Ungaretti's jottings from Petrarch in his margins, the meaning of the vital word *fama* might be obscured and genuinely misleading. The choice of *fama* rather than a more precise noun is of course due to the resonances of time and literary tradition that Ungaretti responds to. But another and more "Alexandrian" reason would be the alliterative and assonantial interplay it makes up with *forma*, so say nothing of its place in a rhyme-system where the *ama*-sound is chimed no less than nine times.

by the Sibyl that justice will be done, that the rock he was broken by will become his tomb, Cape Palinurus.

In the "Recitativo" stages of Palinurus' narrative are slightly altered or elided. Ungaretti's pilot, unlike Vergil's, is a scholarly seer. It is indeed his navigator's "science," the reading of and prophecy by the stars, that leads to his undoing. In the midst the voyage, that is, he becomes suddenly aware of the vanity of all human "measures," of the complete identity of science and dream. This is the blow that wrecks him:

> Senza piú dubbi caddi né piú pace.

> . . . Without further doubts nor further peace I fell.

This, then, is the central originality of Ungaretti's version of the Palinurus story; it was not Somnus, but the pilot's solitary *awakening* into something like a knowledge of Lethe, of the illusion permeating all terrestial activity, that leads to his downfall. For the moment, through what Ungaretti calls his "strenuous fidelity" to the idea of a promised land, he swims after his ship towards the coast upon which he will be dashed to pieces,

> Piloto vinto d'un disperso emblema. . . .

> . . . Conquered pilot of a scattered emblem. . . .

eventually made whole again through the "ironic immortality" of the tomb-headland that now bears his tragic name.

The "Recitativo" is thus a narrative-meditation on the absurdity of the human "measure" and the tragic splendor of keeping faith in it. But the poignant closeness to the subject to Ungaretti's *vita* is obscured by the distracting virtuosity of the expressive means the poet chooses to deploy. The sestina, focused on the adventures in nuance and unfolding connotation of the six terminal words which are its *raison d'être,* is an egregiously complicated artifice whose semantic and musical delights verge on the *tour de force.* At its best it can be the inspired vehicle for an obsessive contemplation of a sextet of images or ideas; at worst, a mere technical exercise. Either way it is not eminently suited for presenting narrative or abstract meditation—that is, the "matter" of the "Recitativo." Ungaretti's six terminals: "fury," "sleep," "waves," "peace," "emblem," and "mortal," like the *-ama* fixation in the "Canzone," seem to master and even pervert his subject. His two experiments in consistent and rich rhyming mark the single deadend of his technically prodigious career.

✿   ✿   ✿

The remaining sections of the *Terra:* the little elegy, the choruses for Dido and the three brief concluding lyrics, are triumphs in his "simpler" style. The exquisite "Variazioni su nulla" employs the sestina device of obsessive repetition of certain key images—a grain of sand, an hourglass, a cloud, a hand—with matchless resource and beauty. But it is the nineteen "choruses descriptive of the inner states of Dido" that should bring our remarks on *La terra promessa* to a close.

The subject is summarized in the notes (which are not necessary) as "the departure of the final glimmerings of youth from a person:

> Here one has wished to give the physical experience of the drama, with recoveries of happy moments, the uncertainties of dream-states, fear-ridden modesties, all in the midst of the delirium of a passionate being watching itself perishing, growing repugnant, desolate, barren.

"Dileguandosi l'ombra," the first chorus begins: "The shadow vanishing," and we as good Vergilians may be forgiven for assuming that the shadow belongs to the departed Aeneas as he disappears over the northern horizon towards Rome. It *is* Aeneas, of course, but it is the ceding of the dark present to the radiantly resurrected past that is also evoked, the trajectory through time of an anguished memory:

> Dileguandosi l'ombra
>
> In lontananza d'anni,
>
> Quando non laceravano gli affanni. . . .

The shadow vanishing,

In the distance of the years,

When sufferings did not lacerate. . . .

The principle governing the sequence of these short lyrics is broadly associative (as in *Giorno per giorno*). What they amount to is a complicated "sentimental" experience, an assortment of affective reactions and oscillations lined out on the axis of *senilità*, with mobility provided by memory. As in the Arcadian landscapes of the *Sentimento* or the Brazilian-Roman evocations of *Il dolore*, *paesaggio* is employed to express mood, as an index to inner state. The same is true, in fact, of all physical detail: the memory of her virginal blush ("April fire on a scented cheek") suggested by the "suspended fire" of sunset brings her to contrast the unexpressed expectancies of long ago with the sterile silence enclosing her now in her abandonment—an intricate counterpoint of interchoral images.

Most of all one finds in these choruses an extraordinary evocative power, the "capture" of a fleeting mood.

> La sera si prolunga
> Per un sospeso fuoco
> E un fremito nell'erbe a poco a poco
> Pare infinito a sorte ricongiunga.

The evening prolongs itself / in a suspended fire / and a shiver in the grass little by little / seems to reunite the infinite to my destined lot.

So all creation seems to "catch" the erotic suspense of an innocent Dido of long ago: a remembered moment less ecstatic but similar to "M'illumino/d'immenso". And in her alternate fascination with and bitter rejection of images, Dido is herself the image of her tormented maker:

> Trarresti dal crepuscolo
> Un'ala interminabile.
>
> Con le sue piume piú fugaci
> A distratte strie ombreggiando,
> Senza fine la sabbia
> Forse ravviveresti.

You would draw from the evening / an interminable wing. / With its most fleeting feathers / casting shadows in distraut streaks, / you would make the sand, / perhaps, endlessly live again.

Compare the ironic portrait of a self-convicted dreamer with the old *L'Allegria* stanza . . .

> Ungaretti
> uomo di pena
> ti basta un'illusione
> per farti coraggio. . . .

An *image* was sufficient, a "measure." It is the desolate wisdom of Dido to recognize the desert that produces the mirage. This is the desolation out of which her vibrant *grido* arises.

❖   ❖   ❖

The last two° installments of the *Vita d'un uomo* are slim and relatively minor Ungaretti. The first, *Un grido e paesaggi,* incorporates poems written between 1949 and 1952. (The large single exception to this, the *grido* itself ["Gridasti: Soffoco"], was composed as part of the Antonietto cycle of 1939–40; we have discussed it above.) *Grido* apart, the book turns out to be this "man of pain's" least anguished collection: for once memory is content to evoke the past without regret, as though for the sake of describing. The effect is of a slender album of snapshots exhibited by an old man in a relatively contented and expansive mood.

Thus "Semantica" is a little philological tour of the Brazilian jungle, its flora and fauna duly and jocosely noted. The *Svaghi* (Amusements, Divertissements) are little picture poems (young lady bicyclists in Holland, pigeons in Ravenna, etc.) which are basically reformulations in terms of hendecasyllables of various passages taken from the *Gazzetta del Popolo* travel-pieces of the early 1930's. The most ambitious of these reminiscings is the long (202 lines) "Monologhetto" (Little Monologue), originally a prose lecture composed for a radio broadcast, then shaped into a loosely structured poetic discourse thereafter, of *vers libres* combined with hendecasyllables. Much of the original lecture was based on passages from the *Gazzetto* articles; the poem, like the concurrent *Svaghi,* often retains their wording.

"Monologhetto" is a monologue *en pantoufles,* too gregarious to quality as soliloquy. It bears the stamp of its occasion (broadcast), and original form (prose). It is an essay on the month of February, the month of the poet's birth, the month of Antonietto's birth and death. To start with it is presented as the season of nature's secret resurrection after the frozen sleep of winter. So the poem begins:

> Sotto le scorze, e come per un vuoto,
> Di già gli umori si risentono,
> Si snodano, delirando di gemme. . . .

Beneath the bark, as in a vacantness, / already the saps feel themselves stirring again, / unknotting themselves, raving with buds. . . .

With this stirring the memory unfolds a series of autobiographical images drawn from various Februaries the poet has known: the piping of birds in the Maremma, a trip by cart from Foggia to Lucera, recollections of Corsica, his landing in Brazil and the

---

° But see headnote to Ungaretti notes below.

stupendous vision of a *delirando* and dancing city during Carnival, finally memories of Alexandria, the Arab quarter and his mother.

The linking and drift of all this material at first seems simply associative and casual. Yet there is a theme that gradually discloses itself in the relaxed succession of lines and moments: the perennial quest for an unearthly and God-centered order of reality . . . the quest but not the discovery.

Images from February's pre-Lenten Carnival thread through the early sections of "Monologhetto": the slaughter of the festival pig in Corsica, the universal Mardi Gras and endless dancing in the streets of Recife, Brazil, the masked riot of the season, all are explicitly linked to the delirium of buds within the secretly burgeoning trees. Yet this movement toward the "ascensions" of primavera and Easter has its darker ramifications in the old Ungarettian motif of our inescapable worldly illusions. Carnival terminates in Ash Wednesday, "il giorno . . . *Del Sei polvere e ritornerai in polvere. . .* " (the day of the "Dust thou art and to dust thou shalt return . . .") and with its evocation the "awakening" which Ungaretti sees as the whole theme of his discourse becomes ironic, futile. This is how the poem concludes:

> Impaziente, nel vuoto, ognuno smania,
> S'affanna, futile,
> A reincarnarsi in qualche fantasia
> Che anch'essa sarà vana . . .
> Non c'è, altro non c'è su questa terra
> Che un barlume di vero
> E il nulla della polvere,
> Anche se, matto incorreggibile,
> Incontro al lampo dei miraggi
> Nell'intimo e nei gesti, il vivo
> Tendersi sembra sempre.

Impatient, in the vacantness, each of us raves, / futilely labors / to reincarnate himself in some fantasy / which too will be vain . . . / There is not, nothing other is there on this earth / than a glimmer of truth / and the nothingness of the dust / —even if, incorrigible maniac, / towards the light of the mirages / in his deepest self and in his acts, the living man / seems forever to reach after.

The impossible thirst for a "glimmer of truth" beyond the dusty answer of mortality, the concurrent awareness that even that glimmer may be mirage, such is the desolate nomad's wisdom which closes not only the "Monologhetto" but the *Vita d'un uomo* as we have it today. The *Taccuino del vecchio* or old man's notebook offers twenty-five "last choruses for the *Terra promessa*"* which in their complex choral totality find that land as intimately haunting, as distant, as before.

> Si percorre il deserto con residui
> Di qualche immagine di prima in mente,
> Della Terra Promessa
> Nient'altro un vivo sa.

One roams the desert places with remnants / of some old early image in mind / —of the Promised Land / a living man knows nothing else.

The quality of the experience offered by the *bella biografia* that Ungaretti leaves behind is extraordinarily consistent—a spiritual self-portrait in the strictest sense. We have had occasion to talk about *spiritus loci* in his poems, the *paesaggi* of Egypt, the Carso, Paris, Lazio, *mezzogiorno*, Brazil, Rome, and surely this old phrase seems peculiarly appropriate if used to designate the evaporative chemistry effected by Ungaretti's imagination when it comes in touch with matter; terrestrial locus rarifies into spirit or idea.

As for the "idea," it is very simple and very terrible: we are dying, all is vanity. Convinced that we inhabit a world of shifting and perishing appearances, this question then becomes metaphysical or, since it is a matter of faith rather than knowledge, religious. Is there a reality beyond appearances?

His three years as combatant in World War I brought him into intermittent contact with a holistic vision of a joyous cosmos in which all things were consumed and spiritualized. In those ecstatic moments of weightlessness and radiance he resembles his own description of the William Blake who wrote *Songs of Innocence:* "the inspired poet if there ever was one." War over and conditions radically altered, it seems he lost his contact and his sense of cosmic *allegria*. The themes grow dark—his songs of innocence become songs of experience. The present grows increasingly spectral; memory becomes both the subject and action of his poetry. His sense of sin, limit and decay becomes increasingly anguished, and the blows that time brings him—his dead—only augment this anguish.

---

* E.g., brief lyrics in the fragmented introspective mode of *Giorno per giorno* or the Dido choruses. These poems were composed between 1952–1960 and were occasioned by moments from the poet's private and public existence— thoughts of his dead, for instance, or a last visit to Egypt, a jet flight from Hong Kong to Beirut. They serve to indicate a final abandonment of any claims on the *Aeneid*.

Against his "horrid cognizance" he has two stays: the religion he was baptized into, and his poetry. The two constitute a connected experience. His tormented awareness of the poem as a mere solipsistic projection or fantasy (a "measure" unrelated to the "mystery") infects the icons of his Catholicism. His characteristic posture is a *pietà*, preferably fashioned by a Michelangelo advanced in years.

Moving toward what he calls in the *Ultimi cori* the "great silence," he wonders whether he will learn at least "whether death only reigns over appearances." His occasional intimations that this might be so—the revisitations of the *Leggende* or the long vigil for Antonietto—make up his hope of salvation. His memories of mortal innocence then become tentatively prophetic, his witness to the ultimately triumphant spirit. But the triumph will only be substantiated by dying.

Ungaretti's poetry is the perfect vehicle for his haunted inwardness. Occasionally, as we have seen, his scholarship can swamp his inspiration, giving rise to a mere "neoclassicism." But the vast majority of the pages of *Vita d'un uomo*—that passionately literary and learned life—constitute a superb demonstration of the vital energy the great Italian tradition has to contribute to the expressive needs of the present. Marinetti sought to be freed of the past by suppressing it. Ungaretti lovingly and urgently solicits that past and finds what is alive in it. Marinetti produced a stillborn "modernism." Ungaretti produces a body of work which is not only an extraordinarily resonant "measure" of one man's spiritual struggles in this difficult century, but a richly instructive lesson to his countrymen of the natural-national resources at their disposal. He has prepared almost single-handedly the ground for what must be the essential condition for modernity in any land: an organic and nutritive relation with the past.

Notes

[1993: Giuseppi Ungaretti died at the age of eighty-two on 1 June 1970. Currently his *Vita d'un uomo* is published on Mondadori in two volumes. The first, subtitled *Tutte le poesie*, is edited by Leone Piccioni. It contains the complete poems (including two very slender late installments published after *Il taccuino del vecchio*), a substantial commentary on his work by the poet himself, critical apparatus and variants, and a bibliography. The second, edited by Mario Diacono and Luciano Rebay, is subtitled *Saggi e interventi* (Essays and Interventions). It gathers all of the poet's considerable prose output on literary and cultural matters (reviews, interviews, essays, lectures), plus notes and bibliography. Ungaretti's translations and travel essays remain in the format described on pp. 135–36 above. In the notes that follow, *TP* = *Vita d'un uomo: Tutte le poesie*, and *SI* = *Vita d'un uomo: Saggi e interventi*.]

1. *TP*, pp. 527–28.

2. *SI*, p. 836.

3. *Il deserto e dopo*, p. 84.

4. Ibid., pp. 26–27.

5. Ibid., p. 169.

6. For many of the details and citations to follow I wish to acknowledge my debt to Luciano Rebay's excellent study of Ungaretti's earlier poetry and the various influences on it: *Le origini della poesia di Giuseppe Ungaretti* (Rome, 1962).

7. Letter to Ardengo Soffici, Rebay, p. 36.

8. From a broadcast made in 1958, at which time the poet read and commented upon "In memoria," Rebay, p. 22.

9. *SI*, p. 741.

10. Interview in the Roman newspaper *Il Tevere*, 18 July 1932: Rebay, p. 14.

11. *SI*, p. 837.

12. *Il deserto e dopo*, p. 135.

13. Interview published in *Les nouvelles lettres*, 24 June 1959, cited in Gianni Pozzi, *La poesie italiana del Novecento* (Turin, 1965), p. 136.

14. *SI*, pp. 742–44.

15. The remark by Reverdy was originally printed in his magazine *Nord-Sud*, March 1918. Its broader circulation comes from its being used by André Breton in the first surrealist manifesto of 1924—this is undoubtedly where Ungaretti found it. Ungaretti quotes Reverdy (at the time he was unable to recall the source) in his interview with G. B. Angioletti (*SI*, pp. 191, 915–16: Rebay and Diacono believe the remark originated with Marinetti, whom Ungaretti was loath to praise).

16. Cited in Rebay, p. 95.

17. *Les cinq livres*, p. 330. See also *TP*, p. 526.

18. *SI*, p. 478.

19. *SI*, p. 744.

20. *SI*, p. 751.

21. *SI*, p. 762.

22. *SI*, p. 154.

23. *SI*, p. 191.

24. *SI*, pp. 751–52.

25. *SI*, p. 839.

26. *SI*, p. 434.

27. *SI*, p. 47–49.

28. *SI*, p. 135.

29. *SI*, p. 1,003.

30. *SI*, p. 490.

31. What follows was first published in slightly different form in *Cesare Barbieri Courier*, spring 1966.

32. *La poesie ermetica* (Bari, 1947), p. 69.

33. Ibid., p. 72.

34. *Zibaldone di pensieri*, ed. Francesco Flora (Milan, 1957), vol. II, p. 1,121 (23 July 1827).

35. Ibid., pp. 1230–31 (30 November 1828).

36. Ibid., p. 459 (16–18 September 1823).

37. Ibid., vol. I, pp. 38–39.

38. *Cento e cento e cento e cento pagine del libro segreto di Gabriele D'Annunzio tentato di morire* (Milan, 1959), p. 128.

39. *Zibaldone*, vol. I (1820), pp. 135–36.

40. Ibid., p. 1,483 (18 June 1822); see also p. 1,275 (5 November 1821).

41. Ibid., vol. II (27 April 1829), p. 1,303.

42. Enrico Thovaz, *Il pastore, il gregge e la zampogna* (Turin, 1948).

43. *SI*, p. 745.

44. *SI*, p. 191.

45. *SI*, pp. 87–89, 753–56, 1,003.

46. *SI*, pp. 135–37.

47. *SI*, p. 154.

48. *SI*, p. 191.

49. Responses as noted by Elio Accrocca in the Ungaretti issue of *Letteratura*, nos. 35–36, September–December 1959, p. 349.

50. Ungaretti's chief *discorsi* on Leopardi: "Il pensiero di Leopardi," [*SI*, pp. 324–43], "Immagini del Leopardi e nostre," [*SI*, pp. 430–50], "Secondo discorso su Leopardi," [*SI*, pp. 451–96], "L'*Angelo Mai* del Leopardi," [*SI*, pp. 497–503]. See also "Ragioni di una poesia," [*SI*, pp. 754–67].

51. Rebay, pp. 134–58.

52. *SI*, p. 478.

53. *SI*, p. 222.

54. *SI*, pp. 839–40.

55. *SI*, p. 746; *TP*, p. 541.

56. Quoted by Leone Piccioni, "Ungaretti e la poesia," Ungaretti issue of *Letteratura*, pp. 77–78.

57. Quoted by Piccioni, Ungaretti issue of *Letteratura*, pp. 77–78.

58. For this and citation directly following, *SI*, pp. 221–22.

59. *TP*, p. 567.

60. Cited in Giacinto Spagnoletti, *Tre poeti italiani del Novecento* (Turin, 1958), p. 5.

61. *Storia*, chapter on *Cuor morituro: Prose*, p. 516.

62. Montale, *Sulla poesia*, p. 306.

63. Rebay, pp. 24–33.

64. *SI*, p. 471.

65. *SI*, p. 488. Leopardi's note can be found in the Moroncini edition of the *Canti*, vol. 2, p. 420.

66. *SI*, p. 473.

67. *SI*, pp. 398–422. Rebay, p. 27.

68. See his remarks in Ungaretti issue of *Letteratura*, p. 327, and "Storia di una traduzione," *SI*, pp. 649–52.

69. *TP*, p. 418.

70. *SI*, p. 841.

71. *SI*, p. 204.

72. "Dante," in *Il poeta e il politico e altri saggi*, p. 85.

73. *SI*, p. 577.

74. *SI*, p. 841.

75. *SI*, p. 577.

76. *SI*, p. 841.

77. Ungaretti's comments on *La terra promessa* will be found in *TP*, pp. 545–67.

78. "La pesca miracolosa," *Il deserto e dopo*, p. 159.

79. "Elea e la primavera, *Il deserto e dopo*, p. 156.

80. Piccioni's study of origins and variants will be found in *TP*, pp. 427–64. A long footnote on the poet's original scenario is omitted here; it can be found in Piccioni's *Lettura leopardiana e altri saggi* (Florence, 1952), pp. 294–96.

81. Quoted by Giuseppe De Robertis in the Ungaretti issue of *Letteratura*, p. 187.

IV   EUGENIO MONTALE

. . . sapere, ecco ció che conta *. . .*

The Riviera di Levante extends southeastward from Genoa along the Ligurian Sea, roughly 120 miles by the Via Aurelia to the industrial town of La Spezia. For the first half of this distance the highway conforms to the shoreline, running in a mildly graded corridor between the sea and the Apennines. Along this sector are the smart resorts (Portofino, Santa Margherita Ligure, urbane Rapallo), the glamorous views of coastline east and west, the villages and coves, beaches and villas, the fleets of fishing smacks and international yachts—all the symptoms in short of that summery *dolce vita* promised by the name of *riviera.* At the town of Sestri Levante however the highway leaves the coast and climbs inland in a sequence of switches and passes through an increasingly mountainous terrain that concludes, at length, in a winding descent to the sea again, the bay of La Spezia, the promontory of Portovenere, the great plain of the river Magra to the south.

From Portovenere, a village dating back to Roman times (Portus Veneris) that seems from the water like a turreted castle hacked out of an almost sheer face of rock, you can look northward toward that portion of the Ligurian coast that is inaccessible by highway: there are the Cinque Terre, the five isolated little villages of Riomaggiore, Manarola, Corniglia, Vernazza and Monterosso. A railroad links them to the great world outside, bringing mail, supplies, the occasional tourist or summer resident, but views of the *paese* are rare from the train, which traverses the rocky and precipitous land in an almost continuous series of tunnels. To know the Cinque Terre one must make an offshore cruise or what Pound—a resident of Rapallo—called "periplum." Otherwise and better, one must walk.

Visitors aside—it is not an easy visit—the country belongs to the fishermen who work its coasts and the owners of its little vineyards which cling between sea and sky to its rocky shoulders and produce a sweetish white wine of "pronounced" bouquet. It is poor land, the living it exacts must be as tenacious as its vegetation—vines, cactus, agave, the occasional fig tree—to coax survival out of the salt- and sun-starved rock. Its houses must cling like its vines, joined by narrow

235

footpaths cut stairwise in the resistant ground. It is ridged and divided in itself by steep Apennine escarpments laced with mountain torrents that do not water the land so much as fall from its back into the sea, sometimes making its waters as sulphur-yellow as the rocks above. It is a *paese* that expresses a kind of massive, dumb resistance, a "long patience"—Eluard's *dur désir de durer* comes to mind—laconic always, refractory.

It has had its poets—Ceccardo Roccatagliata-Ceccardi, Mario Novaro, Giovanni Boine, Camillo Sbarbaro—constituting not a school but assorted sensibilities that drew upon the Ligurian Riviera for local color and veristic imagery. Above all it has had Eugenio Montale, who was born in Genoa on October 12, 1896 and who spent most of the first thirty years of his life either in Genoa—where he grew up, went to school, studied voice and worked as a journalist—or at Monterosso in the Cinque Terre, where his family owned a villa and spent the summers. His first volume of poems in particular—*Ossi di seppia*: Cuttlefish Bones—is permeated by the sensuous experience of Liguria, whether the industrial port of Genoa:

> Paese di ferrame e alberature
> a selva nella polvere del vespro.
> Un ronzío lungo viene dall'aperto,
> strazia com'unghia ai vetri. . . .

Country of iron and masts / forested in the evening dust. / A drawn-out buzzing comes from out there, / lacerates like nails on glass. . . .

or a smart café in Rapallo:

> . . . truccato dai fumi
> che svolgono tazze, velato
> tremore di lumi oltre i chiusi
> cristalli, profili di femmine
> nel grigio, tra lampi di gemme
> e screzi di sete. . . .

. . . masked by the fumes / that cups unfurl, veiled / tremor of lights beyond the closed / show-windows, profiles of women / in the grey amid flashing gems / and whistling silks. . . .

or above all the headland of the Cinque Terre and the sea that grinds against it.

"Curious to think," Montale would write of Monterosso in 1943, "how each of us has a *paese* like this . . . which must remain *his very own* landscape, forever immutable. Curious how the physical order is so slow to filter into us and then so impossible to cancel."[1] It is easy to assume, on the basis of remarks like this and a cursory inspection of the *Ossi*, that we are dealing with a regionalist, a "Ligurian" poet like Ceccardo or Boine or his slightly older friend Sbarbaro. Certainly Montale learned something from his countrymen and predecessors: "Where they adhered most closely to the textures of our land, they undoubtedly represented a teaching for me. . . ."[2] He has pointed out "a common dryness of language," derived not from reading but from living in the same terrain, which links him with the others, "an affinity of roots rather than fruit."[3] But while certain aspects of the physical order of the Ligurian *paesaggio*— namely what critics are fond of calling its *petrosità, scabrezza* and *aridità* (stoniness, roughness, aridity)—are common to *Ossi di seppia* (1925) and the earlier work of Camillo Sbarbaro (*Resine*: 1911), it is the difference in what they make of it that is interesting. It is not just that Montale's horizons expand stupendously in his subsequent volumes. It is not just his infinitely richer verbal *impasto*—in terms of both a more various rhythmic and musical repertoire and of an extremely wide-ranging and adventurous lexicon drawing on historical-literary and scientific-naturalistic usages. It lies in the very meaning, for each, of an experience of "physical order."

For Sbarbaro, Liguria is where he lives and writes. As such, as *surrounding*, it takes its place in his poetry. It provides a backdrop for, sometimes an extension of, his moods. It is a *scene* in which a certain subjective action—his own—unfolds.

Elio Vittorini once tried to distinguish between the Ligurias of the two poets by saying that Sbarbaro only described his, while Montale presented his dramatically, "in action."[4] This is unfair to Sbarbaro but it makes the essential point: that *for Montale the landscape is a coequal presence*. Not only is it not friable or porous or an emanation of spirit like Ungaretti's, not only is it not simply an historically experienced sensation or "view" like Sbarbaro's, but it has its own massive life which impinges upon and sometimes threatens to engulf the poet's.*

This can best be observed in a poem. A good start is the earliest one we know of that he chose to publish, written in 1916 at the age of twenty.

---

* As we shall see this faculty of perception is related to his cult of the talisman or amulet, his confessed "animism." His attitude toward this is superbly reasonable and serene (cf. Ungaretti's): ". . . animism is the spiritual position most worthy of man as well as most logical because man is unable to get outside himself and cannot measure things with a measure that differs from his own."[5]

Meriggiare pàllido e assorto
presso un rovente muro d'orto,
ascoltare tra i pruni e gli sterpi
schiocchi di merli, frusci di serpi.

Nelle crepe del suolo o su la veccia
spiar le file di rosse formiche
ch'ora si rómpono ed ora s'intrecciano
a sommo di minùscole biche.

Osservare tra frondi il palpitare
lontano di scaglie di mare
mentre si lévano trèmuli scricchi
di cicale dai calvi picchi.

E andando nel sole che abbaglia
sentire con triste meraviglia
com'è tutta la vita e il suo travaglio
in questo seguitare una muraglia
che ha in cima cocci aguzzi di bottiglia.

To shelter from the noon sun, pale and abstracted, / by a baking garden wall, / to hear among the thorns and brush / crackles of blackbirds, rustles of snakes./

In the cracks of the ground or on the vetch / to spy upon the files of red ants / that now break up and now reknit / at the tip of miniature heaps. /

To observe through palm leaves the faroff / palpitation of the scales of the sea / while tremulous screaks of cicadas / rise from the bald peaks. /

And moving into the sun that dazzles / to feel with sad wonder / how all life and its travail / is in this following a high wall / topped with broken bits of bottle.

Here we are given a scrupulously observed corner of the world, solidly realized in all its vital weight. Its main sensory features are pervading heat and dryness—even the sea is expressed as a serpentine arrangement of pulsing scales allied to the garden snakes previously introduced. Above all there is a dominant sensation of harshness or abrasiveness that is not only visual and tactile but auditory as well. I have in mind by this not just the citation of certain summer sounds in the poem—the various crepitations, dryish in themselves, of blackbird, snake, cicada—but the "tough" cultivation of dissonance: the progressive dislocation of rhyme sequence so as to preclude any possible *cantilena* movement, the apparent diffidence of the off-rhymes (*veccia/intrecciano*) or the monotonous dactyls terminating the lines of the last stanza (*-aglia, -iglia, -iglio, -aglia, -iglia*), the harping on flat, thin vowel colors and sharp consonantal stops (notably in the crackling succession of k-sounds, shrill i's and flat a's in such a phrase as *scricchi/di cicale dai calvi picchi.*) This is a physical order sensuously—musically—expressed in all its raspish graininess. It is also (and this is the "plot" of the poem) a physical order that gradually extrudes a "metaphysical" one, a moral or spiritual signification sensuously activated by specific and concrete detail.*

That is, we can see not only how the *triste meraviglia* subscribed to in the final stanza but its object as well—life experienced as a weary monotonous passage mapped wholly in terms of exclusions and limits—have been expressed in the textures of the poem from the very beginning. The "wonder" is surely there in the accuracy and clarity of eye and ear that render the experience in the strictest detail. Its "sadness" emerges in the sensitive registration of the process by which such elements as the thorns, the sea-scales, the crack of the blackbird, build a system of minor rejections and bristlings that program a labyrinthine extension of the *muraglia* into nature itself. The monotony and futility of the promenade are indeed suggested by the pallor and abstractedness of the speaker himself, whose introversion severely qualifies any simple "pastoralism" possibly suggested by *meriggiando* and the joys of siesta. The very tenselessness of the verbs upon which the poem is founded—the sequence of infinitives: *meriggiare, ascoltare, spiar, osservare, palpitare, sentire, seguitare*—grammatically implies enforced passivity, lack of transition or consequence, a shadowy perpetuity or prolongation (kin to what Proust found in Flaubert's "eternal imperfect") that coagulates into a "metaphysic" of vicious circle, depletion, radical delimitation.

In his self-conducted interview called "Intenzioni," Montale speaks of "Meriggiare . . ." as his "first fragment *tout entier à sa proie attaché*. . . . The 'prey' was, you understand, *my* landscape: il *mio* paesaggio." Does that possessive pronoun (the italics are the poet's) mean Monterosso, in the Cinque Terre of the Riviera di Levante?

I think not. The *paese* I understand as uniquely Montalean is some harsh and refractory ground lending objective weight and substance to a complicated experience of *blockade*. Early poems like "Meriggiando . . ." present it in the perfectly appropriate image of Liguria: sometimes, as in that poem, explicitly as an episode of walls. Walls,

* In 1934 the critic Pietro Pancrazi distinguished two Montales, one "physical" the other "metaphysical." His phrase has stuck, though not in the dichotomous way he offered it. What is characteristically Montalean is the way in which his "metaphysics" are *there* in his "physics"—and the other way around. When one talks about the *presence* or co-presence of the "outside" world in his poetry, one means its proximity as a substantial intelligence, inscrutable perhaps but felt, acknowledged, and perhaps feared.

his example reminds us, have at least a double function: they exclude or confine. Either way of course, viewed from the outside or the inside, they separate and are accessory to solitude (not necessarily an evil) and "alienation" (solitude regarded as disease). They are also, ideally, unbroken (or even the gates are guarded) in order to create the geometrical condition of a vicious circle. Thus he who walks beside an integral wall will end as he began, either inside or outside. The flavor of such an adventure can be oppressive, providing precisely that "delirium of immobility" suffered by Montale's most famous alter ego or self-caricature, the *raté* and *flâneur* Arsenio.

Mention of Arsenio should remind us that the wall need not be literal: the sensation of blockade in Montale has a large repertoire of ingenious manifestations. A catalogue drawn up from the earlier poetry would include rocky cliffs above a gnawing sea, a trance- or torpor-inducing sun, southwesters, waterspouts and "fleeing horizons." Or a naturalist's notations on a weakening grip or petering-out: a riverbed turned dry gulley, the brittle feathering of a clump of stranded reeds, salt-caked and ripped fishnets drying on a stoney beach, the agave clutching at a wave-worn shoal, cuttlefish bones, a sullen and precarious vegetation. In short, the elements to hand of an edge or limit, a riviera or *finisterre*.

Later on there are other, odder manifestations involving artifacts that suddenly take on portentous life: a defaced garden statue of Pomona, the arthritic wheeze of a pumphandle, a blackened mirror, the revolving door of an English resort-hotel. Still others are elaborate and narrative; his third book of verse *La bufera e altro* (The Storm and Other Matters) comes to what the poet calls a provisional conclusion in the 1950's with image of a prisoner living out his nightmare from the cell of some Kafkan castle. More recently the same prisoner has composed an icy *apologia pro sua vita* from the cloacal subterranea of the Augean stables, no Heraklean prospect even remotely in view.

Still other wall-surrogates are less concise and palpable. There are the interpolations or fissure-moats of history: the phenomenon of fascism produces many ramifications in the later poetry. There is time that cuts one off from parts of oneself and from those who were part of one—Montale likens its action to a scissors (cruel reactivation of the old bottle-crested *muraglia*). There is the wall of space and distancing implicit in the notion of riviera, particularly poignant in the *circa tremila miglia* (roughly three thousand miles) separating the poet of the 1930's and 1940's from his Beatrice, the salvation-bearer Clizia. But this obstacle is the product not only of politics and space but of quality of being. When Montale writes of her that "she is already *outside,* while we are *inside,*"[6] he refers not just to the borders of Italy or Europe but to his *donna's* angelification and the blank wall—the cold taste of purblindness and ignorance, the sour taste of contingency—erected by his own clay.

This catalogue is not exhaustive but it will serve as a preliminary sketch of the variety and coherence of Montale's true *paese,* of which "Liguria" happens to be simply the first definitive formulation. When he looks back on "Meriggiare . . ." as the initial fragmentary crystallization of *his* landscape, it is not on the grounds of its "likeness" to a noon at Monterosso (though his descriptive powers are remarkable) but because of its fidelity to an order of physical-metaphysical experience that can be generalized as "blockade," or so I believe. As for the legitimate question "Blocked from what?" a passage from the indispensable "Intenzioni" seems relevant. He is referring to the period (1921–1925) during which most of *Ossi di seppia* was composed.

> I obeyed a need for musical expression. I wanted my word to be more adherent than that of any other poet that I knew. More adherent to what? It seemed to me I lived under a glass bell, and yet I felt myself close to something essential. A subtle veil, a thread just kept me from the ultimate *quid.* Absolute expression would have been the breaking of that bell, that thread, the end of the illusion of the world as representation. But this was an unreachable limit. And my will towards adherence remained musical, instinctive, nonprogrammatic. I wanted to twist the neck of our old aulic tongue's eloquence, possibly at the risk of a counter-eloquence.

So: blocked from "something essential," an unknown *quid* which words like "freedom" or "completion" do nothing to illuminate.* But we have already noted that the primary character of the experience involves an oppressive sense of being screened or excluded. If one knew from what, one would already be on the way "through" or "out."

❋   ❋   ❋

By "musical expression," Montale seems to mean a high degree of fidelity ("adherence") to the sensuous character of a given experience in the expression of that experience. Our reading of "Meriggiare . . ." shows that he was precocious in this direction, that he found his own expressive voice early with a minimum of apprenticework or *solfeggiando.*✶✶ That he conceives of music as dramatically expressive

---

* In a poem entitled "Crisalide" he refers to it as "liberty, the miracle, the fact that was not necessary. . . ."

✶✶ E.g., running up and down the scales. "A poet mustn't injure his voice by practicing scales too much. He mustn't lose that quality of timbre that later on will never be recoverable" ("Intenzioni").

is a reminder that Montale's first ambitions were not literary but operatic, that he aspired to "debut in the part of Valentine in Gounod's *Faust*" and studied voice in Genoa under the great Verdian baritone Ernesto Sivori. This career ("for which," he says in "Intenzioni," "the prognostications were hopeful,") was broken off by the war—in which he served for several years with the Alpine troops—the death of Sivori and the subsequent ravages of a merciless insomnia. But to judge from *Ossi di seppia* alone, a distinctive poetic timbre was his from the very beginning.

This would be slightly misleading. Recently valedictorian concessions have been made which enable us to witness something of Montale's literary *solfeggiando*—neither long nor apparently arduous but still indubitably there.* The titular description—*Accordi & pastelli* —of this apprenticework is apt, suggesting precisely the sort of sensitive, vagueish, slightly portentous post-symbolist impressionism it contains. The *Accordi* suite, for instance, has seven sections, each named after a musical instrument ("Oboe," "Violins," "Brasses," etc.). Each poem is meant to be an imitation of the "Sensations and Fantasies of a Young Girl" (the general subtitle) as she dreamily experiences the music of each instrument.

What is chiefly interesting in this suite is the evidence it provides of the young author still looking for his voice and his *paese*. The predictable Frenchified elements are all there: *vers libres* (very quickly to be abandoned), envious invokings of the *Azur*, ecstatic abandonments and offerings of the heart to "Life," obligatory intimations of *Liebestod*, void and life's unreality. In short, a set of *fin de siècle* attitudes even unto the final prose *tutti*: "Unissono fragoroso d'istrumenti. Comincia lo spettacolo della vita" (Violent ensemble of instruments. The spectacle of life begins). Of course the elements listed above are not in themselves irrelevant to contemporary experience. But in order not to be mere *idées reçues* from the last century, they require a voice that can ground and energize them. At this juncture Montale was not consistently able to produce it.

Only one of the *Accordi* was able to pass the poet's tough self-

---

* *Accordi & pastelli* (Chords & Pastels) (Milan, 1963) contains a suite of seven poems (*Accordi*) written some time after "Meriggiare . . ." (1916) and before 1920 and, with one exception, never before published in book form, and "Musica sognata" (Dreamed Music), written in 1923, published in the first *Ossi* but dropped from successive editions.

Satura (Medley) (Verona, 1962) contains two new (1961–62) poems and three early (1919–24) ones, one of which—"Minstrels": a new and Debussyan title for "Musica sognata"—was an attempt to catch in words the qualities of the maestro's *Minstrels*. The high incidence of musical allusion in this early work is interesting. [See Montale, *L'opera in versi*, pp.759–72.]

criticism and make the pages of the *Ossi*—this was "Corno inglese" (English Horn), revised and rhythmically structured on the rise and fall of the wind: technically impressive but still in my opinion sub-Baudelairean. A more interesting "survival" of at least the plot of the *Accordi* can be found in the slightly later poem entitled "Falsetto," another portrait of a young girl.

The unnamed adolescent of the suite was a faceless conglomeration of budding desires and premonitory inhibitions. But beyond the stage-direction furnished in the subtitle (e.g., young girl, dreamy), she remains totally unsituated and disincarnate, a pastel repertoire of disjunct moods. One feels that she, along with the musical analogy, is a simple "front" for the young poet's Debussyesque intimations of *senilità*.

In "Falsetto" a focus has been found and by that token similar concerns take on objective validity. The poem is ultimately a meditation on "life" but the meditation is presented dramatically. The speaker is not young: he contemplates youth in the person of Esterina, "menaced"—as he puts it in the first line—by her twenty years. The scene is on the riviera. There is sun, a shore or *lido*, a flat rock glittering with salt, a diving board and—bounding and defining everything—the sea. And there is Esterina whom the observer sees enveloped in the ambivalent "grey-pink cloud" of her young age:

> Salgono i venti autunni,
> t'avviluppano andate primavere. . . .

Twenty autumns rise, / departed springs enfold you. . . .

In the first stanza she emerges phoenixlike in triumph out of the progressively more sinister cloud metamorphosed first into a hellish and windtossed smokiness, then into a *fiotto di cenere* (wave or breaker of ashes). She rises "scorched" (by the sun? by the crowding, cannibalistic, infernal years?—the ambiguity is intended and is pertinent both thematically and dramatically) and, bathed in an atmosphere compounded of the speaker's knowledgeable premonitions and her own "tragic" innocence, is lyrically transfigured:

> . . . proteso a un'avventura piú lontana
> l'intento viso che assembra
> l'arciera Diana.

. . . turned towards a more distant adventure / (is) your rapt face that seems / the archeress Diana.

With this momentary apotheosis the speaker seems to sense a prophecy sounding for her "in the Elysian spheres" and prays—somewhat against his rueful better knowledge at this point—that it may be "an ineffable concert of little bells" rather than the dull *toc* of a "cracked jug struck."

Stanza two develops the lines initiated previously (her fearless grace, the danger that her inexperience means for her: her young years "threaten her"—runs the extraordinary metaphor—as the sunning lizard is threatened by a boy's grass noose) but modifies her "divinity" in more naturalistic and elemental terms:

> L'acqua è la forza che ti tempra,
> nell'acqua ti ritrovi e ti rinnovi:
> noi ti pensiamo come un'alga, un ciottolo,
> come un'equorea creatura
> che la salsedine non intacca
> ma torna al lito piú pura.

The water is the force that tempers you, / in the water you find yourself and you renew yourself: / we think of you as a seaweed, a pebble, / as a marine creature / that saltiness does not corrode / but returns purer to the shore.

Here Esterina has been allied with the natural forces that menaced in stanza one. Amphibian, a *lido* animal, she stretches her bronzed limbs beneath the sun. The second stanza presents her trustfulness, her "impossible" living in the present (according to *noi*, the grown and wounded who know it untenable) as in itself a force sustained by the sea, that immeasurably more powerful presence that according to Thales can create, support, drown and destroy in a pure present unadulterated by harbored memories, principles, anticipations. Montale's sea is something like the blue-fleshed "Hydra absolue" of Valéry's "Cimetière marin" or the "undinal vast belly" of Crane's *Voyages*, an infinite mass of sheer unperspectived fluidity that looks like joyously utter being from the time- and earthborn human viewpoint. Here, precisely through that innocent improvidence or instinctive trust in higher providence which from that viewpoint "threatens" her, Esterina becomes elect.

The third and two-lined fourth stanzas work out the consequences: the momentary marriage of Esterina and the sea (spark and conflagration, granule of sand and salt and ocean). In the midst of the observer's ruminations she rises from her rock, advanced out along

the springboard above the Scylla-like "shrieking whirlpool,"* hesi-
tates "profiled against a ground of pearl," then laughs

> . . . e come spiccata da un vento
> t'abbatti fra le braccia
> del tuo divino amico che t'afferra.
>
> Ti guardiamo noi, della razza
> di chi rimane a terra.

> . . . and as if snatched up by a wind / you cast yourself into the
> arms / of your divine friend who grasps you. /
> We watch you, we of the race / of those who remain on land.

The apotheosis is complete. An absolute distinction has been made
between the elect one (who possesses a certain unworldly or "divine"
faith not just in self but in the elemental powers surrounding and
defining, a total lack of that lacerating sense of contingency and
limit which "blocks" and doubtless stamps the features of the ob-
server *pallido e assorto*) and the rest, *noi*, the earthbound, the pacers,
flâneurs and prisoners whose perfect epithet is Montale's *razza di chi
rimane a terra*. This distinction is fundamental not only for "Falsetto"
but for a great proportion of the physical-metaphysical world of
Montale. That is, the blockade is not absolute: there are those who
penetrate it. As we shall see, the recurrent term used to indicate this
passage from one state or law of being to another is *il varco*: pass,
ford, interstice, gap. The most extraordinary of these creatures who
have the secret of *varco* is the *donna* whom Montale comes to call
"Clizia" in the pages of his later poetry. Esterina can be seen from
our retrospect as one of the harbingers of Clizia, even as Giovanna—
primavera and *prima verrà*—annunciates Beatrice in the pages of the
Vita nova.

A central quality of "Falsetto" wholly lacking in *Accordi* is its
distinctive timbre or voicing—a unique integration of deep emotion
and "worldly" self-ironizing in reaction to that emotion. The title
itself provides an example. *Falsetto* means a vocal "falsification" or
straining in the uppermost registers primarily for purposes of humor
or melodramatic pathos, and the implication for the poem it heralds
is that it will be a squeak or bathetic utterance with some pretentions
to musicality. Such sarcasm is directed by the speaker at himself, not
his subject, and indeed it is the play of his (self-) consciousness

---

* In the text, "sopra il gorgo che stride." This passage echoes the Lorelei-
song of the violins in *Accordi*, where the girl is bid follow "into the whirlpool
of the God who expresses us, echoes of his voice, notes of his scale."

occasioned by the sight of Esterina which constitutes the poem's true subject and "action."

A young girl, a tanned and graceful swimmer, rises from the rock where she has been sunning herself and dives into the sea. In other words, very little happens. But she is observed and it is what the observer makes of her which is everything. He sees her, clearly, with much envy, with certain misgivings and some condescension, and with genuine tenderness throughout. He expresses his feelings with a consolidated irony of language, image and tone which does not nullify or in any way diminish them but intensifies and as it were profiles them in an atmosphere of self-directed dryness and even mockery. Thus the imagery is fraught with "dialectical" opposition—on the one hand the suave neoclassicism of Esterina's apotheosis (Diana, Elysian spheres, Scyllian whirlpool, the sea as "divine friend," and so on), on the other a naturalistic and local specificity (cracked jug and jingling bells, the lizard and the grass lasso, seaweed, pebbles, etc.). In the same way, certain literary archaicisms (*fumea, paventi, assembra, impaura, equorea, lito*) occur throughout the poem and create a sort of phantom and parodic aulicity within the context of its predominantly colloquial language. A similar effect is gained through employing (infrequently) elegant paraphrasis in expressing natural objects: thus a springboard becomes *ponticello esiguo* or *tremulo asse* (slender bridgelet, trembling axis), the white-capped water is parnassianly frozen as "ground of pearl."* Even the dissonanced rhymes (*nube-chiude, intendi-paventi-vento-violento, asse-braccia-razze*) wink at the "correct" cadences of the poem as a whole.

Such elements—in the analysis so indigestible—go to make up Montale's characteristic timbre, pitched slightly towards the sharp. In a tribute composed in 1950, he writes of the sheer *capaciousness* of Eliot's style, opposing it—in words that well define one central element in his own style—to those "'pure poets' who reduce the lyric to the moment of simple contemplation, of elegy."

> In Eliot we find irony, sarcasm, invective. . . . In him the prosaic word dwells beside the aulic, and tone becomes lyric through an inward ascent rather than because it obeys the laws of a metronome. Eliot frequently moves to *canto* from *recitativo*, to the loftiest tone from the most colloquial possible.[7]

---

* In these interpretations context is everything. That which in Montale amounts to "countereloquence," an ironizing humor mounted against self-indulgence or sentimentality, is—when utilized by Ungaretti—a successful commitment to the eloquence of tradition. Angelini suggests that the parody may also be directed at *Ronda* neoclassicism of the time.

Montale's final accolade is significant; Eliot is above all "a poet-musician." We have noted Montale's "operatic" conception of music in poetry. Inevitably it abjures the merely *orecchiabile*, fascinating rhythms for the ear alone. But its model idea is a dramatic expressiveness based upon the whole gamut of significant human experience, open to all senses, moods, faculties, "genres," conditions. His genius is preeminently dramatic, sometimes theatrical—in my opinion his repertoire and range greatly surpass those of the Eliot he so admires in both penetration and catholicity. And as the "poet-musician" par excellence it is little wonder that he works congenially in situations of soliloquy or dramatic monologue. Cast and plot of "Falsetto" are exemplary in this respect: an "I" *solus* contemplates some "you," and in the process produces an intimate *autoritratto* or self-analysis. Beyond Esterina stand Arsenio, Gerty, Clizia or that unspecified *tu* discovered *in medias res* who is the occasion for so many of his lyric meditations.

✿   ✿   ✿

In a note to *Accordi & pastelli* Montale mentions another early poem, written in March, 1920, which "recapitulates my juvenilia." This is "Riviere" (Rivieras) which is notable for its enthusiastic attempt to "run" the blockade by means of d'Annunzian pantheism:

> Oh allora sballottati
> come l'osso di seppia dalle ondate
> svanire a poco a poco;
> diventare
> un albero rugoso od una pietra
> levigata dal mare; nei colori
> fondersi dei tramonti; sparir carne
> per spicciare sorgente ebbra di sole,
> dal sole divorata. . . .

. . . Oh then tossed about / like the cuttlefish bone by the billows / little by little to vanish; / to become / a rugged tree or a stone / polished by the sea; to melt / into the colors of the sunsets; to disappear / as flesh so as to spurt forth as a spring drunken with sun, / devoured by the sun. . . .

It is clear from both its proposed solution and its hortatory style that the young author of "Riviere" was familiar with the archangel's masterpiece, the *Alcyone*; as we shall see, the slightly later suite entitled *Mediterraneo* is in part a parodic reworking of similar materials. "Riviere" concludes in a declamatory vision of *varco* and renewal.

The speaker senses "a mad urging of voices towards an exit" and in a solar ecstasy proposes to "reflower," to

> cangiare in inno l'elegia; rifarsi;
> non mancar piú.

>   . . . change the elegy into hymn; to remake oneself; / to fail no
> more.

This is surely a "premature cure" as Montale puts it in "Intenzioni," as well as one which sits "somewhat ill at ease" amid the *Ossi* proper.* Beyond the fascinating glimpse it gives us of the poet still in the grip of what he calls "eloquence," "Riviere" 's chief interest for us is as a sort of preliminary index of Ligurian *objets trouvés* which will recur again and again in the pages of *Ossi di seppia*. The sun, the sea, the coastal rocks, the cuttlefish bones themselves** are obvious instances. I want to focus on two related presences in particular, as having—under various guises and avatars—extraordinary resonance for his work as a whole.

The first is what the critic Gianfranco Contini calls a "central myth" in Montale's poetry[9]: high noon, *l'ora del meriggio*. Generally speaking, Mediterranean countries seem to unite in attributing to this hour—when the day's work temporarily ceases, when the sun is at its most intense, when human life seems at its most passive through the combination of heat, glare, shadow, food and drowsiness—a special affinity with supernatural visitations, visions, phantasmagoria.*** *Ossi di seppia* is full of *meriggio*: precisely a third of its pages are grouped in a sequence similar to the Ungarettian *capitolo, Meriggi e ombre,* Noons and Shadows. We have seen that Montale's earliest surviving poem, "Meriggiare pallido e assorto . . .", involves a desolating vision of "tutta la vita e il suo travaglio" received under the auspices of this hour; "Riviere" concludes in a noon-inspired dream of disso-

---

* The phrase is Montale's (*Accordi & pastelli*). Despite such misgivings, "Riviere" has always occupied a strategically important position by itself at the very end of *Ossi di seppia*. Coming as it does immediately after such poems as "Arsenio," "I morti," and "Incontro," its placement seems a gross miscalculation, almost impertinently "up-beat."

** An old friend of Montale's, Angelo Barile, writes that the original provisory title for the collection was *Rottami* (Flotsam).[8]

*** "One is still, alone, in shadows: suddenly the crowd of panic fears, suddenly the slamming hearts, suddenly the anguished sweats, the ears pricked to catch each rumor, suspicions, sometimes imaginary visions"—thus Leopardi writes in the 7th chapter ("Sul meriggio") of his youthful *Essay on the Popular Errors of the Ancients* where he compiles a fascinating list of citations from ancient literature, with commentary, on the disquietudes of noon (as seen by a fascinated and nostalgic nonbeliever).

lution; the superb "I limoni" finds in the solar yellow of the lemons a recall to that time of day when "things abandon themselves and seem close to betraying their ultimate secret . . . some disturbed Divinity." The first of the four "Sarcophagi" poems invokes the hour as possible source of a transcendent benignity. Elsewhere in the *Ossi*, *meriggio* is seen as the "one certainty," as token of "divine Indifference," as the bright hue impregnating all apparitions, as the moment when our "secret vein" is touched, as moment of truth. This list is not exhaustive. Underlying it is the sense of *meriggio* as the hour of a conceivable *varco*, as either the moment when one seems to slip or lose one's ground or where "a truth" breaks through—indeed, a truth which may amount to the certainty that there is no *varco* for the speaker.

Allied to the time is a flower, sunflower, heliotrope, *girasole* (turner-to-the-sun), whose bright and solar-rayed physiognomy and leanings have traditionally suggested a special affinity and loyalty to the sun. This bit of Ligurian flora, a "found" object if there ever was one, will in the later books of Montale undergo metamorphosis, via a myth that goes back to Ovid and Dante, into the nymph Clizia, Montale's stupendous emblem for heroic constancy and *coscienza*. But armed with retrospect we can already see her beginnings in the natural landscapes of *Ossi di seppia*, in the "Riviere," for instance, where "sunflower glances" enthrall the speaker in his brief hour of ecstasy or at the end of the "Sarcofaghi" where the sunflower appears as a charmed trifle that might guide and protect the voyager in his quest for exit or *varco*.

But the lyric that strikes one as a remarkable omen of Clizia is the beautiful beseechment that must be given here in its entirety:

> Portami il girasole ch'io lo trapianti
> nel mio terreno bruciato dal salino,
> e mostri tutto il giorno agli azzurri specchianti
> del cielo l'ansietà del suo volto giallino.
>
> Tendono alla chiarità le cose oscure,
> si esauriscono i corpi in un fluire
> di tinte: queste in musiche. Svanire
> è dunque la ventura delle venture.
>
> Portami tu la pianta che conduce
> dove sorgono bionde trasparenze
> e vapora la vita quale essenza;
> portami il girasole impazzito di luce.

Bring me the sunflower that I may transplant it / in my salt-burnt

ground, / that it may show all day to the mirroring blues / of the sky
the anxiety of its yellow face. /
    Dark things tend toward clarity, / bodies exhaust themselves in a
flowing / of tints—these in musics. To vanish / is then the chance of
chances. /
    Bring me, thou, the plant that leads / to where fair transparencies
fountain / and life evaporates like essence; / bring me the sunflower
maddened with light.*

Here the sunflower is conceived of as talismanic, a conductor of
aspirational energies towards some sort of essentiality and unmediated
presence. But very differently than in the *Accordi* or "Riviere," here
there is only a tantalizing *hypothesis* of evaporation—it is *ventura
delle venture* and the phrasing is dry and skeptical. The main features
of the flower in the poem are its anxiety (mocked as it is in the
mirroring blue) and the conclusive detail that it is light-*maddened*.
In such a context, the "philosophical" interlude (second stanza)
which coolly limns a cosmos aspiring to the condition of music à la
Walter Pater has its ironies.** The vision proposed is most devoutly
to be wished, but—if this sunflower is any indication—improbable.
Nevertheless: *portami, portami, portami,* that the two, man and
flower, may lean together in the salt-sown land in a common madness.
The Clizia-to-come will resemble this sunflower in embodying by
her existence not a solution or *varco* but a persisting posture of com-
mitment to such possibilities—a "sign" against encroaching cynicism
or despair.

         *   *   *

". . . they seem to us to be directly in the [true Italian] tradition
who, reflecting in their own work the characteristics of our complex
and difficult time, tend towards a superior dilettantism, saturated
with human and artistic experiences. . . . If it once was said that
genius is a long patience, we would like to add that it is also *cos-
cienza* and honesty." Thus Montale in his essay "Stile e tradizione,"
written in 1925 and published by the active anti-fascist Piero Gobetti

* For a striking parallel one might consider "Portami il girasole" along with
Lawrence's "Bavarian Gentians" (1929). Of course Lawrence uses his blue-
black gentians to go down, not up: his aims are chthonic. But despite the
antithesis of color and direction, the similarity of function is striking. It extends
even to the syntax, the implorings that grow into imperatives: "Reach me a
gentian, give me a torch!" etc. It is tempting but idle to speculate that Lawrence,
a sometime dweller in Spotorno, on the Ligurian riviera west of Genoa, knew
the Montale lyric.
** Even the *fluire* is cluttered and clogged by the *ipermetri* or syllabic surplus
(over and above the normative hendecasyllable) in most lines—the same sort of
effect is produced by the brilliantly placed enjambements in stanza two.

in his magazine *Baretti.** In the same year Gobetti also published
Ossi di seppia.

Of his friend and first publisher, who died in 1926 at the age of
twenty-five, Montale has written how he left

> a seed of doubt and discontentment in the bad conscience of his
> contemporaries, and even of his own friends . . . Gobetti possessed
> what I would call the gift of immanence, the persuasion that life can
> only be explained by life, that man is the sole maker of his des-
> tiny. . . .[10]

If "Stile e tradizione" is a public commitment to the "Gobettian" (as
well as Crocean) virtues of a lucid humanism, to the idea of "style"
as an independent register and witness to a "complex and difficult
time," so is a colophon like "Eugenio Montale/*Ossi di seppia*/Casa
editrice Gobetti/Torino 1925." Despite the strictures of Salvatore
Quasimodo, Montale has always been a political animal, though his
writings have never taken the form of propaganda—as to some extent
the theory and practice of Quasimodo would dictate. If "politics"
means explicit reference to the state of affairs at the Palazzo Venezia,
Ossi di seppia is not a political book. But in fact it realizes the moral
position sketched in "Stile e tradizione" at a time when a hysterical
nationalism and a bread-and-circuses psychology were main features
of Italian life: it bears witness to the supreme values of clarity, intel-
ligence and *conscienza* in the examination and expression of any given
facet of firsthand (and therefore verifiable) experience.** Writing in
Accordi & pastelli of the transitional passage between his juvenilia
and the *Ossi di seppia*, he concludes with characteristic blandness that
"beside a rather turbid vein, or precisely 'within' that vein, there
was developing . . . the leaner but more limpid veining of the *Ossi*."
Precisely, and these qualities constitute the political weapons of a
self-styled dilettante confronting a power system which scorns and
fears them.

It is worth looking at the few poems the *Ossi* contains on the sub-
ject of poetry. What seems to me to be characteristic in both cases
is how the subject of personal limitation and suffering is linked to
and ultimately absorbed in the question of *coscienza*, the moral
values touched upon above. The first stanza of "I limoni" (excepting
the preface poem to be discussed further on, the first poem in the

---

* See chapter I, pp. 19–21 for a résumé of the contents of "Stile e tradizione."
** Cf. "Intenzioni": "The poet's need is the research of a particular truth
(*verità puntuale*) rather than a general one." In "Stile e tradizione": We do
not wish to accept *any* mythology. . . ."

book) abruptly declares where the poet stands in terms of the human values it is implied poetry, or *this* poetry, must express.

> Ascoltami, i poeti laureati
> si muovono soltanto fra le piante
> dai nomi poco usati: bossi ligustri o acanti.
> Io, per me, amo le strade che riescono agli erbosi
> fossi dove in pozzanghere
> mezzo seccate agguantano i ragazzi
> qualche sparuta anguilla:
> le viuzze che seguono i ciglioni,
> discendono tra i ciuffi delle canne
> e mettono negli orti, tra gli alberi dei limoni.

Listen to me, the poets laureate / move only among plants / with little-used names: privet-hedges or acanthus. / I, for my part, love the streets that turn into grassy / ditches where in half-dried / puddles boys grab after / some vanishing eel: / the little paths that follow along those ditches, / that descend among the cane-tufts / and end up in kitchen gardens, among the lemon trees.

Surely the reader is meant to recognize a reference in the first three lines to the luxuriant and exotic vegetation associated with d'Annunzio, above all with the poems of *Alcyone*. Following the Fiume adventure this *fin de siècle* master could justly be thought of as *laureato* by the surgent *fascisti,* who went to school to him for styles of declamation as well as uniform. But these lines, wittily ranging the poet's laurel with systems of power, *luxe,* privilege and exclusion, mainly serve as a contrast to the practices of their author ("Io, per me . . .") who in the remainder of the stanza presents himself as resolutely nonlaureate,* as a poet and man who moves somewhat apart from others amid familiar natural scenes, as one who opposes his personal emblem, the *limoni* discovered in a humble truck-garden, to the official boutonnières involving laurel, privet, acanthus. And if the mood evoked is anti-dithyrambic, the "sprung" metric of the stanza, ranging from seven to fifteen syllables, and the rough approximations of the mainly internal rhyming (*piante-acanti, erbosi-fossi, ragazzi-viuzze,* etc.), provide musical correspondences.

The contentious opening gives way, like the streets and paths it adduces, to the sensuous and finally moral meaning of the lemons. The rich sweetness of their odor is for the moment transported into the tormented being of the walker, stilling "the war . . . of shunted passions" so that the *meriggio* may proffer its secret:

---

* An instance of what Silvio Ramat nicely calls Montale's "proud humility."[11]

Vedi, in questi silenzi in cui le cose
s'abbandonano e sembrano vicine
a tradire il loro ultimo segreto,
talora ci si aspetta
di scoprire uno sbaglio di Natura,
il punto morto del mondo, l'anello che non tiene,
il filo da disbrogliare che finalmente ci metta
nel mezzo di una verità.

See, in these silences in which things / abandon themselves and seem close / to betraying their ultimate secret, / sometimes one expects / to discover a blunder of Nature, / the dead point of the world, the link that doesn't hold, / the thread to disentangle that finally might put us / in the middle of a truth.*

This moment of drastically qualified *varco* ends with the resumption of normal life conditions; specifically, the walker returns to the oppressive tedium of winter life in the city whose deadly flatness is sonically caught in the grating monotony of the ten a's of "*la* luce si *fa avara—amara* l'*anima*" (light grows avaricious—embittered the soul).

Thus the blockade, always there in fact but momentarily obscured by the spell of lemon trees, resumes. And this we understand was and is and will be the perennial condition, like the wall of "Meriggiare . . .", with the occasional exception of such *intermittences du coeur* as are provided by glimpses "through an unlatched gate" of the charm-bearing lemons—

le loro canzoni
le trombe d'oro della solarità.

. . . their songs, / the golden trumpets of solarity.

So the speaker in "I limoni," "Montale," experiences the lemon as a talisman affording a glimmer of another order of reality at certain unpremeditated occasions. The *girasole*, linked to it in a common solarity, works the same sort of magic—consolatory and "maddening"

---

* It should be said that this "vision" like all Montalean visions is no necessary cause for rejoicing or levity. The machine is infernal. The truth glimpsed is made ominous by phrases like "*blunder* of Nature," "*dead* point of the world," "link *that does not hold,*" "*a* truth," "*some disturbed* Divinity"—italics mine. But the point is that it involves a truth, and whether this is beneficent or malificent is secondary. Montale puts his position movingly in his tribute to the dead poet Sergio Fadin in the *Bufera*, a tribute that I believe can stand as epithet for Montale himself—hence I have used it at the head of this chapter. "To be always among the first and *to know,* this is what counts, even if the rationale of the representation escapes us" ("Visita a Fadin").

as we know. Indeed the very eel escaping from the clutching fingers of Ligurian boys in the first stanza will return again and again in the *oeuvre* of the poet as a shorthand sign for escape and *varco*, arriving at last at an extraordinary apotheosis when it becomes an iconic version of Clizia in the final pages of the *Bufera*.* The significance of what originally seemed a "literary" choice at the start of "I limoni" —a program for anti-d'Annunzianism or "counter-eloquence"—has come to have extraordinary "metaphysical" implications in the sequel. This is not surprising perhaps in a poet who consistently conceives of style as one aspect of an overriding moral concern.

The second poem related to poetic matters constitutes the poet's declaration of abilities and intentions:

> Non chiederci la parola che squadri da ogni lato
> l'animo nostro informe, e a lettere di fuoco
> lo dichiari e risplenda come un croco
> perduto in mezzo a un polveroso prato.
>
> Ah l'uomo che se ne va sicuro,
> agli altri ed a se stesso amico,
> e l'ombra sua non cura che la canicola
> stampa sopra uno scalcinato muro!
>
> Non domandarci la formula che mondi possa aprirti,
> sí qualche storta sillaba e secca come un ramo.
> Codesto solo oggi possiamo dirti,
> ciò che *non* siamo, ciò che *non* vogliamo.

Don't ask of us the word that squares on every side / our formless spirit, and in fiery letters / proclaims it and shines out like a crocus / lost in the middle of a dusty field. /

Ah that man who goes secure, / friend to others and to himself, / and has no care that his shadow / is stamped by the dog-star upon a crumbling wall! /

Don't seek of us the formula that might open worlds for you /— rather some syllable as crooked and dry as a branch. / This only we are able to tell you today, / what we are *not*, what we do *not* want.

Surely we are about as far as it is possible to be from the idealistic view of the word (demi-*logos*) expressed by Ungaretti with the term "nominalism." Montale's deformed syllable, crooked and dry as a

---

* Of course the flick and vanishment of the *sparuta anguilla* is also related to the dive and disappearance of quicksilver Esterina in "Falsetto," to the quick glint of a fish or the whirr and explosion of some bird into its flight, to countless other moments in the poems when the transfixed and trapped speaker sees something or someone moving "outside."

branch, that cannot open worlds, seems a parody or perverse reminiscence of the Vergilian bough, crocus-golden, that lights Aeneas' way to his vision of the mechanism of divine providence. "Non chiederci . . ." baldly proposes poetry as a critical operation for defining *what is* (negatively, to be sure), as the desolating perception of limit. As for its politics, Vittorini once asserted (apropos the last two lines) that "all contemporary (that is, the Italian 1930's) literature might be ultimately understood as a research into the meaning of that *non*."[12]

❋   ❋   ❋

The *Ossi di seppia* of 1925 is a book built upon two suites or lyric sequences: the twenty-two diversified short lyrics which give the book its name, and the nine-part speech to the sea called *Mediterraneo*. These two core sections are preceded and followed by other groups of varying size and character. The first pages contain relatively early poems like "I limoni," "Corno inglese," and "Falsetto," followed by a set dedicated to Camillo Sbarbaro and a faintly *Ronda*-esque "Sarcofaghi" or *tombeaux* sequence. Following the *Ossi* proper and *Mediterraneo* comes a group of somewhat longer and more diffuse poems, *Meriggi e ombre,* combining disconsolate reminiscing with an observant naturalism somewhat in the vein of "Riviere"; "Riviere" itself terminates the volume.*

"Non chiederci la parola . . ." is in fact the preface-poem for the *Ossi* section. Certain of these are already known to us—"Meriggiare . . ." is the second in the series, the *girasole* poem the sixth. Together, the two of them inscribe a typically vicious circle: an awareness of the absolute limit (no exit) and the thought of imminent exit (*varco*) whose absurdity to the intelligence in no way diminishes the complicated pleasure of the idea. "One is required to live out ceaselessly one's own contradictions . . ." ("Intenzioni").

But the series as a whole develops no story beyond this. As its title suggests, it offers the remains or relics of a riviera life (the *seppia* or cuttlefish familiar to its shores is equipped to protect itself by ejecting an inky fluid—a possible instance of Montalean black humor), an anthology of occasions or epiphanaic moments from an existence set along the Mediterranean coast, specifically the Cinque Terre. The initial "Non chiederci . . ." skillfully establishes the dominant note of anguished awareness of limit that threads the sequence to the very end, where the sky's arch seems to terminate on a graffiti-covered

---

* Montale is not a fanatic revisionalist like Ungaretti. The second (1928) edition of the *Ossi* will have six poems added, four of them immeasurably strengthening the *Meriggio e ombre* section. We shall deal with these new poems as transitional—in chronology, theme and style—to the *Occasioni* volume of the 1930's.

wall. The eighth ("Ciò che di me sapeste": What you knew of me)
is a self-parodying canzonetta by the Montalean *raté*-persona whose
conviction of blockade is so intense that he speaks of himself in the
past definite or historical tense. This apparitional voice concludes
with a horrid grimace:

> Se un'ombra scorgete, non è
> un'ombra—ma quella io sono.
> Potessi spiccarla da me,
> offrirvela in dono.

If you glimpse a shadow, it is not / a shadow—but what I am. /
Would I could pluck it from me, / to offer you it as gift.

Such bitterness is relatively unusual; more characteristic is a kind of
wry acceptance (wry because in fact there is no choice) of blockade
as a fact of life. We can think of this as Montale's precocious *senilità*,
kin to Eliot's but how much more to Italo Svevo's, who precisely in
this period, 1925–1926, was being discovered in Italy and abroad,
largely due to Montale's public championing.* His most recent tribute
to Svevo, delivered in Trieste in 1963, focuses on a point as relevant
to himself as to the novelist. Svevo, he says, "in three successive self-
portraits [the novels] created the myth of himself, the image and I
would almost say the category of a *senilità* which is not due to time
(*non è temporale*) but is the state of being of whoever feels he has
already lived for himself and others, suffered and lived for all." Later
on he speaks of such *senilità* "understood as a fact of being and
vocation."[13] We shall return further on to this suggestion of sacrifice
and substitution which has major importance in the work of Montale,
though not in the sequence we are considering now. But surely
"vocational" *senilità* is the burden of the beautiful fourth *osso*:

> Mia vita, a te non chiedo lineamenti
> fissi, volti plausibili o possessi.
> Nel tuo giro inquieto ormai lo stesso
> sapore han miele e assenzio.
>
> Il cuore che ogni moto tiene a vile
> raro è squassato da trasalimenti.
> Cosí suona talvolta nel silenzio
> della campagna un colpo di fucile.

* The documents of the relationship between the two writers—*vecchio e giovane*—are now
conveniently available in Italo Svevo-Eugenio Montale, *Carteggio, con gli scritti di Montale su
Svevo,* ed. Giorgio Zampa (Milan, 1976), which contains their correspondence from 1926 to
Svevo's death in 1928 and all of the poet's many articles (thirteen in all) on the novelist, from
1926 to 1963.

My life, I do not ask of you fixed / lineaments, plausible faces or possessions. / In your restless circuit by now / honey and absinthe have the same taste.

The heart that holds all movement vile / but rarely is shaken by surprises. / Thus sometime sounds in the silence / of the countryside a rifleshot.

Clearly such a position need not be humble or "resigned." In Montale *senilità* is often Promethean and exalted, closer to Dante's Farinata standing upright in his fiery tomb "come avesse lo inferno in gran dispetto" than Eliot's faintly complacent aged eagle.

Infrequently there are intermittences—cracks or fissures—in this *impasse:* glimpses of "a truth," a momentary relaxing of the rules, a sort of *varco.* Thus sun can induce a torpor and slackening of consciousness, as in the eleventh lyric ("Gloria del disteso mezzogiorno: Glory of expansive noon), though even here well-being feels ironic and inconclusive—"l'ora piú bella è di là dal muretta" (the loveliest time of all lies on the far side of the wall). Indeed, the fragility of "felicità raggiunta" (happiness regained) is the subject of the twelfth: the conclusion is that the most passionate lover of happiness will respect its frailty by relinquishing it.

Another sort of epiphanaic glimpse is the subject of two other *ossi.* In "La farandola dei fanciulli sul greto" (The snake-dance of the children on the dry riverbed) the walker witnesses the sheer uninhibited energy of the children's play and painfully feels his own "detachment from ancient roots" where "even a name, a garment was a vice." The ninth, "Portovenere," places us directly at what it calls "the origins"; the old village, just to the south of the Cinque Terre, in which pagan and Christian remnants jostle, gives off an air in which "ogni ora prossima è antica" (each new hour is ancient):

> Là non è chi si guardi
> o stia di sé in ascolto.
> Quivi sei alle origini
> e decidere è stolto:
> ripartirai piú tardi
> per assumere un volto.

There no one scrutinizes himself / or stands apart hearkening. / There you are at the origins / and to decide is foolish: / you depart later / in order to assume a face.

Volto for Montale means finalization, a crystallized identity which signifies implacable condition and therefore limit. It need not be an accurate sign or measure of one's "true" inwardness—thus in the grotesque eighth *osso* the *false* face has stuck, and stifled the head behind it. Portovenere, then, is the physical-metaphysical *locus* for a fabulous or hypothetical state of sheer potentiality and fluidity, "ancient" because it is prior to the hardening of features brought about by choice and action.*

Other *ossi*, such as the famous fourteenth, recount moments where the wall gives way and the void it diked out floods in:

> Forse un mattino andando in un'aria di vetro,
> arida, rivolgendomi, vedro compirsi il miracolo:
> il nulla alle mie spalle, il vuoto dietro
> di me, con un terrore di ubriaco. . . .

Perhaps one morning moving in a dry and glassy air, / turning around I shall see the miracle achieved / —nothingness at my shoulders, the void behind / me—with a drunkard's terror. . . .

Against such terrors other lyrics in the series invoke, for luck, certain recollected objects that serve to ward off, for the moment at least, the consciousness of *male di vivere*. Montale's Dora Markus will carry an amulet, a white mouse made of ivory, in her purse as a fragile witness to at least the theoretic possibility of good fortune. So certain *ossi* offer a little collection of "amulets" against evil: the smile of a certain "K." who, somewhat like Oedipus or Piero Gobetti, wanders far away "bearing his suffering with him like a talisman"; a name ("Valmorbia") with a memory in its syllables that holds peace for he who articulates them; the thought of a woman whose very absence creates a kind of maelstrom of passionate longing more vibrant by far than the sun-stunned landscape she has abandoned.

Such are the varieties of experience expressed in the *Ossi di seppia* group. Perhaps words like "suite" or "sequence" which suggest a scheme of development are misleading—certainly they were not conceived under any unifying rubric ("story of a soul," and so on) or plot-line. Montale himself refers to them as fragments. The *Ossi*, in fact, constitute a lyric diary kept by the poet over a period of four years, between 1921 and 1925. Entries are brief; the moods, as one would expect in a diary, vary in intensity and direction and are frequently contradictory. Nevertheless, there is a general thematic strand running through them all: the experience of blockade mo-

---

* Cf. the conclusion to the great "Incontro" (Meeting): "Forse riavrò un aspetto" (Perhaps I shall have a face again). Saba appropriates the conclusion to "Portovenere" for his own uses in "Felicità" (*Parole*).

mentarily punctuated or burst by flashes of something "other." The diaristic or fragmented mode first employed in the *Ossi* will recur in both of Montale's later volumes of verse. With certain developments in the direction of a quicker and more elliptical movement, a more idiosyncratic system of references, the *Ossi* are precedent for the "motets" of *Le occasioni*, the *Lampi e dediche* (Flashes and Dedications) of *La bufera e altro*.

❋   ❋   ❋

Mediterraneo, on the other hand, is a genuine suite of nine parts which, as the name indicates, faces away from the baked and stony land towards the sea. "I am a tree burnt out by sirocco," Montale wrote to Svevo in 1926, apropos of the life expressed in the pages of his recently published book,[14] and this is an image which in its desolation and suggestion of helpless capitulation to "superior" powers certainly corresponds to a major portion of the experience given by the poems. In "Intenzioni," however, Montale uses a different gathering metaphor: "In *Ossi di seppia,* everything was drawn and absorbed by the fermenting sea. . . ."

The sea indeed is the other aspect of riviera, experienced not only as "distance" or barrier but as Thalean *source,* a power in and through which change into something rich and strange is conceivable, *varco* and/or transfiguration a possibility. In the early "Riviere," for example, the sea is hailed as a Dionysian force bearing the individual beyond himself into some renovative communion with all Nature. In "Falsetto" the sea is Esterina's divine lover, reinvigorating and purifying the creature who dares its protean arms, though a mocking menace to the race of those who remain on earth. Doubtless part of what makes Portovenere a place of "origins" is its intimate involvement with the sea. But *Mediterraneo* is Montale's major poem based on this dispensation.

The adjectival title modifies not just the sea but the speaker as well: he too is "Mediterranean" and must call the sea not only *antico,* ancient one, but *padre.* The suite begins and ends—as it must, spoken as it is by he who must finally remain on earth—with the rocky summer coast. At its opening, he lies in siesta on the ground, vacantly registering the sound of the waves along the shore. His reverie is broken by "a sound of strident jeers" and as he raises his head he sees two jays, feathered blue and white and with the speed of arrows, shoot toward the sea. No comment here: merely a happening or occasion which directs the *flâneur's* roused attention to the great presence beside him. And with this stagesetting event the poem's main movement begins: the high speech (eloquent, formal, solemn as befits speech addressed to a Power) of a Mediterranean speaking to the Mediterranean, which is given the *tu* as is right when that Power is fathering.

In the second section, the speaker recalls the "solemn admonition" breathed by the sea now as in summers long ago:

> . . . che il piccino fermento
> del mio cuore non era che un momento
> del tuo; che mi era in fondo
> la tua legge rischiosa: esser vasto e diverso
> e insieme fisso:
> e svuotarmi così d'ogni lordura
> come tu fai. . . .

> . . . that the tiny ferment / of my heart was only a moment / of yours; that in my deepest being was / your risky law: to be vast and various / and stable at once, and so to purge myself of every filth / as you do. . . .

Here the speaker feels himself "no longer worthy" of that great lesson. Yet in the third section he recounts a recent vision in which the rocky shore that is his *paese* seemed to consent amorously and thrust itself towards the waters' "invisible embrace":

> Tu vastità riscattavi
> anche il patire dei sassi:
> pel tuo tripudio era giusta
> l'immobilità dei finiti.

> You, vastity, redeemed / even the suffering of stones: / through your exultation / the immobility of finite things was made just.

Now the speaker, standing in and allied with the finitude of rocks, is touched to joyous worship by this prospect of infinitely free power. Yet, this same "suffering of stones" provokes the main note of the fourth section where, from the thought of a city sunken beneath the sea that is suggested by the images of clouds reflected in the water, there comes the reminder of the "severe law" governing all finite existence (here called "nameless suffering turned to stone"): the implacability of process, of sea,

> . . . l'informe rottame
> che gittò fuor del corso la fiumara
> del vivere.

> the formless rubbish / thrown aside by the torrent / of living.

The fifth section broods on this opposition between power and impotence, exultation and suffering, infinitude and finitude, and so develops an exacerbated awareness of the cruelty in things. His life, he says, is a dry slope slowly crumbling away, or perhaps this plant—brother to Leopardi's broomflower growing on Vesuvius—born in the "devastation" of the careless pounding of wind and sea. He is the daisy thrusting from a crack soil:

> In lei títubo al mare che mi offende,
> manca ancora il silenzio nella mia vita.

. . . In it I waver towards the sea that offends me; / silence still lacks in my life.

Such "silence" of course would be the stillness of perfect submission. At the end of the section, however, a sort of "filial" yielding occurs—the speaker gazes at the peaceful riviera scene presently before him and his poor rebellion gives way to a rueful rephrasing of infelicity as "perhaps the rancor that every son has, Sea, for his father." This modification of personal defiance through the sheer presence of the fathering sea is increasingly apparent as *Mediterraneo* moves to its conclusion.

In the sixth section, the poet meditates on heredity (the experience of Liguria and the *Ossi di seppia*) in terms of a voice transmitted from sea-father to son:

> un poco del tuo dono
> sia passato per sempre nelle sillabe
> che rechiamo con noi, api ronzanti.

. . . a little of your gift / has passed forever into the syllables / we bear with us, buzzing bees.

Such an inheritance, speech with the savor of *sale greco* (sea brine and/or Attic salt), is an apt enough description of not only the saline flavor of irony that is present in so much of Montale (e.g., in the *api ronzanti* who constitute the epithet for poets in the passage above) but of the "Homeric" resonance of which he is capable when he chooses—as, for example, in the opening eight lines of section six, where aulicity of diction and phrasing fully responds to the ceremonial piety expressed.

Section seven returns to matters raised in section two; that is, his "unworthiness" of the sea's example: to be vast, manifold, and "fixed" or integral at once. Here the speaker is aware that his perversion of the sea's qualities is a paralyzing sense of flux and dis-integration—that he himself is torn and dispersed through his perception of infinite possibilities of action. This section proceeds by a series of rhetorical alternatives: what he would like to be and what he is or is not. Thus, he would wish himself to be "rough and ele-mental," as integral as a pebble rolled in the sea, and instead of this he is at once a consciousness of and identification with the fume of "fugitive life." In language and aspiration reminiscent of the vision of the infernal machine in "I limoni," he would wish

> . . . cercare il male
> che tarla il mondo, la piccola stortura
> d'una leva che arresta
> l'ordegno universale. . . .

> . . . to seek out the evil / that gnaws the world, the little twist / of a lever that halts / the universal machine. . . .

but instead of this he is a helpless witness to the chaos implicit in each instant. Once, we recall, at Portovenere, to "decide" seemed stupid; now he could not decide if he wanted to. So the sea has been a bad master. But the section ends with a drastic change of heart similar to that of section five. The mere presence of the sea is con-versional, finite consciousness is drowned:

> Ma nulla so rimpiangere: tu sciogli
> ancora i groppi interni col tuo canto.
> Il tuo delirio sale agli astri ormai.

> . . . But I can regret nothing; again you loosen / the knots within me with your song. / Now your frenzy rises to the stars.

The same sort of resolution by drowning occurs in section eight which resumes the subject of section six. But the certainty expressed in that section (that something of the sea would forever reverberate in his voice) is now known to be a dream. What, he inquires with bitter sarcasm, has such vital power to do with his sort of tempera-mental *senilità*, "my melancholy of an aged child who ought not to have thought"? Instead of the sea's *salmastre parole* (salty words), he has only *lamentosa letteratura*, the faded language of the diction-aries, words like public women (the witty Italian for this is *donne pubblicate*, published women). The final straw is to have even these "tired phrases" stolen tomorrow and integrated in a genuine poetry (*versi veri*) by studious *canaille*. The gamut of resentments here, the commonplace nature of his complaints and the ridiculousness of the final flareup about the *studenti canaglie* is extraordinarily rich and dramatic, and the modulation or shift at the end—again like section five and section seven—gains enormously in dramatic impact as a result of it. The agent of conversion is, again, the presence of the Mediterranean:

> Ed il tuo rombo cresce, e si dilata
> azzurra l'ombra nuova.
> M'abbandonano a prova i miei pensieri.
> Sensi non ho; né senso. Non ho limite.

And your booming grows, / and the new shadow spreads blue. / My thoughts race to abandon me. / I have no senses; nor sense. I have no limits.

The ninth and last section returns us to where we began: land and *meriggio*. Ecstasy, even wishfulness, have gone. In their place there is the grim clairvoyance we associate with the *Ossi* group. The speaker now stands beside what he felt as the fathering sea, now "like a muted memory when someone recalls his home," resigned to his transience and eventual obliteration "like an ephemeral scrawl on a blackboard." His lesson from the sea has been learned in this *meriggio desolato* in which the dream of *varco,* the hope of in some way assuming or incorporating in himself the sea's glorious energy, has evaporated. And so the sequence ends in a capitulation, not so much to the sea as to the sea's infinite difference, to the "wall" separating the limited from the limitless:

> . . . a te mi rendo in umiltà. Non sono
> che favilla d'un tirso. Bene lo so, bruciare,
> questo, non altro, è il mio significato.

. . . to you I surrender in humility. I am / only spark from a beacon. Well I know it—to burn, / this and no more, is my meaning.

Perhaps that culminating *tirso* of which the speaker finds he is only a byproduct provides a useful point from which to appraise the qualities and originalities of *Mediterraneo.* Primarily *tirso* is a "literary" noun, part of a standard poetic lexicon where it means "thyrsus," the ivy-wreathed and phallic staff carried by Dionysus and his followers. As such it relates to one central thematic strand of the sequence, the "filial" connection between man and nature (here the *fermenting* Mediterranean). Under the sign of the thyrsus, then, the speaker aspires to his source, to nature, and would reject, if he could, his "face," his individualized and finite self. According to the myth expressed in *Mediterraneo* the suffering stone is "redeemed" by the sea, and the sequence reaches its climax in this direction as the speaker feels his thoughts abandon him in a rush: "Sensi non ho; né senso. Non ho limite."

And under the aegis of the thyrsus we are led to make a curious connection between Montale's *Mediterraneo* and—of all possible predecessors—Gabriele d'Annunzio's book of summer *Alcyone* (Halcyon). *Alcyone*, written in 1903 as part of the *Laudi* cycle, exhibits d'Annunzio's considerable talents at their most genial. The book purports to be a lyric journal of a summer spent in the coastal region just to the south of the Riviera di Levante. It begins in June and ends in September. As one might expect from this poet, the mood *passim* is ecstatic and dithyrambic. Creatures of the Dionysian dispensation, satyrs, nymphs, naiads, and so on, abound and are constantly evoked and embraced; the rhythms are ebullient and skillfully martellated to create an exultant and somewhat hypnotic effect. Stress is all on the sphere of physical sensation and the brake or "inhibition" of intellect or *coscienza* is utterly absent. We know that the d'Annunzio of this phase loved to ride horseback along the edge of the Ligurian Sea, galloping "centaurlike" at the foam lip between surf and sand, at the edge of another dispensation where, when the speed was high enough he could sense his unity with the world whistling around him and achieve an ecstatic communion with the scheme of things. He even reports a high point where he was thrown from his horse and, one foot still in the stirrup, dragged a certain distance down the beach. The dizzily dislocated *lido*'s-eye view he then had of the waves breaking on the shore was for him a spectacular epiphany.

The point of the d'Annunzian experience in *Alcyone*, then, is elemental—he loses his name, his historical and psychological identity, and becomes his environment. His style works to render this experience in dithyrambic terms:

> . . . e il fiume è la mia vena,
> il monte è la mia fronte,
> la selva è la mia pube,
> la nube è il mio sudore. . . .
> E la mia vita è divina.
>
> ("Meriggio")

. . . and the river is my vein, / the mountain my forehead, / the wood my loin, / the cloud my sweat. . . . / And my life is divine.

Accompanying this merger, votive offerings to the Graces, Bacchantes and nymphs, aspects all of presiding Dionysus and his transforming thyrsus.

But such a *tirso* represents a very different thing in the world of *Mediterraneo*. For one thing, the sweeping consummation it represents is only momentary in the Montale sequence: an abolition or evasion of consciousness which, while it lasts, also abolishes the sense of limits. And while it lasts this is felicity. But, the narrative movement of the poem reminds us, consciousness is only dispersed momentarily: one returns to oneself, "comes to" at a reformed wall. Even Montale's rhythms in this sequence—a kind of Italian "blank verse" grounded on an approximate hendecasyllable that can be expanded or contracted to fit the tempo of thought—suggest meditation and a highly speculative mind rather than any sort of dithyrambic release. (For example, despite the "d'Annunzian" climaxes of sections eight and nine—*Non ho limite*, etc.—not a single exclamation point.)

This brings us back to the meaning of *tirso* in this poem. In my trot I have translated it as "beacon," and this, a seaside structure emitting warning signs by means of flags and lights, is an alternate, secondary sense of the word.* But here, at the desolately sane conclusion, this sense is primary, the "thyrsus" an ironic reminiscence. "I am a tree burnt out by sirocco": "to burn, this and nothing else is my meaning." Here the sense of a continuing deterioration and disintegration is very clear; the suffering speaker is fatally "of the race of those who remain on earth."

But one other point should be made. His staying, his burning, constitutes in itself a sort of witness: he becomes a sign and warning for others. And in this sense a commitment and relation *is* established—not with "nature" but with other men. Can it be called "sacrifice" when such an action (absence of action?) has no alternative, is in fact a sentence? Here intention is everything. This climactic *bruciare* that is the speaker's signification might, given the intention, be understood *not only* as hellish suffering but as vocation, as a service offered up to others who move "outward" towards some inconceivable *varco*.

❋   ❋   ❋

> Penso che per i piú non sia salvezza,
> ma taluno sòvverta ogni disegno,
> passi il varco, qual volle si ritrovi.

---

* Thus the dictionary I use, Nicola Zingarelli's *Vocabolario della lingua italiana*, offers "thyrsus" first as "carried by Bacchus and every Bacchante at the holidays," then "pole with globes, lights, pennants for signals at the top."

. . . I think that for most there is no salvation, / but that someone
overturns every design, / passes the ford, recovers that which he
wished to be.

So, gazing outward through the sea haze towards Capraia and Cor-
sica, a Montalean "I" tentatively offers his "hypothesis of Grace."
With its stoic despair over the fate of "most" and its Farinata-like
pride, it is hardly an acceptably Christian concept: "Doubtless there
is some Christian ferment in me, but I am not a practicing Christian.
I respect *all* Churches as institutions."[15] Briefly, salvation is for some,
for certain others, certainly not for "me."

The idea relates to his conception of vocational *senilità*—"the state
of being of whoever feels he has already lived for himself and for
others, suffered and lived for all." Most simply are *della razza di chi
rimane*. A few, unaccountably, are chosen to go "beyond," to essay
the *varco*. Between the suffering and the chosen one, however, there
can be a bond or sodality.

The poem cited above concludes with a double offer on the part
of the speaker. His journey is finished, but "before yielding" he can
indicate (to you) a way of escape as "labile as spray"; he can also
transfer the object of his "wretched hope":

A'nuovi giorni, stanco, non so crescerla:
l'offro in pegno al tuo fato, che ti scampi.

. . . Weary, I cannot grow it toward new days: / I offer it as
forfeit to your fate, that you may be freed.

His accepted role then is to stay behind, *bruciare,* to mark (beacon-
like) the perilous coast and, conversely, the direction outward. Be-
yond this there is the concept of intentional sacrifice, the ceding of
personal hope in the interests of another, a shift and deposit of
aspirational energy which psychic "surplus" may serve to release
that other.

Such a program of course relates to orthodox beliefs in the validity
and power of selfless prayer, the idea of a willing substitution made
in love and the assumption of another's burdens. In Montale the
notion is complicated by an absolute conviction that he himself (or
the "I"s of his monologues and soliloquies) is eternally fixed in his
suffering—"Grace is for others." But suffering, it seems, can be of
use, may—burning—supply a light for others who are outward bound.
And man himself can become the Christopher, the "Christ-bearer,"
the bearer of an agony that might be redemptive—for others.

The lines cited above are taken from "Casa sul mare," the last poem before "Riviere" in the original *Ossi di seppia*. The preface-poem for this volume, "In limine" (Threshold-inscription) was surely written in the same phase (1924–1925). The *In limine* at the entrance to Dante's hell was one terrible imperative: to abandon all hope. Montale's inscription makes a distinction between the speaker ("I") and *tu;* we are at the threshold of a garden, but hardly the earthly paradise.

> Godi se il vento ch'entra nel pomario
> vi rimena l'ondata della vita:
> qui dove affonda un morto
> viluppo di memorie,
> orto non era ma reliquario.

Rejoice if the wind entering the fruit garden / bears with it the surging of life: / here where there settles a dead / tangle of memories,/ there was no garden, but a reliquary.

Even the rhymes in this initial stanza, *pomario* as against *reliquario, morto* as against *orto,* sound out the harsh discrimination self-drawn between the possibilities for "you" and "me"—growth versus decay, upsurge versus sinking, life versus death. Already with the presence of the wind in the garden, there is a sense of stirring, possibility, viable hope *for the addressee;* the speaker on the other hand will aid and abet but stay, Sidney Carton to your Darnay, your substitute this side of the "sheer wall."

> Un rovello è di qua dall'erto muro.
> Se procedi t'imbatti
> tu forse nel fantasma che ti salva. . . .
>
> Cerca una maglia rotta nella rete
> che ci stringe, tu balza fuori, fuggi!
> Va, per te l'ho pregato,—ora la sete
> mi sarà lieve, meno acre la ruggine. . . .

A frenzy is on this side of the sheer wall. / If you keep on you will come upon / perhaps the phantom that saves you. . . . / Seek a broken mesh in the net / that holds us, leap outside and flee! / Go, I've prayed for this for you—now my thirst / will be light for me, less biting the rust. . . .

Even the possibility of a salvation sketched here tastes salt and wry— the verb *imbattersi* means "bump into" or "fall in with" and suggests, augmented by the adverb *forse* (perhaps, maybe), mere happenstance. The salvationary agent itself, *fantasma,* seems insubstantial, slightly implausible—something like Dora Markus' "amulet which perhaps will save." *Così è se vi pare;* at any rate evasion or *varco* seems a matter of gratuitous luck, though even the *chance* of breakthrough can constitute an "hypothesis of grace" from the viewpoint of he who must stay. The thought affords an ironic consolation: *meno acre le ruggine . . .*

Between them, the initiatory "In limine" and the penultimate "Casa sul mare" at least provide a point or purposiveness to suffering which lends some slight basis to the premature optimism of "Riviere." To them should be added "Crisalide" (Chrysalis), a fulldress dramatic rendering in "blank" hendecasyllables of the situation and proffered resolution more schematically dealt with by the others. It seems to me a key poem which looks forward to the great achievements of the next five years (1925–1930)—the poems augmenting the second (1928) edition of *Ossi di seppia* and the elaborate dramatic "portraits" which eventually initiate *Le occasioni.*

Once again we are in an *orto,* a small domestic orchard. It is April, new leaves and flowers appear from moment to moment, the warm wind—as in "In limine"—bears life with it in waves. But here things are more gnomic. In the prefatory poem the characters were two: the speaker-counsellor who might be the poet, and you, *tu,* possibly the reader, anyway someone addressed in restrained but intimate emotion.

In "Crisalide" the speaker has recognizable connections with him of "In limine" in his bitter sense of the ironies of a springtide which may bring renewal to others but not himself. He stands, a meditative onlooker, in a "dark corner" of the garden, repeatedly associating himself (verbally) with shadow. He thus seems a "vegetable shade" in the Dantean sense,* peering on the living (spring, you) with a

---

* This image is recurrent in Montale. In "Scirocco" he sees himself "the agave bearding the crevice of a rock" with shut buds unable to burst, in an "immobility like a torment." Arsenio, that wry variation on Pascal's *roseau pensant,* is presented as a *giunco,* a reed dragging his roots with him. The climax poem of the definitive *Ossi di seppia* involves a vegetal *incontro,* a strange encounter in which submerged lymphatic lives grope, brush and fall away. The image is at least as old as Ovid—see *Meta.* II and the agonized transformation of Phaeton's sisters into trees. Dante used it for the *contrapasso* in the wood of suicides (*Inf.* XIII) where the self-destroyers are ironically gratified by painful investiture into bloody wood. Generally Montale's usage involves the sense of a potential unable to express or extropolate itself—the Syrinxian presence within a tree which then dies baffled or strangled for lack of air or recognition. The connection to "wall" or blockade is clear. Cf. the poem "Vasca" where "something" is seen reflected on the surface of a little pool (*vasca*):

> . . . di erompere non ha virtú,
> vuol vivere e non sa come;

mixture of resignation and envy from what he calls his "squalid limbo of maimed existences."

As the poem develops his presence takes on a darker, "sicker" note:

> Siete voi la mia preda, che m'offrite
> un'ora breve di tremore umano.
> Perderne non vorrei neppure un attimo. . . .

. . . You are my prey, who offer me / a brief hour of human tremor. / I will not lose even a moment of it. . . .

His contemplation thus has its succubic or vampirical side—the speaker "preys" upon the life-energies about him. As the poem amply illustrates, even the pangs involved in spring's renewal have their value to him as being symptomatic of real life, prized by one for whom even pain has become routine.

The "you" is not the customary *tu,* but *voi,* a plurality. A precise identification of the addressee in Montale's poetry is not always easy or even possible. The main function of such pronouns is to lend the discourse the dramatic immediacy associated with the vocative, and *who* exactly is spoken to often seems of minor importance. Always, of course, the vocatives work to bring the reader into the story, and the *voi* of "Crisalide," like the *tu* elsewhere, assuredly covers each and every one of us perusing Montale. But beyond this, *voi* seems to refer here to the myriad aspects of burgeoning natural life within the garden, a kind of Aprilic composite or coalition fermenting about the staring shade:

> Son vostre queste piante
> scarse che si rinnovano
> all'alito d'Aprile, umide e liete.
> Per me che vi contemplo da quest'ombra,
> altro cespo riverdica, e voi siete.

. . . Yours are these scattered / plants that are renewed / in April's breath, moist and joyous. / For me who contemplate you from this shadow, / another bush grows green again: and you are.

> se lo guardi si stacca, torna in giù:
> è nato e morto, e non ha avuto un nome.

. . . it has no strength to burst out, / it wants to live and doesn't know how; / if you look at it it ceases, returns below: / it was born and is dead and never had a name.

But this life also involves specifically "human" features. At one moment in the poem "you" are transfixed by a memory and a sudden sense of time's rapid passage, and the "human tremor" that betrays this event is watched, almost gulped, avidly from the shadows. At another moment "you" seem infected by the grim despair of the witness or spy you are probably quite unconscious of, and then you are "reclaimed" by the shade who sucks you into its own despair:

> . . . anche la vostra
> rinascita è uno sterile segreto,
> un prodigio fallitio come tutti
> quelli che ci fioriscono d'accanto.

> . . . even your / rebirth is a sterile secret, / a failed prodigy like all / those that flower beside us.

Now "you" and "I" become "we" as gradually the relation revealed in the first third of the poem (life and light scrutinized by death and shadow) blurs into common depression. We look out to sea at this point, observe its mists and clouds "shaped like a schooner" and in conscious self-irony fantasticate upon our approaching salvation:

> . . . nel meriggio afoso
> spunta la barca di salvezza, è giunta:
> vedila che sciaborda tra le secche,
> esprime un suo burchiello che si volge
> al docile frangente—e là ci attende.

> . . . in the sultry noon hour / the boat of salvation appears, has arrived / —see it where it rolls between the sand dunes, / as it puts out its longboat that turns / to the mild breaker—and there awaits us.

This detailed "hypothesis of Grace," enunciated in sarcasm, constitutes the cruellest moment of the poem. At this point the speaker turns in a shudder of revulsion from his own contaminating bitterness to a simpler, less contorted expression of his suffering. And here the *voi* is given a summary name— *crisalide*, butterfly-in-the-making with its promise or future of flight. The name reestablishes original distinctions between those who stay and those who may move out, but for the moment the general destiny is contemplated in terms already familiar to us:

> . . . e noi andremo innanzi senza smuovere
> un sasso solo della gran muraglia;
> e forse tutto è fisso, tutto è scritto,
> e non vedremo sorgere per via

> la libertà, il miracolo,
> il fatto che non era necessario!

> . . . and we shall go on without dislodging / a single stone of
> the great wall; / and maybe everything is fixed, everything is writ-
> ten, / and we shall not see rising on our way / liberty, the miracle, /
> the fact that was not necessary.

With this evocation of *varco* the final movement begins; the ten-
derness implicated in the climax-vocative of "chrysalis" is realized
through a pledge of substitution-sacrifice such as ended "In limine."
The poem's concluding image even recapitulates the burning sign
(*tirso*) of *Mediterraneo*. The speaker makes his "pact with destiny,"

> . . . di scontare
> la vostra gioia con la mia condanna.
> È il voto che mi nasce ancora in petto,
> poi finirà ogni moto. Penso allora
> alle tacite offerte che sostengono
> le case dei viventi; al cuore che abdica
> perché rida un fanciullo inconsapevole;
> al tagio netto che recide, al rogo
> morente che s'avviva
> d'un arido paletto, e ferve trepido.

> . . . to redeem / your joy with my sentencing. / It is the prayer
> that is born even now in my breast; / then every motion will cease.
> I think, then, / of the silent offerings which sustain / the houses of
> the living: of the heart that renounces / so that a child may laugh,
> unknowing; / of the clean cut that severs, of the dying / pyre that
> quickens / with a dried-up stick, and blazes trembling.

So in the setting of an April garden by the sea a conversion of a
sort occurs. Alternately a psychic rape is conceived, initiated and
ultimately relinquished or sacrificed. But to speak of mild sea, bud-
ding plants, warm breeze, shade, chrysalis as "setting" obscures a
central characteristic of Montalean vision: the fact that there is no
hard and fast bounding line to be drawn between a consciousness
and the world it inhabits. "Everything is internal and everything is
external for today's man, without the so-called world being neces-
sarily our representation,"* he writes in "Intenzioni." "I do not know

---

* This view then is not at all related to Ungarettian "nominalism," where
the world is man's invention. For Montale, the world exists, is *there*, and
not as our invention, representation, idea or projection. We are a part of it,
though a nice division of real estate—how much mine, how much thine or its—
is impossible to say for a rough and radical skepticism like his.

up to what point the external world (the non-I of the philosophers) includes or excludes my physical person."[16] Such a notion as the phenomenological "bracketing" (*epoché*) of Husserl—the intellectual operation by which some *quid* of life can be separated out and mounted in parentheses as a "pure" object for study—would be, for Montale, comic were it not for its disastrous social consequences. The self, the "I", is inextricably bound up in what we call its "environment," surrounding conditions. And hence it follows that the most satisfactorily precise view of man will have to be specific, even dramatic—in Montale's phrasing (italics his): "not the individual, then, but *this* individual, in *this* place, in *this* situation."

The matters touched upon here are not remote from "Crisalide" and the development of Montale's poetry after *Ossi di seppia*. The "I" of "Crisalide," for example, is not presented as a more or less stable entity upon which other entities press or impinge but as a consciousness in continuous flux and process. It can be defined only from moment to moment, "*this* individual . . . *this* place . . . *this* situation"; it has no "definitive" or final identity except in terms of its continually shifting relationships with presences and conditions edging its very local jurisdiction. It acts and is acted upon; its motions involve an astonishing range of rhythms and vocal modulations covering the starts, feints, shifts and realignments it lives through until the moving and heroic coda, its formulation of a "pact." "Crisalide" is the dramatization of the fortunes of a consciousness moving from an obsessional and lacerating sense of its own impotence to a commitment, *nevertheless*, to the well-being of another; a dramatic aria— if one wishes—of an evolving *coscienza*. In both theme and dramatic richness it anticipates the major work to come.

❖   ❖   ❖

In the years 1926–27 Montale not only wrote several of the poems that would eventually initiate *Le occasioni*, but six which were to be added to *Ossi di seppia* for the second edition of 1928. In my opinion, five of these—"Vento e bandiere," "Arsenio, "I morti," "Delta," "Incontro"—are masterpieces.

As we might expect, they are dramatic monologues. They are also— with the exception of "Arsenio" which, as we shall see, falls into another category——ironic fulfilments of the change proposed in the final lines of "Riviere" in the last pages of the first *Ossi:*

> . . . cangiare in inno l'elegia; rifarsi;
> non mancar piú.

No doubt the poet who wrote these lines in 1920 had a different idea of "hymn" than what turned out eventually to be the case—something celebrative no doubt, joyously affirmative. Ungaretti's definition of his own *inni*—compositions exactly contemporanous to the work we are considering—as expressions of metaphysical crisis ("extreme disquietude, perplexity, anguish and fright over man's destiny") seems relevant to the Montale of this phase.

But there is an enormous difference. Ungaretti sought to resolve his crisis by desperately soliciting another order of being—an idea or memory of unearthly innocence, the supernatural. "Cerco un paese innocente." For Montale such a "vertical" evasion or *varco* is impossible. The Gobettian "gift of immanence" ("the persuasion that life can only be explained by life, that man is the sole maker of his destiny") is his own. There is no way in which a human being can transcend or bracket himself from the conditions that make him human. Even "Grace" in Montale is humanoid—only human sacrifice or transfer of energy can "save" another human. And the famous formulation of the poet's function which concludes the first of the *ossi*

> Codesto solo oggi possiamo dirti,
> ció che *non* siamo, ció che *non* vogliamo. . . .

incorporates a *positive* program: poetry will divest itself of its traditional licenses—sonorous dreams, ideals, regrets (in a word, "poetry")—and adhere to the known conditions.

The fourth section of *Mediterraneo* had evoked the image of life as a "torrent" moving toward the sea, casting aside in its course the detritus of used-up individual lives. This amounts to a "philosophy". It is present everywhere in the poems now added to *Ossi di seppia*: in the "descent" of Arsenio from what could be the *corso* in Rappallo to the sea breaking in a summer storm, in the expiring of the ghosts of both the living and the dead on the "iron coast" in "I morti," in the very title of "Delta" with its sense of silted deposits thrown up in ditches where the river meets the sea. The second stanza of the great "Incontro'" places it with a fierce eloquence of which no other contemporary poet has been capable:

> La foce è allato del torrente, sterile
> d'acque, vivo di pietre e di calcine;
> ma piú foce di umani atti consunti,
> d'impallidite vite tramontanti
> oltre il confine
> che a cerchio ci rinchiude: visi emunti,

> mani scarne, cavalli in fila, ruote
> stridule: vite no: vegetazioni
> dell'altro mare che sovrasta il flutto.

The rivermouth straddles the torrent, sterile / of water, alive with stones and lime, / but more the rivermouth of used-up human acts, / pallid lives setting / beyond the confines / that close us in a circle: emaciated faces, / fleshless hands, horses in a file, screaming / wheels: lives, no—vegetations / of the other sea that overhangs the flood.*

The voices arising from this fluid cortège are full of suffering, prayers, curses, complaints. For the speaker, there is only his sorrow—"sole living portent in this swarm" and he begs it to stay as a kind of talisman of vital resistance (like K's suffering or the maddened sunflower) against the gathering blankness. Its precarious actuality momentarily seems to attract other life, a submerged copresence—kin to the *voi* in "Crisalide"—which might bring nourishment and the strength to defy: "To it I hold out my hand, and feel another life make itself mine." Then it fades. But in the brush with another life, what was "elegy" has been transformed into the will to endure and, if possible, to conclude with integrity. What follows is one of the few radiant moments of the *ventennio nero:*

> Poi piú nulla. Oh sommersa! tu dispari
> qual sei venuta, e nulla so di te.
> La tua vita è ancor tua: tra i guizzi rari
> dal giorno sparsa già. Prega per me
> allora ch'io discenda altro cammino
> che una via di città,
> nell'aria persa, innanzi al brulichio
> dei vivi; ch'io ti senta accanto; ch'io
> scenda senza viltà.

Then nothing more. Oh submerged one! You disappear / as you came, and I know nothing of you. / Your life is still your own—dispersed already / among the rare glints of day. Pray for me / while I descend another road / than a city street, / in the dim red air, before the swarm / of the living; that I may feel you beside me, that I / may descend without vileness.

---

* The other sea, that is, the flux of life itself. This image finds an adequate commentary in a sentence from "Intenzioni": "In the *Ossi di seppia* everything was drawn and absorbed by the fermenting sea; later I saw that the sea, for me, was everywhere, and that even the classic architectures of the Tuscan hills were in fugitive movement." One of the poems of *Le occasioni,* "Tempi di Bellosguardo" (Times at Bellosguardo), literally surveys Florence and environs from this viewpoint.

"Vento e bandiere" (Wind and Flags) deals with a similar move-ment—from the elegiac and sorrowful to, via an "encounter," a quick-ened *coscienza*—in Riviera imagery. Again we are in a summer garden. The object of the first-person consciousness is a *donna lontana*, a faroff lady, as she reappears to the memory on the wings of the wind. The poem begins with a series of recollections of her, moulded and shaped by the various moods and modalities of wind—gentle breath, gust, blast, etc.—culminating in stanza three with what seems to be a curious anticipation of Clizia: you (*tu*) the remembered *donna* reclining in a hammock in the garden, "cradled" by a now attendant wind "in your flights without wings." (Clizia, stormy petrel or angel, will grow wings.) But at this point in the poem, where the past seems to have swamped the present, the idyll is suddenly broken off by the turn of thought on itself—

> Ahimé, non mai due volte configura
> il tempo in egual modo i grani!

Alas, never twice does time order / its grains in an identical way!

Fond fantasies are interrupted by the prompting of the wakened intelligence: there is no repetition and memory cannot "return" or revive what is over.* And with this recall to authentic conditions the poem's movement reverses itself towards the present. We are perhaps near Monterosso, and the last two stanzas revive its shapes and meager consolations (its flags and holidays):

> . . . ed or fa vivo
> un gruppo di abitati che distesi
> allo sguardo sul fianco d'un declivo
> si parano di gale e di palvesi.

---

* Cf. Ungaretti. The last word on memory is Clizia's in one of the *Bufera* poems ("Voce giunta con le folaghe": Voice arrived with the coots):

> Memoria
> non è peccato fin che giova. Dopo
> è letargo di talpe, abiezione
> che funghisce su sé. . . .

. . . Memory / is no sin while it serves. After, / it is sloth of moles, abjectness / sprouting on itself like fungus. . . .

Fin che giova: while it is auxiliary to, rather than substitute for, the present. For Montale, as certain *ossi* and the later motets (that is, a suite of obsessive memories of another—perhaps the same—*donna lontana*) remind us, the objects served up by memory can be an intermittence or interstice in the wall, but they never really displace his continuing awareness of being blocked.

> Il mondo esiste. . . . Uno stupore arresta
> il cuore che ai vaganti incubi cede,
> messaggeri del vespero: e non crede
> che gli uomini affamati hanno una festa.

> . . . and now a group of dwellings / come alive that, spread out /
> to the eye along a sloping face, / are decked with bannerets and
> pennants. /
> The world exists. . . . Amazement stops / the heart that cedes
> to wandering incubi, / messengers of evening: and that does not
> believe / that famished men have holiday.

This, like the resolution of "Incontro," is the stoic triumph of *coscienza*, where the insistence on awareness, lucidity and discrimination amounts to a heroic resistance to the incursions of intellectual sloth, sleep, commerce with incubi. Poems like "Vento e bandiere," "I morti" and "Incontro" look forward to later apocalyptic poems like "Nuove stanze" (New Stanzas) where Clizia's steely eyes unflinchingly oppose in *conscienza* the "hell-hoards" sacking not only Florence but all Italy of the 1930's.

The later 1920's witness the creation of another sort of dramatic poetry by Montale—the "portrait" of a given character, as observed with a certain affectionate irony and understanding from the outside. Of course Esterina might be cited as a prior example of the same sort of thing, but "Falsetto" is rather a portrait of the speaker occasioned by the twenty-year-old goddess who remains ideally remote throughout. Portraits such as "Arsenio," "Dora Markus I," and "Carnevale di Gerti" (Gerty's Carnival) are products almost entirely confined to this phase of Montale's career.* Clizia is no more a portrait than Beatrice or Laura, though the genre is briefly resumed towards the end of the subsequent decade in his poems on the vissitudes of two Jewish women forced into exile by the fascist "racial" policies of the period.**

---

* As we shall see below, possibly prompted by the examples of Browning and Eliot, whom he was reading in this period.

** E.g., the fragment "A Liuba che parte" (To Liuba Departing) of 1938 and "Dora Markus II" of 1939. Their Jewishness (which might be overlooked) is declared in Montale's postwar notes. The name Dora Markus, by the way, is an invention of the late 1930's, when Montale concluded her story by presenting her in political exile. Part I, written 13 years earlier, shows her in Ravenna looking eastward across the Adriatic towards her "true country" in Central Europe, and whether or not she is Jewish is simply irrelevant because the poem as originally projected appears to have had no special political overtones. That is, if she is a victim in "Dora I" it is owing to "human" rather than fascist conditions.

All three of the portraits of 1926–1928 are related in subject and treatment. All three deal with urban *ratés*, restless and lonely creatures of empty lives who seek some opening in the closed and vicious circle hemming them in through the constructs of dream or superstition. The "lake of indifference" that is Dora's heart* lies at the core of a tempestuous and neurotic personality that is fed by nostalgia (a dream of Carinthia) and some private "charm" (the white ivory mouse beside the lipstick in her purse) that represents at least the hope of a benign fortune. Gerty, the lonely wife of an absent soldier, walks city streets in the midst of carnival festivities and dreams of setting back the clock, of miraculously regaining another and earlier world where the sun "saluted her grace" and all absent friends could be reunited smiling around a holiday table laden with the presents of her childhood. Like Dora, Gerty has her lucky piece: not merely the "trembling bubble of air and light" that is the world of memory but the favoring auspices indicated by an old and preferred oracle, the prophetic shape once upon a time assumed by a spoonful of melted lead suddenly dipped in cold water.

Dora must return from the pier looking eastward out upon the high sea to sooty Rimini "in the lowlands where a sluggish spring was sinking without memory"; so too time cannot pause or reverse itself for Gerty and she too must return to her lonely room and (a similar image) "to springs that do not flower." As in "Arsenio" a dazzling barrage of ironically rhetorical questions is directed by the speaker at his subject—its extravagant imagery (crystallizations of her retrospective fondness) undercut by the interlocutor's awareness of ceaseless change and dissolution, of how memory runs to fiction:

> Chiedi
> tu di fermare il tempo sul paese
> che attorno di dilata? Le grandi ali
> screziate ti sfiorano, le logge
> sospingono all'aperto esili bambole
> bionde, vive, le pale dei mulini
> rotano fisse sulle pozze garrule.
> Chiedi di trattenere le campane
> d'argento sopra il borgo e il suono rauco
> delle colombe? Chiedi tu i mattini
> trepidi delle tue prode lontane?

* "I do not know how, so weary, you resist in the lake of indifference which is your heart." The image is an old one for Italians. See Dante, *Inf.* I, 19–21 where it is used, perfectly in keeping with medieval medical terminology, as the cavity within the heart where blood is gathered and dispersed. Boccaccio comments: "Vital spirits inhabit the lake of the heart . . . which is the receptacle for all our passions."

> Do you ask / to stop time over the countryside /that spreads
> around? Great speckled / wings graze you, colonaded galleries /
> thrust out into the open thin, / blonde, live dolls, the blades of wind-
> mills / turn fixed above garrulous streams. / Do you ask to hold back
> the silver bells / above the town and the hoarse sound / of the doves?
> Do you ask the shy mornings / of your distant shores? . . .

No, the portrait concludes, her life is *quaggiú,* down here, in the
blaring city streets, "amid heavy walls that do not open" where both
she and the portraitist (*fratello*) are destined to live out the pre-
mature evenings of their lives.*

Arsenio, whose name seems to pun on a burnt-out case and whose
poem concludes with an evocation of cinders, is the most famous
of Montale's portrait-subjects.** Like "Gerti" and "Dora Markus
I" the portrait deals with a *varco* glimpsed and lost, a return to
definitive confinement. One might regard it as a dramatization of
the situation lyrically elaborated in *Mediterraneo:* that is, a man's
relation to the sea, his sense of its presence and power, his hope for
some sort of escape or renewal through immersing himself in it.
Paralleling d'Annunzio, Esterina and "I" of *Mediterraneo,* Arsenio
turns his back on the land and moves towards the bounding and
fluid element. He carried no talisman and conforms to no told
fortune, yet he reads in the pre-storm stillness of the air punctuated
by the *ritornello* of castanets and violins from the smart hotels behind
him what may be the correct omens for breakthrough into what he
thinks of as "another orbit" from the "motionless moving" that is his
life. But the storm strikes and passes and nothing has changed
except his heightened consciousness of immobility, of a hypothetical
chance somehow missed and now forever irrecoverable.

❊   ❊   ❊

In 1927 Montale moved to Florence, where in the following year
he was appointed director of the Gabinetto Vieusseux, the distin-
guished book collection which is the largest lending-library in Europe.
He retained this position until 1938, when the government forced
him to relinquish it as the price of his influential anti-fascism.

---

* "Carnevale di Gerti" could have been titled "Senilità" insofar as it consti-
tutes a recall of the protagonist to her true vocation. Svevo's second novel was
set in Trieste during that pre-Lenten festival; its original title had been *Il
carnevale di Emilio.*

** Arsenio might also be considered a "version" of Eugenio Montale, who
has been known to sign letters with that name. Other sardonic self-appellations:
"Eusebius"—the name given by Robert Schumann to the gentle, dreamy, con-
templative and "poetic" side of his "split" personality; "Tiresias"—the passive
prophet-androgyn resuscitated by Eliot; "Mirco"—the lovelorn shepherd (see
commentary on the *mottetti* below).

Montale describes the *intenzione* behind the move as the wish to live "with the detachment of a foreigner, of a Robert Browning," and certainly the mask of an "English" reserve is related to the ideal of *dilettantismo superiore* proposed in "Stile e tradizione."* But the mention of a Browning-model is worth examining briefly for its connections with Montale's poetry as well as his style of living.

Portraits of the sort discussed above are a relative novelty in the history of Italian poetry. Critics have suggested the influence of the crepuscular Guido Gozzano on the Montale of this phase, and certainly there is something in this. Gozzano's character-portrait of the *raté* Totò Merùmeni can be looked upon as an Italian precedent for "Arsenio," and Montale himself has written brilliantly on the genius of this near-contemporary (1883–1916) in terms that recall his praise of Eliot's catholicity of style. Thus Gozzano was "born to be an exceptional narrator or *prosatore* in verse"; his best lines "sing but don't sing lyrically . . . and more than sing they recount, describe, comment."[18] Like Eliot, Gozzano was a Laforgian; unlike Eliot he never had a chance to assimilate this influence. As a result his narratives are finally limited, made "minor," by the prevailing irony of tone which drastically curtails the dramatic possibilities of his verse. Like Laforgue then, Gozzano is more of a liberating influence on a select posterity than a richly satisfying poetic presence on his own account.

But the mention of what Pound has called the "prose tradition in verse" brings us back to the wholesale creator of "dramatic monologues" "dramatic lyrics," "dramatic romances," "dramatic idylls," and a whole *Dramatis Personae:* Robert Browning. For Pound, it might be recalled, Browning is ranked with Crabbe and the Eliot of *Prufrock and Other Observations* in a great tradition of dramatically oriented verse that is concrete, socially observant and hospitable to subjects, diction and tonalities felt to be infelicitous and nonpoetic to the various Victorian-Edwardian-Georgian establishments. Montale knew Pound personally, having visited him occasionally at Rapallo where they read and discussed Pound's preferences in this tradition.[19]

---

* See his amusing analysis of the anglophile Italian—the "false Englishman"— in *Farfalla di Dinard* ("Signore inglese"); it is clear that he sees himself as a case in point. Eliot's Englishness is another one. In "Invito a T. S. Eliot" Montale writes how "T. S. Eliot, bourgeois poet, ex-bank clerk and still member of a London publishing firm which does good business publishing books on gardening and hence can afford to print poetry at a loss . . . is separated from other poets by his aristocratically neutral aspect of the man on the street. He is the true Englishman as people who have never been to England imagine him to be: reserved, well-bred, incapable of raising his voice and gesticulating. An Englishman, to tell the truth, who is not at all English. . . ."[17]

Surely Montale's remarks on Browning as a *prosatore* in verse are to some extent derived from his knowledge of Pound:

> . . . A verse that is "also" prose is the dream of all modern poets from Browning on; it is the dream that the integrity of style which makes Dante and Shakespeare the newest and most relevant of poets will once more be possible. . . . There has been, starting with Baudelaire and a certain side of Browning, and sometimes from their confluence, a current of poetry that is not "realistic" nor "romantic" and not even strictly "decadent" but which very broadly one can call "metaphysical". I was born in that furrow.[20]

The epithet "metaphysical" relating to an "integrity of style" is familiar to English-speaking readers through Eliot's famous essay on the English metaphysical poets where he cites with approval their capacious sensibilities in which "disparate experiences" such as the reading of Spinoza and kitchen odors are imaginatively integrated into new wholes. "The Metaphysical Poets" is precisely where Montale found his terminology—*metafisico* in the sense he employs it here has no previous history in Italian literature until the coming of Eliot—through, we may add, the cultural ambassadorship of Montale's friend Mario Praz.* Far more than the superficial similarities between Eliot's Old Testament image of the wasteland and Montale's Cinque Terre, it is their common quest for an "integrity of style" that links Eliot (and Pound) with Montale. Their achievements have been very different, but there is no doubt that the Italian found the strictures and exempla (for example, a "metaphysical" Browning) furnished by the two American expatriots pertinent to his own independently-conducted researches for a viable dramatic music.

❖   ❖   ❖

For Montale, then, Eliot has had particular value as a poet seeking "to construct objects that set feeling free without declaring it."[22] In 1940 he responded to the critic Pancrazi's charge that *Le occasioni* was "hermetically" obscure by writing that

* According to the critic Oresti Macrí it was Praz's anthology of 19th-century English poetry (*Poeti inglesi dell'Ottocento*: 1925) that gave Montale his introduction to Robert Browning. It was Praz again who made the first translation of Montale into English ("Arsenio" for Eliot's *Criterion* of June 1928) and at the same time, sensing an affinity between the two, lent Montale a copy of Eliot's poems, two of which ("A Song for Simeon" and "La figlia che piange") Montale translated in 1928–9. According to Praz the two poets struck him as very like in manners and temperament. He found "a family likeness in their outward appearance of sallow, prematurely aged men [vocational *senilità*!], slow and unemphatic in their manners, seemingly incapable of strenuous physical effort, reserved and concentrated in an inner vision like priests of an unhallowed religion."[21]

on the most favorable hypothesis, the so-called *obscure* poet is he who works on his own poem as if it were an object, accumulating in it instinctively sensory and supersensory things, reconciling there the irreconcilable, until he makes of it the firm and definite correlative of his own interior experience.[23]

This notion of the poem as *object*, as an articulation apparently independent of the expressive or subjective needs of the poet—as, in other words, a scientific instrument—is of course related to Eliot's famous formulation of the "objective correlative" in his essay on "Hamlet and His Problems." The "artistic inevitability" that Eliot and Montale desire lies in a way of expressing emotion directly without talking about it, by finding (in Eliot's words) "a set of objects, a situation, a chain of events which shall be the formula of that particular emotion. . . ." And while the dates of the *Ossi di seppia* poems with their extraordinary use of "external" elements (weather, landscape, architecture) as "formulae" for complex inwardnesses show that Montale's objectivism was under way well before he was familiar with Eliot's poetry or criticism, he obviously found a precious parallel and *riconoscimento* in the work of this other, equally saturnine, "false Englishman."

For Montale of the late 1920's and 1930's, the *Ossi* seemed overly self-centered, expressionistic. He has commented on his opinions during this period in "Intenzioni":

> During this time I felt born in me the need for a stricter lyric poetry, more intensely *attachée à sa proie*, less explanatory . . .[24] and I feared that in my old efforts the old dualism between lyric and comment, between poetry and preparation or impulsion towards poetry . . . still clumsily persisted. I did not want a pure lyric poetry in the sense it was then understood in Italy, and interplay of sonorous suggestions. [This may be a crack at Ungaretti and Quasimodo.] I wanted, rather, a fruit that could contain its motives without revealing them, or better, without flaunting them. Granted that in art there exists a balance between the inside and the outside, as between the occasion and the art-objectification, it was necessary to express the object and leave the impelling occasion in silence. A new, non-Parnassian method of plunging the reader *in medias res*, a total absorption of intentions in objective results.

The poems produced out of this need and method are gathered in *Le Occasioni* (1939), Montale's second* book of verse.

---

* Not counting the pamphlet *La casa dei doganieri e altre poesie* (The Customs House and Other Poems) whose five poems are all printed in *Le occasioni*. The title-poem won an important literary prize (Premio dell'Antico Fattore) in 1931.

An "occasion" is literally a falling-together, a juncture of circumstances that may suggest some pattern or purpose. It could refer to one's sense of the significance or auspiciousness of the juncture, or to the need or responsibility it seems to give off—as with the occasion for writing a poem. Such an idea of occasion is of course distinctly related to Montale's predilection for the talismanic and hypothetical moment of grace (*varco*). It involves some sort of concentrated experience, a scintilla of vital energy that effects one as either propitious, ominous, or riddlingly "meaningful."

Le occasioni was ticketed as an integral manifestation of the "hermetic movement" on its first publication. This simply means that it struck its first readers as unduly difficult; it has no relation whatever to the elaborate evocative stratagems underlying a genuine hermetic product like *Sentimento del tempo*. For Montale at any rate the obscurity of a book like *Le occasioni*, when it *is* obscurity and not critical obtuseness, is born from either the poet's "excessive confidence in his materials" (that is, what he thought was public knowledge turns out to have been private) or "an extreme concentration."[25] In the first case the poet can supply postfacto notes, which has been Montale's practice for both *Le occasioni* and *La bufera*; in the second, it is largely a matter of adjustment: the public simply will or will not catch on, in time, to a poet's timing.

There is no doubt in my mind that most of the difficulty encountered in *Le occasioni* has to do with Montale's need to produce a dramatic lyric quite purged of narrative omniscience and entrepreneurism, of editorializing and comment; that is, a "total absorption of intentions in objective results." A book of occasions is a book of concentrates, intensities; as Montale himself has written, it is a short step from the intense poem to the obscure one.[26] We are not talking of any grammatical-syntactical ellipsis here but of the nature of the poet's dramatic methods, his procedural assumptions. To be plunged, with minimal or no preparation, *in medias res*, which is to say, into the midst of an occasion dense with its own particular history, cross-currents, associations and emotional resonances, seems to me to be a fair description of the difficulties typically encountered in certain of the *Occasioni* poems. These can be relative. The sense and grasp of the whole of a given sequence (like the *Mottetti*) will help elucidate certain specific opacities within it. In other cases it is a question of information not really "withheld" but perhaps too carelessly *assumed* in the overriding interests of dramatic intensity and immediacy. Here notes can help, though Montale's, like Eliot's, are frequently either reserved or facetious. More often than not matters are left to the reader's own engaged interest and good will, his sensibility and, most of all, his common sense.

Examples are in order. In the first section of *Le occasioni* there is a pair of poems, "Buffalo," "Keepsake" (both English titles, both composed in 1929), which offers a perfect example of the Montalean "plunge." The first eight lines of "Keepsake" run as follows:

> Fanfan ritorna vincitore; Molly
> si vende all'asta: frigge un riflettore.
> Surcouf percorre a grandi passi il cassero,
> Gaspard conta denari nel suo buco.
> Nel pomeriggio limpido è discesa
> la neve, la Cicala torna al nido.
> Fatinitza agonizza in una piega
> di memoria, di Tonio resta un grido. . . .

Fanfan returns victor; Molly / sells herself at auction: a reflector sizzles. / Surcouf paces the poopdeck with great strides, / Gaspard counts coins in his den. / In the limpid afternoon the snow / has fallen, the Grasshopper returns to his nest. / Fatinitza agonizes in a fold / of memory, only a cry remains of Tonio. . . .

So the extraordinary catalogue continues for its twenty-two lines to the abrupt and poignant conclusion:

> Larivaudière, magnetico, Pitou,
> giacciono di traverso. Venerdí
> sogna l'isole verdi e non danza piú.

. . . Larivaudière, enchanter, Pitou, / lie crossways.   Friday / dreams of the green isles and dances no more.

In fact, as Montale's note to the poem indicates, it constitutes a repertory of characters ("reduced to a purely nominal existence, *flatus vocis*") drawn from international light opera of the late nineteenth century—Fanfan, for example, the hero of Varney's *Fanfan la Tulipe*, Molly the soubrette in *The Geisha* by Sidney Jones, and so on. The note is wholly "musicological" in intent, and apart from alerting the poor reader to the *genre* of the *dramatis personae* it is probably overspecialized.

Certainly much more relevant is the title, "Keepsake," which points to the real stage, the memory of the past and the rosary or charm-bracelet of affectionately recollected names that can magically accrue to a somewhat Proustian *temps retrouvé* for the poet Montale and whilom student of *bel canto*. The poem rehearses certain key moments in the lives of its trifling cast, but in so doing functions above all as correlative for the real emotion and vein of self-irony at that emotion experienced by the memory screening them. The pathos of this cumulative keepsake is produced by such details as the shivering grasshopper, the anguishes of Fatinitza and Tonio, the culminating pastoral melancholia of Crusoe's faithful Friday. Its concurrent counter-vein of ironic detachment is made up of such interruptive "stage" business—kin to Brechtian *Verfremdung*—as the "frying" reflector, the used-up puppet's limpness of Larivaudière and Pitou, the brusque pacing of the hendecasyllables (*vivace* rather than the obligatory *largo* of reminiscence), the sudden breaks and forced enjambments, the sonic playfulness of the irregular rhyming *passim* (for example, *ritorna-riflettore-percorre-torna, Fatinitza-ago-nizza, Pitou-non danza piú,* and so on). In short, "Keepsake" is just that: a catalogue of *moments musicales* made into hendecasyllables and kept "for luck," a fairly private and slight "charm" whose odd vivacity endows it with a geniality which, at least, is public. It stands by itself, *cul de sac* or extreme, in the *opera* of Montale.

What I suppose is the more genuinely difficult poem, "Buffalo," is also more characteristic of *Le occasioni*. As a naming-poem it bears a certain relation to "Keepsake," but a more interesting comparison can be made with an earlier example of this miniature genre. The fifteenth lyric in the *Ossi di seppia* sequence ("Valmorbia, discor-revano il tuo fondo . . . ": Valmorbia, there flowed across your depths . . .) is one of the few poems where the poet has permitted himself a reference to his experiences with the infantry in the Alps during World War I.* In this unusually pastoral lyric, Valmorbia, a little valley by the river Leno in the northern mountains near Trento, is a name that concentrates and preserves a certain memory; uttered (as it promptly is with the first three syllables of the poem) that stored memory is momentarily released and expanded. And as one might expect from the sonorous texture of the name, the memory is peaceful and idyllic, a charmed resonance bearing with it a recollected pause in hostilities, where rifles are silenced and only the murmur of the Leno is heard, where even a shellburst is experienced as "fire weeping into air." With the name a blessed *oblio del mondo* (forgetting of the world) is resurrected, and so the poem concludes:

---

* Specifically, besides *osso* #15, the third motet with its reference to the "ballerina" bomb and, in the fourth, the placenames Cumerlotti and Anghébeni: like Valmorbia, war and Alpine locales.

> Valmorbia, un nome—e ora nella scialba
> memoria, terra dove non annotta.

. . . Valmorbia, a name—and now in pale / memory, land where there is no night.

"Buffalo" provides as exemplary contrast and should be cited in its entirety. Like "Keepsake" it is a sequence of hendecasyllables made jagged and quick by means of abrupt caesurae and enjambments.

> Un dolce inferno a raffiche addensava
> nell'ansa risonante di megafoni
> turbe d'ogni colore. Si vuotavano
> a fiotti nella sera gli autocarri.
> Vaporava fumosa una calura
> sul golfo brulicante; in basso un arco
> lucido figurava una corrente
> e la folla era pronta al varco. Un negro
> sonnecchiava in un fascio luminoso
> che tagliava la tenebra; da un palco
> attendevano donne ilari e molli
> l'approdo d'una zattera. Mi dissi:
> Buffalo! — e il nome agí.
>   Precipitavo
> nel limbo dove assordano le voci
> del sangue e i guizzi incendiano la vista
> come lampi di specchi.
> Udii gli schianti secchi, vidi attorno
> curve schiene striate mulinati
> nella pista.

A glozing hell was thickening by bursts / in the sounding throats of loudspeakers / its multicolored crowds. Autobuses / emptied themselves in floods into the evening. / A smoky heat vapored / above the swarming gulf; below, a gleaming / arch evoked a river / and the crowd was ready for the crossing. A negro / was dozing in a luminous bundle / that slashed the shadow; in a grandstand, / gay, free and easy ladies were awaiting / the landing of a raft. I said to myself: Buffalo!—and the name worked. /

I plunged / into the limbo where the voices of the blood / are deafening and glintings burn out the sight / like mirrors flashing. / I heard the dry cracks, I saw all about / bent striped spines pumping / on the track.

Here is an occasion that clearly calls for—and gets—a stage direction. It seems that "Buffalo" is the name of the vélodrome or arena housing six-day bicycle races at Montrouge in the Parisian suburbs. *Le Six-day*, we may know from other sources—for example, expatriate Americans' memoirs of the 1920's—ranked high in the period as the last word in fashionable imports from the U.S.A. (hence the exotic name of the arena). It had its obligatory Negro jazz band, its loud-speakers and limelights, flask parties and film stars, cacophony of hot music, cheers, imprecations and the roar of the motorcycles preceding the bicyclists (or "stayers") in order to break air-resistance during their periodic tries for records. And having summarily named the occasion through his title—minimally amplified it is true by a note—Montale plunges us into a chaotic *medias res* whose lineaments literally look like Hell. The first twelve lines are an impersonal inventory of the inferno of this *dolce vita*, the milling mobs, the shouts, the violent alteration of light and shadow, smoke arising from the "burning gulf," the bright blond wood of the track, which I take to be the gleaming arc or arch, suggesting an Acheron at the side of which the giggling and hysterical damned line up.

In a reversal parallel to the "recall" by intelligence in "Vento e bandiere," but far more abrupt and desperate, the entranced speaker awakens and enters the poem to wrench himself from his vision and force a kind of saving return to the more tenable reality that is the arena at Montrouge. "I said to myself: Buffalo!—and the name worked": the hendecasyllable is hinged like the plot at this crucial point. For exotically American "Buffalo" is the name for a local reality or occasion and its utterance works like a charm to reestablish the possibly false but more bearable existence of race, moment, milieu. The last six lines narrate the rise back into the body and the teeming grandstands: impressions of recognizable life take over the brutish surface-symptoms (we know now) of the inferno below.

What makes "Buffalo" a characteristically Montalean *occasione* is its nervous and sinewy speed, its immediacy, its effect of private life revealed, its dramatic thrust. One can read "Valmorbia" without knowing previously where that valley is located or what its role is in the poet's biography; that is, the poem itself supplies the necessary information so that an adequate background can be assembled by the reader. In "Buffalo", on the other hand, clearly a real risk of obscurity is run. The problem, quite unlike what I conceive to be the problem involved with Ungarettian hermeticism, is simply a paucity of information, plus the poem's own self-confident speed, plus, above all, the novice reader's fear of trusting his own guesses which, after all, are directed and influenced by the poem itself. As we have seen, the risk is incurred deliberately in the name of dramatic intensity.

*   *   *

As is perhaps suggested by the two poems discussed above, the world of *Le occasioni* is a far larger one, more cosmopolitan, more European, than that of the *Ossi*. It leaves "regional" isolation to take account of others, unhappy or accursed ones like Dora, Gerty, Liuba, faces in a crowd in Paris, Eastbourne or Florence, Tommaso Landolfi's valet, a swimmer in the Danube near Vienna. The seascapes of Liguria yield to the *viali* of Florence, Rimini, Caserta, Venice, to souvenirs from Switzerland, Austria, France and England.

Le occasioni is divided into four sections, none of them titled except the second, the *Mottetti*. While the poems of each section are arranged in roughly chronological order, the sections themselves run more or less concurrently—that is, section one spans the period between 1929–39, and so does section four. Like the second edition of the *Ossi*, the *Occasioni* as a whole seems to move from a consideration of specific problems and experiences towards a more inclusive and contemplative view. Fitting the larger themes of the second half, the style grows less terse and "fragmentary," slower and more deliberative.

Thus the first section, which contains all the poems we have discussed so far, makes up a chapter of specific "cases": compressed and highly particularized memories like "Keepsake" or "Buffalo," or dramatic portraits of individuals like Dora and Gerty. The second section is the *Mottetti,* a very personal series of love poems addressed to a particular *donna lontana*. The third and fourth sections combine the atmosphere of the specific plights in the first with the erotic longing and amorous worship of the second to produce a new synthesis that is vaster and more inclusive. These sections are begun and ended with a pair of tripartate "vista" poems, long meditations from *heights* which are geographical as well as spiritual: the well-named Bellosguardo that surveys Florence from the left bank of the Arno and Mount Amiata in the mining country of southern Tuscany. Despite this widening of focus and, to a certain extent, heightening of style, the commitment to dramatic objectification that is one of the features of the volume remains normative throughout.

The love motif is not a novelty in the early poetry of Montale, though it does not become obsessive and exclusive until the *Mottetti*.*

---

* In a postcard to Piero Gadda Conti Montale specifies his view of the motifs of *Ossi di seppia*.[27] Besides the Ligurian landscape and the "lay miracle" of possible escape or *varco*, he instances, "love, under the form of phantasms that frequent the various poems and provoke the usual 'intermittences of the heart.'" We can cite the 13th and 16th of the *Ossi* group, the absent *tu* of "Vento e bandiere," "Delta," and "Incontro," the saved one of "In limine," "Crisalide"

One of these, "Il balcone" (The Balcony), has been detached from the sequence to act as the dedicatory poem for the entire volume, thus, in intention at least, putting the book under the sign of Eros or Amor. Several of the poems in the first section of *Le occasione*—notably "Verso Capua" (En route to Capua) and "Accelerato" (Express)—seem to look forward to the experience recorded in the second.

The story of the writing of the *Mottetti* has been told by Montale, with customary self-irony and Arcadian nomenclature, in an article written for the *Corriere della sera* in 1950, some ten to fifteen years after their composition (between 1933 and 1939, the bulk of them 1937 to 1938).

> Many years ago, Mirco, a noted poet who today has changed his trade [an ironic reference to Montale's postwar work for the *Corriere della sera* in Milan, and of course to this very article], composed mentally and then transcribed onto certain bits of paper kept balled up in his vest pockets, and at length published, a series of brief poems dedicated—and even addressed by airmail (but only on the wings of imagination)—to a Clizia who lived roughly three thousand miles distant from him. Clizia, in point of fact, was not called Clizia . . . nor was Mirco called Mirco, but necessary circumspection does not invalidate this little note. Let it suffice that we have identified the typical situation of that poet, and I would say of almost every lyric poet who lives besieged by the absence and presence of a faroff lady. . . . The little poems of Mirco, which evolved into a series, an autobiographical novelette that was anything but shadowy, were born from day to day. Clizia knew nothing of them and perhaps didn't read them until many years later; but sometimes news of her which reached Mirco furnished him with the stimulus for some motet, and thus new epigrams were born and were sped like arrows beyond the seas, without the lady concerned offering—even involuntarily—the pretext.[28]

As we shall see, the relation between the poet and his Clizia undergoes certain remarkable alterations in the course of *Le occasioni* and *La bufera*. The *Mottetti* simply trace the first and largely erotic phase of this affair. We can compare them in "plot" to roughly the first half of Dante's *Vita nuova* (that is, before the death of Beatrice) insofar as they deal with the suffering caused by the lover's separation from his beloved, his perturbation mixed with recollected images

---

and "Casa sul mare." Whether these are the same woman is impossible to say. We have noted Montale's predilection for an open *tu* designed to involve the reader. [See "Afterword on Montale" below.]

of her presence and ardent praises. They also mark the beginning of the vision vouchsafed him of her miraculous nature: increasingly she will come to represent that possibility of suspension of law, the *varco*, the veritable *fantasma che ti salva*.

The preface poem for *Le occasioni*, "Il balcone," ("part of the *Mottetti* but printed *in limine* for its dedicatory value," the author notes) is a brilliantly executed parody-canzonetta complete with lovers' balcony, a change of heart, an adoration. As popularized in the eighteenth century by such as Metastasio, the canzonetta was conceived of as a neat, bright, liltingly rhythmed artifact occasioned by love; one of my favorites is the opening pairing of quatrains from Jacopo Vittorelli's "Anacreontics for Irene":

> Guarda che bianca luna!
> Guarda che notte azzurra!
> Un'aura non susurra,
> Non tremola uno stel.
> L'usignoletto solo
> Va dalla siepe all'orno,
> E sospi rando intorno
> Chiama la sua fedel. . . .

The effect is all in the breathless music: translating ("See what a white moon! See what a blue night!" etc.) only confirms the old Italian saw, *traduttore-traditore*. But it is against this exquisite convention that the three quatrains of "Il balcone" have to be heard.

> Pareva facile giuoco
> mutare in nulla lo spazio
> che m'era aperto, in un tedio
> malcerto il certo tuo fuoco.

It seemed an easy game / to change the space open to me / into nothingness, into uncertain / tedium your certain fire.

Giorgio Baiardi has cleverly called the gambit announced here a "sort of 'Infinito' in reverse,"[29] and certainly this grim metaphysical juggling with spatial illusion is a feature of both lyrics, though Montale ends with a change of heart that rejects Leopardian "wrecking" or fantasy-annihilation. The speaker is here reviewing a mental operation habitually performed in the past—the reduction or decimation of his world to a contemptuous zero, the cynical acceptance of a world sans *varco* by an Arsenio who will not be lured by the dream of "other orbits." And everything is grist for this subjective mill, even the clear flame of the beloved smokes and gets dispersed in the virtuosity of his despair.

Played against such nihilism, the rhythmic suggestion of the *canzonetta d'amore* tugs oddly, with a certain gloomy humor. The short octosyllabics framed by the tidy *giuoco-fuoco* rhyme (to be wrenched in the middle of the first line of the next stanza by the slanted *vuoto* [void]), the accelerative elisions—as in the third line— and syncopation of the closely clustered internal rhymes (*aperto-malcerto-certo*), all work to build a light, skipping cadence which is made lame and *malcerto* by the jokey half-rhymes (*facile-spazio-tedio*) and flatfooted enjambing (especially lines 3 and 4). This in fact is the musical strategy governing the whole poem, the creation of tension by crossing the emphatic *orrechiabilità* of canzonetta with rhythmic dissonances, facetious rhymings, a deliberately dry language.

The last two stanzas express the speaker's "conversion," the effect of encountering his saving phantom.

> Ora a quel vuoto ho congiunto
> ogni mio tardo motivo,
> sull'arduo nulla si spunta
> l'ansia di attenderti vivo.
>
> La vita che dà barlumi
> è quella che sola tu scorgi.
> A lei ti sporgi da questa
> finestra che non s'illumina.

Now at that void I have assembled / each of my latent needs, / upon sheer nothing the longing / stirs to attend you, alive.
The life that gives off glimmerings / is the only one you recognize (*or:* the one that only you recognize). / Towards it you lean from this / unillumined window.

Clizia's posture is perfectly heliotropic: she bends towards the living light (not defined, except as the opposite of the dark and negative subversions recalled by the speaker in the first stanza) from her bleak balcony, a sign of vital aspiration. Towards what, at this stage, hardly matters. But she has moved and modified the author of this serenade who, if he must have the last harsh word, the final *che non s'illumina*, has nevertheless found a service beyond solipsism. To "attend" her, in the several senses of "to await" and "to wait upon," will henceforth be his life.

"Il balcone" is a fitting preface for *Le occasioni* since its subject is renewal through love, a renaissance of purpose and integrity through the *donna* who supports the lover against his temperamental despair, sardonic self-knowledge and precocious *senilità*. The twenty brief lyrics of the *Mottetti* proper have as their motto a phrase culled from the nineteenth century Spanish poet of love Gustavo Bécquer. "Sobre el bolcán la flor": Above the volcano the flower—the problematic nature of this epigraph (is the flower triumphant or threatened?) is a fair directive to the oscillations between utter despair and exaltation, passionate longing and fears of self-delusion, that characterize much of the drama these lyrics offer.

They begin in hell. The poet is alone in an industrial Genoa which intensely embodies his sense of the pointless brutality of a world without Clizia, a world which works to obliterate even the possibility of her dispensation:

> . . . Un ronzío lungo viene dall'aperto,
> strazia com'unghia ai vetri. Cerco il segno
> smarrito, il pegno solo ch'ebbi in grazia
> da te.
> E l'inferno è certo.

. . . A drawn-out buzzing comes from out there, / lacerates like nails on glass. / I search for the mislaid sign, / the single pledge I had from you / in your mercy. /
And hell is certain.

The second motet expresses, via a steadying memory of a previous return of Clizia (a note indicates that the "harder year" is one she spent in a sanatorium), the impassioned committment felt by the solitary lover. It is accomplished with a stilnovistic and operatic flourish which is one of the many sides of this extraordinary poet.

> Molti anni, e uno più duro sopra il lago
> straniero su cui ardono i tramonti.
> Poi scendesti dai monti a riportarmi
> San Giorgio e il Drago.
>
> Imprimerli potessi sul palvese
> che s'agita alla frusta del grecale
> in cuore . . . E per te scendere in un gorgo
> di fedeltà, immortale.

Many years, and one harder spent above the foreign / lake on which sunsets burn. / Then you descended from the mountains bringing back to me / St. George and the Dragon. /
Oh that I might inscribe them on the shield / that twists in my

heart at the flailing of the northeast wind. / . . . And that I might
descend for you into a maelstrom / of fidelity, immortal.

Here Montale's taste for the elegant, often recondite emblem is
very clear. St. George is the patron saint of Genoa, and his image
slaying the beast of evil is the heraldic sign for that city. (There
is even something heraldic about the epithet for the Swiss (?) lake
of line two, and of course the main image of the hung shield in the
second stanza is in perfect decorum.) But to paraphrase this passage,
then, as "You brought back Genoa, or memories of Genoa, to me"
would be to miss the main point. If Montale is not being simply
dandiacal, he would call Genoa Genoa if that were what he meant.
The sign of St. George and the Dragon must be, besides Genoa
and a probable reference to where Clizia and the poet met or loved,
an allusion to the miraculous struggle against evil which is the
essence, as we shall see, of Clizia's angelicity. The vow then under-
taken at the conclusion would then be to take that struggle upon
oneself, to make it one's own, to give oneself up to it. And even as
the emblem of St. George and the Dragon works on several levels,
so even the final *immortale* has its various polysemous functions:
grammatically it can be an epithet for Clizia ("O immortal one"),
an adjective asserting no bounds to the lover's fidelity to Clizia and
her struggle, a possibility for the salvation, via Clizia and "works,"
of the lover's own immortal soul. We need not select here but
accept them all as we would with Dante.

A very good case can be made for considering the *Mottetti* as a
whole as an experience of signs, a story in which from day to day a
lover seeks some signal or omen of his *donna lontana*. "Cerco
il segno smarrito," as he writes in the first motet. Besides Clizia
leaning towards the light from her balcony and the heraldic emblem
of St. George, there are the fringe of palm-leaf of motet eight, the
ineffable ("rich and strange") insignia of the ninth, the two shining
crosses of the nineteenth, the coin set in a lava paperweight ("sobre
el bolcán la flor") of the twentieth and last. The most scandalously
renowned of these signs, however, occurs in the sixth motet, here
quoted in full.

> La speranza di pure rivederti
> m'abbandonava;
>
> e mi chiesi se questo che mi chiude
> ogni senso di te, schermo d'immagini,
> ha i segni della morte o dal passato
> è in esso, ma distorto e fatto labile,
> un *tuo* barbaglio:

(a Modena, tra i portici,
un servo gallonato trascinava
due sciacalli al guizaglio).

The hope of even seeing you again / was deserting me; / and I asked myself if this that cuts me off / from every sense of you, this screen of images, / bears the signs of death or if from the past / there is in it, though distorted and elusive, / some brightness that is *yours:*
(at Modena, beneath the arcades, / a beribboned servant hauled along / two jackals on a leash).

In the *Corriere della sera* article Mirco-Montale amplifies on that apparently true moment at Modena:

Clizia loved odd animals. How she would have been amused to see them! Mirco thought. And from that day on he never read the name of Modena without associating that city with the idea of Clizia and the two jackals. Strange, persistent idea. What if the two beasts had been sent by her, almost as emanations? What if they were an emblem, an occult citation, a *senhal?* Or perhaps they were only an hallucination, the premonitory signs of his decay, his end?

Thus the parenthetical material that concludes the motet must be understood as an example of, or, better, a sampling from what the poet calls the "screen of images" confronting him and walling him off from his *donna.* If their destinies decree that he cannot attend *her,* he can attend her sign, some possible configuration on the screen before him.

A somewhat parallel situation occurs in two later, larger poems. In "Iride" (Iris) scattered signs of Clizia-Iris penetrate through to the hermet-poet in his ossuary. In the quite recent testamentary poem "Botta e risposta" (Thrust and Parry), the prisoner observes some invisible hand work mementoes of freedom through chinks or "invisible airholes." But in these later cases, the signs, if rare, are clear enough: the poet in solitary has no difficulty in recognizing the provenance of the emanations reaching him.

In the jackal-motet on the other hand, what might be interpreted as a sign (so extraordinary that it must have been "sent") is what Francesco Flora would call hermetic—not just to critics but to Mirco as well. This is the point: the poem is predicated by a mystery, it dramatizes an interpretive dilemma, the first two stanzas abstractly posing its nature, the last submitting a concrete instance. It seems to me that extraneous difficulties and consequent exasperation arise when one tries to do what the speaker of the poem explicitly says he cannot do: that is, interpret the sign. Does the heraldic ensemble of the flamboyant servant and his strange task imply some sort of medieval and "courtly" amorous vassalage? Do the leashed jackals mean an unhealthily balked eroticism or a healthily controlled id?, and so on. The search for the missing sign undertaken by the Mirco of stanza one in the hell of Clizia's absence is the apt *motto* for stanza six—the search though not the finding.

The route of the entire *Mottetti* sequence, then, beginning with its anguished sense of separation and ending with a kind of weary acceptance (" . . . ma cosí sia": but so be it) of Clizia's otherness, is mapped amidst signs—some of her, some of his condemnation to solitude, some baffling. The last motet finds a resigned poet seated amidst souvenirs that have lost their numinous function as talismanic signs and have become merely objects with a past. The past is past:

> . . . ma cosí sia. Un suono di cornetta
> dialoga con gli sciami del querceto.
> Nella valva che il vespero riflette
> un vulcano dipinto fuma lieto.
>
> La moneta incassata nella lava
> brilla anch'essa sul tavolo e trattiene
> pochi fogli. La vita che sembrava
> vasta è piú breve del tuo fazzoletto.

. . . but so be it. A winding horn / converses with the bee swarms in the oak grove. / In the shell that reflects the evening star / a painted volcano smokes happily. /

The coin stuck in lava, / it too shines on the table and holds down / a few sheets of paper. The life that seemed / so vast is briefer than your handkerchief.

An obsession with signs is of course related to that cult of talismans and amulets we have already noted as characteristic of Montale. Gerty and Dora immediately spring to mind, but this ascription of prophetic function or luck to various more or less arbitrary things is also a feature in many of those poems in which the poet may be assumed to be speaking for himself sans persona—one thinks of the sunflower, the lemons, the cloud that looks like a schooner, word-incantations like "Valmorbia" or "Buffalo"; the heraldic blazons and zodiacal figures that are a feature of the *Bufera* poems are other instances. "I only know," the poet has said in an interview, "that I have been so to say *hypnotized* by certain animals, objects and things. And I have had them recur many times in my verses."[30] He has referred to such items—a certain shoehorn, for example—as "concentrates of the past, assuming the function of totem for their bearers"[31] and as we know conceives of such animism "as the spiritual position most worthy of man as well as most logical."[32] At any rate it is a further instance of his inability to draw a clear line between the so-called external and internal spheres of experience. In poetry, I think, it is a power, a "gift" for discerning, imagining, or detecting immanence, which is a central source of his greatness.

❋   ❋   ❋

The conclusion of the phrase of experience represented by the *Mottetti* by no means concludes the poet's attendance on his absent lady's signs. The witness of desperate longing in the book's third and fourth sections is less personal and exclusive, far more comprehensive than in the first two. They involve a world and an era; her signs are not only clearer, to the poet at least, but have expanded in scope from the special case, the occult charm, to materials for universal apocalypse, "good" for everybody. Many Italians have recorded their sense, at the time, of the *Occasioni* poems as a heartening and heroic testament of moral resistance to the regime and what it stood for in the years just before the outbreak of world war. At the center of this opposition stands the fabulous presence of Clizia, now no longer simple source of "Mirco's" anguish or ecstasy but, as he invokes her in "Eastbourne," *Lux-in-Tenebris,* the embodied principle of fidelity to the light, of ravaged but persisting resistance to the "dark forces of Ahriman" both within and abroad, of that selfless "daily decency" which for this poet is the seed of divinity in all men's keeping.

This transfiguration of Clizia is not instantly accomplished in the few blank pages separating the last motet from the long "Tempi di Bellosguardo" (Times at Bellosguardo) which constitutes the whole of section three. Certainly the effect of this poem, strategically placed as it is, is quite literally to "elevate" the point of view at least as high as the hill of Bellosguardo, from which can be surveyed not just Florence and the landscape of Tuscany, but what the speaker calls the life of *tutti,* of all men "down there"

> . . . moto che si ripete
> in circolo breve: sudore
> che pulsa, sudore di morte,
> atti minuti specchiati,
> sempre gli stessi. . . .

. . . motion that repeats itself / in brief circle: sweat / that pulses, sweat of death, / tiny mirrored acts, / always the same. . . .

lived out amidst the historic stones with their silent witness to "great images—honor, unbending love, the rules of the game, immutable fidelity." So the view involves something like a panorama of all human life, its furtive and transient gestures as well as those that seem permanent, its pathos and its grandeur. And at the poem's end, the prospect opens out to include elements of apocalypse: the storm, the *bufera* that will give title to Montale's next volume, makes its violent appearance accompanied by Biblical omens (surely the locusts are black-shirted) and supernatural connivances:

> Un suono lungo
> dànno le terrecotte, i pali appena
> difendono le ellissi dei convolvoli,
> e le locuste arrancano piovute
> sui libri dalle pergole; dura opera,
> tessitrici celesti, ch'è interrotta
> sul telaio degli uomini. E domani. . . .

. . . The terracottas / give off a long-drawn hum, the gardenstakes scarcely / support the ellipses traced by the convolvuli, / the locusts limp that rained / on the books from the arbors: hard work, / celestial weavers, now interrupted / on the loom of men. And tomorrow. . . .

So the poem breaks off, ominously, to be followed by Montale's motto for section four, a citation from Shakespeare's fifth sonnet:

> Sap check'd with frost, and lusty leaves quite gone,
> Beauty o'ersnowed and bareness everywhere.

A grim prognostication certainly, which the basic mood of this section does nothing to alleviate.*

It begins with the well-known "La casa dei doganieri" (The Customs Station) which evokes a shack on a cliff above a breaking sea (in many ways kin to the *casa sul mare* of the *Ossi* and parallel to the "rented house" in which Eliot's Gerontion stiffens) and its inhabitant, the forgotten one with memories of "you," the abandoned sea-watcher who cannot follow you out:

> Oh l'orizzonte in fuga, dove s'accende
> rara la luce della petroliera!

* Though the Shakespeare sonnet, beyond what is cited, is finally optimistic— the flowers' distillation as perfume ("liquid prisoner in walls of glass") can triumph over time. So too the presence of Clizia abides, even gains in splendor, through these anguished pages.

Il varco è qui? (Ripullula il frangente
ancora sulla balza che scoscende. . . .)
Tu non ricordi la casa di questa
mia sera. Ed io non so chi va e chi resta.

Oh the fleeing horizon, where rarely flares / the tanker's light! /
The pass is here? (Still swarms the breaker / against the cliff that
breaks it. . . .) / You don't remember the house of this / my evening.
And I don't know who goes and who remains.

"La casa dei doganieri" also inaugurates a geometrical image—
the circle—which is a kind of existential descendant of the old wall
and is clearly related to the life seen as "motion that repeats itself in
brief circle" in "Tempi di Bellosguardo." Besides imprisonment, the
image incorporates various senses of mechanistic monotony and
vertigo; it also has connections with the mindless vortex of the
imminent *bufera.** So, in the "Casa," the compass spins crazily and
the smoke-blackened weathervane on the roof turns on itself *senza
pietà;* the whirlwind or whirlpool or mill (*mulinello*) of fate is
cited in "Sotto la pioggia" (Under the Rain); in "Eastbourne," muti-
lated men take the air in wheelchairs, the revolving doors of hotels
flash signals to one another, the tourist speaker finds himself shaken
by the sight of a carousel that "sweeps up everything within its
whirling," and concludes that goodness is unarmed, that "Evil
wins. . . . The wheel does not stop"; "Palio" begins and ends with
the sign of a spinning top.

Related to these images of circularity—the line that goes nowhere—
are other ones of drift, aimlessness, of being carried imperceptibly
by another power. Drift can be literal as in "Barche sulla Marna"
(Boats on the Marne) where Sunday boaters glide without effort
in a blurred felicity of *farniente* punctuated with twinges of malaise:

. . . ma dov'è
la lenta processione di stagioni
che fu un'alba infinita e senza strada,
dov'è la lunga attesa e qual è il nome
del vuoto che ci invade.

---

* Which I associate with Dante's *bufera infernal*
. . . che mai non resta,
mena gli spirti con la sua rapina:
voltando e percotendo li molesta. (*Inf.* V, 31–33)
The infernal storm, that never rests, / leads the spirits in its fury— /
turning and lashing it vexes them.

. . . but where is / the slow procession of seasons / that was an
infinite uncharted dawn, / where is the long expectation and what
is the name / of the void that invades us.

Or drift can be the shrug of capitulation, the wry grimace of an
Arsenio, the "realistic" perception of personal impotence that may
tempt stoicism to a sort of passive connivance. A repeated phrase in
this section is "Tutto è uguale"—the dispirited "all's one" of the
fatalist. Poems such as "La casa dei doganieri," "Costa San Giorgio,"
"Eastbourne," "Barche sulla Marna" and "Notizie dall'Amiata" are
the superbly varied dramatizations of this sense of no exit, impotent
dread and paralysis that made the book so timely.*

Yet, just as in "Tempi di Bellosguardo," the "brief circles" traced
by human lives were juxtaposed to the stones of Florence and "great
images" of honor, love, fidelity, so in section four the presence of
Clizia marks a curious resistance to what seems to be the triumph
of Evil. In "La casa dei doganieri," the stress is on her absence—the
reproachful refrain is "tu non ricordi"—and the anguished bewilder-
ment of he who stays behind. In his pain, of course, she is also
present, and as the section proceeds, Clizia can be seen to emerge,
chrysalis-like, out of that knot of lover's anguish into a life and mission
of her own that transcends the original, personal-erotic "occasion."
Perhaps the best graph of this metamorphosis is afforded by two
poems written at either end of a decade and plainly meant to be
linked by their titles: the "Stanze" (Stanzas) of 1929 and "Nuove
stanze" (New Stanzas) of 1939.

In "Stanze" the topic is the mystery of Clizia, her provenance,
the miracle she is, her paradoxical presence-in-absence.

> Ricerco invano il punto onde si mosse
> il sangue che ti nutre, interminato
> respingersi di cerchi oltre lo spazio
> breve dei giorni umani,
> che ti rese presente in uno strazio
> d'agonie che non sai, viva in un putre
> padule d'astro inabissato. . . .

I search (lit.: research) in vain the point whence moved / the
blood that nourishes you, endless / spread of circles beyond the
brief / space of human days, / that rendered you present in a tearing /
of agonies you know not, alive in a putrid / swamp of buried star. . . .

---

* However, as Montale has written, "the prisoner is not *solely* a political
prisoner."

The network of her nerves, fervor of her eyes, throb of her temples—
to paraphrase the second stanza—all "recall" her fabulous journey
from her origins, a journey described literally as a descent and in-
carnation. The beautiful third stanza evokes her *signs* as a play of
correspondences with the unknown agency which sent her:

> In te converge, ignara, una raggéra
> di fili; e certo alcuno d'essi apparve
> ad altri: e fu chi abbrividí la sera
> percosso da una candida ala in fuga,
> e fu chi vide vagabonde larve
> dove altri scorse fanciullette a sciami,
> o scoperse, qual lampo che dirami,
> nel sereno una ruga e l'urto delle
> leve del mondo apparse da uno strappo
> dell'azzurro l'avvolse, lamentoso.

In you, unknown to you, converges an aureole / of threads; and
certainly some among them appeared / to others: and one there was
who shivered one evening struck by a flying white wing, / and there
was one who saw wandering ghosts / where others glimpsed swarms
of young girls, / or discovered, like branching lightning, / a wrinkle
in the calm sky and the shock of the / levers of the world appeared
through a crack / in the blue and enveloped him, lamenting.

For the speaker however she is a fading revelation of the light ("a
last corolla of light embers that does not last but flakes and falls")
while he returns to his painful solitude:

> La dannazione
> è forse questa vaneggiante amara
> oscurità che scende su chi resta.

. . . Damnation / is perhaps this raving bitter / dark that des-
cends on he who stays.

That is, for him the miracle has failed, blocked or obscured by his
excruciated sense of privation.

In "Nuove stanze"—composed like its predecessor in an unusual
pattern of four symmetrical stanzas—all vain search and doubt are
at an end. We are in a room in Florence; a bejewelled Clizia sits
reigning above a chessboard whose pieces watch "stupified" as the
smoke from her cigarette ascends to the ceiling, composing not only
rings but heraldic towers and bridges in the air. But this "game"
is interrupted by another: a window is opened, the smoke is roiled,
the *fata morgana* dispelled.

> Là in fondo,
> altro stormo si muove: una tregenda
> d'uomini che non sa questo tuo incenso,
> nella scacchiera di cui puoi tu sola
> comporre il senso.

. . . In the distance there, / another host is moving: a hellhorde / of men who do not know this incense of yours / on the chessboard whose sense / you only can compose.

To the faint tolling of La Martinella (the alarm-bell of the Palazzo Vecchio) two worlds are in contention: the forces of evil and "murderous folly" involving not only blackshirted militarism but racial persecution as against the heraldically rendered *via contemplationis* embodied by Clizia as she surveys the board. In stanza three the speaker recalls his little faith of one time, his doubt as to whether Clizia herself knew the terrible nature of the game, of the harrowing "fires" of passion and suffering it involved. But now, with the vision evoked by the poem, his faith is made firm:

> Oggi so ciò che vuoi; batte il suo fioco
> tocco la Martinella ed impaura
> le sagome d'avorio in una luce
> spettrale di nevaio. Ma resiste
> e vince il premio della solitaria
> veglia chi può con te allo specchio ustorio
> che accieca le pedine opporre i tuoi
> occhi d'acciaio.

Today I know what you wish; la Martinella strikes / its weak hour and terrifies / the ivory forms in a spectral snowy light. But he resists / and wins the solitary vigil's prize / who can, with you, to the burning glass / that blinds the pawns oppose your / eyes of steel.

The vigil's prize is surely one's authentic *mortal* soul. The virtù of resistence resides in *coscienza,* the persisting consciousness of good and evil. The guiding blazon is contemplative Clizia, keeper of the faith, she who says no, who realizes the divinity of man through her absolute commitment to human dignity, justice and the good. Clizia, as our lady of the chessboard, is the climactic sign of the *Occasioni* volume, while "Nuove stanze" is the culmination of the thematic shift, under Amor, from suffering and negation to the idea of service and sacrifice first touched upon at the close of *Ossi di seppia* in "Casa sul mare" and "Crisalide."

In the fourth section the mood is increasingly apocalyptic, Clizia increasingly remote and unearthly. The stage is set for the terrestial-cosmic concerns of *La bufera e altro*. *Le occasioni* concludes with a last view from a height, transcribed in "Notizie dall'Amiata" (News from Amiata) as a letter to Clizia. Amiata is an extinct volcano in southern Tuscany, at present heavily mined for mercury—a perfect set, then, for a poem bearing the bitter bad news of Italy in 1938. To write to absent Clizia is of course to make her present—the poet's writing-table, the hearth where chestnuts explode, the "veins of saltpeter and mould" are details of the solitary setting "into which in a moment you will burst." The first section of this tripartate poem ends with that blessed apparition:

> La vita
> che t'affàbula è ancora troppo breve
> se ti contiene! Schiude la tua icona
> il fondo luminoso. Fuori piove.

. . . Life / that fables you is still too brief / if it contains you! The luminous ground discloses / your icon. Outdoors it rains.

Fuori piove; once more there are premonitions of the gathering storm. The next two sections fall away from the vision of her presence into torment and despair. In what is surely an ironic reminiscence of the cosmic optimism of Shelley's "Ode to the West Wind," Montale invokes destruction:

> Ritorna domani piú freddo, vento del nord,
> spezza le antiche mani dell'arenaria,
> sconvolgi i libri d'ore nel solai,
> e tutto sia lente tranquilla, domino, prigione
> del senso che non dispera! Ritorna piú forte
> vento di settentrione che rendi care
> le catene e suggelli le spore del possibile!

Come back colder tomorrow, north wind, / shatter the ancient sandstone hands, / overturn the books of hours in the attics / and let all be as a tranquil lens, dominion, prison / of non-despairing sense! Come back stronger / northern wind who makes our chains dear / to us and seals up the spores of the possible!

So the poem ends darkly amidst intimations of catastrophe—such is the news from Mount Amiata. Yet the short third section of the

"Notizie" terminates with one staving image out of the prisoner's vigil—porcupines sipping from the artery of pity (*pietà*) that links him to his absent *donna*.* Unobtrusively, then, the lady of the chessboard sponsors what is literally the last word in the book—*pietà*.

＊　　　＊　　　＊

> *Le occasioni* were an orange—better, a lemon—that lacked one component . . . *pedale*, a more profound music of contemplation. The poems [that followed] . . . carry to its extreme limit my so-to-speak Petrarchan experience. I projected the Selveggia, Mandetta or Delia—call her what you will—of the *Mottetti* onto the background of a pointless and irrational cosmic and terrestrial war, and gave myself into her keeping, lady or cloud, angel or stormy petrel. The motif was already prefigured in "Nuove stanze," written on the eve of the war.

Thus Montale, recapitulating his "*Intenzioni.*" Certainly the poems that follow the *Occasioni*—*Finisterre* of 1943 and *La bufera e altro* of 1956 (*Finisterre* comes to be its opening section)—would be extremely difficult going for anyone unfamiliar with the evolving myth of Clizia as charted in the poetry of the earlier volume. And since she provides the thematic link between Montale's middle and late periods—insofar as *La bufera* represents an intensification of her prodigious immanence—we should be clear as to her significance.

Originally, of course, she must have been a "real" woman, one perhaps first known to the poet in Genoa and Florence. From the *Mottetti* we understand that she was once dangerously ill, hence "exiled" (motets two and three) to a sanatorium. She sings and is often evoked (motets eleven, thirteen, and fourteen) in conjunction with musical occasions. From other sources[33] we learn that she is apparently Jewish—this in part explains her absence—and possibly of German origins. Frequent evocation of the seas separating her from Mirco, the "roughly three thousand miles" of the *Corriere* piece, occasional references to North American places, even the "starry banner" she waves in "Verso Capua" may suggest that she is either American or living there.

But Montale's recent remark apropos of Dante's *donna petrosa* seems relevant to Clizia: "Perhaps the stony lady really existed; but insofar as she is a product of style (*avventura stilistica*) she can never coincide with a real donna."[34] Whoever she originally was, she has been "translated" and wholly transformed as "Clizia." While retaining certain of her "real" attributes—a cursory listing might include the

---

* These deliberate and bristling creatures anticipate Lowell's resisting skunks ("Skunk Hour"). While Lowell has "imitated" "News from Mount Amiata" he traces his skunks' genealogy back to an armadillo belonging to Elizabeth Bishop.

intensity of her eyes, the forelock of ash-blonde hair she habitually clears with her hand or toss of her head, a pair of coral earrings, a jade bracelet, etc., she has become what Montale calls "a visiting angel," an idea or principle.

Like Beatrice, she has accessory names or *senhals**—Artemis, Diotima, Iris—and countless epithets: "goddess," "annunciator of dawn," "sister," "daughter of the sun," "messenger," "heart of amethyst," "sphinx," "my angel," "chosen of my God"—the connotations range from self-abasement to the ecstatic. But the crucial *senhal*—the one which provides the main clue to the idea or principle she incarnates—is "Clizia."

The seventy-fourth poem in Gianfranco Contini's edition of Dante's *Rime* is a sonnet bemoaning the beloved's cruelty. The sestet begins:

> Né quella ch'a veder lo sol si gira
> e'l non mutato amor mutata serba,
> ebbe quant'io già mai fortuna acerba.

> Nor did she who turns to see the sun / and, changing, preserves her love unchanged, / have ever as bitter fortune as I.

The *quella* is Clizia, according to Ovid (*Meta.* IV, 234–70) a daughter of Ocean who, smitten with the Sun, was transformed by the god into the heliotrope or sunflower—the emblem, then, of an "impossible" passion and persisting fidelity.** Given Montale's Ligurian background and his addiction to certain magical components of its *paesaggio* (*girasole, meriggio*) it is not strange that he would be attracted to their formulation in the ancient myth of Clizia.

It is in one of the *Bufera* poems—"La primavera hitleriana": Hitlerian Spring—that this *senhal* is employed for the first time, with the first line of the Dante sonnet cited above serving as motto below the title and the second embedded in the poem's conclusion:

> Guarda ancora
> in alto, Clizia, è la tua sorte, tu
> che il non mutato amor mutata serbi,
> fino a che il cieco sole che in te porti
> si abbàcini nell'Altro e si distrugga
> in Lui, per tutti.

* *Senhal:* the Provençal troubadour's term for the protective pseudonym that at once screens his *donna* from unseemly publicity and celebrates her virtue. As regards Beatrice, Montale has remarked how "there is no lack of other ladies, other names that are perhaps *senhals.* . . ."[35]

** Cf. the English *locus classicus*, Blake's sunflower "weary of time, / Who countest the steps of the Sun, / Seeking after that sweet golden clime / Where the traveller's journey is done. . . ."

> . . . Look still / on high, Clizia, this is your fate, you / who,
> changing, preserve your love unchanged, / until the blind sun you
> bear within you / is eclipsed in the Other and is destroyed / in Him,
> for everyone.

Possibly the best commentary on these lines would be to juxtapose
them to a pertinent precedent; for example, the first canto of the
Paradiso where the angelic Beatrice gazes eaglelike at the flaming
sun (image of the omnipotent "Other," or God) and the pilgrim
Dante, gazing in turn upon her, feels himself to *trasumanar*, to be
lifted up out of his heavy flesh towards what the poet Dante calls
"the Love that governs heaven." The traditional figure for this
spiritual transmutation—dramatized by Dante as a vital chain of
amorous gazes—is the ladder of ascent whereby one mounts from the
sensible world with its shadowplays of distorting *solarità* to the world
of spirit, luminous with intellectual light.[36] In "La primavera hitler-
iana" and other poems of the *Bufera* volume which Montale calls
Silvae, Clizia seems to occupy a position broadly analogous to Bea-
trice on this ladder.

Indeed one may talk with some point of the *stilnovismo* of Montale
in a considerable portion of his poems from the *Mottetti* onwards.
The very notion of a "motet" historically suggests a vocal music of
liturgic origins which was later secularized and appropriated for the
amorous song of the troubadours. As we have seen, Montale himself
refers to his *donna* in the context of the *dolce stil nuovo* ("the Sel-
vaggia or the Mandetta or the Delia—call her what you will—of the
Mottetti"), ranging his *senhal,* and the miracle it clothes, with those
of two members of that Tuscan school, Cino da Pistoia and Guido
Cavalcanti, plus a predecessor out of antiquity, the Augustan elegist
Tibullus. The inspiration investing the new poetry of Dante and
his friends

> . . . Io mi son un che, quando
> amor mi spira, noto, ed a quel modo
> che ditta dentro, vo significando. . . .

> I am one who, when / love inspires me, make note, and in that
> mode / with which he speaks within me, so set it forth . . . (*Purg.*
> XXIV, 52–54).

certainly relates to Montale. The result is a formally intricate music,
passionate, allusive, recondite, even "scholastical," arising from the
central mystery of Amor, with that deity's elected, the *donna,* at the
heart of an esoteric cult. The *Silvae* will show that Montale even

tracks Dante to the all but blasphemous verge of envisaging his *donna* as a miraculous intercessor between the lost man in the dark wood and abiding Love Divine, *Amor che move il sole e l'altre stelle.*

      ❋   ❋   ❋

> Non martirio per me—estasi di pensiero e di preghiera
> né la visione estrema. . . .

so runs Montale's translation of lines 29–30 of Eliot's "Song for Simeon" ("Not for me the martyrdom, the ecstasy of thought and prayer,/not for me the ultimate vision"). From a Christian point of view, Montale is Simeon (though by no means so plangent about it as Eliot's)—not only is "salvation for others" but the nature and extent of that salvation, that "hypothesis of Grace," is schismatic and heretical.

"This Christian agony [*rissa cristiana,* perhaps with flavor of "agonizing"] that has nothing but words of shadow and lament"— the phrase is from a passage from the letter to Clizia, "Notizie dall'Amiata." Several of the poems in the last section of *Le occasioni* refer sardonically to Christian orthodoxy, implicitly or explicitly contrasting its worship to Clizia's. Thus in "Costa San Giorgio" the God of the churches is a fetish called *El Dorado;* in "Palio" the bars of the cross merge into prison bars; in "Elegia di Pico Farnese" the phenomenon of pious pilgrimages to the catacombs is rudely dismissed as a sentimental sideshow:

>   Ben altro
> è l'Amore e fra gli alberi balena col tuo cruccio
> e la tua frangia d'ali, messaggera accigliata!

> . . . Other indeed / is Love and it flashes among the trees with your anger / and your fringe of wings, O frowning messenger!❋

The point of these criticisms is not that he rejects out of hand the notions of supernatural intercession and/or the miraculous. Grace, we have seen, is at least an "hypothesis"; he writes in "Intenzioni" that "miracle" is as evident to him as "necessity," that "immanence

---

❋ Ten years later, in "Le processioni del 1949" in *La bufera,* Montale expresses similar contempt for the "pilgrim mariolators" in the processions which, on the eve of Holy Year, celebrated the consecration of Italy to the Virgin. They are dismissed from serious consideration at a gesture from the "furiously angelic" Clizia. His "Little Testament" of 1953 expresses pride that the thought he bequeaths "is not light of church or factory on which red or black clerics have thrived."

and transcendence are inseparable."* In "Crisalide" he had spoken of "liberty, the miracle, the fact that was not necessary" as a conception worthy of prayer and sacrifice; in the fourth motet he considers his having been spared during the war for his destiny with Clizia—years before he met her he was "already aided, all unknowing, by her star, the parasol of her sunflower."[37]

But the miraculous divinity incarnated by Clizia and the object of Montale's cult is primarily distinguishable by its insistence on "Gobettian" humanism, on man as the supreme value and responsibility. The "daily decency (most difficult of the virtues)" of his dead friend Sergio Fadin, for example, may have been literally divine:

> Exit Fadin. And now to say that you are no longer here is only to say that you have entered into a different order, insofar as that order in which we sluggish ones move, insane as it is, seems to our mind to be the only one in which divinity can unfold its proper attributes, to be recognized and tasted within the limits of a proposition whose significance we do not know. (Even divinity, then, also has need of us? If this is blasphemy, alas, it is hardly our worst.)

This was written in 1943; the following manifesto during the days of *Resistenza* in 1944:

> . . . today the arts and sciences are only worth something insofar as they express, in and through themselves, a superior force that is within us. This is by no means related to that irrational obscurantism, that furious activism with which Nazi fascism and its pseudo-cultural manifestations (the degeneration of philosophic idealism) wished to create an alibi and banner. Very simply it is the old battle of good and evil, the struggle of the divine forces within us against the unleashed forces of the man-beast, the dark forces of Ahriman. In and through us a divinity thus realizes itself, at first terrestrial and then perhaps celestial and incomprehensible to our senses, though without us it could not be formed or known. And for this to happen we must simply say *no* to all abuses that come from man to man, to all the flatteries of reaction masked as a cult of order and return to ancient values, to all the over-facile and unilateral certainties prompted by desire for instant profit. Simply, to say *no*: to act so that the *trahison des clercs*, on the grand scale, will no longer be possible for us.

This is from "Augurio"—now collected in *Auto da fé*—and it develops

---

* Cf. his remark at the Dante Congress to the effect that Beatrice is a miracle "not a priori unacceptable . . . for whoever believes, as I do, that miracles are possible and always in wait before our doors, and that our very existence is wholly a miracle. . . ."

the position first assumed in "Stile e tradizione." Both stress "daily decency," a refusal to submit to or condone what one knows to be ungenerous, unjust, untrue. Both affirm the value—in "Augurio" the *divine* value—of solitary integrity and *coscienza*. Both propose to say no to the "dark forces of Ahriman." And the famous climax to the first *osso*—"Codesto solo oggi possiamo dirti,/ciò che *non* siamo, ciò che *non* vogliamo"—which may once have looked like a simple admission of impotent despair, now in retrospect takes on the lineaments of the heroic, of *Resistenza* before the letter.

If Clizia is an angel, she is so not because she dwells in another world but because her mission is to "visit" this one. Montale calls her *Cristòfora*—Christ-bearer—and her mission is described in "Intenzioni" as that of being "continuer and symbol of eternal Christian sacrifice. She pays for everyone, she expiates for everyone." One can conceive of this Jewess, then, as Daughter of Man. She does not come in triumph; she is not only the angel of the victimized but herself victim incarnate—in this she is sister of Christ. In one of the late motets she is described as a frozen bird with torn feathers, who has, however, arrived. Elsewhere she is threatened by savage beasts, wears rags, is shot. "Her task . . . does not allow her other triumph than what seems failure here below: separation in space, misery, vague phantomlike reapparitions. . . . Her features are always tormented and proud, her fatigue is mortal, her courage indomitable: . . . she preserves all her earthly attributes."[38]

In one characteristic and recurrent image, then, Clizia is in flight: in flight from persecution, in flight to succor others. There is another, however, in which she is very still: this is the image of her eyes, steady and unflinching, attentive to our world, sign of persisting *coscienza*. Beside the opposing eyes of steel celebrated in "Nuove stanze," there are her eyes that fix the present ("Palio"), her flashing brows ("Verso Finistère"), hard crystal gaze ("L'orto"), burning eyes ("Voce giunta con le folaghe"), etc. Perhaps these are all consummated in the image-epithet of Iris, where "eye" and God's contractual rainbow linking heaven and earth, man and divinity, are conjoined.

Montale once dreamed a name for his cult. In "Iride"—"dreamed and then translated from a nonexistent language"—he refers to himself as *povero Nestoriano smarrito* (poor strayed Nestorian). We are told that Nestorius was a fifth-century patriarch of the Eastern Church whose doctrine of the fundamental humanity of Christ was condemned in 431 by the Council of Ephesus. His relation to the old "gift of immanence" ought to be clear. "The Nestorian," Montale writes in "Intenzioni," "[is] the man who best understands the affinities that bind God to incarnate creatures—not, certainly, the stupid spiritualist or rigid and abstract Monophysite" (that is, the catacomb-tourist or doctrinaire legalist of official Church councils).

With this in mind we can recognize the seriousness underlying the whimsy of a little *Bufera* poem like "Vento sulla mezzaluna" (Wind Over the Crescent) occasioned by an encounter Montale once had in the streets of Edinburgh.

> L'uomo che predicava sul Crescente
> mi chiese "Sai dov'è Dio?". Lo sapevo
> e glielo dissi. Scosse il capo. Sparve
> nel turbine che prese uomini e case
> e li sollevò in alto, sulla pece.

The man who was preaching on the Crescent / asked me "Do you know where God is?" I did know / and I told him. He shook his head. He vanished / in the whirlwind that seized men and houses / and lifted them on high, into the pitch-black.*

The encounter was between a Monophysite and a Nestorian. The latter had answered "Here."

❋   ❋   ❋

Le occasioni had run through four small editions in the war years between 1939 and 1943—a sign in itself of its (largely underground) pertinence and vitality. Dismissed from the directorship of the Gabinetto Vieusseux in 1938—the year of "Notizie dall'Amiata"—and forced to take on a heavy load of translation (chiefly from the English language, mostly Shakespeare plays) in order to survive, Montale stayed in Florence and wrote the poems to be gathered in the small war-book called *Finisterre*.

With its pointed epigraph taken from Agrippa D'Aubigné's "À Dieu"

> Les princes n'ont point d'yeux pour voir ces grands merveilles,
> Leurs mains ne servent plus qu'à nous persécuter. . . .

Finisterre was unpublishable in the Italy of this tormented period. The manuscript was smuggled out to Switzerland where an edition of 150 copies was published in Lugano in 1943 just before the *coup*

---

* Cf. the version of this meeting in a prose-piece written concurrently ("Sosta a Edimburgo" in *Farfalla di Dinard*) where the dour presbyterian answers his own question ("God is not here, Sir") and rejects out of hand "all those places where life presents itself as easy, pleasant and where truly God might be sought and found."

d'état of July 25th which marked the beginning of the end of Mussolini.

In his essay on "Eliot and Ourselves," Montale has remarked on the *stilnovismo* of Eliot and Pound, their common cult of Dante and their *docte* allusiveness that "works itself out in inlay work and the glittering game of quotations and recollections." The same might be said of *Finisterre;* it is entirely appropriate that the second edition of this book (Florence, 1945) included a facsimile of Montale's never-finished translation of the first two stanzas of *Ash-Wednesday,* Eliot's stilnovistic season in purgatory. The poems are similar in their tendency towards recondite allusion, occult citation, a certain exclusive and "aristocratic" approach to the traditions involved. The themes of course are entirely different, and Montale's style has grown increasingly compressed and elliptical. *Finisterre,* he writes in "Intenzioni,"

> is a matter of a few poems, born under the incubus of the years '40–42, perhaps the freest I have ever written, [in which] the research effected in *Le occasioni* is carried to its extreme consequences, the interlacings of rhymes and assonances become even more dense, and I am surprised that nobody has brought up the name of Gerard Manley Hopkins. In a certain fashion I too was searching for my own "sprung rhythm."

Montale conceives of sprung rhythm as involving not only the *crammed* quality of much of Hopkins' (and his own) verse but as a dramatic instrument: "the musical investiture of the act of inspiration that doesn't degrade music to a simplistic 'auroral' ineffability."[39]

Another facet of this heightened "interlacing" is Montale's use of the sonnet for the first and only time in his published career—seven out of the fifteen short lyrics in *Finisterre* move in some sort of relation to the form. In several the sonnet is only there as a covert allusion or witty possibility, identifiable only in the context of other definitely "committed" sonnets on either side. Thus "Serenata indiana" (Indian Serenade: given what happens here the allusion to Shelley's breathless lyric can only be sardonic) is made of fourteen hendecasyllables exactly halved (that is, between lines seven and eight) by a large space. The lyric, then, is broken into two sub-lyrics of seven lines apiece, and these in turn—perfectly symmetrically—into two triads and a concluding single line. The rhyming is largely slanted (*sera-mare-potere, aloè-follia*), irregularly placed but as noticeable as is generally the case with sonnets. Each of the two halves is devoted to a contrasting perception of Clizia's power. The first celebrates her domination of reality, the second unhappily evokes her as a victim of brutal natural forces ("the inky tentacles of the polyp") in a reversal kin to that of "unarmed goodness" by Evil in "Eastbourne." Thus this sonnet bisects into sections of ecstasy and anguish, unified by adoration, with the halfway break working something like the hinge of alteration between octave and sestet in the orthodox model. Pursuing Montale's citation of Hopkins, one could call "Serenata indiana" a sprung- or curtal-sonnet, where the various pleasures of symmetry, sound-chiming and thematic modulation are cultivated in a drastically restricted area.

More characteristic of *Finisterre* sonnetry, however, are poems like "Nel sonno" (In Sleep), "Gli orecchini" (The Earrings), "La frangia dei capelli" (The Bangs), and "Il ventaglio" (The Fan), where Montale's familiarity with the so-called Shakespearian sonnet is apparent. (He has published translations of sonnets 22, 33, and 48 in the *Quaderno di traduzioni*). Unlike Ungaretti's more literal and less adventurous renderings in *40 sonetti di Shakespeare*, Montale's insist on something of the pace, metre and rhyme-patterning of the originals. Here are their versions of the octave to Shakespeare's thirty-third sonnet ("Full many a glorious morning have I seen . . ."):

Ungaretti

Ho veduto piú d'un mattino in gloria
Con lo sguardo sovrano le vette lusingare,
Baciare d'aureo viso i verdi prati,
Colorire con alchimia celeste i rivi pallidi,
E poi a vili nuvole   permettere
Di fluttuargli sui celestiale volto
Con osceni fumi sottraendolo all'universo orbato
Mentre verso ponente non visto scompariva, con
                    la sua disgrazia. . . .

Montale

Spesso, a lusingar vette, vidi splendere
sovranamente l'occhio del mattino,
e baciare d'oro verdi prati, accendere
pallidi rivi d'alchimìe divine.
Poi vili fumi alzarsi, intorbidata
d'un tratto quella celestiale fronte,
e fuggendo a occidente il desolato
mondo, l'astro celare il viso e l'onta. . . .

In almost every instance Montale tries for speed and concentration (for example, the *spesso* for "full many" as opposed to Ungaretti's more courtly *piú d'un* [more than one], or his radical telescoping of the elaborate metaphor of the first two lines as opposed to Ungaretti's more approximative procedure). His version is more crammed, more "Hopkinsesque," not only than Ungaretti's but than Shakespeare's. Apart from what seem to me to be his intelligent verbal-syntactical liberties, one also notes his loyalty to the metrical patterns of the original: the hendecasyllable is reasonably equivalent to our pentameter, the three cross-rhymed quatrains are preserved along with an approximation of the concluding couplet. One obvious divergence from the original is Montale's use of slant-rhymes (a procedure that gives him more sonic freedom, of course, though we know that in any case he favors its opportunities for wit and edgy dissonance—for example, the clever *terrestre-celeste* of the final couplet). His liberties with the letter serve his fidelity to the spirit of playful elegance and wit in the original.

"Gli orecchini" is one of Montale's own sonnets written on the Shakespeare model. It focuses on one of the talismanic appurtenances —signs, icons—belonging to Clizia: her earrings.

Non serba ombra di voli il nerofumo
della spera. (E del tuo non è più traccia.)
È passata la spugna che i barlumi
indifesi dal cerchio d'ora scaccia.
Le tue pietre, i coralli, il forte imperio
che ti rapisce vi cercavo; fuggo
l'iddia che non s'incarna, i desideri
porto fin che al tuo lampo non si struggono.
Ronzano èlitre fuori, ronza il folle
mortorio e sa che due vite non contano.
Nella cornice tornano le molli
meduse della sera. La tua impronta
verrà di giù: dove ai tuoi lobi squallide
mani, travolte, fermano i coralli.

The tarnished mirror does not conserve the shadow / of flights. (And of yours there is no longer a trace). / The sponge has passed over that / hunts out defenseless glimmerings from the circle of gold. / Your stones, the corals, the strong imperium / that snatched you—I search for them there: I flee / that goddess who is disincarnate, I bear my desires / until they are consumed in your lightning. / Outside the coleoptera are buzzing, the mad cortège is buzzing / —it knows two lives don't count. / Within the mirror-frame the jellied / medusae return. Your seal / will come from below: where, at your earlobes, emaciated / anguished hands affix the corals.

Beyond the prosodic features of Shakespearean sonnet "Gli orecchini" has other high-Renaissance qualities. *Concettismo*, the athletically-deployed conceit, is very evident in the modulations of imagery

through which a gold-framed looking-glass becomes a well of prophetic memory yielding first blackness (absence) then a murky sub-humanity (the low-level organic activity of beetles and jellyfish whose technical name, *medusae,* adds a classic danger to the forces beleaguering the poet and his *donna*), and finally, in the strange triumphant couplet, the regal insignia of Clizia attended by her people, the poor and wretched, the sacrificed ones of this world.*
Language too is remote from "spoken" Italian—either aureate (such as *spera* which is a literary Tuscan archaicism for "mirror," *cerchio d'oro* and *cornice* for the "frame," *forte imperio, iddia*) or unusual technical terms like *èlitre,* "elytra," the hard outer wing-casings of beetle-like insects which cover and protect the hindlegs, and vibrate and "buzz"—here intended to suggest the subhuman sound of war-mechanisms like tanks and planes.

The coral earclips of "Gli orecchini" are a good example of "private" objects treated by Montale in such a way that they preserve their occult meanings for "two lives" while simultaneously working as public emblems for a great humane ideal. Indeed, there is an heroic equivalence between the images of the pale martyred hands attending the toilette of Clizia and the arming of Achilles. Another *Finisterre* sonnet, "Il ventaglio," demonstrates the virtù of her fan, amounting to a holy relic in time of war. It is also a perfect example of the allusive density, transitional-abruptness and nervous intensity of tempo of the Montale of this phase.

The poem must begin with its title, since the fan, never mentioned in the sonnet *per se,* is surely not only the source of the mother-of-pearl in line nine, contributing several associative functions (wings, wind), but is the *là* of line three whereon the poet vainly tries to "paint" or fix his memories of happier, prewar days of love.

> *Ut pictura* . . . Le labbra che confondono,
> gli sguardi, i segni, i giorni ormai caduti
> provo a figgerli là come in un tondo
> di cannocchiale arrovesciato, muti
> e immoti, ma piú vivi. Era una giostra
> d'uomini e ordegni in fuga tra quel fumo
> ch'Euro batteva, e già l'alba l'inostra
> con un sussulto e rompe quelle brume.
> Luce la madreperla, la calanca

---

* See for a brilliant reading of this sonnet which eventually involves a study of all recurrent Montalean imagery, D'Arco Silvio Avalle's " 'Gli orecchini' di Montale," in *Tre saggi su Montale* (Turin, 1970), pp. 9–90. In a private communication to Avalle, Montale suggested that the hands could be thought of as emerging from the tombs of those who have been gassed or massacred ("Jews, like the phantasm . . ." *op. cit.,* p. 66).

vertiginosa inghiotte ancora vittime,
ma le tue piume sulle guance sbiancano
e il giorno è forse salvo. O colpi fitti,
quando ti schiudi, o crudi lampi, o scrosci
sull'orde! (Muore chi ti riconosce?)

Ut pictura . . . Lips that mingle, / gazes, signs, days now fallen
away / —I try to fix them there as in an eyepiece / of a reversed
telescope, mute / and immobile, but more living. There was a whirling
clashing [*giostra* combines "joust" and "carousel": we should prob-
ably think of the wheeling motion of Evil in poems like "Eastbourne"
or, in the *Silvae*, "Ezekial Saw the Wheel"] / of men and machines
fleeing in that smoke / that Eurus [god of the cold southeast wind;
probably also meant to suggest sonically a wind-beaten "Europe"]
flailed, and already the dawn empurples it [*inostrare* can also mean:
"grant the hat of the cardinalate to" as well as, in pun, "in-Auster,"
i.e. "dawn sponsors a warmth-bearing counterwind to chilling
Eurus"] / with a bound and breaks up those wintrinesses. / The
mother-of-pearl grows resplendent, the dizzy / vortex [*calanca* is
literally a little bay or cove; I associate it here with the *giostra* of line
five] still swallows victims, / but your feathers whiten on their cheeks
[*le guance* leaves *whose* cheeks an open question; I would say both
Clizia's and the victims'] / and perhaps the day is saved. Oh the
steady strokes, / when you reveal yourself, oh the raw flashes, oh the
roars / above the horde! (Does he who recognizes you die?)

Even providing a fairly literal translation, one can see, involves real
difficulties, so dense with associative energy are the words. And
there are some authentic obscurities in this dense sonnet which so
admirably illustrate Dr. Johnson's witty definition of the metaphysi-
cal poem.* Yet the main action seems clear enough. The poem is
about the power residing in Clizia's fan which, since it is present
(*là*), she has presumably left behind her—as it turns out, as a sign
of her mission. "Il ventaglio" is also a triumphant affirmation of her
genuine and abiding presence—as contrasted with the sad images of
her, lips, gazes, reduced and crystallized by memory.

Ut pictura . . . : the sonnet starts with Horace's famous phrase
from the epistle *Ad Pisones* ("Art of Poetry," line 361: *Ut pictura
poesis*—"As with painting, so with poetry") which serves as a stage-
direction for what follows: the poem-image of the loveable past that
the poet is occupied in trying to "fix" on his absent lady's fan. The
desperation informing this effort to take refuge in the past is indi-

---

* That is, ". . . a kind of *discordia concors;* a combination of dissimilar
images, or discovery of occult resemblances in things apparently unlike . . . ;
nature and art are ransacked for illustrations, comparisons, and allusions; their
learning instructs, and their subtlety surprises; but. . . ."

cated in the first clause of the second sentence with its references to military debacle and the heavy clouds of war and winter storm, while the second clause, with its startled *già* and shift into the present tense shows the miracle of the relic as it starts—not a return via memory but a resurrected presence in a replenished present. Thus "already" through the mere contemplation of her fan the light begins to dawn, the storm begins to abate, while simultaneously the fan assumes— kin in this to the various *éventails* of Mallarmé—its coordinate roles as purveyor of winds (here a beneficent southern variety) and wing carrying back the angel of the storm. But no longer is she a mere "refuge," a fixed image or snapshot which the poet projects for the sake of his sanity. Here toward the poem's climax she is present, is directly addressed, and the miraculous possibility dawns that she is able to alter the balance of things (". . . il giorno è forse salvo"). The wing feathers that were her fan now bear light to the drowning visages of "the victims"* and also retributive justice to the fleeing hordes of Ahriman. The extraordinary *mana* of her coming prompts the final question. What is the fate of those, like the Nestorian or the guilty ones, who must sustain her radiance face to face? The query, and its strenuous abruptness after the string of exclamations pre- ceding it, sounds out the panting ecstasy with which, fanlike, the poem snaps shut.

One more remark should be made on the point and pertinence of the Horatian citation at the beginning. Besides setting the scene for subsequent action, *Ut pictura* also suggests that this poem should be seen as a picture—which it is; indeed, it is a succession of them. The full passage in the epistle deals with the matter of perspective, how poems, like pictures, vary with distance, with conditions of light and shadow, with familiarity. But "Il ventaglio" itself incorporates several perspectives and viewpoints—contrasting chiefly the tiny "plane" of fixed memory with the immense living present that succeeds it. That is to say, the citation functions not only to place the action of the poem but to capsulize a major thematic concern of the poem itself. One has to know Horace to get the full point, but this is part of the instructive surprise and "scholastic" pleasure offered by the Montale of *Finisterre*. For some—for Montale in fact—such poems are "of a texture possibly too rigorous," as he puts it in "Intenzioni." Surely "Il ventaglio" qualifies as one of the microfilmed "euphuistic sonnets" over which Clizia dozes in one of the poet's last testaments, "Botta e risposta."

* Compare the conclusion of "Gli orecchini" as well as Montale's relevant remark in "Intenzioni" regarding the "sphinx" of "Nuove stanze," who left the east to bring light to the wintry North.

Such is *Finisterre*. The title itself is self-explanatory and familiar: land's end, the Breton cape looking westward from Europe "roughly three thousand miles" across the sea to Clizia—an emblem of terminus, an end of one world and expectation of another. From here as before, he searches for signs: her earrings or her fan:

> Anche una piuma che vola può disegnare
> la tua figura, o il raggio che gioca a rimpiattino
> tra i mobili, il rimando dello specchio
> di un bambino, dai tetti. . . .

Even a feather floating in the air can trace / your shape, or the ray that plays at hide-and-seek / among the furniture, reflection from a child's / mirror on the roofs.

Later her features will be found in an eel, a fox, a torpedofish; this weird totemism founds its surreal climax in the search-poem "Per album" (Lines for an Album) written in the early 1950's:

> . . . Ho continuato il mio giorno
> sempre spiando te, larva girino
> frangia di rampicante francolino
> gazzella zebú ocàpi
> nuvola nera grandine. . . .

. . . I resumed my day / forever spying on you, larva tadpole / fringe of ivy ptarmigan / gazelle zebu okapi / black cloud hailstone. . . .[40]

But Montale's *Revelation*, his personal apocalypse of signs, will be found in the oneiric "Iride" (Iris).

The second edition of *Finisterre* was augmented by several autograph reproductions (one of them the *Ash-Wednesday* fragment), two prose-pieces and four poems of varying length. *In chiave, terribilmente in chiave* (key to it all, terribly so) as Montale writes in "Intenzioni" was "Iride," "a poem I dreamed [twice] and then translated from a nonexistent tongue; I am perhaps more the medium than the author." "Iride" does not constitute a "key" that opens, or unlocks or in any way defines the poet's relation to his *donna;* even Montale, usually scornful of his readers' perplexities, grants that it might legitimately be considered obscure—"but even so I see no reason to throw it away."

Nor do I. How after all does one correct a dream? Certainly "Iride" is a poem that is extremely dependent upon the reader's knowledge of Montale's prior work—it does not stand by itself. But fragmentary and genuinely obscure as it frequently is, it is also a poem in which many of the strands of *l'affaire Clizia* come to their exacerbated and "heretical" conclusion, and in this sense is indeed *terribilmente in chiave*.

"Iride" is a diptych representing two aspects of the cult of Clizia. The first is composed about her annunciatory signs, this time drastically occult and as "closed" to her priest, apparently, as to ourselves. Here, for example, is "Iride I"'s extremely convoluted opening clause, deployed over three verse paragraphs in a labyrinthine series of imagistic amplifications and qualifications:

> Quando di colpo San Martino smotta
> le sue braci e le attizza in fondo al cupo
> fornello dell'Ontario,
> schiocchi di pigne verdi fra la cenere
> o il fumo d'un infuso di papaveri
> e il Volto insanguinato sul sudario
> che mi divide da te;
>
>   questo e poco altro (se poco
> è un tuo segno, un ammicco, nella lotta
> che me sospinge in un ossario, spalle
> al muro, dove zàffiri celesti
> e palmizi e cicogne su una zampa non chiudono
> l'atroce vista al povero
> Nestoriano smarrito);
>
>   è quanto di te giunge dal naufragio
> delle mie genti, delle tue. . . .

When all of a sudden Saint Martin shifts / his embers and kindles them deep in the dark / furnace of Ontario, / snapping of green pinecones in the ashes / or the steam from a poppy infusion / and the bloody Face on the napkin / that divides me from you /

—this and little else (if little / is a sign of yours, a wink, in the struggle / that condemns me to an ossuary, back / to the wall, where celestial sapphires / and palm trees and storks on one foot don't shut out / the atrocious sight from the poor / strayed Nestorian)—

—this is how much of you gets here from the wreck / of my people, of yours. . . .

A heretic's dream of salvation, expressed in the images of the orthodoxy from which he is excommunicate—that would be one way of describing what is going on here. "Iris," the title of the poem and the *donna's* newest *senhal*, is not only a flower and thus part of the company of floral presences with which the poem is tissued,* not only synecdoche for the eye of *coscienza* which is one of her main signs, not only the name of the rainbow goddess and messenger for the Olympians, but also and above all—as the poem will say—*Iri del Canaan,* the rainbow of the Promised Land, the Lord's own sign of covenant with the lost and wandering.

The first three lines of the passage cited lend the dream a cryptic time and place; St. Martin's summer (our "Indian" summer) is the brief period of mild weather that can occur in late autumn, so that St. Martin's intervention in chilly Ontario implies a kind of trans-Atlantic thaw which joins the western world in a brief season of saving warmth. But grammatically it is not the season but the saint who performs this miracle, and we are reminded of his cloak and mission of holy and heroic charity. In this context even *braci* may have dream-connections with the Ember Days of fasting and prayer that frame autumn in the church calendar.

Or, to take the signs themselves, the first—the crackling pinecones in the ashes—is introduced by St. Martin's fires and its connotation of renewal (green against grey, sudden explosive energy out of depletion) is familiar enough to the attentive reader of Montale.** But those that immediately follow are more strange, though they clearly function to remind us of the visionary sphere in which the poem operates. The poppy infusion (whose fumes are produced by the same heat that cracks the pinecones) is at once an extract that is part of the poem's "botanical" collection, an opiate and pain-killer possibly suggested, if we go outside the poem, by the medications required by Montale's very sick wife in the same year, 1943 (see "Ballata scritta in una clinica" [Ballad Written in a Clinic]) and a producer of other, exalted states of consciousness. This last can guide us to the third sign, and second saint: the sudarium or sweatcloth with the face of suffering Christ upon it, Clizia's napkin which—like Saint Martin's cloak and Saint Veronica's handkerchief—testifies to

---

* E.g., the sunflower (implicit), pine cones, poppies, palms, rosaries or rose-chains, berries and resin, laurel, sycamore, mistletoe and holly, desert plants, vines; even Clizia's work or mission is said to be "flowering."

** Such interstices or *intermittences du coeur* have been mentioned previously—cf. the sudden apparition of Clizia in the vicinity of Pico Farnese at the crack of a rifle and shattering of a clay pigeon ("Elegia di Pico Farnese") or, on Mount Amiata, at the popping of chestnuts on the hearth. The whole idea of an occasion involves the notion of an abrupt disclosure of a certain reality; a similar notion is indicated in *La bufera* by the section of brief, concentrated lyrics called *Lampi,* "magnesium flashes." And see Montale's remark in "Dov'era il tennis," one of the prose-pieces in that volume: "One would say that life can only flare up in flashes, nourishing itself solely on what accumulates and goes gangrenous in these abandoned zones."

her mission of pity and ministration to the sick and suffering, as well as to the perfect faith that divides her from the "poor strayed Nestorian" dreaming her.

The remaining images are less recondite. That of the prisoner (whose prison is, appropriately enough for an Italian and European in 1943, a morgue or charnel house) is an old one. What I take to be the sardonically listed images of traditional otherworldly consolation (the celestial sapphires will be found in Dante—*Para.* XXIII, 101–2— though the reference is not needed to comprehend this Blue Heaven; the storks and palms seem out of some child's guide to the Holy Land)[41] are too out of phase and insubstantial to blinker the wretched Nestorian to atrocity—the mangled bones and torn flesh of Europe, the suffering God consubstantial with a wrecked humanity. The long parenthesis of stanza two not only identifies the dreamer but underlines his desperate need for signs of his angel's immanence, the "rosary" of sacred images that he may hold and count over to stave off his rational despair.

At the same time the prisoner's cult is no longer private. Its erotic origins have been sublimated into a complicity with her mission whose blazon is—as "Iride II" dealing with the prisoner's recognition and renunciation informs us—the Face, "that effigy in purple on the white cloth."

> . . . Perché l'opera tua (che della Sue
> è una forma) fiorisse in altri luci
> Iri del Canaan ti dileguasti. . . .

> . . . So that your work (which is a form / of His) might flower in other lights, / Iris of Canaan you disappeared. . . .

The old images, so much a part of the erotic texture of the *Ossi* poems of the late 1920's and the earlier *Occasioni,* are now swiftly recapitulated: the garden where they were together, "our river," the lonely shore, the disappearing boat—and are found to be irrelevant to the new dispensation. "If you return you are not you, your terrestrial story is changed . . ."; or, as the poem concludes (italics are the dreamer's):

> . . . non hai sguardi né ieri né domani;

> *perché l'opera Sua* (che nella tua
> si trasforma) *dev'esser continuata.*

> . . . you have no eyes [that is, for me], no yesterdays, no to-

morrows; / *because His work* (which transforms itself / into yours) *must be continued.*

❋   ❋   ❋

"Iride" is not a wholly satisfactory poem. It is an impassioned and vehement dream, with all the liabilities as regards a clear transmission that such a genre suggests. But its total engagement (very clear) and the strange exaltation of its feverish rhetoric make it an excellent passage into the apocalyptic world of *La bufera*'s climax section, the eleven lyric hymns called *Silvae*.

The etymology of this title—woods, woodlands—suggests poetry of a pastoral or bucolic variety, and in fact many of the *Silvae* occur in a garden. It also suggests a forestlike abundance and variety and was in fact appropriated as a literary metaphor by Quintilian, implying an assortment of hastily composed occasional poems. Statius wrote *Silvae* as did the Renaissance humanist Politan. The *Oxford Classical Dictionary* quotes Ben Jonson on *Sylva* as an antique term for "works of divers nature and matter congested," while the *OED* notes an eighteenth-century use in which a "Sylva" is "in Poetry, a poetical Piece, composed, as it were, at a Start, in a kind of Rapture or Transport." All of these senses seem applicable to this section of the *Bufera*.

Montale's *Silvae* all seem to "occur" in an exceptional state of consciousness that verges on the visionary. In the case of "Iride," this is called dream. The other *Silvae* are not so distinguished by the poet, though they all seem exalted, peopled by phantoms, omens, emblems drawn from classical, Biblical, and astrological lore. Perhaps the sourcing state is best described as the hollow spoken of in one of the *Silvae* themselves: "Voce giunta con le folaghe" (Voice Arrived with the Coots):

> . . . il respiro mi si rompe
> nel punto dilatato, nella fossa
> che circonda lo scatto del ricordo.
> Cosí si svela prima di legarsi
> a immagini, a parole, oscuro senso
> reminiscente, il vuoto inabitato
> che occupammo e che attende fin ch'è tempo
> di colmarsi di noi, di ritrovarci. . . .

. . . my breath breaks off / at that pregnant point, in the ditch / encircling the burst of memory. / So there unveils itself, before tying itself / to images, words, a dim sense / of reminiscence, the uninhabited void / we occupied and that awaits the time / to fill itself with us, to rediscover us. . . .

We normally live in less than ourselves. Occasionally, at such "pregnant points" as the poem evokes and dramatizes, we expand to our fullness and so include our beloved presences—as, in "Voce giunta con le folaghe," the poet's dead father and the absent Clizia. In a note on this hollow written for Angelini's translation of the poem Montale calls it "that which is formed in us just before we *are*, before we say Yes to life; the hollow that forms in the pendulum a second before the hour strikes."

> Dicevano gli antichi che la poesia
> è scala a Dio. Forse non è così
> se mi leggi. . . .

The ancients said poetry / is a ladder to God. Perhaps it's not so / if you read me. . . .

This is the wry start to "Siria" (Syria), one of the *Lampi* written in the black-humored, fantastical vein characteristic of the post-*Silvae* period.* With the proviso that they are dedicated to God's immanence in Clizia—but she is increasingly a *senhal* for "Nestorian" deity— such a Plotinian aesthetic is pertinent to the *Silvae*, hymns and laddering *commedie* that they are. Such faith is never serene. The two brief quatrain-poems immediately following "Iride" evoke moments of daemonic-angelic possession in, respectively, a greenhouse and a park. In both a certain "sylvan" or pastoral reality—composed of the odor of quinces and lemons, the glitter of dew on a scythe, a *meriggio* beneath a magnolia tree—is swamped by her Coming, accompanied in the first by the "obscure thought of God," in the second by "a laughter not my own." But his ecstasy is qualified by a simultaneous sense of his removal from her in a scabrous world—so reminded (in the conclusion to "Nel parco") by the nudge of the "boney" magnolia roots he reclines upon and the insubstantial though beloved face which he pierces rather than caresses with his idle straw.

In "L'orto" (The Garden)—stylistically a new version of the matter of "Iride" in Ligurian terms—Clizia is hailed as "descending messenger," as "chosen one of my God, yours too perhaps." There is bewilderment as to her identity—was the angel implicit in the *donna* who once played and sang for him or is she "other"?—but such essentially private considerations are swept away in the thought of her terrestrial-cosmic mission:

* *Farfalla di Dinard* (The Butterfly of Dinard) is a collection of Montale's fictionalized memories, grotesques and arabesques written in prose in a similar vein. Montale's reputation as a "dark" poet should not blind us to his extraordinary wit and charm—the *Farfalla* is the creation of a highly civilized humorist.

. . . o diti che smorzano
la sete dei morenti e i vivi infocano,
o intento che hai creato fuor della tua misura. . . .

. . . O fingers that quench / the thirst of the dying and inflame the living, / O purpose that you have created beyond your own measure. . . .

Such increasingly passionate invocations dispel the perplexities of the start, enabling the supplicant to sacrifice his suffering, to submit and subscribe to the purpose revealed that renders criteria of personal privation simply irrelevant. It is his fate to "remain on earth," triumphantly if absurdly convinced of their strange bond or elective affinity:

Se la forza
che guida il disco *di già inciso* fosse
un'altra, certo il tuo destino al mio
congiunto mosterebbe un solco solo.

. . . If the force / that guides the record *already cut* were / another, surely your destiny conjoined with mine / would show a single track.

"L'orto" is characteristic of the *Silvae* in its evocation of recent history in Biblical-apocalyptic terms: the war is not only *bufera* but "hour of torture and laments," "Day of Wrath which time and again the cock announced unto the perjured."[*] In "La primavera hitleriana" Clizia appears at the historical occasion of a gala held for Hitler and Mussolini near the Teatro Communale in Florence. The Walpurgisnacht of the jubilant "monsters," announced by howling sirens and the *alalà*—war cry of Fascist stormtroopers—of their henchmen, is framed by a "mystic gulf lit and bedecked with hooked crosses"; to this is opposed the fireworks of St. John (whose feastday this is), the silent pledges of the "faithful," and Clizia's heliotrope ("tu che il non mutato amor mutata serbi"). In "L'ombra della magnolia" (The

---

[*] See the great "Ballata scritta in una clinica" for the fantastic culmination of this tendency: a bomb-shelter "the whale's belly," the German bombardment of Florence from Fiesole in Aug. 1943 conducted under the sign of Taurus ("horned monster . . . not ours") and opposed by Aries the Ram (just war, the Liberation). Add to this a comet and a talismanic wooden bulldog on a bedside table and, over all, "the God that colors with fire the lillies of the ditch," evoking not only the martyrized meek and lowly—Clizia's special care—but the red lillies that are the ancient blazon of embattled Florence. The "Ballata" is a veritable dance of esoteric apocrypha.

Magnolia's Shadow) the chatter of a locust in the treetop suggests to the speaker the mechanical "unisons" of public life under Fascism—

> . . . il tempo del nume illimitato
> che divora e rinsangua i suoi fedeli. . . .

   . . . the time of that god without limits / who devours and gives new blood to his faithful. . . .

—while the chill of coming autumn evokes cold war and the increasingly difficult task of preserving integrity under the subtler conditions of postwar life. Against locust, chill and the voracious god are placed the magnolia—like the sunflower "rooted, eaten by sun"—and a wren in its branches, and out of this cluster of oppositions (eating and eaten, failing and persisting, rootedness and flight) emerges Clizia, marked with the stigmata of the suffering Man-God (*tuo Sposo:* your Bridegroom), undeflected by the "shiver of frost" in the air. The magnolia's bare and unflowering shade is evoked once more as the poem closes, but now as a possible beginning rather than a terminus and *momento mori.* It is a question of a "leap" of faith, leading— who knows?—through the unknown to oblivion or Clizia:

> . . . l'ombra è livida,—
> è l'autunno, è l'inverno, è l'oltrecielo
> che ti conduce e in cui mi getto, cèfalo
> saltato in secco al noviluno.
> > Addio.

   . . . its shadow is livid— / it is the autumn, it is the winter, it is the beyond / that guides you and into which I throw myself, mullet / leapt onto dry land in the new moon.

Addio, (a Dio), the last word, can mean either parting or the hope of miraculous *varco.*

   The *Silvae* conclude with "L'anguilla" (The Eel), a single sentence of thirty lines in which that Ligurian creature—first seen escaping from the hands of children in "I limoni"—is transfigured into the heraldic emblem of Clizia. The sentence is a question ("The eel . . . can you not believe it is your sister?") but between the first and last lines which assemble its subject and predicate the answer has been given in a crescendo of passionately assertive images which culminate in the sign of the eye of *coscienza:*

> . . . l'anguilla, torcia, frusta,
> freccia d'Amore in terra . . .
> l'anima verde che cerca
> vita là dove solo
> morde l'arsura e la desolazione,
> la scintilla che dice
> tutto comincia quando tutto pare
> incarbonirsi, bronco seppellito;
> l'iride breve, gemella
> di quella che incastonano i tuoi cigli
> e fai brillare intatta in mezzo ai figli
> dell'uomo, immersi nel tuo fango. . . .

> . . . The eel, torch, whiplash [cf. Emily Dickinson's snake, "a Whip lash unbraiding in the sun"], / arrow of Love on earth . . . / the green soul that seeks / life where only / dry heat and desolation gnaw, / the spark that says / everything begins when all seems / carbonized, a buried stump; / the minute iris, twin / to that framed by your lids / that you make shine intact in the midst of the sons / of man, immersed in your mud. . . .

And so the *Silvae* end on the same Nestorian image-icon with which they began—the *iride* first encountered in dream and now celebrated in this final waking dithyramb of immanence.

✼   ✼   ✼

The *Silvae* constitute the *positive* culmination (thus far)[42] to not only *La bufera* but Montale's poetry taken as a whole—if we want a happy ending we should stop with "L'anguilla." But in the two "provisory conclusions" which end *La bufera*, "Piccolo testamento" (Little Testament) and "Il sogno del prigioniero" (The Prisoner's Dream), and the perhaps definitive one written in 1961, "Botta e risposta" (Thrust and Parry) published in *Satura*, the focus shifts from the revelation according to Clizia to "I," the Mirco that was, the prisoner, Arsenio.

It is not that Clizia is traduced or denied. The *piccolo testamento*, the feeble light that flickers in the cup of the valedictorian's thought, is precisely *quest'iride*, this iris:

> Solo quest'iride posso
> lasciarti a testimonianza
> d'una fede che fu combattuta,
> d'una speranza che bruciò piú lenta
> di un duro ceppo nel focolare.

> . . . Only this iris can I / leave you in witness / of a faith that

was fought for, / a hope that burned more slowly / than a tough log in the grate.

Further on: "Giusto era il segno": the sign was a just one. Thus far, then, instances of Montalean "proud humility." But the little irridescence he bequeaths comes from something that is now extinguished for him: his slow-burning hope has at last consumed itself:

> Conservane la cipria nello specchietto
> quando spenta ogni lampada
> la sardana si farà infernale
> e un ombroso Lucifero scenderà su una prora
> del Tamigi, del Hudson, della Senna. . . .

> . . . Keep its powder in your compact / when, every light gone out, / the dance grows infernal / and a shadowy Lucifer descends upon a prow / on the Thames, on the Hudson, on the Seine. . . .

Such a powder is the deposit left by an order of experience that is now over, pathetic kin to the ivory mouse amulet kept by Dora Markus beside her lipstick and nailfile. Perhaps these chilling lines are the poem's true testament:

> . . . ma una storia non dura che nella cenere
> e persistenza è solo l'estinzione.

> . . . but a story endures only in its ashes, / and persistence is only extinction.

In "Sogno del prigioniero" ("my prisoner can be a political prisoner, but he can *also* be a prisoner of the existential condition"[43]) everything that is *not* part of the experience of confinement is ruthlessly categorized as dream, merciful dream. "The straw is gold, my wine-red lantern is hearthside if, sleeping, I think myself at your feet."

> . . . mi son guardato attorno, ho suscitato
> iridi su orizzonti di ragnateli
> e petali sui tralicci delle inferriate. . . .

> . . . I have looked about, I have conjured / irises on horizons of spider webs / and petals on the iron-barred grating. . . .

The *botta* of the latest testimonial is a letter from "her"/"you" addressed to Arsenio bidding him awaken out of his "somnambulist's torpor," "spread sail." And the *risposta*, at once parry and counter-thrust, is an autobiography of forty-nine lines detailing a life lived in a prison conceived of as the Augean stables, presided over by an unknown ruler ("He Himself was never seen"), surrounded by the excrement and bellowing of human cattle.

Such a life had its *occasioni*, its *intermittences du coeur*:

> Poi d'anno in anno—e chi piú contava
> le stagioni in quel buio?—qualche mano
> che tentava invisibili spiragli
> insinuò il suo memento: un ricciolo
> di Gerti, un grillo in gabbia, ultima traccia
> del transito di Liuba, il microfilm
> d'un sonetto eufuista scivolato
> dalle dita di Clizia addormentata,
> un ticchettìo di zoccoli (la serva
> zoppa di Monghidoro)
>
> > > finché dai cretti
> il ventaglio di una mitra ributtava. . . .

Then from year to year—and who went on counting / seasons in that darkness?—some hand / that tried invisible chinks / slipped its memento through: Gerty's / curl, a cricket in a cage (last trace / of Liuba's passage), the microfilm / of a euphuist sonnet slipped / from the fingers of sleeping Clizia, / the click of wooden clogs (the lame maid / from Monghidoro) /
Until from the cracks / the spray of a machinegun threw us back. . . .

The last words interrupt the autobiography for a parenthetical final address to "you," closing the story with a sour self-evaluation:

> > > > (Penso
> che forse non mi leggi piú. Ma ora
> tu sai tutto di me,
> della mia prigionia e del mio dopo;
> ora sai che non può nascere l'aquila
> dal topo.)

(I think / that perhaps you no longer read me. But now / you know everything about me, / about my imprisonment and my there-after; / now you know that the eagle cannot be born / of the mouse.)

The *botta* and its *invitation au voyage* ("Don't tell me that the season is a dark one . . .") have been rejected out of hand.

*   *   *

"Botta e risposta" and the other testimonial poems return us full circle, with a rueful humor worthy of Franza Kafka, to the glass-crested *muraglia* of "Meriggiare pallido e assorto . . ." of 1916. The circle is always vicious in Montale, and we have stressed from the beginning the consistency of his central fable—the sensation of blockade—as well as reviewing something of the rich varieties of physical-metaphysical experience that ensue from it—above all, the hypothesis of *varco* and its extraordinary embodiment in the person of Clizia.

But the "Arsenic" taste of the last poems (where contempt is both centripetal and centrifugal, directed at both the impotent "mouse" and the mindless "cattle") is not an adequate keepsake or hangover to take away from a reading of his three fairly slender volumes. I believe that critics have made too much of Montale as a wastelander, a poet of desolation and despair. I do not mean that the mouse is an eagle, but if he knows he is a mouse then this is something—perhaps he is a "lucky" mouse, even a bat, even a real man. "*Sapere,* ecco ciò che conta,*"* as he writes of Sergio Fadin; it applies just as well to himself. If the obsession of Saba is to *belong* ("d'essere come tutti/gli uomini di tutti/i giorni"), and if the obsession of Ungaretti is to evade or become pure spirit ("Cerco un paese/innocente") Montale's is *to know* and, since knowledge imposes limits, to act according to what is known. One is not always *pallido* and self-absorbed as one patrols one's wall; if one facet of the prospect of life from Bellosguardo—or wherever—is "motion that repeats itself in brief circle . . . tiny mirrored acts, always the same . . ." another reveals "great images, honor, unbending love . . . faith that does not alter" and above all the induplicable gesture of one human being, prisoner of his time and space, to another:

> Il gesto rimane: misura
> il vuoto, ne sonda il confine:
> il gesto ignoto che esprime
> se stesso e non altro: passione
> di sempre in un sangue e un cervello
> irripetuti. . . .

The gesture remains: it measures / the void, sounds its confines: / the unknown gesture that expresses / itself and nothing else: lasting passion / in one irrepeatable blood and brain. . . .

The lovely *Finisterre* poem addressed to the poet's dead mother rejects her helpless spirit "in the shadow of the crosses" for the corporeal actuality he is able to conserve of her in his loving thought:

> . . . La strada sgombra
> non è una via, solo due mani, un volto,
> *quelle* mani, *quel* volto, il gesto d'una
> vita che non è un'altra ma se stessa,
> solo questo ti pone nell'eliso
> folto d'anime e voci in cui tu vivi. . . .

> . . . The straight and narrow / is not a road—only two hands, a face, / *those* hands, *that* face, the lifetime's gesture / that is nothing but itself, / this alone places you in the elysium / thick with spirits and voices where you are alive. . . .

So, despite "Piccolo testamento," a story may survive its ashes.

There are many vividly rendered and beautiful acts or gestures in the poetry of Eugenio Montale, not only those that reconnoitre and "sound the confines" but those which express "daily decency," endurance *senza viltà*, faithful attendance on and selfless exchange with another, love, *coscienza*. From the unaffiliated human viewpoint, these are not hopeless matters. From the "Nestorian" point of view, they are divine. Despite backsliding, Montale has always been fundamentally Nestorian.

Aesthetically, the three volumes of his poetry offer one of the richest *oeuvres* of this century.[44] Montale is always an original, even when touched by Dante, Browning or Eliot. He is an excellent *raconteur*, never predictable, seldom without some tonal or imagistic or conceptual novelty. He is an authentic dramatic poet, with a repertoire ranging from "practical" joke to melodrama, drawing-room sketch to tragedy. Yet, it is misleading to talk of genres; he mixes them all in the space of a stanza, blending *verismo* with *stilnovismo*, physics with metaphysics, local color with technology, to achieve his own characteristically complex tone and timbre. Such gifts, indeed, at the service of an imagination combining high seriousness with wit and considerable erudition, constitute his own authentic gesture, an heroic and enduring one that has done his country credit during the difficult period in which he chanced—or was chosen—to play his part.

Notes

[1993: Eugenia Montale died, nearly eighty-five years of age, on 12 September 1981. With the exception of a small collection of posthumous verse (see Bibliography), all of his poetry is included in *L'opera in versi*, a critical edition edited by Rosanna Bettarini and Gianfranco Contini, published in 1980 by Einaudi. His literary and cultural criticism is chiefly in *Sulla poesia*, ed. Giorgio Zampa, Mondadori 1976; see also *Auto da fé*, (Milan, 1966). In the notes to follow, *OV* = *L'opera in versi* and *SP* = *Sulla poesia*.]

1. "Dov'era il tennis . . .," *OV*, p. 215.
2. "Intenzioni (intervista immaginaria)," *SP*, p. 263.
3. *Il mestiere di poeta*, ed. Ferdinando Camon, p. 81.
4. *Diario in pubblico*, p. 32.
5. "L'angiolino," *Farfalla di Dinard*, p. 154.
6. "Giorno e notte," *SP*, p. 92.
7. "Invito a T. S. Eliot," *SP*, p. 463.
8. Angelo Barile, "La veglia genovese di Montale," *Letteratura*, nos. 79–81, Jan.–June 1966 (Montale issue), p. 258.
9. In a 1933 essay on the *Ossi*, in *Esercizî di lettura* (Florence, 1947), pp. 83–84.
10. In an article (1951) for the *Corriere della sera*; cited in Ramat, *Montale* (Florence, 1965), p. 33. Ramat's study, the most comprehensive to date on Montale's work through *La bufera*, very usefully assembles a large number of citations from both Montale and his critics, which are otherwise hard to obtain.
11. Ramat, *Montale*, p. 17.
12. *Diario in pubblico*, p. 32.
13. Svevo-Montale, *Carteggio*, pp. 125, 139.
14. Ibid., p. 40.
15. *Il mestiere di poeta*, p. 81.
16. "Variazione IX," *Auto da fé*, pp. 191–95.
17. "Invito a T. S. Eliot," *SP*, p. 458.
18. "Gozzano, dopo trent'anni," *SP*, p. 57.
19. On Montale's relations with Pound, see Piero Gadda Conti's memoir, "Montale nelle Cinque Terre (1926–8)" in the Montale issue of *Letteratura*, esp. p. 279. See also "Lo zio Ez," *SP*, pp. 481–86 and "Eliot e noi," *SP*, pp. 441–46.
20. "Gozzano, dopo trent'anni," *SP*, p. 58; "Dialogo con Montale sulla poesia," *SP*, p. 581.
21. See Oreste Macrí, "Esegesi del terzo libro di Montale," *Letteratura* (Montale issue), p. 23; Praz, "T. S. Eliot and Eugenio Montale," in *T. S. Eliot: A Symposium*, ed. Richard March and Thurairajah Tambimuttu (Chicago, 1949).
22. "Invito a T. S. Eliot," *SP*, p. 462.
23. "Parliamo dell'ermetismo," *SP*, p. 560.
24. This first sentence was added by the poet for the French translation of "Intenzioni," (Angelini, *Os de seiche*, p. 15).
25. *OV*, p. 894; "Due sciacalli al guinzaglio," *SP*, p. 87.
26. "Parliamo dell'ermetismo," *SP*, p. 560.
27. *Letteratura* (Montale issue), p. 279.
28. "Due sciacalli al guinzaglio," *SP*, pp. 84–87.
29. "'Segni' della *Bufera*," *Letteratura* (Montale issue), p. 117.
30. *Il mestiere di poeta*, p. 81.
31. "L'uomo nel microsolco," *Auto da fé*, p. 265.
32. "L'angiolino," *Farfalla di Dinard*, p. 184.
33. See "Afterword on Montale" below for a listing and discussion of the materials needed for a study of Clizia.
34. "Dante ieri e oggi," *SP*, p. 21.
35. Ibid., p. 20.

36. See Irma Brandeis, *The Ladder of Vision* (New York, 1962), esp. pp. 129–32, a book praised by Montale himself (at the Dante Congress) as "one of the most suggestive I have read on the argument of the ladder that leads to God . . ." ("Dante ieri e oggi," *SP*, p. 31). Irma Brandeis was the historical prototype for Clizia (see "Afterword on Montale" below).

37. "Due sciacalli al guinzaglio," *SP*, p. 85.

38. "Giorno e notte," *SP*, pp. 91–92.

39. "Invito a T. S. Eliot," p. 461.

40. But see "Afterword on Montale" below.

41. But see Irma Brandeis's comment in Luciano Rebay, "Montale, Clizia e l'America," *Forum Italicum* 16, no. 3 (Winter 1982), 198: "My father and Louis D. Brandeis were second cousins. Both branches of the family were Austrian (for I do not know how many generations) before coming to the United States in mid-century. My grandfather married an English Jewess and my father married the daughter of a German Jewish family. I tell you this so that you will avoid reading Montale's references to Palestine or Canaan or the East as colorful background rather than as awareness of a two thousand year old heritage—and therewith a confraternity which deserves more thought than I think it has had."

42. But see "Afterword on Montale" below.

43. "Dialogo con Montale sulla poesia," *SP*, pp. 579–80.

44. But see "Afterword on Montale" below.

Chronological Tables #1 [b. = born; d. = died]

	Italy	Literary Elsewhere	Historical/Biographical
1880			b. Apollinaire d. Flaubert
1881	Verga, *I malavoglia*	Ibsen, *Ghosts* Flaubert, *Bouvard et Pécuchet* Verlaine, *Sagesse*	
1882			b. Joyce, V. Woolf, F. D. Roosevelt d. Longfellow, Emerson
1883	Collodi, *Avventure di Pinocchio*	Nietzsche, *Thus Spake Zarathustra*	b. Gozzano, Mussolini, Saba, W. C. Williams d. De Sanctis, Marx, Wagner
1884		Twain, *Adventures of Huckleberry Finn*	
1885		Laforgue, *Complaintes* Zola, *Germinal*	b. Campana, Pound, Moretti, Palazzeschi d. Hugo
1886			
1887		Rimbaud, *Les Illuminations*	b. Eluard, Saint-John Perse, Corazzini
1888			b. T. S. Eliot, Sbarbaro, Ungaretti d. M. Arnold
1889	d'Annunzio, *Il piacere* Verga, *Mastro Don Gesualdo*		b. Hitler d. G. M. Hopkins, Browning
1890			
1891	Pascoli, *Myricae*		d. Rimbaud, Melville

330

Chronological Tables #2 [b. = born; d. = died]

	Literary		Historical/Biographical
	Italy	Elsewhere	
1892	Svevo, *Una vita*		d. Tennyson
1893		Yeats, *The Celtic Twilight*	
1894	d'Annunzio, *Trionfo della morte*		Dreyfus Trial
1895			
1896		Housman, *A Shropshire Lad*	b. Montale / d. Verlaine
1897		Mallarmé, *Un coup de dés* / Yeats, *The Secret Rose*	
1898	Carducci, *Rime e ritmi* / Svevo, *Senilità*	Hardy, *Wessex Poems*	b. Brecht, Hemingway / d. Mallarmé
1899			b. Crane, Lorca
1900			d. Wilde, Ruskin, Nietzsche / Boxer Rebellion
1901	Croce, *Estetica*	Mann, *Buddenbrooks*	b. Quasimodo, Malraux / d. Queen Victoria, McKinley
1902		Gide, *L'immoraliste*	d. Zola
1903	d'Annunzio, *Alcyone* / Pascoli, *Canti di Castelvecchio* / *Leonardo* (periodical: 1903–07)	James, *The Ambassadors*	

Chronological Tables #3 [b. = born; d. = died]

	Italy	Literary	Historical/Biographical
		Elsewhere	
1904	Pirandello, *Il fu Mattia Pascal*	Hardy, *The Dynasts* (1904–08) Chekhov, *The Cherry Orchard*	d. Chekhov
1905			b. Sartre
1906	Pascoli, *Odi e inni*		d. Ibsen
1907		Bergson, *Creative Evolution*	b. Auden, MacNeice d. Carducci, Corazzini Saba in infantry (Florence/Salerno: 1907–08)
1908	*La Voce* (periodical: 1908–16)	Pound, *A lume spento*	b. Pavese
1909	Marinetti, Futurist manifesto Corazzini, *Liriche*	Pound, *Personae, Exultations* *NRF* founded	
1910	Moretti, *Poesie scritte col lapis* d'Annunzio, *Forse che sì forse che no*	Claudel, *Cinq Grandes Odes* Rilke, *Malte Laurids Brigge*	d. Tolstoy

	Italian literature	International literature	History
			Tripolitan War [Italy vs. Turkey] 1911–12
1911	Gozzano, *I colloqui* Saba, "Quello che resta da fare ai poeti" Sbarbaro, *Resine*	Saint-John Perse, *Éloges* Pound, *Canzoni*	
1912	Papini, *Un uomo finito* Saba, *Coi miei occhi*	*Poetry* (Chicago) founded. Cendrars, *Les Paques à New York* Pound, *Ripostes*/HJC Grierson ed. of Donne's Poems	d. Pascoli Ungaretti leaves Egypt for Paris
1913	*Lacerba* (periodical: 1913–15)	Frost, *A Boy's Will* Mann, *Death in Venice* Apollinaire, *Alcools* Proust, *À la Recherche du temps perdu* (1913–28)	b. Camus
1914	Campana, *Canti orfici* Sbarbaro, *Pianissimo*	Pound, *Des Imagistes* Joyce, *Dubliners* Yeats, *Responsibilities* Frost, *North of Boston*/*Blast* (periodical)	b. Dylan Thomas World War I 1914–18
1915		Pound, *Cathay* Ford, *The Good Soldier* Masters, *Spoon River Anthology* Stein, *Tender Buttons*	Italian intervention

Chronological Tables #4 [b. = born; d. = died]

	Literary		
	Italy	Elsewhere	
1916	Ungaretti, *Il porto sepolto* Montale composes "Meriggiare..."	Joyce, *A Portrait of the Artist as a Young Man* Pound, *Lustra*	Dada 1916–22 d. Gozzano, H. James
1917		Eliot, *Prufrock and Other Observations* Valéry, *La Jeune Parque* Williams, *Al Que Quiere!*	Bolshevik Revolution Caporetto U. S. Intervention
1918	Pirandello, *Così è (se vi pare)*	Apollinaire, *Caligrammes*, "L'esprit nouveau et les poètes", Hopkins, *Poems* (ed. Bridges).	d. Apollinaire, W. Owen Ungaretti in Paris 1918–21
1919	Ungaretti, *La guerre, Allegria di naufragi* *La Ronda* (1919–25)		Versailles d'Annunzio at Fiume 1919–20 Mussolini founds Milan *fascio*
1920	Saba, *Cose leggere e vaganti*	Spengler, *Decline of the West* Eliot, *The Sacred Wood* Valéry, "Le Cimetière Marin" Pound, *H. S. Mauberley*	Saba founds Libreria antica e moderna

1921	Saba, *Canzoniere* (1900–21) Pirandello, *6 personaggi in cerca d'un autore*	Marianne Moore, *Poems*	Ungaretti moves to Rome Mussolini elected to Parliament
1922	Pirandello, *Enrico IV* Saba, *Preludio e canzonette*	Eliot, *The Waste Land* Joyce, *Ulysses* Valery, *Charmes* Williams, *Spring and All* *Criterion* (Eliot [ed.] 1922–39)	Fascist "March on Rome" Mussolini assumes power 1922–43 d. Proust
1923	Svevo, *La coscienza di Zeno*	Rilke, *Sonnets to Orpheus* Stevens, *Harmonium*	Munich putsch—Hitler writes *Mein Kampf* 1923–27
1924	Saba, *Autobiografia, I prigioni*	Perse, *Anabase* Breton, *Surrealist manifesto* Mann, *The Magic Mountain*	Murder of Matteotti
1925	Montale, *Ossi di seppia* Montale, 1st Svevo article, "Stile e tradizione"	Kafka, *The Trial* Pound, *Draft of XVI Cantos* Yeats, *A Vision*	Manifestoes of Italian intellectuals (Croce vs. Gentile)
1926	Saba, *L'uomo* *Solaria* (1926–36)	Crane, *White Buildings* Hemingway, *The Sun Also Rises* Tawney, *Religion and the Rise of Capitalism*	
1927		Woolf, *To the Lighthouse*	Montale moves to Florence

Chronological Tables #5 [b. = born; d. = died]

	Italy	Literary Elsewhere	Historical/Biographical
1928	Montale, *Ossi di seppia* (2nd ed.) Praz trans. of "Arsenio", in *Criterion* *Solaria* (Saba issue) Saba, *Preludio e fughe*	Yeats, *The Tower*/Joyce, 'Anna Livia Plurabelle' Lorca, *Romancero Gitano* Eliot, *For Lancelot Andrewes*	d. Svevo, Hardy
1929	Moravia, *Gli indifferenti*	Eliot, *Dante* Faulkner, *The Sound and Fury*	Montale, director of Gabinetto Vieusseux Depression
1930	Quasimodo, *Acque e terre* Silone, *Fontamara*	Crane, *The Bridge* Michaux, *Un certain Plume* Pound, *Draft of XXX Cantos*	d. D. H. Lawrence
1931	Ungaretti, *L'Allegria*	Edmund Wilson, *Axel's Castle* Woolf, *The Waves*	Japanese occupy Manchuria
1932	Montale, *La casa dei doganieri e altre poesie* Quasimodo, *Oboe sommerso*	Auden, *The Orators* Yeats, *Words for Music Perhaps* *Scrutiny* 1932–53	d. Campana
1933	Ungaretti, *Sentimento del tempo* Saba, *Tre composizioni* Vittorini, *Il garofano rosso*	Neruda, *Residencia en la tierra I* Malraux, *La condition humaine*	Hitler German chancellor/Reichstag Fire

336

1934	Saba, *Parole*	*James, The Art of the Novel* *Pound, ABC of Reading*	
1935		*Pound, Jefferson and/or Mussolini* *Stevens, Ideas of Order* *Cavafy, Alexandria*	Italian-Ethiopian Campaigne 1935–36 Soviet purges 1935–38
1936	Quasimodo, *Erato e Apollion* Flora, *La poesia ermetica*	*Auden, Look, Stranger!* *Eluard, Les yeux fertiles*	Rome-Berlin axis Spanish Civil War (1936–39) d. Lorca; Ungaretti in Brazil 1936–42
1937	Silone, *Pane e vine* *Letteratura* 1937–	*Auden, Spain* *Pound, Fifth Decad of Cantos* *Warner, The Wild Goose Chase*	Japan invades China
1938	Quasimodo, *Poesie* Vittorini, *Conversazione in Sicilia*	*Sartre, La Nausée* *Beckett, Murphy*	Fascist racial edicts Anschluss "Peace in our Time" (Munich) d. d'Annunzio
1939	Montale, *Le occasioni*	*Joyce, Finnegans Wake*	d. Yeats, Freud World War II (1939–45) German-Russian non-aggression pact.

Chronological Tables #6 [b. = born; d. = died]

	Literary		Historical/Biographical
	Italy	Elsewhere	
1940	Quasimodo, *Lirici greci*	Lorca, *Poet in New York* Aragon, *Les yeux d'Elsa*	Fall of France Battle of Britain 1940–41 Italy invades Greece
1941		Auden, *New Year Letter* Ransom, *The New Criticism* Warner, *The Aerodrome*	d. Joyce, Frazer, Woolf Pearl Harbor Germany invades Russia
1942	Quasimodo, *Ed è subito sera* Ungaretti works issued as *Vita d'un uomo*	Camus, *L'étranger* Saint-John Perse, *Exil*	Allies land in Africa Ungaretti returns to Italy—at Univ. of Rome
1943	Montale, *Finisterre* (pub. in Switzerland)		Allied invasion of Italy; Stalingrad Italy surrenders, Mussolini flees, Germans seize Rome Resistenza
1944	Saba, *Ultime cose* (pub. in Switzerland.)	Eliot, *Four Quartets* Auden, *For the Time Being*	Normandy invasion Battle of Bulge

1945	Saba, *Il Canzoniere* (1900–45) Ungaretti, *Poesie disperse*	Ransom, *Selected Poems*	d. Valéry, Mussolini, Hitler, Roosevelt End of War—Pound in Pisa Potsdam, Yalta A-bomb, Hiroshima
1946	Saba, *Mediterrenee, Scorciatoie e raccontine* Quasimodo, *Con il piede straniero sopra il cuore*	Williams, *Paterson I* Prevert, *Paroles*	
1947	Ungaretti, *Il dolore* Quasimodo, *Giorno dopo giorno*	Camus, *La peste* Graves, *The White Goddess*	
1948	Saba, *Storia e cronistoria del Canzoniere* Montale, *Quaderno di traduzioni*	Pound, *Pisan Cantos* Char, *Fureur et mystère*	Berlin airlifts Montale moves to Milan
1949	Quasimodo, *La vita non è sogno* Pavese, *La bella estate*		NATO
1950	Ungaretti, *La terra promessa, Fedra di Jean Racine* Saba, *Uccelli* Pavese, *La luna e il falo*	Neruda, *Canto generale*	Korean War 1950–53 d. Pavese
1951	Saba, *Quasi un racconto*		

Chronological Tables #7 [b. = born; d. = died]

| | Literary | | Historical/Biographical |
	Italy	Elsewhere	
1952	Ungaretti, *Un grido e paessaggi*		H-bomb tested by U. S.
1953	Quasimodo, *Il falso e vero verde*	Ungaretti-Lescure tr., *Les Cinq Livres*	d. Stalin Saba honored by Univ. of Rome
1954			
1955			d. Stevens
1956	Saba, *Ricordi—Racconti*		Hungarian revolt Suez crisis Krushchev denounces Stalin
1957	Montale, *La bufera e altro*		d. Saba
1958	Quasimodo, *La terra impareggiabile* *Letteratura* (Ungaretti issue)	Ungaretti, *Life of a Man* (tr. Mandelbaum)	
1959	Saba, *Epigrafe, Ultime prose*	Pound, *Thrones*	Quasimodo, Nobel Prize for Literature
1960	Ungaretti, *Il taccuino del vecchio* Quasimodo, *Tutte le poesie; Il poeta e il politico e altri saggi* Montale, *Farfalla di Dinard*	Robert Lowell, *Poesie di Montale*	d. Camus Eichmann Trial
1961	Saba, *Il Canzoniere 1900-54* Ungaretti, *Il deserto e dopo* Montale, "Botta e risposta"		
1962	Montale, *Satura*	*Quarterly Review of Literature* (Montale issue)	
1963	Montale, *Accordi e pastelli* Saba, *Antologia del Canzoniere*		Ungaretti president of European Community of Writers

340

Chronological Tables #8 [b. = born; d. = died]

	Literary		Historical/Biographical
	Italy	Elsewhere	
1964	Saba, *Prose*	Eugenio Montale, *Poesie/Poems*, tr. Kay	Ungaretti's seminar on Leopardi at Columbia University Fall of Krushchev
1965		Angelini et al, *Montale: Poèsies* I, II, III Montale, *Selected Poems* (Cambon, ed.).	
1966	Quasimodo, *Dare e avere* *Letteratura* (Montale issue) Montale-Svevo, *Lettere* Montale, *Auto da fé*, "In memoria della moglie" Ungaretti, *I visioni di William Blake*		
1967	Ungaretti, *Morte delle stagioni*		Montale, honorary degree Cambridge University Montale made Senator for life by President Saragat.
1968			d. Quasimodo

afterword on SABA
(1993)

IL CANZONIERE AS CONSTRUCT

A *canzoniere* may be broadly defined as a collection of lyric poems, often of an amorous nature, composed in Italian by (usually) an individual author: thus poets from Dante on have left behind what can and have been called their *canzonieri,* their assembled shorter verses. But the singular example of Petrarch's *Canzoniere,* his poems inspired by the life and death of the woman named Laura, has given the term a more rigorous and more artistically ambitious sense. When, for example, Gianfranco Contini undertook his great edition of Dante's lyric work outside of the *Commedia,* he chose (diverging from respectable precedents) to call the volume *Rime* rather than *Canzoniere,* on the grounds that the latter, post-Petrarch, suggested "the idea of a unitary work, of the organic adventure of a soul, . . . of a conscious psychological as well as stylistic construction supported by the armature of a clear-cut history or story [*storia perspicua*]."[1] Something along the lines of this scope and intent, even though his own *storia* in process might seem very far from clear-cut, was certainly in the mind of Umberto Saba when he chose *Il canzoniere* (note the aggressive definite article) as the title for his on-going, ostensibly collected (but actually very much selected) poems.

His first written mention of such a rubric occurs in letters to friends in 1913, when he was thirty years old and a little-known author of two books, *Poesie di Umberto Saba* (1910) and *Coi miei occhi. Il mio secondo libro di versi* (1912), for which he had written the aborted manifesto "Quello che resta da fare ai poeti" (see above, pp. 14–18 and 45–47). A letter of 20 November 1913 to the critic Emilio Cecchi is worth quoting nearly in its entirety.

> I've transcribed with pleasure the enclosed poem ("A mia madre" [the "A mamma" discussed above, pp. 45 and 54–56] which perhaps you will have read in my book (*Poesie*) but which as it stands now, through formal elaboration, is almost another thing. In the crisis of turning 30 it has happened to me to refeel as actual the feelings of ten years ago, and I have taken advantage of this to place myself with today's expressive means at the window of those times, and to

redo—either more or less depending on their defects—those few lyrics from *Poesie* that I think of keeping for the edition of the "First part of my *Canzoniere.*" For the remaking of "A mia madre" I have been helped by a forgotten earliest version in possession of a friend, and I have found out that in the printed version I had, through an evil inspiration, spoiled the design [*sciupata la linea*], inflating certain details and suppressing others . . . I have no idea whether this poem will be as pleasing to you as it is now to me (it seems to be absolutely my best) but please accept it in homage . . .[2]

The entire undertaking would be a complicated and, over the years, a frequently vexed one, particularly as regards the earliest poems in the projected "First part of my *Canzoniere,*" the ones to be called "Poesie dell'adolescenza e giovanili (1900–1907)" in a 1919 draft of contents.

Saba says he generally composed these poems in his head while walking. He then copied them out from memory—revising as he went—to send to his elected circle of "exactly six" friends.[3] We know that in 1913 he was contacting certain of those friends for return of "earliest versions" of poems he himself remembered imperfectly, or knew only in their subsequently revised state: the reworking of "A mamma" mentioned in the letter to Cecchi indicates that such a procedure could be immensely helpful to him. But it should be noted that the retrieved "forgotten earliest version" was not—or not necessarily—the version to be included in the anticipated *Il canzoniere*. Such drafts, or miraculously recovered memories of drafts, mainly aided him in imaginatively "refeeling" himself as he had been ten years earlier, a creature he could now, with the "expressive means" at his present disposal, express for the first time with authenticity. And by no means all of those earlier poems (only "those few . . . that I think of keeping") were to be retained for the new collection.

The proud assertion of "formal elaboration" made to Cecchi in fact echoes an old rebuke made in a postcard from Croce to whom Saba had sent copies of some of the military sonnets and "A mia moglie": "Your poems have here and there some lively moments, but they still lack any trace of formal elaboration." (With pleasant irony Saba quotes these words in the *Storia,* adding that many years later he sold the postcard "at a steep price" to one of his bookshop customers.[4]) But how do such procedures—not only formal reworking but what might be called "suppression of evidence"*—square with the profession of a conscientiously unelaborated and "honest" poetry made in "Quello che resta da fare ai poeti" the year before?

---

* By my count, Saba published, either in periodicals or in his two books, *fifty-four* poems from the years 1900 to 1907; versions of only *sixteen* of these make up the "Poesie dell'adolescenza e giovanili" of the final *Il canzoniere.*

Such a question arises only when one mistakenly looks upon *Il canzoniere* as a "diary" (see above, p. 31) or as some sort of documentary record, as Saba himself sometimes seemed to think (as in his preface to the 1921 volume: see above, p. 44). But a term thrown out half-humorously in the *Storia*—"we would have nothing against calling it a 'novel' [*romanzo*], even, if one wished, a 'psychological novel'"—comes closer to the point. *Il canzoniere* is an artifact, a historical romance, a gradually incremented projection or myth of self. From 1913 onward, Saba was engaged, by way of poetry, in the task of creating his *storia*, his story based on—but certainly not identical with—his history; of "forging"—to borrow from another literary artist's portrait—himself.

A similar but simpler task had been successfully accomplished a few years earlier when Umberto Poli at last discovered his ideal name as poet. Always—and for reasons we readily understand—dissatisfied with the name life had given him, he signed his earliest poems "Umberto Chopin Poli" before inventing the D'Annunzian "Umberto da Montereale" used during his Florentine *vagabondaggio* of 1905 to 1907. (This name also contains an allusion to his father's family, Italian and Christian, which came from Montereale Valcellina in the province of Udine.) When the D'Annunzian magic wore off, he tried the anagram Umberto Lopi before pre-empting "Saba" from his mentor and fellow townsman the philosopher Giorgio Fano, who had been using it as a pseudonym of his own.

Saba does not mean "bread" in Hebrew, as stated above on p. 35. The poet was attracted to the name because of its resemblance to that of his Slovenian nurse and preferred mama, Peppa Schobar, who may have even informally christened her Berto with a baby or dialect version of her own name.[5] In choosing *Saba* over the prior "art" names linking him with music and eloquence, Saba chose to place himself and his poetry under the star of simple piety and tender mother-love. (No matter about the bitter anguish of his real mother!) The title of his first book, *Poesie di Umberto Saba,* thus makes a secret declaration. As it is glossed in the final tercet of "La casa della mia nutrice" (but see above, pp. 50–54), his final name evokes one of the central, recurrent motifs of *Il canzoniere* in its entirety: "It seems to me that I am still living in that serene age / when, tired of play, I watched rise from the rooftop / the blue smoke of supper."

Like his book and his *nom de plume,* Saba's "doctoral dissertation," the *Storia e cronistoria del Canzoniere* of 1944–47, offers what Contini called "a conscious psychological as well as stylistic construction," this time in the form of highly specialized information and commentary as to how the poet wished his *poema* to be read and valued after some thirty years of intensive work on it. A distinguished Saba scholar like Mario

Lavagetto calls the *Storia* "that odd, faithless, irritating book."° On the other hand, it must be said that very few readers of poetry were taken in by the fictive Carimandrei's mastery of the dates and names and intimate circumstances of so much of the poet's history, and that even Carimandrei allowed Saba's occasional "unevenness" and prosaicism, as well as the fact that the first part of *Il canzoniere* in particular had undergone substantial cuts and revisions. (What was really misleading, however, was the implication that such changes were always made on veristic and moral grounds—that is, because of their failure to express accurately the view from "the window of those times"—rather than in conformity to a gradually developing myth or portrait of the artist.)

So the *Storia,* like "Umberto Saba" and *Il canzoniere* itself, is what Leopardi would have called without disapproval a *dolce menzogna,* a sweet lie. And every so often a sweetening one. One can read all that Saba wrote and never guess, for instance, that the author of the idyllic *Casa e campagna* was coldly furious when his wife confessed to him that they were going to have a child (*his* view of *her* family function being to cater to the poet Saba's needs; just as soon as she was born, Linuccia, like Umberto Poli before her, was sent out of the house to nurse); or that, underlying the bitter scenes of the "Nuovi versi alla Lina" in *Trieste e una donna* (see above, pp. 70–75) is the fact that, reacting to her husband's angry neglect, poor Lina had fallen in love with another man, a Triestine painter of Saba's circle, and had taken Linuccia and left home. (The entire Lina-Carmen parallel working through this section of *Il canzoniere* creates a false impression because it suggests that the poet, a long-suffering Don José, has been wronged by his tempestuous red-shawled paramour.°°) *And yet,* withheld biographical particulars notwithstanding, what is more devastatingly and essentially "honest" than his presentation of his own deep self-absorption in those same "Nuovi versi" through which Lina's rebuffed generosity and undeserved pain are made

---

° The full charge runs: "with all its grace, its excess of 'adjectives,' and praises . . . [the *Storia*] is, precisely, a faithless book, ready to spring-to like a trap and entangle the reader if, for a single second, he forgets that there before him—on the page and on the proscenium—there is a poet who is constructing his own character [*figura*], for this purpose making use of a scapegoat, a patient exegete, a boundless admirer [i.e., 'Giuseppe Carimandrei'] . . ."6 For context it might be noted that Lavagetto is here writing the introduction to Arrigo Stara's edition of *Tutte le poesie* of Saba, an edition including not only the complete *Il canzoniere* (425 poems) but also a *Canzoniere apocrifo* of all the poems excluded by the poet from his canon (178 poems, 144 of these of the period from 1900 to 1920). If an apocrypha means a writing of doubtful authenticity, the standard of authenticity here has been the poet's, corresponding to the composite *figura* he has chosen to present.

°° In the *Storia* Carimandrei disingenuously remarks of the parallel, "we do not know if it is objectively exact, but [it was] dear to the poet." He points out that *Coi miei occhi,* as published by *La Voce* in 1912, had a yellow cover with the title in red, "the colors of Carmen."7

very clear? Saba's portrait of himself is not a self-exculpatory one. And honesty is more than a matter of sufficient fact: it is truth to feeling. (But this is difficult since "windows" alter, time can bring insight or a different humor, the view and thus the feeling changes.)

Sometimes the altered feeling will bring what may seem a jarring disclosure. Probably the last and for some the most scandalous "fact" included within *Il canzoniere* occurs in a poem mentioned quite casually above on p. 90 which begins "Un vecchio amava un ragazzo" [An old man loved a boy]. It was written in 1947 but first published in 1959, two years after the poet's death, in a small set of poems entitled *Epigrafe*, placed with correct dates (1947–48) at the very end of the book. The possibility of Saba's having been "all the time" homosexual, or anyway bisexual (compounded in 1975 by the publication of the incomplete novel *Ernesto*—see above, p. 40—with its opening episode of a sixteen-year-old's sexual initiation in a Trieste warehouse by a middle-aged day-laborer) has raised again in a sensational manner the issue of what Lavagetto calls his *faithlessness*. (Even the late Giacomo Debenedetti, Saba's oldest and most discriminating critic, called "Vecchio e giovane" a confession, "a risky, cruel attempt at exorcism."[8])° But whether or not the old man and the youth are—as Lavagetto says they are—"in bed" together seems to me to be quite beside the point: "Vecchio e giovane" is a noble poem about the immutable difference between the two, between the untested sleeping "angel" with his grave life's suffering all still to come, and the watching lover, an old man alone with his still impatient heart awaiting his own death. Surely the poem is a final variacion on the motif of the inevitably doomed *cose leggere e vaganti* discussed above on pp. 87–93. It is a rare "fusion of sensuality and tenderness" which, as we have seen, Saba denies to Petrarch's *Canzoniere* but by implication claims for his own.

And I would alter the too-absolute judgment made in the middle of p. 69 above to read: "Saba's poetry will certainly have its erotic, sensual side, but *usually* [instead of *always*] compartmentalized from what he calls 'tenderness,' meaning by this a fraternal or human reverence devoid of all lust." Besides, that Saba could be erotically stimulated by the "heart-breaking" beauty of the young of either sex has always been as clear as crystal: I am thinking not only of the newly wedded Lina, Linuccia, Paolina and Chiaretta (of whom he wrote but chose not to

---

° For what it is worth, I agree with Saba's biographer Stelio Mattioni that Saba was not really homosexual; friends of his who frankly were, like the poet Sandro Penna or the novelist Giovanni Comisso, have borne witness that he was not.[9] The adolescent Ernesto, after all, goes on to have "normal" relations with a kind-hearted female prostitute closer to his own age, and in any case his story is not the story of a homosexual but of a young man's discovery of his "vocation" as artist.[10]

publish some sexually explicit verses[11]) but of *ragazzi* like the blond, sailor-suited Glauco of one of his earliest poems, or the clumsy street-urchin "with hands too big / to give a flower" who personifies Trieste, or the "Telemachus" evoked in the late Ulysses poems (see above, pp. 129–30), or indeed himself, the "baldo giovane" (the "bold youth" admonished in the very first poem of *Il canzoniere*), the *piccolo Berto* Schobar/Saba of the legendary nurse's house, resurrected with the help of Freud and needy memory and the art of poetry.

Is the messianic claim to an extraordinary and exclusive suffering made in the closing lines of "La moglie" (see above, p. 73) a sign of a monstrously inflated ego or a necessary precondition to Saba's greatness as a poet? Or both? (I think both: what do you make of a largely unknown versifier setting about to perfect his juvenalia at the age of thirty?) It is, at any rate, a recurring presumption—one related to the refrain-image of *cantuccio,* the place apart which is "made for me"—which runs the entire length of *Il canzoniere.*° And in its different apparitions it is treated differently.

The term "affective ambivalence" (see above, p. 39) is employed often in the *Storia* to help define "scientifically"—*psychoanalytically*—Saba's divided feelings toward those close to him as well as toward the world about him. It might also be applied to his shifting and conflicted presentation of self, of his internalized "two races in an ancient quarrel," of the inner space separating "Poli" from "Saba," separating *l'uomo* (a man like other men among other men) from *il poeta* (the keeper of the "golden thread" of Italian lyric tradition, the heir to Count Giacomo Leopardi, the maker of *Il canzoniere*). Central and crucial among the formal elaborations shaping the emergent work is the poet's expert management of the "musical" motif, the repeat-with-a-difference (Pound would call it subject-riming) of situations and characters together with the varying feelings they arouse, which elevates "affective ambivalence" from a mere psychobiographical diagnostic symptom into a powerful agent for poetic coherence. *Il canzoniere* is a true *canzoniere* in Contini's sense of the word, a conscious whole and soul's adventure, a *poema.*

But here, certainly, as even in Italy, and as is not the case for his peers Ungaretti and Montale, Saba's time has yet to come.

° And beyond. Cut into the small gravestone in the Catholic cemetery of Sant'Anna in Trieste is the "motto" chosen (by whom? Linuccia? Carlo Levi? Saba himself?) for his actual epitaph: *Pianse e capí per tutti,* "He mourned and understood for all," quoting from a poem to the muse written in his old age.[12] (And curiously similar to Montale's 1963 definition of vocational *senilità:* see above, p. 256.) Above the citation is *Umberto Saba* and below, like afterthoughts (one might say visually matching the claim made in "La moglie"), two familiar first names: *e la Lina* to the left and *e Linuccia* to the right.

Notes

1. Dante Alighieri, *Rime,* ed. Gianfranco Contini, p. vii.

2. *Per conoscere Saba,* ed. Mario Lavagetto, p. 122.

3. See "Prefazione per *Poesie dell'adolescenza*" (*Prose,* p. 731) and "Ai miei lettori: Prefazione al *Canzoniere 1921*" (*Prose,* p. 664).

4. Chapter on *Casa e campagna* (*Prose,* p. 437).

5. For more on "Saba," see Cary, *A Ghost in Trieste;* see also Lavagetto's remarks in "Cronologia," *Tutte le poesie,* pp. lxxiii, lxxvii–lxxviii.

6. "Introduzione," *Tutte le poesie,* pp. xi–xii.

7. Chapter on *Trieste e una donna* (*Prose,* pp. 441, 449).

8. Quoted in *Tutte le poesie,* pp. 1,092–93.

9. Stelio Mattioni, *Storia di Umberto Saba,* pp. 18–20, 121–22.

10. *Ernesto,* p. 121.

11. "La fanciulla egoista," *Tutte le poesie,* pp. 945–50.

12. "Tre poesie alla musa" #3, *Tutte le poesie,* p. 532.

afterword on
UNGARETTI (1993)

THE HEAVY HEART OF GIUSEPPI UNGARETTI[1]

. . . sursum corda . . .

"This also is Thou; neither is this Thou." The phrase—origin unknown—I appropriate from the writings of the late Charles Williams, who used it to epitomize what he regarded as the two main modes ("ways") of being conscious of God.[2] The way of affirmation ("this also is Thou") testifies to the inherence of the Creator in the creation and experiences the things of this world as traces or signatures of His presence. The way of negation stresses the radical limitations of fallen creaturely consciousness, urges a ruthless self-scrutiny and *ascesis* as means of coping with human frailty and ignorance, and invokes God as the absent one, the wholly other, the unimaginable ("neither is this Thou"). By the way of affirmation, images of experience—natural or devised, inspired through the senses or expressed through the responsive imagination—are, so to say, numenal and to be cherished; by the way of negation, such images are intrinsically corrupt and to be rejected. The exemplary "saint" for the first would be Francis; for the second, John of the Cross.

It seems reasonable to say that poets belong, by definition, to the affirmative way. Their calling, after all, is to be makers of images, "priests of eternal imagination" in Joyce's glamorous phrase or—a Valéry notwithstanding—at least believers that what they make somehow signifies something in the order of objective reality. Even St. John of the Cross, master of spiritual negation, composes celebrative poems and loads them with erotic images drawn from the hot heart of the fallen world: dark nights and occult rendezvous, the lover's weight upon the breast, the killing caress, and so on. Or, to take a less ecstatic instance: Eliot's Sweeney *has* to use images ("I knew a man once did a girl in—") and so must Eliot, though neither is very happy about it. But among even Eliot's devotions is the ideal of a perfected language ("a complete consort" of word and grammar and image "dancing together") and it becomes clear in the course of the *Four Quartets* that his recurrent misgivings about his calling arise from the gap he perceives between this ideal and his own performance. His unhappy humility, then, does not really call the *métier*, with its premise of the objective viability of images, into question; quite the contrary. Something similar could be said with regard to the notorious gripings of Flaubert or, I think, the frequent cagey superciliousness of Paul Valéry.[3]

From this point of view, the concluded *bella biografia* of Ungaretti is of extraordinary interest. It constitutes the intimate record of a particular individual's inner schism: on the one hand, his impulse to create images ("poesia / è il mondo l'umanità / la propria vita / fioriti dalla parola"); on the other, his continuing awareness of these images as phantasmagoria, *nonnulle* ("Regno sopra fantasmi"). I consider Ungaretti primarily a mystical poet not because of his "return" to Roman Catholicism at the age of forty but because of his persistent sense of a reality—at times referred to liturgically as *Eterno* or *Dio*, but more often affectively as *silenzio, mistero* or as the implied secret cause of anguish—beyond the shiftings of appearances, dreams, or even spiritual longings. I think of him as a poet of the way of negation (like his nominally "atheist" master Leopardi) because of his tormented questioning of all his feelings, thoughts, and images directed toward that reality. Even in his most joyous poems where his dearest dead—Antonietto, Jeanne—are resurrected in a nimbus of unearthly light, a word like *dream* occurs to raise the ironic specter of his solipsism. Thus the original title of "Segreto del poeta" (see above, p. 218) was "Vattene, sole, lasciami sognare"[4] [Begone, sun, and let me dream], while the initial verb of the very beautiful "Per sempre" (". . . sognerò . . .") casts a disquieting reservation on the culminating vision itself. The words written by Ungaretti to characterize the poetry of Davide Turoldo apply perfectly to his own: "poetry that bursts from the fracture caused by the absence-presence of the Eternal: presence in a torment of desire, absence since our ephemeral earthly state, to which we in our foolishness cling so [*tiene tanto*], separates us from the Eternal."[5]

In the *plaquette* of his verse in French, published in 1919 as *La Guerre*, there is one which consists of a single line—"corruption qui se pare d'illusions" [corruption that is dressed in illusions]—titled "Vie," Life. More aphorism than poem, "Vie" illuminates for me, through the perspective of contrast, the typical quality of Ungarettian negation: far more tortured and divided than the flat judgment sounded by *corruption*. One still clings so—*tiene tanto*—to the things of this familiar world, and such a holding-on bears its own sweet but groundless comfort, as the title of Ungaretti's first large collection, *Allegria di naufragi*, reminds us. The pages of this volume are unified not only by their historical occasion, the First World War, but by the theme of consoling illusion which momentarily transfigures that occasion and its theater, the ravaged Carso: "Ungaretti / uomo di pena / ti basta un'illusione / per farti coraggio . . ." And the possibilities are endless: either prompted by geography and landscape (the sun turning Alexandria into brilliant motes of dust, the tear-colored mists that liquify Paris or Milan, the magical permutations available through the colors of dawn or sunset, glint of dew, sigh of breezes) or induced by one's own "creative" mechanisms (eyes half or wholly shut, skin's response to grass or warmth or water, erotic hankering, memory, dream . . .). Even the famous "Mattina" (see above, pp. 153, 166), which seems so much a natural "cosmic" affirmative, has a secret history of image-making, of imaginative transformation; originally titled "Cielo e mare," Ungaretti transcribed it in a letter to Serra as "M'illumino / d'immenso / con un breve / moto / di sguardo" [I illuminate me / with immense / by a brief / movement / of gaze].[6]

"Vie" notwithstanding, in the earlier poetry the tendency is to treat the state of being-in-illusion with some sympathy as being in any case unavoidable and, in a historical dilemma (the war and its aftermath), a human easement. One image which in some version or other ranges through the entire *Vita d'un uomo* is that of the miracle of grace whereby the laws governing matter are apparently suspended and one becomes weightless, levitating like the blessed souls of *Paradiso*. Both *L'Allegria* and *Sentimento del tempo* end with such an image ("Preghiera" and "Senza più peso"). If the characteristic ecstasy of the first volume is first-person and centrifugal ("Ungaretti" in a flash integrated into the scheme of things, "docile fibra dell'universo"), that of the second volume celebrates the weightless *trasumanarsi* of certain of the poet's legendary dead: to the memory at least, the persons of *il capitano* and Ofelia D'Alba have become feather-light and pure. These legends of levitation are in fact prayers for the suspension of natural law and as close as Ungaretti ever gets to wholehearted *sursum corda*.

Simone Weil has written: "Creation is composed of the descending movement of weight, the ascending movement of grace and the descending movement of grace to the second power. Grace is the law of the descending movement. To lower oneself is to rise with regards to moral weight. Moral weight makes us fall towards the heights."[7] But for Ungaretti there is no "grace to the second power," no "works" of moral gravity or renunciation through which a living man may be raised (as he puts it in "Preghiera") "dal barbaglio della promiscuità / in una limpida e attonita sfera" [from the dazzle of promiscuity / into a limpid and astonished sphere]. The sole solution is death, after which a man is either "changed" (St. Paul's word) or nonexistant. But man fears death; *tiene tanto.*

In his own late legend of his life (see his *nota introduttiva* to *Tutte le poesie*), Ungaretti has insisted upon two determining presences: desert and mirage. His destiny thus gave him at the start two colossal objective "facts" which taught him, *nelle vene*, that nothing is permanent, that we are nothing and shall return to nothing; and that in our thirst for something we are subject to mirage, to the illusion of renewal in a benevolent world-oasis. These two presences are reciprocal: one cannot exist without the other. And beyond desert and mirage is a possible third that cannot be named so much a fact as a need: this is "God," who may be a mirage.

In the same *nota* Ungaretti writes of his early "passion to throw myself, plunge myself, squeeze myself into mirages"; he was a creature, clearly, very like his own Cain, "made in the heart's own image." His approach to religious belief, to the possible third presence, was much the same—quite as ardent, as violent, and as desperate. In an otherwise brilliant essay, Georges Poulet speaks of his poetry as "la poésie du détachement,"[8] and the phrase is ill-considered if detachment means— and it surely does—a standing-off, a noninvolvement in which the centers of awareness, head and heart and body, keep calm and clear. Ungaretti's poetry, particularly in its later stages, is tense, entangled, caught and divided. (One remembers his portentous and explosive way of reading his work aloud.) His word for all this was *barocco;* he meant by this the style of desperation. It enacts, in all senses of the word, a passion.

Or when not a passion, a *pietà* of a special sort. For the image that constantly obsessed Ungaretti from the composition of his own "Pietà" in 1928 to the end of his life was that carved by Michelangelo in his old age: the so-called Pietà Rondanini in Milan: "When Michelangelo represents Christ in his last work, the Pietà Rondanini, Christ is an inanimate body, an empty body . . . The idea of resurrection is an idea that he never managed to assimilate."[9] Ungaretti goes on to say: "Michelangelo was a good Christian, but . . . was Michelangelo truly a Christian?" The question is impossible to answer. But the dilemma is his own. Christ is that empty body, that dead-weight subject to the inexorable laws of matter.

That dead-weight, on the other hand, is Christ.

FOR A READING OF "VARIAZIONI SU NULLA"[10]

Quel nonnulla di sabbia che trascorre
Dalla clessidra muto e va posandosi,
E, fugaci, le impronte sul carnato,
Sul carnato che muore, d'una nube . . .

Poi mano che rovescia la clessidra,
Il ritorno per muoversi, di sabbia,
Il farsi argentea tacito di nube
Ai primi brevi lividi dell'alba . . .

La mano in ombra la clessidra volse,
E, di sabbia, il nonnulla che trascorre
Silente, è unica cosa che ormai s'oda
E, essendo udita, in buio non scompaia.

That less-than-nothing of sand that streams / Through the hourglass, mute, and comes to its resting, / And, fleeting, the impressions on the flesh, / On the rosy flesh that dies, of a cloud . . .

Then hand that reverses the hourglass, / The return to its moving, of sand, / The tacit silvering of cloud / At the first brief pallors of the dawn . . .

The hand in shadow turned the hourglass, / And, of sand, the less-than-nothing that streams / Silent, is sole something henceforth heard / And being heard, in darkness does not vanish.

I wonder how many readers of *La terra promessa* have been dissatisfied, as I have been, with the poet's own gloss on his beautiful lines. "The theme is earthly duration beyond the particularity of persons. Nothing but a disembodied timepiece that alone, in the void, continues to distill the minutes." According to this interpretation, the running sand evoked in the opening halves of the first and second stanzas and throughout the third would signify *durata terrena,* a sort of geological or planetary time-scale against which the mutations of light upon a cloud or a hand, expressions of *durata umana,* would seem fugitive, ephemeral, "nothing." Indeed some such theme is obsessive throughout the *Vita d'un uomo,* the very first poem of which sounds an awareness of the *inesprimibile nulla* investing every human value; its grand last chapter is a wintry oratorio in which the poet's voices (Dido, Palinurus, the *vecchio* himself) sing their several senses—his compound experience—of perishing. And for the astute reader of Ungaretti's achieved *bella biografia,* the hourglass sands may well range themselves with the desert sands which are at once the "spectral foundations" and the confines of his native city, that "friable" Alexandria where he received, as it were by birthright, the linked *sentimenti* of time, of attrition, of an encroaching *nulla.*

Against such an amply precedented reading—and against, it seems, the poet's own self-understanding—I would argue that "Variazioni su nulla" is a lyric celebration of *durata umana* insofar as this implies, following Ungaretti's master Bergson, human consciousness itself. A mortal and therefore tragic consciousness to be sure, since there is scarcely a trace in these lines of that "secret" and tormented hope for an immortal soul that is touched upon in (to mention only the contextual *Terra promessa*) the "Canzone," the "Segreto del poeta," and the terminal "Per sempre." "Nothing will come of nothing," says Lear, but in the remarkable evocation of impermanence which is the "Variazioni," something abides and, for the first time—for the life of a man at least—lasts.

It seems important to be precise about the hourglass *as it is presented.* Its function is not primarily to be the emblem of an idea or concept, though the poet's comment appears to say that it is. It is neither "alone" nor "disembodied," as would be the equivalent allegorical figure encountered on a sundial or graveyard headstone, silent sign for *tempus fugit.* It is, rather, an object of consciousness, "embodied" in a consciousness, and it is the flow of that consciousness rather than the flow of the sand which constitutes the poem's true movement.

Quel nonnulla di sabbia: the demonstrative adjective seems to me to indicate the specific direction of a particular attention. The attention belongs to the speaker of these lines, and his is the hand that turns the hourglass. The lines move with the attention, from the fall and all-but-imperceptible coming-to-rest° of sand, to the shifting shadows on a cloud's surface—but here the noun *carnato* (awkwardly translated as "rosy flesh," though the obsolete "carnation" or "incarnadine" might be preferable) could suggest either the pinkish tints of a cloud at sunset or the speaker's cloud-dappled hand at that hour: in any case a useful ambiguity linking cloud and man in a common waning.

In the second stanza the hand, only suggested in the first, is observed distinctly at what I take to be its key operation: the reversing of the glass so that the flow of sand resumes and, with it, an explicit sense of duration. Again the attentive eye moves naturally to the sky, now fixing on a cloud that has caught the ominous paleness (*brevi lividi*) heralding day to come. It seems a night has passed.

The first two stanzas sustain a mood of bemused or entranced attentiveness. They operate out of what could be called a pure present, created by a close to paratactic conjuration of things seen (whose governing verb—*guardo*, "I see"—is silent), the suave movement of the "blank" hendecasyllables, the tenuous and fluid imagery, the hypnotic repetition of key images and words, the "timeless" use of verb forms as substantives, the commas and the terminal dots suggesting a process *ad infinitum.* The final stanza, while retaining the base images of hand and running hourglass, abandons the mood of suspended constatation for, first, a statement of completed action (the *volse* of line nine is *passato remoto,* a past absolute), and, second, an affirmation. There is another novelty. The first two stanzas are entirely visual, with the only other sense involved, the auditory, specified only in terms of nonpresence: for example, the *mute* sand, the *tacit* silvering of the cloud. But in the final

---

° The verb *posare,* something like our "pause" or "repose," has a special quality of peaceful gentle cessation in Italian. Ungaretti's casting it as a present participle further removes it from any suggestion of abruptness or break in motion. (The same strategy, by the way, governs the use of infinitives as substantives—*muoversi, farsi*—in the middle of the poem.) *Posare* also has strong literary-historical vibrations for Ungaretti, who, in his second discourse on Leopardi (1944), devotes over a page to the "miraculous" use both Petrarch and Leopardi made of it.[11]

stanza the hearing takes over; the hand is lost in shadow, the clouded sky is wholly absent. The sand, it is true, still runs in silence, *but it is heard and so does not disappear.* It is the nature of this hearing that must be understood in order to be clear about the climactic affirmation.

The night has meant a vigil for the speaker: *he has watched,* and it is entirely appropriate that the hourglass with him is a manner of watch. Attentively, with its aid, he has measured the time into minutes and hours, night and day. He has occupied himself with "nothing" (or variations on it: a few grains of sand, some clouds, the permutations of light and dark) and arrived at a scale for his true condition: not the flickering intimation of mortality that occurs to us from time to time, but a deep and circumstantial sense of it, timed "in the veins."

The lovely "Sentimento del tempo" written some fifteen years earlier dramatizes a similar realization. Its "I" watches the gradually increasing proportion of shadow to light upon a distant range of mountains and hears simultaneously what has always been there, his rhythmically beating heart timing the approach of dark, measuring the vast and mysterious spaces surrounding him, sounding a *sentimento del tempo*—the intimate feel of time—in his breast. Surely its crucial lines—

> . . . Ogni mio palpito, come usa il cuore,
> Ma ora l'ascolto . . .

> . . . My heartbeat, the heart's custom, / But now I hear it . . .

are directly applicable to the climax of "Variazioni su nulla."

Such a *sentimento* may or may not lead to the horror and sickening despair to be found in, say, certain of the *Inni* or Dido's choruses. In the "Variazioni," as in "Sentimento del tempo," the mood is serene and affirmative. I have written above of what can be called Ungaretti's "Egyptian nominalism," his sometimes desperate search for a scale of names or images that might stand against time and make the perishing moment imperishable. He wrote in *La Ronda* in 1922 of the *donnée obscure,* the "mystery," which he finds at the heart of all life, and of the specially human mode of coming to grips with this which he calls "measure"; ". . . not the measure of the mystery, which is humanly absurd, but the measure of something which is in a certain sense opposed to the mystery while at the same time constituting for us its highest manifestation, the terrestrial world considered as man's continual invention." One such measure, of course, is time itself, "a part of our mind," as Leopardi wrote in his notebooks, "a name . . . a mode of considering existence" (*Zib.*, 14 December 1826). The risk here—and the famous "La pietà" is Ungaretti's consummate expression of it—is the risk of solipsism, of "peopling silence with names." In his travel journal of the 1930s Ungaretti ruefully mocks the tragic aspiration of the desert peoples of antiquity to "conquer" time through the construction of heroic monuments: obelisks and pyramids like colossal clock-hands pointing forever to a fixed meridian. Measure, it is clear, cannot "refute" that mysterious reality it is meant to witness. It is a manifestation, after all, not of desire but of recognition, and hence must be just "fair measure" . . . like an hourglass.

"Variazioni su nulla" is a poem of recognition and also, finally, of memory, for it is memory—*profondeur de l'homme* is Ungaretti's phrase for it—that can preserve what is seen, heard, and felt against the dark. If he who remembers happens to be a poet, then what he remembers may survive his lifetime, even as we can still be touched by dead Ungaretti. This comes at the end to a last variation on *nulla*, which must mean not only the "nothingness of dust" to which, as he writes in the late "Monologhetto," we must return, but also whatever he raised long ago from his buried port—

> quel nulla
> d'inesauribile segreto

"that nothing" of quenchless secret which is the poem itself, miraculous survival, light measuring the darkness.

Notes

1. First published in *Forum Italicum* 6, no. 2 (June 1972): 247–52.

2. See *The Descent of the Dove* (London, 1939), pp. 57–62, and *The Figure of Beatrice* (London, 1950), pp. 8–11.

3. For example, Monsieur Teste versus the Pythoness, who concludes with this affirmative:

> Honneur des Hommes, Saint LANGAGE,
> Discours prophétique et paré,
> Belles chaînes en qui s'engage
> Le dieu dans la chair égaré,
> Illumination, largesse!

4. The "segreto" refers to a hidden hope, not a certainty, as the poem's last verb (*parvero,* referring to the "immortality" of Antonietto's earthly gestures) reminds us. The implication is that the hope is "secret" not only to the reader but to the poet as well. See *SI,* p. 843: "The secret alone still keeps its value . . . Human knowledge augments the secret . . . The more we know the more things are removed from us . . ."

5. Davide Maria Turoldo, *Udii una voce,* premessa di Giuseppe Ungaretti (Milan, 1952), p. xi. See also *SI,* pp. 772–75.

6. See Ettore Serra, *Il tascapane di Ungaretti* [&} *Il mio vero Saba* (Rome, 1983), pl. 4.

7. *La pesanteur et la grâce* (Paris, 1948), pp. 4–5.

8. "Ungaretti et la poésie du détachement," *Nouvelle Revue Francaise*(April 1961): 757–60.

9. *TP,* p. 534.

10. First published in *Books Abroad* (special issue: "Homage to Ungaretti"), vol. 44, no. 4 (Autumn 1970), pp. 588–91; journal currently named *World Literature Today.*

11. *SI,* pp. 465–67, 481.

afterword on
MONTALE (1993)

AS A MAN GROWS OLDER

"The *Silvae* constitute the *positive* culmination (thus far) to not only *La bufera* but Montale's poetry as a whole . . ." This barely provisional conclusion (made on p. 323 above) seemed sensible enough in 1968. Montale was seventy-two years old and had been famously unprolific from the very beginning of his life as a poet—a charter member, in fact, of the "Slow Club" described so delightfully in *Farfalla di Dinard*.[1] Since 1954, two years before the publication of *La bufera e altro*, he had ceased to write poetry almost entirely. The two slim volumes published in 1962–63 (see p. 242) contained just two new poems; the rest was early work rightly excluded from the *Ossi*, of interest simply because anything written by Montale is interesting. The privately circulated *Xenia* of 1965 printed fifteen brief poems in memory of the wife who had died three years previously; if a few professors likened them to Thomas Hardy's similarly inspired *Veteris vestigia flammae*, judged by Montale himself as "one of the peaks of modern poetry,"[2] the fact is that the two suites are deeply different.* In any case, the *senex* Hardy maintained a vein of versifying that "thus far" was nonexistent in Montale, who in 1962 believed that he had said "everything essential" in his three main books of verse. Perhaps, he hoped, "something" might still come, "not a proper book but an appendix . . ."[3] Perhaps (one thought in 1968) the handful of *Xenia* poems was that appendix.

But if he had been unprolific as a poet, his situation as a producer of prose since 1948 was quite otherwise. In that year Montale transferred from Florence to Milan to take up a career as regular contributor—contracted minimum five pieces per month—to two major newspapers, the *Corriere d'Informazione* and the *Corriere della Sera*. The fifty "rac-

---

* Not only in terms of word- or line-count. Hardy's vestiges of his old flame haunt and taunt him: the "original air-blue gown" is gone forever or survives in mocking memory only. Whereas Montale, though technically bereft, in his *xenia* (guest-offerings) bemusedly and most un-elegiacally hosts a persisting if elusive—flylike—presence flickeringly *there* in his wife's relics ("calendars, jewel cases, medicine bottles, and creams"), *keepsakes* which encapsulate and preserve her essential being.

conti non-racconti [*cum*] poesie non-poesia" of *Farfalla di Dinard*,[4] the bulk of the articles on culture and society in *Auto da fé* and on poets and poetry in *Sulla poesia*, the travel essays and "star" interviews—Brancusi, Mauriac, Malraux, Char, Stravinsky—of *Fuori di casa* [Away from Home] and the music criticism (opera especially) of *Prime alla Scala* [First Nights at the Scala]—all of it work of a superior order and some of it, such as *Farfalla*, not "journalism" at all even though written to deadline—were almost entirely generated in the twenty years' span between 1948 and 1968. Under such conditions, poetry, rare enough in any case, must suffer. "The activity of journalism," he remarked in 1962, "does not permit that sort of *otium*, of interior vacancy, which for me at least is necessary for poetry."[5]

His partial retirement from newspaper work in 1968 changed things again. Renewed *otium* revealed that *Xenia* was not to be an appendix at all but part of the first section of a big new book of poems, *Satura*, published in 1971 and not to be confused with the slender collection of five poems issued in 1962. In the ten years remaining him, Montale wrote three further collections of verse: *Diario del '71 e del '72, Quaderno di quattro anni* [Notebook of Four Years, 1973–77], and *Altri versi e poesie disperse* [Other Verses and Uncollected Poems, 1981], by my count a total of 448 poems as opposed to the 177 poems of the first three volumes, or a total of over five hundred pages in the complete *L'opera in versi* as opposed to the slightly over half of that taken up by the others. But the change was not merely quantitative.

After all, there is a sense in which *La bufera e altro does* mark the "positive culmination" of Montale's poetry as a whole, if we mean by that phrase his aspiration (voiced in "Intenzioni") toward a poetry of "*pedale*, of profound music, of contemplation." My remarks on the *Lampi* or "flash" poems (on p. 320 above), that is, on the post-*Silvae* lyrics included in *La bufera*—on their "wry . . . black-humored, fantastical vein" somewhat akin to the witty prose arabesques of *Farfalla*, composed in roughly the same period (1948–52)—indicate something of the nature of Montale's later music: *secco* and more satirical, aphoristic, less adventurously "operatic" (less "musical") than before. The same point is made by his unplangent later cover-titles: "diary," "notebook," and especially "satura."

A *satura* is a medley, a miscellany, a mixed-dish, a stew, a mélange of attitudes and speech-styles.° The related ideals of a "prose tradition in

---

° The 1962 *Satura* was meant to be modest but is really a misnomer. The name for the 1971 *Satura* was originally less generic, *Rete a strascico* [Trawl-Net], dropped presumably because of its unwanted link with the "marine and Mediterranean" world of *Ossi di seppia*.[6] Giorgio Zampa has pointed out that Montale's first published use of the word *satura* occurred in 1952 in the course of a preface to an anthology of ancient Chinese poetry: "a civil, social, I would say almost humanitarian, poetry . . . lyric and satire set freely cheek by jowl in this very vast *satura* . . ."[7]

verse" à la Pound or a "metaphysical poetry" à la Eliot—see above, pp. 246–47, 279–80—suggest that every poem might constitute its own satura, its own mix of high and low, of *canto* and *conversazione*. But Montale's own metaphors for describing his poetry *up through* and *after* *La bufera*—written in *frac* or in pajamas, *recto* or *verso*, one or the other side of a medal[8]—emphasize the difference overtaking his *Opera*. A major change of mood-key has happened: the tone is lower, the norm of verse-structure is "free" and more like a cadenced prose. The old themes can recur—talismanic objects, the lay miracle of *varco*, the sudden flash or burst of vital life, the visiting angel—but they are treated with a diffused intensity, often with a quizzical humor.

Take, for example, the second stanza of "Divinità in incognito" [Divinity Incognito] from *Satura:*

> Io dico
> che immortali invisibili
> agli altri e forse inconsci
> del loro privilegio,
> deità in fustagno e tascapane,
> sacerdotesse in gabardine e sandali,
> pizie assorte nel fumo di un gran falò in pigne,
> numinose fantasime non irreali, tangibili,
> toccate mai,
> io ne ho vedute più volte
> ma era troppo tardi se tentavo
> di smascherarle.
>
> [*OV*, p. 367]

I say / that immortals invisible / to others and perhaps unaware / of their privilege, / deities in corduroy with rucksacks, / priestesses in gabardine and sandals, / Pythias wrapped in the smoke / of a huge bonfire of pinecones, / numinous phantoms not unreal, tangible / though never touched, / I have seen them more than once / but it was too late if I tried / to unmask them.

Verso, surely, of a familiar *recto:* any reader of Montale will spot this passage's connections with, say, the motets of the 1930s or the great *canzoni* ("Nuove stanze," "Notizie dall'Amiata," the *Silvae*) of the war and immediate postwar period. But *that* Montale was above all a dramatic poet, the poet of (italics his) "*this* individual, in *this* place, in *this* situation," and the product was matchless: a powerful, impassioned vocal music moving through its various specific occasions of ecstasy and anguish, metrically intricate, *ore rotundo*. The new manner exemplified by "Divinità in incognito" is very different.

It lies in a distancing or de-dramatizing of the subject (as with a telescope reversed) by various stylistic means. In this sample one may note the discursive tendency of the free verse itself, the focus upon a general phenomenon (deities, priestesses glimpsed more than once) rather than a unique situation, the amusing touches of modish *vie de bohème* in the broad details of disguise, the wry-rueful note in the final clause—all of which contribute to the benign humor lightening this later work, its casual, free-floating, "prosaic," and *désengagé* mood. Perhaps it is the appropriate voice for a certain sort of old age and retirement. But the ghosts of Yeats and Giuseppe Ungaretti are there to give me the lie.

Late Montale is a richly moving Montale, but only—perhaps I mean mainly—if you know the tremendous achievement of his first three books.

He was awarded the Nobel Prize for Literature in 1975. "There is a negativism," said the Swedish Academy, "based not on misanthropy but on an indelible feeling for the value of life and the dignity of mankind. That is what gives Eugenio Montale's poetry its innate strength."

> Codesto solo oggi possiamo dirti,
> ciò che *non* siamo, ciò che *non* vogliamo.

TU

> " . . . dantesche, dantesche . . . "

Satura starts with a brief poem set in italics entitled "Il *tu*":

> *I critici ripetono,*
> *da me depistati,*
> *che il mio tu è un istituto.*
> *Senza questa mia colpa avrebbero saputo*
> *che in me i tanti sono uno anche se appaiono*
> *moltiplicati dagli specchi. Il male*
> *è che l'uccello preso nel paretaio*
> *non sa se lui sia lui o uno dei troppi*
> *suoi duplicati.*
>
> [*OV*, p. 275]

Critics repeat, / put off the track by me, / that my *tu* [i.e., my "thou," my second-person singular intimate *you*] is an institution. / Without this mea culpa they would have known / that in me the many are one even if they appear / multiplied by mirrors. The trouble / is that the bird caught in the net / does not know if it is itself or one of its too many / duplicates.

One instance of the duplicity proudly claimed in the second line of "Il *tu*" may be found in Montale's remark to his biographer Giulio Nascimbeni, made well before the poem's publication three years later, regarding the famous pronoun: "it is an institutional 'tu,' the other [*l'antagonista*] that would have to be invented if it did not exist."[9] *Istituto* seems to designate a customary rhetorical practice, this poet's habitual use of a mode of direct address, a confidential vocative in the service of drama which, he urges, *need not refer* to a particular, personal autobiographical other (although it might, as the if-clause to Nascimbeni allows . . . and in fact he then goes on to identify the uninvented *tu* of "Casa sul mare" and "Crisalide.") But "Il *tu*" goes on to disclose that the *tu* is really not institutional at all, not at all a manner of speaking, and that there *is* a "one" underlying the multiplicity of appearances—those semblances, those merely reasonable facsimiles, those *senhals* (see p. 303 above)—but that even the "one," the secretly marked winged creature, cannot be sure if it is really *she* (since *tu* is invariably a *donna*). Is Montale being disingenuous with his readers here? Or, as he responded toward the end of his life to one of the last of his inquisitors, is he being "dantesque, dantesque"?[10]

We know from *Vita nuova* that Dante consciously set out to put his townspeople off the track by using what he calls a *donna schermo*, meaning the troubadour device of choosing a "screen lady" or decoy who would seem to be the object of his uncounterfeit passion—thus protecting that passion as well as its true object, Beatrice, from prying eyes and knowingness. (We know also that Beatrice herself was taken in by this ruse—if it was entirely a ruse—and later rebuked her lover for it.) In the *Flashes* and *Private Madrigals* framing the Clizia-centered *Silvae* appears what Montale has termed an "Antibeatrice" or earthly "counterfigure" to Clizia, the vivid female presence called *la Volpe*, the vixen; it is in fact in the interplay between the two (or more accurately between the two sorts of voice—the one grave and contemplative, the other playful and bizarrely satirical—that the two inspire in him) that he has located a parallel with the amorous double-dealing of *Vita nuova*.[11] But la Volpe is never in any sense a "duplicate" or "screen" for Clizia; she is entirely her own jagged, passionate self, a radically contrasting crystallization of that overarching theme of "love, under the form of phantasms who frequent the various poems and provoke the usual 'intermittences of the heart.' "[12] What in my opinion is more profoundly dantesque about Montale's poetry is its evidence of the transformatory power of an imagination which, like Dante's, can create a sensuously polysemous life—physical as well as metaphysical, literal as well as symbolic, moral, and anagogical—of whatever it plays upon and finds the words and music for: whether a branch set in a vase at the door of an inn, or a photograph sent by a friend of a pair of "marvelous" legs belonging to someone never met named Dora Markus, or a young American scholar with strong green eyes and ash-blond bangs studying Dante and "lives of half-known saints and baroque poets of small reputation"[13] at a desk in the Gabinetto Vieusseux in the 1930s.

Bice, 1266–90, daughter of Folco Portinari and wife of Simone dei Bardi, does not "equal" the *donna* Dante chose to call by the full name of Beatrice in honor of the blessing he felt she conferred upon him. By the same token, the American scholar named Irma Brandeis, 1906–90, who published "An Italian Letter" on Montale's poetry in *The Saturday*

Review for 19 July 1936, and to whom *Le occasioni* was dedicated ("a I. B."), and who later taught literature at Bard College and wrote a distinguished study of Dante's religious imagination—see notes 36 and 41 to chapter four above—does not "equal" the salvation-bearing Clizia. For Clizia, like Beatrice, is what Montale would call an *avventura stilistica:* which is to say that she can "never coincide with the real *donna*"—the striking scholar with coral earrings poring over a manuscript—who provided the historical "occasion" and inspiration for her.[14]

In a very late memory-poem ("Previsioni," Previsions) addressed to a *tu* who is certainly I. B. rather than the "C." mentioned toward its end, the poet recalls her speaking sardonically of the pathetic fate of *donne dei poeti* "made to pad out unreadable odes," and, despite his rather pompous denial through appeal to the mystery of imagination, her murmured forecast: *Così sarà di me* [So it will be with me]. So it was, although each of them, in her or his own way, was right. You forget, the poet had protested, that the bullet [that is, the poem] knows neither its target nor who fired it.[15] And certainly Professor Brandeis was strictly accurate when, at a 1966 gathering in New York in honor of the poet's seventieth birthday, speaking purely as—like those in the audience—a devoted reader of his poetry, she cited Montale's "code of images that excludes the personal." Surely that too was included in her "prevision" of thirty years earlier. *Così sarà di me.*

In his old age, Montale made arrangements so that posterity might know something of the historical basis of things imagined.[16] We now know, for example, that the preface poem for *Le occasioni* ("Il balcone": see above pp. 289–91) as well as the first three *mottetti* were occasioned by *donne* other than her who later in the volume would be given the name of Clizia. We now know, thanks chiefly to the elucidations of the poet's confidante Luciano Rebay of Columbia that a number of the *tu*-poems of the *Ossi* and *Occasioni* were addressed to a young girl, Arletta or Annetta, whom he had known in the Cinque Terre ("she died young," Montale once wrote, "and there was nothing between us"), and who makes her reappearance as a blackcap—*capinera,* a small European bird, grey with black crown—in the last three books; the entire *Opera in versi,* excluding the translations and uncollected poems, closes in fact with "Ah!," a poem that voices her initial. The "one" is, if not many, certainly multiple.

And yet, thinking of the names of *tu* threading the *Opera,* remembering Esterina, Gerti, Dora, Liuba, la Volpe, Mosca his wife, Annetta, and above all Clizia, it is right I believe to feel that they are indeed, as he said, in some sense *one,* not just as human instances of saving Amor which impinged upon his life and poetry, but as something vulnerable, in peril, brave and resistant. Something therefore lovely, and inspiring.

Notes

1. "Slow," *Farfalla di Dinard*, pp. 138–41.

2. Eugenio Montale, *New Poems: A Selection from Satura and Diario del '71 e del '72*, translated with an introduction by G. Singh and an essay on *Xenia* by F. R. Leavis (New York, 1976), pp. xiv, xxvi–xxx. A portion of what follows has been adapted from my review of this book, "Count Your Dead: They Are Alive," in *The Nation* (9 October 1976): 341–44. Montale's opinion of *Veteris vestigia flammae*, written in 1968 as a preface to a selection of Hardy's poems in translation, is in *SP*, p. 528.

3. "Queste le ragioni del mio lungo silenzio. Dialogo con E. M.," *SP*, p. 593. It is worth recalling that the collection called *Finisterre*, which opens *La bufera e altro*, was originally conceived as "simply an appendix to *Le occasioni*" (*OV*, p. 937).

4. Montale, *Trentadue variazioni*, p. 42.

5. "Queste le ragioni . . .," *SP*, p. 593.

6. See Luciano Rebay, "La rete a strascico di Montale," *Forum Italicum* 5 no. 3 (September 1971): esp. pp. 338–40.

7. "Liriche cinesi," *SP*, p. 44.

8. "Ho scritto un solo libro," *SP*, p. 606; *Profilo di un autore: Eugenio Montale*, ed. Cima and Segre, p. 192.

9. Nascimbeni, *Eugenio Montale*, p. 58; see also Greco, *Montale commenta Montale*, p. 50.

10. *Profilo di un autore . . .*, p. 194.

11. *Profilo di un autore*, p. 194; *Montale commenta Montale*, pp. 48, 51. On *la Volpe*, see also Maria Luisa Spaziani, "Un carteggio inedito di Montale," *La poesia di Eugenio Montale* (*Atti del Convegno Internazionale a Genova dal 25 al 28 nov. 1982*), pp. 321–24.

12. Montale, quoted by Piero Gadda Conti in *Letteratura* (Montale issue), p. 329.

13. "Clizia nel '34," *OV*, p. 696.

14. "Dante ieri e oggi," *SP*, p. 21; "Giorno e notte," *SP*, p. 91.

15. *OV*, p. 697.

16. See, above all, the biographical and critical articles by Luciano Rebay, listed in the Select Bibliography below. The Clizia-Brandeis connection was first mentioned publicly by Montale's friend, the scholar Gianfranco Contini, in his opening remarks to a round-table on the poet, though he gave her first name as "Iris." See *Antologia Vieusseux*, no. 64 (October–December 1981), p. 16. See also Nascimbeni, pp. 92, 122; *Profilo di un autore*, pp. 194–95; *Montale commenta Montale*, p. 33.

select bibliography
(1993)

UMBERTO SABA

Poems
   Il canzoniere 1921. Edited by Giordano Castellani. Milan, 1961.
   Il canzoniere 1900–1954. Turin, 1965.
   Tutte le poesie. Edited by Arrigo Stara. Milan, 1988.

Prose
   Ernesto. Turin, 1975.
   Prose. Edited by Linuccia Saba. Milan, 1965.
   Ricordi-racconti (1910–47). Milan, 1956. [Included in *Prose.*]
   Scorciatoie e raccontini. Milan, 1946. [Included in *Prose.*]
   Storia e cronistoria del Canzoniere. Milan, 1948. [Included in *Prose.*]

Anthologies
   Antologia del Canzoniere. Edited by Carlo Muscetta. Turin, 1963.
   L'adolescenza del Canzoniere e undici lettere. Edited by Folco Portinari. Turin, 1975.
   Per conoscere Saba. Edited by Mario Lavagetto. Milan, 1981.

Letters
[For undisclosed reasons, the complete *Epistolario di Umberto Saba,* edited by Linuccia Saba and Aldo Marcovecchio, in typescript by 1961, has not as yet been published. Over the ensuring thirty years, sections have been issued as follows.]

   Atroce paese che amo. Lettere famigliari (1945–1953). Edited by Gianfranca Lavezzi and Rossana Sacconi. Milan, 1987.
   Il vecchio e il giovane: Umberto Saba / Pierantonio Quarantotti Gambini, Carteggio 1930–1937. Edited by Linuccia Saba. Milan, 1965.
   La spada d'amore. Lettere scelte 1902–1957. Edited by Aldo Marcovecchio. Milan, 1983.
   Lettere a un'amica (74 lettere a Nora Baldi). Turin, 1966.
   Lettere a un amico vescovo. Vicenza, 1980.
   Lettere sulla psicoanalisi. Carteggio con Joachim Flescher 1946–1949. Edited by Arrigo Stara. Turin, 1991.
   Saba Svevo Comisso (lettere inedite). Edited by Mario Sutor. Padua, 1967.
   Ettore Serra, *Il tascapane di Ungaretti. Il mio vero Saba.* Rome, 1983.
   See also *Per Conoscere Saba.*

Biographical Materials

Baldi, Nora. *Il paradiso di Saba*. Milan, 1958.

Cary, Joseph. *A Ghost in Trieste*. Chicago, 1993.

Cecchi, Ottavio. *L'aspro vino (Ricordi di Saba a Firenze '43–'44)*. Milan, 1967.

Fano, Anna. "L'amicizia tra gli scaffali della Libreria Antiquaria." *Il piccolo* (25 August 1967): 3.

Lavagetto, Mario. "Nascere a Trieste nel 1883." *Paragone* (June 1972): 4–32.

Mattioni, Stelio. *Storia di Umberto Saba*. Milan, 1989.

Pittoni, Anita. *Caro Saba*. Trieste, 1977.

Pierantonio Quarantotti Gambini. *Il poeta inamorato*. Pordenone, 1984.

Saba, Umberto. *Amicizia: Storia di un vecchio poeta e di un giovane canarino*. Edited by Carlo Levi. Milan, 1976.

Stuparich, Giani. *Trieste nei miei ricordi*. Milan, 1948.

Voghera, Giorgio. *Glí anni della psicanalisi*. Pordenone, 1985.

Zorn Giorni, Lionello. *Saba e il cinese a altri racconti*. Gorizia, 1987.

Translations into English or French

Cary, Joseph. "Trieste Poems from the *Canzioniere*." In *A Ghost in Trieste*. Chicago, 1993.

Gilson, Estelle. *The Stories and Recollections of Umberto Saba*. Riverdale-on-Hudson, New York, 1993.

Renard, Philippe. "Umberto Saba/Épigraphe-Oiseaux.' In *Cahiers pour un temps: Italo Svevo et Trieste*, pp. 241–301. Paris, 1987.

Stefanile, Felix. *Umberto Saba: Thirty-one Poems*. New Rochelle, 1978.

Thompson, Mark. *Ernesto*. Manchester, England, 1987.

Critical Materials

Atti del Convegno Internazionale. *Il punto su Saba*. Trieste, 1985.

Caccia, Ettore. *Lettura e storia di Saba*. Milan, 1967.

David, Michael. *La psicanalisi nella cultura italiana*. Turin, 1966.

Debenedetti, Giacomo. *Saggi critici*. Milan, 1952.

———. *Intermezzo*. Milan, 1963.

galleria (fasciola dedicato ad Umberto Saba). Edited by Aldo Marcovecchio. Anno X, nos. 1–2 (January–April 1960).

Intellettuali di frontiera (Triestini a Firenze (1900–1950). Edited by Marco Marchi et al., Florence, 1983.

La critica e Saba. Edited by Francesco Múzzioli. Bologna, 1976.

Lavagetto, Mario. *La gallina di Saba*. Turin, 1974.

"Omaggio a Saba." *Nuovi argomenti (nuova serie)*, no. 57 (January–March 1978): 9–93.

Portinari, Folco. *Umberto Saba*. Milan, 1963.

Solaria [Saba issue]. May 1928.

See also works listed in "General Critical Materials" below: Bàrbari Squarotti; Contini, *Un anno . . .*; DeRobertis, *Scrittori;* Gargiulo; Mariani; Solmi; Tita Rosa.

GIUSEPPE UNGARETTI

Poems

Il porto sepolto. Udine, 1916.

Derniers jours. Edited by Enrico Falqui. Milan, 1946.

L'allegria di naufragi. Florence, 1919.
L'allegria. Milan, 1931.
Sentimento del tempo. Florence, 1933.
Poesie disperse. Milan, 1945.
Il dolore. Milan, 1947.
La terra promessa. Milan, 1950.
Un grido e paesaggi. Milan, 1952.
Il taccuino del Vecchio. Milan, 1960.
Morte delle stagioni. Turin, 1967.
Vita d'un uomo: Tutte le poesie. Edited by Leone Piccioni. Milan, 1969.

Prose
Il Carso non è più un inferno. Milan, 1966.
Il deserto e dopo. Milan, 1961.
Vita d'un uomo: Saggi e interventi. Edited by Mario Diacono and Luciano Rebay. Milan, 1974.

Translations by Ungaretti
Traduzioni. Rome, 1936.
40 sonnetti di Shakespeare. Milan, 1946.
Da Gongora e da Mallarmé. Milan, 1948.
Fedra di Jean Racine. Milan, 1950.
I visioni di William Blake. Milan, 1966.

Recordings
Ungaretti legge se stesso. Cetra CL 0430.
Ungaretti legge Ungaretti. RCA Italiano, 30 L 502.

Translations of Ungaretti into English or French
Chuzeville, Jean. *Vie d'un homme, suivi de La douleur, La Terre promise.* Lausanne, 1953.
Creagh, Patrick. *Selected Poems: Giuseppe Ungaretti.* Harmondsworth, 1971 [Penguin].
Jouve, Jean Pierre. *Giuseppe Ungaretti tradotto da Pierre Jean Jouve.* Milan, 1960.
Lescure, Jean. *Les Cinq Livres.* Paris, 1953.
Mandelbaum, Allen. *Selected Poems of Giuseppe Ungaretti.* Ithaca and London, 1975.
Ponge, Francis. *Nouveau recueil.* Paris, 1967.

Anthology
Per conoscere Ungaretti. Edited by Leone Piccioni. Milan, 1971.

Biographical Materials
Piccioni, Leone. *Album Ungaretti.* Milan, 1989.
————. *Vita di un poeta.* Milan, 1970.
Serra, Ettore. *Il tascapane di Ungaretti. Il mio vero Saba.* Rome, 1983.
Ungaretti, Giuseppe, and Jean Amrouche. *Propos improvisés.* Paris, 1972.

Critical Materials
Baroni, Giorgio. *Giuseppe Ungaretti, introduzione e guida allo studio dell'opera ungarettiana.* Florence, 1981.

Books Abroad ("Homage to Ungaretti"), vol. 44, no. 4 (Autumn 1970).

Cambon, Glauco. *Giuseppe Ungaretti* (Columbia Essays on Modern Writers #50). New York, 1967.

———. *La poesia di Ungaretti.* Turin, 1976.

Cavalli, Gigi. *Ungaretti.* Milan, 1958.

Forum Italicum ("A Homage to Giuseppe Ungaretti"), vol. 6, no. 2 (June 1972).

galleria: Omaggio a Giuseppe Ungaretti nel Suo ottantesimo compleanno. Edited by Ornella Sobrero. Fasc. no. 4–6 (November 1968).

Jones, Frederick J. *Giuseppe Ungaretti, Poet and Critic.* Edinburgh, 1977.

La critica e Ungaretti. Edited by Giuseppe Faso. Bologna, 1977.

L'approdo letterario: Omaggio a Ungaretti. Edited by Mario Luzi. No. 57 (nuova serie), anno XVIII (March 1972).

Letteratura (Ungaretti issue), nos. 35–36 (September–December 1958).

L'Herne #11: Ungaretti. Edited by Piero Sanavio. Paris, n.d.

Pea, Enrico. *Vita in Egitto.* Milan, 1949.

Picon, Gaëton. *L'usage de la lecture.* Paris, 1960.

Portinari, Folco. *Giuseppe Ungaretti.* Turin, 1967.

Rebay, Luciano. *Le origini della poesia di Giuseppe Ungaretti.* Rome, 1962.

See also works listed in "General Critical Materials" below: Bàrbari Squarotti; Contini, *Esercizi;* DeRobertis; Flora; Frattini; Gargiulo; Mariani; Petrucciani; Piccioni; Solmi.

EUGENIO MONTALE

Poems

Ossi di seppia. Turin, 1928.

Le occasioni. Turin, 1939.

La bufera e altro. Venice, 1956.

Satura. Verona, 1962.

Accordi & pastelli. Milan, 1963.

Satura [definitive version]. Milan, 1971.

Diario del '71 e del '72. Milan, 1973.

Quaderno di quattro anni. Milan, 1977.

Altri versi e poesie disperse. Edited by Giorgio Zampa. Milan, 1981.

L'opera in versi. Critical edition edited by Rosanna Bettarini and Gianfranco Contini. Turin, 1980.

Diario postumo (prima parte: 30 poesie). Edited by Annalisa Cima. Milan, 1991.

Prose

Auto da fé: cronache in due tempi. Milan, 1966.

Farfalla di Dinard (enlarged edition). Milan, 1973.

Fuori di casa. Milan-Naples, 1969.

Nel nostro tempo. Rome, 1972.

Prime alla scala. Edited by Gianfranca Lavezzi. Milan, 1981.

Quaderno genovese. Edited by Laura Barile. Milan, 1983.

Sulla poesia. Edited by Giorgio Zampa. Milan, 1976.

Trentadue variazioni. Milan, 1987.

Translations by Montale

Quaderno di traduzioni. Milan, 1948 [included in *L'opera in versi*].

T. S. Eliot tradotto da Eugenio Montale con un saggio introduttivo. Milan, 1963.

Letters
  Italo Svevo-Eugenio Montale. *Carteggio con gli scritti di Montale su Svevo.* Edited by Giorgio Zampa. Milan, 1976.
  Lettere a Salvatore Quasimodo. Milan, 1981.
  See also "Autocommenti" section in *Sulla poesia* and works by Luciano Rebay in "Biographical Material" below.

Translations of Montale into English or French
  Angelini, Patrice, et al. *Os de seiche.* Paris, 1966.
  ———. *Les occasions.* Paris, 1966.
  ———. *La tourmente et autres poèmes.* Paris, 1966.
  Arrowsmith, William. *Cuttlefish Bones.* New York-London, 1993.
  ———. *The Occasions.* New York-London, 1987.
  ———. *The Storm and Other Things.* New York-London, 1985.
  Farnsworth, Edith. *Provisional Conclusions: A Selection of the Poetry of Eugenio Montale.* Chicago, 1970.
  Galassi, Jonathan. *Otherwise: First and Last Poems of Eugenio Montale.* New York, 1984.
  ———. *The Second Life of Art: Selected Essays of Eugenio Montale.* New York, 1982.
  Hamilton, Alistair. *Poet in Our Time.* New York, 1976.
  Kay, George. *Eugenio Montale, Poesie/Poems.* Edinburgh, 1964 [In Penguin as *Eugenio Montale: Selected Poems.* Baltimore, 1969.].
  Lowell, Robert. *Poesie di Montale.* Bologna, 1960.
  ———. *Imitations.* New York, 1961.
  Morgan, Edwin. *Poems from Eugenio Montale.* Reading, England, 1959.
  Singh, G. *It Depends: A Poet's Notebook (Quaderno di quattro anni).* New York, 1980.
  ———. *New Poems: A Selection from Satura and Diario del '71 e del '72.* New York, 1976.
  ———. *The Butterfly of Dinard.* Lexington, Ky, 1971.
  Various Hands, *Quarterly Review of Literature* (Montale issue). Edited by Irma Brandeis, vol. 11, no. 4, 1962.
  Various Hands, *Eugenio Montale: Selected Poems.* Edited by Glauco Cambon. New York, 1966 [revised edition of *Quarterly Review* Montale issue].

Anthology
  Per conoscere Montale. Edited by Marco Forti. Milan, 1976.

Biographical Materials
  Antologia Vieusseux #64 (conference dedicated to Montale by Rosanna Bettarini, Gianfranco Contini, Dante Isella, and Giorgio Zampa), pp. 13–25. Florence, 1981.
  Bazlen, Roberto. "Lettere a Montale 1925–1930." In *Scritti,* edited by Roberto Calasso, pp. 356–89. Milan, 1984.
  Cambon, Glauco. "Summer Days with Eugenio Montale." *Canto: Review of the Arts* (Spring 1978): 71–97.
  Cima, Annalisa. *Incontro Montale.* Milan, 1973.
  Contorbia, Franco, ed. *Eugenio Montale—immagini divna vita.* Milan, 1985.
  Mercedes Gibelli, Flavia. *Una domanda infinita: ricordi intorno a Eugenio Montale.* Genoa, 1988.

Nascimbeni, Giulio. *Montale: biografia di un poeta*. Milan, 1986.

Rebay, Luciano. "I diàspori di Montale." *Italica* (Spring 1969): 33–53.

———. "La rete a strascico di Montale." *Forum Italicum* 5, no. 3 (September 1971): 329–50.

———. "Montale, Clizia e l'America." *Forum Italicum* 16, no. 3 (Winter 1982): 171–202.

———. "Sull' autobiografismo di Montale." In *Innovazioni tematiche espressive e linguistiche della letteratura italiana del Novecento*, pp. 73–83. Florence, 1976.

———. "Un cestello di Montale, le gambe di Dora Markus e una lettera di Roberto Bazlen." In *La poesia di Eugenio Montale (Atti del Convegno Internazionale a Genova dal 25 al 28 nov. 1982)*, pp. 107–17. Florence, 1984.

Spaziani, Maria Luisa. "Un carteggio inedito di Montale." In *La poesia di Eugenio Montale (Atti del Convegno Internazionale a Genova dal 25 al 28 nov. 1982)*, pp. 321–24.

Bibliography

Barile, Laura. *Bibliografia montaliana*. Milan, 1977.

Critical Materials

Almansi, Guido, and Bruce Merry, *Eugenio Montale. The Private Language of Poetry*. Edinburgh, 1977.

Atti del Convegno Internazionale [Milan-Genoa, 12–15 September 1982]. *La poesia di Eugenio Montale*. Milan, 1983.

Atti del Convegno Internazionale [Genoa, 25–28 November 1982]. *La poesia di Eugenio Montale*. Florence, 1984.

Avalle, D'Arco Silvio. *Tre saggi su Montale*. Turin, 1970.

Becker, Jared. *Eugenio Montale*. Boston, 1986.

Biasin, Gian-Paolo. *Montale, Debussy, and Modernism*. Princeton, 1989.

Brandeis, Irma. "An Italian Letter." *The Saturday Review* (18 July 1936), p. 16.

———. "Montale, Eugenio." *Columbia Dictionary of Modern European Literature* [first edition]. New York, 1947.

Cambon, Glauco. *Eugenio Montale* [Columbia Essays on Modern Writers #61]. New York, 1972.

———. "Eugenio Montale's 'Motets': The Occasions of Epiphany." *PMLA* 1967, no. 7.

———. *Eugenio Montale's Poetry: A Dream in Reason's Presence*. Princeton, 1982.

———. "Eugenio Montale's Poetry: A Meeting of Dante and Brueghel." *Sewanee Review* (Winter 1958).

Contini, Gianfranco. *Una lunga fedeltà: scritti su Eugenio Montale*. Turin, 1974.

Forti, Marco. *Eugenio Montale: la poesia, la prosa di fantasia e d'invenzione*. Milan, 1974.

Greco, Lorenzo. *Montale commenta Montale*. Parma, 1980.

Huffman, Claire de C. L. *Montale and the Occasions of Poetry*. Princeton, 1983.

Letteratura (Montale issue), 79/81 (January and June 1966). Edited by Silvio Ramat. [Now expanded and issued in book form as *Omaggio a Montale*, Milan, 1966.]

Praz, Mario. "T. S. Eliot and Eugenio Montale." In *T. S. Eliot, a Symposium*, edited by Richard March and Thurairajah Tambimuttu. Chicago, 1949.

Profilo di un autore: Eugenio Montale. Edited by Annalisa Cima and Cesare Segre. Milan, 1977.

Ramat, Silvio. *Montale.* Florence, 1965.

Singh, G. *Eugenio Montale: A Critical Study of His Poetry, Prose and Criticism.* New Haven-London, 1973.

West, Rebecca J. *Eugenio Montale: Poet on the Edge.* Cambridge, MA, and London, 1981.

See also works listed in "General Critical Materials" below: Bo; DeRobertis; Flora, *Scrittori;* Gargiulo; Macrì, *Esemplari;* Pancrazi (vols. III and IV); Pasolini; Petrucciani, *Poesia;* Solmi.

GENERAL CRITICAL MATERIALS

Anceschi, Luciano. *Le poetiche del Novecento in Italia.* Milan, 1962.

Bàrbari Squarotti, Giorgio. *Astrazione e realtà.* Milan, 1960.

Bo, Carlo. *Otto studi.* Florence, 1939.

Brandeis, Irma. *The Ladder of Vision: A Study of Dante's Poetry.* New York, 1962.

Bremond, Henri. *La poésie pure.* Paris, 1926.

Camon, Ferdinando. *Il mestiere di poeta: autoritratti critici.* Milan, 1965.

Contini, Gianfranco. *Esercizi di lettura.* Florence, 1947.

———. *Un anno di letteratura.* Florence, 1947.

Croce, Benedetto. *La poesia.* Bari, 1953.

———. *Poesia e non poesia.* Bari, 1923.

Dante Alighieri. *Rime.* Edited by Gianfranco Contini. Turin, 1946.

De Robertis, Giuseppe. *Altro Novecento.* Florence, 1962.

———. *Scrittori italiani del Novecento.* Florence, 1940.

Dombroski, Robert S. *L'esistenza ubbidiente: letterati italiani sotto il fascismo.* Naples, 1984.

Eliot, T. S. *Selected Essays 1917–1932.* New York, 1962.

Flora, Francesco. *La poesia ermetica.* Bari, 1947.

———. *Scrittori italiani contemporanei.* Pisa, 1952.

Frattini, Alberto. *Da Tommaseo a Ungaretti.* Bologna, 1958.

Gargiulo, Alfredo. *Letteratura italiana del Novecento.* Florence, 1958.

Jones, F. J. *The Modern Italian Lyric.* Cardiff, 1986.

Leopardi, Giacomo. *Tutte le opere,* edited by Francesco Flora. Milan, 1953–58.

Macrì, Oreste. *Caratteri e figure della poesia italiana contemporanea.* Florence, 1946.

———. *Esemplari del sentimento poetico contemporareo.* Florence, 1941.

Mariani, Gaetano. *Poesia e tecnica nella lirica del Novecento.* Padua, 1958.

Marinetti, F. T. *Les mots en liberté futuristes.* Milan, 1919.

Pacifici, Sergio. *A Guide to Contemporary Italian Literature from Futurism to Neorealism.* Carbondale, 1972.

Pancrazi, Pietro. *Scrittori d'oggi, serie I–VI.* Bari, 1946–53.

Papini, Giovanni. *Un uomo finito.* Florence, 1932.

Pasolini, Pier Paolo. *Passione e ideologia.* Milan, 1960.

Pavese, Cesare. *La letteratura americana e altri saggi.* Turin, 1962.

Petrucciani, Mario. *La poetica dell'ermetismo italiano.* Turin, 1955.

————. *Poesia pura e poesia esistenziale*. Turin, 1957.

Piccioni, Leone. *Lettura leopardiana e altri saggi*. Florence, 1952.

Pozzi, Gianni. *La poesia italiana del Novecento da Gozzano agli ermetici*. Turin, 1965.

Pullini, Giorgio. *Le poetiche dell'Ottocento*. Padua, 1959.

Quasimodo, Salvatore. *Il poeta e il politico e altri saggi*. Milan, 1960.

Ragusa, Olga. *Mallarmé in Italy*. New York, 1957.

Ravegnani, Giuseppe. *I contemporanei*. Milan, 1960.

————. *Uomini visti*. 2 vols. Milan, 1955.

Solmi, Sergio. *Scrittori negli anni*. Milan, 1963.

Svevo, Livia Veneziani. *Vita del mio marito con altri inediti di Italo Svevo*, edited by Anita Pittoni. Trieste, 1958.

Thovaz, Enrico. *Il pastore, il gregge e la zampogna*. Naples, 1926.

Titta Rosa, Giovanni. *Poesia italiana del Novecento*. Siena, 1953.

Vittorini, Elio. *Diario in pubblico*. Florence, 1957.

acknowledgments

Acknowledgments are made to the following publishers for their kind permission to quote and/or translate copyrighted materials:

Excerpts from Eugenio Montale's *Auto da fé,* copyright © 1966 by Casa Editrice Il Saggiatore; reprinted by permission of Casa Editrice Il Saggiatore.

Excerpts from Giuseppe Ungaretti's prefatory "Quelques réflexions suggérées à l'auteur par sa poésie" in *Les Cinq Livres,* translations of Giuseppe Ungaretti into French by Jean Lescure with the assistance of the poet, copyright © 1953 by Les Editions de Minuit; reprinted by permission of Les Éditions de Minuit.

Excerpts from Umberto Saba's *Il Canzoniere (1900–1954),* copyright © 1961 by Giulio Einaudi Editore; reprinted by permission of Giulio Einaudi Editore.

Excerpts from prefatory statements by Giuseppe Ungaretti and Eugenio Montale in Giacinto Spagnoletti's *Poesia Italiana contemporanea (1909–1959),* copyright © 1964 by Ugo Guanda Editore; reprinted by permission of Ugo Guanda Editore.

Excerpts from T. S. Eliot's "A Note on War Poetry" in *Collected Poems, 1909–1962,* copyright © 1936 by Harcourt, Brace & World, Inc; copyright © 1963, 1964 by T. S. Eliot; reprinted by permission of Harcourt, Brace & World, Inc.

Excerpts from interviews with Giuseppe Ungaretti, Eugenio Montale, and Salvatore Quasimodo in Ferdinando Camon's *Il mestiere di poeta: autoritratti critici,* copyright © 1965 by Lerici Editore; reprinted by permission of Lerici Editore.

Excerpts from Umberto Saba's *Prose,* edited by Linuccia Saba, copyright © 1964 by Arnoldo Mondadori Editore; reprinted by permission of Arnoldo Mondadori Editore.

All poetry by Giuseppe Ungaretti and Eugenio Montale, copyright © by Arnoldo Mondadori Editore; reprinted by permission of Arnoldo Mondadori Editore.

Italian texts of poems by Eugenio Montale from Montale's *Selected Poems,* edited by Glauco Cambon, © by New Directions Publishing Corporation, New York; reprinted by permission of New Directions Publishing Corporation.

[For current information on more recent editions of Saba, Ungaretti, and Montale, see the Select Bibliography (1993) in this edition.]

index of proper names
and literary terms

Historically, Italian poetic genius has appeared in installments of three. *Three Modern Italian Poets* focuses on the most recent triad: Umberto Saba, Giuseppe Ungaretti, and Eugenio Montale. Through careful readings of the work of these giants of literary modernism, Joseph Cary facilitates our understanding of their poetry. Cary also presents striking biographical portraits—a complex and poignant Saba, a spiritually nomadic and tormented Ungaretti, and Montale, poet of *coscienza*—all the while guiding us through the first half of twentieth-century Italy, a most difficult period in its literary and cultural development.

"*Three Modern Italian Poets* is without doubt one of the very best books on modern Italian poetry available in English. Cary in effect reconstructs the history of modern Italian poetry in a comprehensive, succinct, rigorous way. A true classic in the best sense of the term."
—Robert Pogue Harrison, Stanford University

"A pioneering work of very real importance. . . . Cary was, I believe, the first critic, Italian or non-Italian, to identify the great 'triad' of Montale, Ungaretti, Saba; his critical discussion of each of these three great poets is exemplary: trenchant, acute, elegantly written, astutely perceived. *There is no better introduction to Italian poetry in this century.*"
—William Arrowsmith, Boston University

JOSEPH CARY is professor emeritus of English and comparative literature at the University of Connecticut, Storrs. He is the author of *A Ghost in Trieste*, published by the University of Chicago Press.

THE UNIVERSITY OF CHICAGO PRESS

Cover photograph: *Parable, 1991,* by Ruth Thorne-Thomsen.

ISBN 0-226-09527-4